D1273929

A HISTORY OF PIANOFORTE-PLAYING *and* PIANOFORTE-LITERATURE

Da Capo Press Music Reprint Series
GENERAL EDITOR
FREDERICK FREEDMAN
VASSAR COLLEGE

A HISTORY OF PIANOFORTE-PLAYING *and* PIANOFORTE-LITERATURE

by C. F. Weitzmann

DA CAPO PRESS • NEW YORK • 1969

A Da Capo Press Reprint Edition

This Da Capo Press edition of C. F. Weitzmann's *A History of Pianoforte-Playing and Pianoforte-Literature* is an unabridged republication of the first edition published in New York in 1897 by G. Schirmer.

Library of Congress Catalog Card Number 74-90209

Published by Da Capo Press
A Division of Plenum Publishing Corporation
227 West 17th Street
New York, N. Y. 10011

Printed in the United States of America

A HISTORY

OF

PIANOFORTE-PLAYING

AND

PIANOFORTE-LITERATURE

BY

C. F. WEITZMANN.

NEW YORK: G. SCHIRMER.
1897.

A HISTORY

OF

PIANOFORTE-PLAYING

AND

PIANOFORTE-LITERATURE

BY

C. F. WEITZMANN.

WITH MUSICAL APPENDICES AND A SUPPLEMENT CONTAINING THE HISTORY OF THE PIANOFORTE ACCORDING TO THE LATEST RESEARCHES, AND SUITABLY ILLUSTRATED.

WITH A BIOGRAPHICAL SKETCH OF THE AUTHOR, AND NOTES
BY
OTTO LESSMANN.

FROM THE SECOND AUGMENTED AND REVISED GERMAN EDITION
BY
DR. TH. BAKER.

NEW YORK: G. SCHIRMER.
1897.

BIOGRAPHICAL SKETCH OF THE AUTHOR.

By Otto Lessmann.

Carl Friedrich Weitzmann departed this life soon after the appearance of the second edition of his principal work; on Nov. 7, 1880, the keen eyes of the manful champion closed for ever, in the 73rd year of his age. Weitzmann was born on Aug. 10, 1808, at Berlin, where he began, under the guidance of the violinist C. W. Henning and the composer Bernhard Klein, his practical and thereotical studies, which he finished in Cassel, from 1827 onward, under Ludwig Spohr and Moritz Hauptmann. In 1832 he entered the theatre orchestra at Riga as violinist, being at the same time engaged as chorus-director. Together with Heinrich Dorn, then Kapellmeister at Riga, Weitzmann founded a Singing Society in that city, for which he composed a number of pieces for vocal chorus. In 1834 he relinquished his position in Riga for that of Musikdirector in Reval, where some dramatic compositions by himself—"Räuberliebe", "Walpurgisnacht", and "Lorbeerbaum und Bettelstab"—were brought out. Two years later Weitzmann joined the orchestra of the Imperial Opera at St. Petersburg as first violinist, becoming at the same time Musikdirector in the Church of St. Anne. Here, too, he founded a German Liedertafel, which he conducted until, on the expiration of an eleven years' service as musician to the Russian Court, he left St. Petersburg, generously pensioned, first making a concert-tour through Finland with the oboe virtuoso Henry Brod, and afterwards settling in Paris. There he applied himself assiduously to the study of the history and theory of music, which he continued successfully after removing to London in 1847, where he was engaged as a violinist in the Italian Opera. During this same year he returned to Berlin, where he settled permanently, enjoying a high reputation as a teacher of harmony and counterpoint, at first in Stern's Conservatory, and later in Tausig's "Schule des höheren Clavierspiels" (School for advanced Pianoforte-playing), and also as a private instructor.

Armed with the panoply of the well-equipped musical theoretician, Weitzmann, as a champion of the artistic conceptions of Liszt and Wagner, first entered the arena, in which was raging the battle waged for and against the justification of progress pioneered in music both in regard to harmony and form. In a number of writings he took his stand decidedly on the side of these two masters, and his "Harmoniesystem", to which a prize was awarded in 1860, established on a firm logical basis the practical acquisitions which, in the works of the "neo-German" school, were a stumbling-block to the theoreticians of the old school. While earlier writings, such as "The Augmented Triad" (1853), "The Diminished Chord of the Seventh" (1854) (publ. by Th. Chr. Fr. Enslin—Richard Schoetz—, Berlin), and the "History of the Ch. of the Seventh", had discovered Weitzmann's revolutionary tendencies in the field of music, his "Harmoniesystem" won him for good and all the reputation of being the thereotical henchman of the musical radicals. Weitzmann showed this to be his unmistakable wish in the sub-title of his "Harmoniesystem" by designating the latter as "An explanatory disquisition on and musico-theoretical justification of the transformation and evolution of Harmony through the recent creations of Art''. His opponents, the champions of the musical "Zopf" (literally "pigtail", the obstinate prejudice of narrow-minded pedantry), who fell upon the work to tear it to pieces according to the rules of their worn-out musical grammar, were answered by Weitzmann in a second paper, "The New Science of Harmony versus the Old" (C. F. Kahnt, Leipzig, 1861). That he after all had the last word in the hotly contested battle, is proved by the revolution of public opinion in regard to the masters Schumann, Liszt, and Wagner.

His controversies concerning modern music did not hinder Weitzmann from attentively studying antiquity; the fruits of this study he garnered in a "History of Grecian Music" (Th. Chr. Fr. Enslin, Berlin, 1855). In 1863 was issued, as Part III of the Lebert-Stark Pianoforte School, the "History of Clavier-playing and Clavier-Literature", published later as a separate work, in a second edition augmented by a "History of the Pianoforte".—A number of meritorious articles have appeared in various musical journals, among them a warm encomium of Carl Tausig, "the last of the virtuosi". Weitzmann's contrapuntal skill was very considerable, as is sufficiently attested in his "Studies in Counterpoint" (Schuberth & Co., Leipzig,) "Musical Puzzles", Canons for 4 hands, 2 Books (same publ.) and his "1800 Preludes and Modulations", Book 1, classic; Book 2, romantic (Th. Chr. Fr. Enslin, Berlin); likewise an analytical treatise on the 2-part Fugue (autographed).

As a composer Weitzmann did little to attract public attention. Besides the above mentioned dramatic compositions he published only a few books of songs and vocal works, and some pianoforte pieces for 2 and 4 hands, among the latter being a few "Valses Nobles" (Bote & Bock, Berlin), which are simple and natural in feeling and pleasing in effect.

Weitzmann's character was upright and frank, and before long years of sickness had diminished his powers he was animated by the liveliest interest for everything which concerned his art and his calling as a writer on art. His opinions, which he defended with circumspection, readiness and tenacity, were for him the sole guide in all his actions; for, as Tappert wrote after Weitzmann's death, "He needed neither office nor preferment, sought neither honors nor renown".

May the memory of this able man live on as that of a well-deserving champion in the triumphal progress of our sublime art.

Charlottenburg, October, 1887.

Otto Lessmann.

AUTHOR'S PREFACE and INTRODUCTION.

Every thinking pianist, who would avoid the appearance of colorlessness and one-sidedness in his compositions and performances, will perceive the necessity of attaining familiarity not merely with the more important productions of the present day, but with the prominent works in the earlier literature of his art as well. Hitherto, however, an orderly historical view, comprehending the entire field of clavier-literature, and at the same time calling to mind the names of those masters to whose activity we owe the perfection and extension of our art, has been wanting. It is the purpose of the present work to bridge over this sensible gap in writings devoted to the history of music.

The author feels it incumbent upon him to give some explanation concerning the arrangement and grouping of the contents of his work. The *earlier history* of clavier-playing closes with the disappearance of the older keyboard instruments—the Clavichord, the coyly tremulous tone of which was produced by metallic pins or tangents, striking and setting in vibration the strings when the keys were depressed; and the sweeping Harpsichord, the strings of which were twanged by quills; the author regarded it as most practical to trace successively the earlier schools in Italy, England, France, and Germany down to the above period. The *modern history* of clavier-playing begins with the predominance of the Pianoforte, in which hammers, striking the strings gently or powerfully, admitted of the greatest variety in the shading of the tone, and gradually evolved the most manifold effects in playing and means of expression. And henceforward the creative masters follow each other at such short intervals, that the author considered it needful to point out the influence of each one, even down to his pupils and imitators, before taking up any contemporary eminent in other ways, though at the same time never losing sight of momentous meetings between celebrated musicians and rivals in art.

The earliest history of clavier-playing goes hand in hand with that of organ-playing; not until the beginning of the 16th century do the clavier performances of noted organists sometimes find special mention. At that time the two chief species of claviers alluded to above were already in existence; their compass, with the chromatic scale, embraced 3 octaves (A—a), and sometimes even 4 octaves (F—f), the succession of white and black keys being the same as at present.* In their tuning, the claviers were already tempered to snch an extent, that the diatonic ecclesiastical keys predominant down to about the 17th century, to which a chromatic tone was seldom added, and which also occurred transposed by a fifth lower (then in every case with one flat in the signature), might be employed with tolerable purity.** By the establishment of the equal temperament, about 1700, Sebastian Bach and his contemporaries were enabled to write compositions in all the modern major and minor keys for the clavier; the ecclesiastical modes then vanished entirely as far as their peculiar and purely diatonic character is concerned, and the widest field was thrown open to modulation.

In some manuscript specimens of counterpoint of the 13th century, the oldest which have as yet been discovered, the notes of vocal music for two or more parts are in some cases written one above the other on a single staff of 8, 9, 10, or 12 lines. In various more recent, though equally rare, specimens we find similar staves of 10 lines, the lowest of which is marked with a Γ (Gamma), the fourth with the F-clef, the sixth with the C-clef, the eighth with the G-clef, and the tenth with dd, the notes of the several parts thus standing in conjunction. For greater distinctness, the notes of the several parts were sometimes distinguished by color or shape, the soprano and bass having square red notes, the alto triangular green notes, and the tenor round black notes. In still later similar attempts, music for the organ and clavier was written on 6 lines intended for the right hand and 8 for the left. Strange to say, besides these

---

*See "Musica getutscht und aussgezogen durch Sebastianum Virdung", Basel, 1511.

**See Toscanella in musica di messer Piero Aron, Venice, 1529, Divisione del Monarchordo per tuoni e semituoni, cap. XXXX; and also De la participatione et modo de accordare l'instrumento, cap. XLI.

and similar attempts made only by isolated composers, not a single actual score, either written or printed, of any vocal or instrumental composition in several parts of the 13th, 14th, 15th, or even of the first half of the 16th century has been found, so that it almost looks as if the contrapuntists of that time wrote out all their compositions immediately in separate parts, without sketching them at first in score. Further, as the *bar* did not appear until the second half of the 16th century, together with the **score,** it is evident, that previous to that time only the most skilful and thoroughly trained singers or players could successfully undertake the performance of a new composition, especially when the composer himself was not present at rehearsals. Still greater difficulties were to be overcome by the organist who either could or would not at all times follow simply the dictates of his own fancy. For as organ music, like all instrumental music of the period, was merely an echo of the vocal music, the organist was obliged, before attempting to play a piece intended for voices, to study the several parts, which were either printed separately or at best on opposite pages of the music-book in such wise, that the upper half of the left-hand page bore the highest part, the lower half the lowest part, while the two middle parts were similarly ordered on the right-hand page. Until toward the end of the 16th century it was the duty of church-organists in Italy to introduce the regular *a cappella* compositions by preludes and intonations, to connect the various divisions of the vocal mass by interludes, to answer certain vocal strains on the organ, and at times to perform the verses of hymns on the organ in alternation with the singers. The choir was but seldom supported by the organ, in the psalm tunes and chorales. The papal choir at Rome has retained pure vocal music exclusively down to the present day in full simplicity; but about the year 1600, so important in the annals of music, there was initiated the so-called "seconda pratica di musica", the singers being thenceforward continually supported or accompanied by the organ or other instruments. Vocal music pure and simple thus disappeared entirely from the church, and the difficulties of the organist accompanying the various vocal and instrumental parts continually increased, till at length he was furnished with a continuous bass part to his accompaniment, over the notes of which the harmonies of the other parts co-operating were indicated by figures. Such a bass part, supporting the whole harmonic structure, was styled a *basso continuo, basso per l'organo, basso principale*, or *basso generale.*

In Germany, on the other hand, where, as in other countries, the singers had sung from notes since the appearance of the first contrapuntists, the instrumentalists employed from the very beginning of the 16th century a kind of notation with letters, which Virdung mentions as early as 1511, with reference to which Martin Agricola, in his Musica instrumentalis (1529), gives instructions "for playing on the organ, harp, lute, violin, and all instruments and stringed instruments, according to the rightly established tabulature". In this German Tabulature, in accordance with a usage handed down to our time, the tones of the lowest octave were indicated by capital letters, those of the next octave by small letters, and the others in succession by small letters with lines drawn above them, being called the once-lined, twice-lined, thrice-lined octave, etc.

C D E F G A H (B) c d e f g a h (b) $\bar{c}$ $\bar{d}$ $\bar{e}$ $\bar{f}$ $\bar{g}$ $\bar{a}$ $\bar{h}$ ($\bar{b}$) $\bar{\bar{c}}$ etc.

and set one above the other in two, three, four, or more rows as required, in movements having several parts to be executed by the organist. The relative length of the tones was indicated by dots, hooks, or cross-lines over the letters in question, the rests being marked by other special signs. This organ tabulature, immediately after its invention, was also used for compositions for the clavier, and down to 1650 was exclusively employed in Germany for keyboard instruments. The organists in Italy, on the contrary, never took to the alphabetic tabulature; in that country, as said before, various kinds of note tabulatures were tried for giving the player a convenient view of the several parts of a composition, until finally he was provided with a *full score* for the execution of pieces in several parts, such as obtains to-day. But the compression of all the parts of a movement in more than 2 parts on only *two staves* is not found, even in Italy, until after the appearance of the *basso continuo* or thorough-bass, i. e. not until the first half of the 17th century. The setting of separate parts of a composition on an equal number of staves one above the other was also brought into use in Germany about the middle of the 17th century, and there styled the "Italian Tabulature" (intavolatura), or "Partitur" (partitura, score), though the German alphabetic tabulature still found adherents and defenders down to the beginning of the 18th century.

TABLE OF CONTENTS.

MODERN HISTORY.

THE FORTEPIANO.

III. The Lyrical Clavier Style.

IV. The Dramatic Pianoforte Style.

V. The Brilliant Style.

VI. The Romantic Style.

HISTORY OF THE PIANOFORTE.

ERRATA.

Page 6, line 3, for *Vincentino* read *Vicentino*.
" 47, " 3 from below, for *Ritter* read *Bitter*.
" 67, " 2 " " after *is employed* supply: "as the Rondeau or Rondo."
" 133, " 9 " " for *Kittel* read *Kittl*.
" 219, " 17, after *mathematical accuracy* supply: "The instrument was therefore also called the *Canon*, as forming a *rule* for the determination of the intervals."
" 221, foot-note, for *Vicento* read *Vicentino*.
" 231, last line, for *Zente* read *Zenti*.
" 238, line 2, for *Werkmeister* read *Werckmeister*.
" 250, " 2, for *Oesterlin* read *Oesterlein*.
" 251, " 12 from below, for *Christofori* read *Cristofori*.
" 252, " 13 " " for *Lemmi* read *Lemme*.
" 254, " 5 " " for *Rish* read *Risch*.
" 267, " 8 " " for *Spath* read *Spaeth*.
" 279, " 14 " " for *Croma* read *Chroma*.

EARLIER HISTORY OF CLAVIER-PLAYING.

The Clavichord.

I. The strict contrapuntal Organ Style and the freer Clavier Style.

The earlier Italian Clavier School.

Among the Italian capitals, Rome took the lead in the cultivation of sacred music, Naples in the refinement of popular, profane song, and Florence in the development of the homophonic style and the musical drama; while Venice devoted herself more particularly to the culture of instrumental music, and to a style of composition suited to the same and differing from that proper to vocal music. We therefore begin our historical researches with the last-named commercial republic, so powerful in the Middle Ages, whose victorious fleets wafted thither all the wealth of the Orient, and whose active intercourse with the most various people of the Old World caused the arts and sciences to flourish in early and marvelous perfection. From the 14th century on, Venice was famed for her eminent organists, engaged at the cathedral of San Marco, and for co-operation with whom a there was appointed, in the latter half of the next century, a conductor *(maestro di cappella)* able to lend fresh impetus to the vigorous musical life of the city. The fame of these remarkable musicians attracted a great number of zealous students of art, who either remained as successors of their masters in Venice, or transplanted the knowledge there acquired to other places. But even the distinguished artists of Italy, Germany, and the Netherlands visited the flourishing Island City, to seek positions in the same or to measure their strength with her renowned musicians. Thus appeared in Venice, about 1364, the blind Florentine **Francesco Landino,** the highly extolled poet and organist, during the brilliant festivities given by the Doge Lorenzo Celsi in honor of the King of Cyprus and the Archduke of Austria. At one of these solemnities, and in the per-sence of the universally revered Petrarch, Landino was crowned as poet with the laurel wreath, though **Francesco da Pèsaro,** appointed organist at San Marco in 1336, was his successful rival for the prize for organ-playing. Distinguished among the later successors of the latter was also **Bernhard the German,** to whom the invention of the organ-pedals is likewise ascribed, and who is entered on the records of the church as Bernardo di Stefanino Murer. From 1527 **Adrian Willaert** of Flanders, frequently called Maestro Adriano by the Italians, was *maestro di cappella* at San Marco; he became the founder of the afterwards so famous Venetian School of music, and especially to him and his pupils do we owe the development of a more vigorous and artistic instrumental style. Willaert was the originator of compositions for two and three choruses, the harmony of each having to be complete in itself, and was distinguished as a composer of sacred masses and motets, as well as of profane madrigals and *canzoni.* In Venice first appeared those Fantasias and "Ricercari", originated or suggested by him, which were originally intended for the voice, or else for the organ or other instruments, but whose performance was later abandoned to the organ alone. In 1541 the Fleming **Jachet de Buus** was appointed to the second organ in San Marco. He published in 1547 a book entitled "Ricercari da cantare e sonare d'organo et altri stromenti" (Venice: Antonio Gardane), followed by a similar one in 1549. His *ricercari* are free fugal movements. One of the parts begins with the theme in the principal key; that following takes up the same transposed a fifth higher or a fourth lower, but without quitting the original key; the other parts on entering take up the subject and answer alternately in like manner. In most cases, the parts progress diatonically in the principal key, modulations occurring only transiently to the keys of the dominant or sub-dominant. The instrumental compositions of the period still lack a distinctive, positive character, and the flow of the melodies has too little of pleasing animation, to claim more than an historical interest. Buus leaving Venice in 1551, Willaert's pupil **Giròlamo Parabosco** succeeded to his office in the cathedral. At this early date, the free fantasias and improvised "sonatas" of this excellent organist on the "Instrumento da penna" (harpsichord) found special commendation.*

---

* S. Caffi, Storia della musica sacra etc. Venice 1854, Vol. I, pp. 111 and 113.

As in England the Virginal perhaps derived its name from the predilection of young damsels for this miniature clavichord, in Italy, too, the *monacordo* (clavicordo) was already the favorite instrument of young girls. In the 16th century it was the custom there to educate the daughters of the wealthier classes in convents, where they received instruction in the arts and sciences, more particularly in music. We learn, that at the time of Adrian Willaert's labors in Venice, he himself and the organists at San Marco were likewise clavier-teachers in such convents, and that about 1529 Elena, daughter of the renowned poet and man of letters Pietro Bembo, begged her father to allow her to take part in this instruction. Bembo's written reply has been preserved for us; and the passage in his letter, wherein he speaks of the fondness for clavier-playing already becoming universally prevalent, runs thus: "Touching thy request for leave to play the 'monacordo' I answer, that by reason of thy tender years thou canst not know, that playing is an art for vain and frivolous *(leggiera)* women. And I would, that thou shouldst be the most amiable and the most chaste and modest maiden alive. Besides, if thou wert to play badly, thy playing would cause thee little pleasure, and no little shame. But in order to play well, thou must needs give up ten or twelve years to this exercise, without even thinking of aught else. And how far this would befit thee, thou canst see for thyself, without my telling it. Should thy schoolmates desire thee to learn to play, for their pleasure, tell them that thou dost not care to have them laugh at thy mortification. And content thyself with the pursuit of the sciences and the practice of needlework."*

Willaert, beloved and honored by all his contemporaries, and above all revered by his numerous pupils, died at Venice in 1562. How liberal and comprehensive his teaching must have been is proved by the circumstance, that many of his pupils are mentioned as most zealous reformers during the total revolution in music which began shortly after his death. The eight Ecclesiastical Modes, distinguished from each other by the places of their semitones, were at that time still taught and employed in their full diatonic purity. But Willaert called attention to the fact, that each whole-tone interval can be divided into two semitones, and consequently the whole octave, as the Greeks had already taught, into twelve semitones quite equal in their

* Caffi, Vol. 1, p. 95.

mutual proportions. Although he himself may not have wished to draw practical conclusions from this theory, his distinguished pupils, **Nicolo Vincentino** and **Cipriano de Rore,** took a leading part in introducing and defending the newly appearing chromatic music, by which the diatonic was later to be superseded. Their fellow-pupil **Gioseffo Zarlino** also stands out as the most eminent and liberal theoretician of his period, his authority being recognized almost exclusively and universally until the appearance of Rameau in the 18th century.

Of the compositions of Willaert and his pupils, bearing on our subject, the following were published by Ant. Gardane in Venice, 1549: "Fantasie o Ricercari dall' eccelentiss. Adr. Vuigliart e Cipr. Rore, suo discepolo, a 4 e 5 voci"; further, in 1559: "Fantasie, Ricercari, Contrapunti a tre voci di M. Adriano et altri autori, appropriati per cantare e sonare d'ogni sorte di stromenti".—The Fantasias and Ricercari are built up from motives of the composer's own invention; while in the Contrapunti the counterpoint is added to a selected sacred melody or a given *canto fermo.* The motives, generally short, enter in the several parts in fugue style, in the fifth above, the fourth below, or the octave, and the building up of the composition is often effected by imitations in the various parts.

Besides the above-mentioned organists for the two organs in San Marco, **Claudio Mèrulo da Correggio** is deserving of special mention. He was born in Correggio in 1533, was a fellow-student of Cipriano de Rore under Willaert, and while still very young was appointed organist of the cathedral at Brescia. But when, at the decease of Parabosco in 1557, the position of second organist in the cathedral at Venice became vacant, Merulo was chosen therefor over the heads of nine distinguished rivals. He and his colleague **Annibale Padovano** now frequently performed simultaneously or in alternation upon the two organs at solemn celebrations; and after the death of the latter, Merulo was appointed to his position as first organist, while **Andrea Gabrieli,** afterwards so famous, undertook the control of the second organ. Merulo's friends and fellow-students, Cipriano de Rore and Gioseffo Zarlino, successively followed their master Willaert in office, and when Merulo left Venice in 1584, in response to his flattering appointment as Court Organist of the Duke of Parma, his position was given to **Giovanni Gabrieli,** a highly meritorious and influential composer and teacher, and nephew of the Andrea Gabrieli before spoken of. Now, all these artists were devoted to the liberal tendencies by which Willaert's teaching was marked; *and to their co-operation do we owe, foremostly, the gradual emancipation of instrumental music from the shackles of diatonics and the limitations of vocal style.* Claudio Merulo worked in Parma for twenty years longer as an organist, composer, and music-teacher, marks of favor of all kinds being lavished upon him, and the Duke distinguishing him by the golden chain and the title of *Cavaliere.* He died in Parma in 1604. While his numerous 3 to 6-part Madrigals had the greatest influence on the development of a more animated style of profane song, his Toccate and Ricercari for the organ and other instruments, published in Rome and Venice, similarly promoted the evolution of the instrumental style proper, as distinguished from vocal style. They appeared under the title: "Toccate d'intavolatura d'organo di Claudio Merulo da Correggio, organista del sereniss. Sig. Duca di Parma e Piacenza. Libro secondo, 1604"; and further: "Ricercari d'intavolatura d'organo, lib. primo. In Venetia, 1567, 1605, and 1607; lib. secondo, 1608". The **Toccata,** with its broken chords, more rapid runs, and livelier figures, was originally intended for the quickly vanishing tone of the clavier, and later transferred to the organ. In Merulo's toccatas an inner coherency already shows more distinctly; the figurate runs are taken up, now in one part and now in another, and supported by sustained tones, and simple melodious periods likewise alternate with more animated passages in manifold variety.

Like the Toccata through Claudio Merulo, the Canzone and Sonata attained to a more finished artistic form at the hands of the above-mentioned Andrea and his nephew Giovanni Gabrieli:— A. Gabrieli, "Canzoni alla francese per l'organo", Venezia, 1571 and 1605; "Sonate a cinque per i stromenti", Venezia, 1586; and by G. Gabrieli, "Intonazioni d'organo", lib. 1, Venezia, 1593; "Ricercari per l'organo", lib. 2, 1595; lib. 3, 1595. In the **Canzone** (originally marked "per sonar" to distinguish it from the canzone for the voice) a principal melody appears, frequently changed in measure and rhythm when reappearing in the course of the piece; and like the *sound* (harmony) in the **sonata,** the melody in the **canzone** was the bearer of the motives and their imitations. In the canzoni by Giovanni Gabrieli we already meet with varied and interestingly turned forms; an essentially melodious idea is the theme of the composition; the passages of the toccata are employed therein, rhythmical contrasts appear, and in the frequent imitations the subject and answer, regularly alternating with each other, are distinctly recognizable. The distinction between *Sonatas* and *Canzoni* is given by Michael Praetorius, in his Syntagma musicum, Tom. 3, P. 24, A. D. 1620, as follow . "*Sonata a sonando* is thus named, because it is not performed by human voices, but by instruments alone, like the Canzone; of which kind very beautiful ones may be found in Giov. Gabrieli's and other authors' Canzonibus and Symphoniis. But in my opinion there is this distinction:—That the Sonatas are written right seriously and rarely in motet-style, whereas the Canzoni speed along blithely and merrily with many black notes".

The *Preludes, Intonations,* and *Fantasias* were compositions intended for organ as preludes, interludes, or postludes, written in chord-style, and often interspersed with more animated runs. But the *Symphonies* of that period were not only for the organ; they were sometimes extended pieces for 4, 5, 6 or more independent instruments, which contained shorter imitations, and were set, in particular, in very full harmony.

Fuga was originally the name of a composition for two, three, or more parts. One of these begins with a melody, which is exactly imitated by the other parts entering in succession, the part first entering continuing its melody to the close,. regularly followed by all the rest in the same manner. Tinctoris (sic) therefore defines the Fugue, in his earliest musical dictionary, published about 1474, as a strict imitation of the parts of a song.* Such a fugue could be executed by the performers to whom it was entrusted from a single part, when the author set at the beginning a rule or "canon" ordering the successive entrance of the parts (whether after one or more measures, on the strong or weak beat, in augmentation or diminution, etc.) Such directions were often given in enigmatical form. For instance, if there stood, above the one part intended for all performers, the words "Canon: Crescit in duplo", the contrapuntist meant, that the next part should follow in double augmentation; with "Canon: Qui se exaltat humiliabitur" the direction was given, that the answering part should ascend when the leading part descended, and *vice versâ.* Tinctoris defines the word *canon* as a direction, which obscurely indicates the composer's pleasure** As early as 1558. when

---

* Fuga est idemtitas partium cantus quo ad valorem, nomen, formam et interdum quo ad locum notarum et pausarum suarum.

** Canon est regula voluntatem compositoris sub obscuritate quadam ostendens.

Zarlino published his celebrated work "Le institutioni harmoniche" in Venice, "some musicians of little understanding", as he disapprovingly says, called the strict fugue spoken of above a "canon". The Venetian contrapuntists, too, desired to distinguish their freer fugue from the strict one, the *fuga legata,* and therefore named it the *fuga ricercata* (choice, well chosen). A composition so carefully wrought out might further be termed *una Ricercata* or *un Ricercare,* terms never employed by the scrupulously exact Zarlino, although he lived and labored for 23 years in the midst of his colleagues, the *ricercari* composers just mentioned. The practical theoretician G. M. Bononcini, in his "Musico prattico" (Bologna, 1688), discusses the *Fuga sciolta ò libera* (free fugue), and also the *Fuga legata overo obligata* (the "bound" or strict fugue), and various others, adding the remark (p. 78): "The strict fugue is the same as the canon".

At the present time the word "canon" is used to denote a composition constructed throughout in strict imitation, whereas under "fugue" we understand only the former, artistically wrought composition whose independent parts progress with greater freedom. Our modern "strict fugue" should properly be developed organically only from motives of the subject and counter-subject; whereas our "free fugue" decorates its tissue, especially in the episodes, with fresh motives symmetrically repeated.

All compositions as yet named were also written in different forms by different composers. The contrapuntal movements also took at times an introduction and coda in chord-form, from the motives of which the imitations of the middle movement were worked up; or the several parts of a canzone or some other serious composition had various motives for modulatory work, in order to keep the hearer's interest continually alive by this or similar means.

To these monotonous, academical works a novel and fructifying element was, however, added in the airs of the folk-songs and folk-dances, which, more sympathetic in melody and more symmetrical in rhythm, had found loving and fostering care at all times in Italy and in all other countries. Even before the beginning of the 16th century, learned composers had based their works, including masses and sacred motets, on such popular melodies, which they surrounded by ingenious counterpoint. Although such a *cantus firmus* was usually set in the tenor, or most prominent part, it could nevertheless exercise no important influence on the character of the composition as a whole, as its melody and, in particular. its rhythm were quite covered up by the other parts. Not until writers began to set melodies of a popular cast in the naturally most prominent part, the soprano, and to develop the accompanying parts harmonically rather than contrapuntally, did these readily intelligible profane songs show a more pulsing animation.

Instrumental music also adopted this improvement, and its *canzoni villanesche*, *napolitane*, and *francesi*, as well as the likewise homophonic dance-melodies of the Gagliardi, Correnti, Ciacone, etc. everywhere met with a most favorable reception. Later, several such serious or gay pieces written in the popular style of the folk-song would be put together, wrought out more artistically, furnished with an introduction and a lively Finale (often a Giga), and maintained unity amid this diversity by a principal key sustained throughout, and a similarity in the working out of the different movements. Cyclic compositions of this order were called *Partite*, *Suites*, or *Parthien*.

The above-mentioned *Ricercari da cantare e sonare* by Buus, published in Venice, 1547, were the first contrapuntal works printed in Italy which were intended, besides for singing, for the organ and other instruments. They were followed by "Fantasie, Ricercari, Contrapunti a tre voci di M. Adriano (Willaert) et altri autori appropriati per cantare e sonare d'ogni sorti di stromenti. Venezia, A. Gardane, 1549." Two years later the same publisher issued: "Intabulatura nova di varie sorte di balli da sonare per Arpichordi, Clavicembali, Spinette e Manachordi, raccolti de diversi excellentissimi Autori. Libro primo." In the Pass' e mezi, Gagliardi, a Pavane and a Saltarello contained therein, the soprano is supported by a very simple harmonic accompaniment. In the collections of such dances printed later in Venice and other places, the accompaniment to the soprano already exhibits a more interesting harmonic form.*

From a chapter of the extremely rare book "Compendium musices descriptum ab Adriano Petit Coclico, discipulo Josquini de Pres. Impressum Norimbergæ — — — 1552" it appears, that as early as the 16th century a distinction was made between the science of

---

* Of most of the compositions hitherto named—the Ricercari, Canzoni, down to the last-mentioned dances—characteristic specimens may be found in the carefully edited and richly made-up book: "History of Instrumental Music in the XVI. Century", by W. J. von Wasielewsky Berlin, 1878, J. Guttentag (D. Collin).

Counterpoint (employed in working out the Ricercari and other scientifico-artistic compositions), and the science of Harmony, according to whose freer and more easily mastered rules the accompaniments to the greater part of the collections of dances just mentioned were set. This chapter begins on sheet L II^b, or on page 84, if one choose to number the pages from the title-page. It not having been noticed hitherto, I quote so much of it as bears on our subject:

"On the Rules of Composition, and on the Syncopation and Tying of the Notes."

"Many have boasted of being composers, because, following the rules and consonances of composition (compositionis), although not in accordance with the existing usage of counterpoint, they have composed much. Dominus Josquinus despised such, and made sport of them, saying that they would fain fly without wings."

"Thus the first thing required of a good composer is, that he should be able to sing an extemporized counterpoint (contrapunctum ex tempore canere); else he is none."

"The second: That he should be drawn to composition by a great desire, by a certain natural impulse, so that neither food nor drink may tempt him before his song be finished. For in one hour he will do more, when driven by this natural impulse, than otherwise in a whole month. Incapable, therefore, are those composers, who lack this special impulse."

"The third: That he should understand the employment of the perfect consonances *(species perfectas,* the Prime and the Fifth, likewise their doublings, the Octave and the Twelfth, etc.) and the imperfect consonances *(species imperfectas,* the Thirds and Sixths, with their doublings) in the proper place, as is taught in rule of Counterpoint. For the rule of composition differs in a measure from the rule of counterpoint. The rule of composition is freer, and more is allowed in this than in counterpoint. For the *bad* varieties (of intervals), i. e. the Second, the Fourth, and the higher octave of either, are very good in composition, wherever an Octave or a Sixth in one of the lower parts excuses them; and this is termed in French "faubordon" *(faux bourdon)*, i. e. bad intervals with the highest part (e. g. g—$\bar{c}$) are excused by Sixths or Octaves in the lowest part (e. g. e—g—c, or c—a—$\bar{c}$)."— — —

"It is likewise allowed in composition, to ascend and descend with perfect consonances *(cum speciebus perfectis)* and to set *fa* against *mi (f—b)* by writing a ♭ before *b (f—b♭)*, which is not permitted in counterpoint."

"But in composition, too, one should take the greatest care not to let two perfect consonances (*species perfectae)* follow each other immediately, such as two Octaves, or two Fifths, or their higher positions; unless one part should ascend and the other descend (e. g. $\genfrac{}{}{0pt}{}{g}{c} \times \genfrac{}{}{0pt}{}{a}{d}$)."—

Coclius informs us in this chapter, that the compositions of the 16th century were not always contrapuntal, but sometimes in a freer, homophonic style. This latter gave rise later to the epoch-making invention of the *basso continuo* for the organist accompanying a vocal piece,—this being a bass part, whose notes were soon provided with figures indicating the chords to be performed over the same.

It was in Venice, too, that the first systematic Organ and Clavier Method, by P. **Giròlamo Diruta,** appeared, bearing the title: "Prima parte del Transilvano, diàlogo sopra il vero modo di sonar organi ed instrumenti da penna", which latter term included the harpsichord, spinet, and other instruments whose strings were made to sound by crow-quills. The dedication to the Prince of Transylvania, with whom the author holds these dialogues, and to whom the work owes its title, bears the date of 1593. The second part, also printed in Venice, appeared in 1609. In the first part Diruta explains the keyboard, shows the position of the hands and the use of the fingers, explains the Intavolatura (Tabulature or Score), and then proves the truth and necessity of his rules by giving several Toccatas of his own, by Claudio Merulo and Andrea Gabrieli, whose compositions he praises very highly, and by others; calling special attention to the difference between organ-playing and clavier- (harpsichord-) playing. The second part teaches how a melody is to be noted down, gives contrapuntal rules, and directions for improvization with examples from Luzzasco Luzzaschi, Gabriele Fattorini, and Adriano Banchieri —all celebrated organists of that period. He treats further of the ecclesiastical modes and their transposition, teaches how to accompany a chorale harmonically, and gives at the close short directions for singing. The numerous editions of both parts of this book, demanded in the beginning of the 17th century, bear trustworthy testimony at the same time to its clearness, intelligibility, and practical utility.

Concerning the **fingering** of keyed instruments, even one hundred years later, we may draw information from a work whose fifth edition was issued in Antwerp, 1690, its first having been published in Bologna, 1656. It is entitled: "Li primi albori musicali", and the author, Lorenzo Penna, a distinguished organist of the time, gives therein the following general rules for the fingering (p. 195): In ascending, the fingers of the right hand move one after the other; first the middle finger, then the ring-finger, and then the middle finger again; thus they run on in alternation, whereby care must be taken that the fingers do not strike at the same time. But in descending, the middle finger moves first, then the forefinger, then the middle finger again, etc. The left hand observes the reverse order; i. e. in ascending it takes the middle finger first, then the forefinger, etc., and in descending the middle finger first, then the ring-finger, etc.—The author gives the additional rule, that the hands must not lie lower than the fingers, but high, and that the fingers should be stretched out.

Even in the following century the fingering was no more rationally developed, as we see from a book with a very happy poetical introduction by Mattheson. It bears the title: "J. F. B. Caspar Majer's, Organistens bey St. Catharein in Schwäbischen Hall, neueröffneten theoretisch- und praktischer Music-Saal" etc. (Newly opened Theoretico-practical Music-Hall). Second edition, Nuremberg, Joh. Jac. Cremer, 1741. In the chapter "von denen Instrumentis Pulsatilibus, oder die da geschlagen werden" (on the instruments of percussion, or such as are struck) we find the following remarks: The white keys are named c d e f g a h (b) c and so on through the four octaves of the clavier. "But the black keys, which stand between the white, though further back and higher than the latter, derive their names from the white keys, and the first black key from below is named *cis* (*c*♯), because derived from *c*, the second *dis* (*d*♯), because derived from *d*, that following *fis* (*f*♯), the next *gis* (*g*♯), because it stands next the *g*. Only this must be noticed; that the black key following the *a* is named *b* (*b*♭) through the four Octaves." On pages 64 and 65 a view is given of the 24 musical modes. Here we find under *G*♯-major, for instance, the *notes* *a*♭ *b*♭ *c* *d*♭ *e*♭ *f* *g* *a*♭, without signature, yet provided with all the necessary chromatic signs; though under these *notes* there stand the *names* then in general use for the same: *g♯ b♭ c c♯ d♯ f g g♯*. In like manner we find under *D♯*-minor the *notes e♭ f g♭ a♭ b♭ c d e♭*, and below the same their *names d♯ f f♯ g♯ b♭ c d d♯*.

To introduce his discussion of the clavier-fingering, the author first gives the signs for the fingers of either hand: O indicates the but seldom used thumb, 1 the forefinger, 2 the middle finger, 3 the ring-finger, and 4 the little finger. This numbering still prevails in the United States of North America. [This statement may have been correct when penned; but at present (1891) the fingering 1 2 3 4 5 is decidedly and justly preferred. In more conservative England the former fingering, with a cross × for the thumb, is still, perhaps, the prevalent one. **Transl. Note.**] In the "Music-Saal" under consideration the theory of fingering is very concise, and is illustrated by the following table:

Left hand takes the		with the		right hand	
	seconds ascending		forefinger and thumb		middle and ring-f.
	seconds descending		middle and ring-finger		middle and fore-f.
	thirds and fourths		ring and forefinger		ring-finger and foref.
	fifths and sixths		ring-finger and thumb		forefinger and little f.
	sevenths and eighths		little finger and thumb		little f. and thumb

We owe the first fingering for the clavier based on rational principles to Carl Philipp Emanuel Bach, son of the great composer Sebastian Bach, whose "Versuch über die wahre Art das Clavier zu spielen" (Essay on the true Method of playing the Clavier) was published in Berlin, in the year 1753.

On the first appearance in Italy, about 1580, together with Monody and recitative song, of a principal part not enveloped, as until then, by contrapuntal parts of equal importance, but merely supported harmonically by an appropriate instrument, like the lute or harpsichord, this principal part was furnished with a bass, to serve the player as a guide for the harmonies accompanying the former. Lodovico Viadana, in turn *maestro di cappella* at several cathedrals in the States of Urbino, at Venice, and at last in Mantua, invented thereafter (about 1596, at which time he was in Rome) a new kind of vocal compositions, which he called *"concerti ecclesiastici"*, and in which now one voice alone, and anon two, three, or four voices together would appear, an accompanying bass part for the organ, a **basso continuo,** being added thereto. One hundred of the same were, however, first printed at Venice in 1602 as four separate voice-parts, together with a fifth: "il basso continuo per sonar nell' organo". In the preface he gives the organist the advice, to play only the voice-parts belonging to each movement, to look through these before the performance, and not to obscure the same by embellishments. But as yet the *basso continuo* of this first edition shows no figures over the notes, or any other sign indicating the harmonies to be taken therewith.

Recitative and solo singing, which came into vogue in Florence, together with the first attempts at a drama supported by music throughout, in the last decade of the 16th century, and which was actively promoted by the Florentines Vincenzo Galilei and Jacopo Peri, and the Romans Emilio del Cavaliere and Giulio Caccini then in Florence, had also made necessary a similar bass part for its accompaniment. The sacred musical drama, designed for the oratory, also took its rise in that time of mental and vital activity. In such an Oratorio by the above-named Emilio del Cavaliere, "La rappresentazione di anima e di corpo", printed in 1600, and in the opera "Eurydice" by Giulio Caccini, published at Florence in the same year, likewise in Jacopo Peri's opera of the same name which appeared in Venice in 1608, the bass parts already have *figures* and *chromatic signs* over the notes; and the editor of the Oratorio, Alessandro Guidotti, already furnishes some observations on the meaning of this figuring in his accompanying "Avvertimenti particolari per chi canterà recitando e per chi sonerà". Now, as Ludovico Viadana, in the second edition of his "Cento concerti ecclesiastici" (published in Venice, 1609, i. e. later than the work mentioned above), first added to the same a *basso continuo* with figuring, yet already provided it with detailed directions for playing, it is doubtful whether we owe the invention and introduction of thorough-bass to this composer, or to Emilio del Cavaliere, Caccini, or Peri. But, as the execution of such figured basses in profane compositions was usually entrusted, from that time onward, to a clavier-player, the latter was obliged, like the organist who had to accompany sacred music in a similar manner, to be familiar with **thorough-bass playing**; and the science of accompanying formed henceforward an important part of the musical education of every clavier-player.

The course of our observations has shown, how in Venice, firstly there were gradually developed from compositions intended for the voice those forms of art, which were adapted to the character of instrumental music in general and to that of keyed instruments in particular; and how thereafter, in Florence, the clavier was not as formerly used exclusively for the performance of works in contrapuntal style, but also for the freer harmonic support of dramatic solo singing, whereby its easily evoked harmonic fulness was brought out. We now turn to Rome, where **Giròlamo Frescobaldi** and **Bernardo Pasquini,** two men prominent in the annals of Music, *at length treated the clavier, with its non-sustained, quickly vanishing tones, in a manner corresponding to its peculiarities, so that compositions written both artistically and in true clavier-style made their appearance.* As teachers of Frescobaldi are named the two excellent organists and composers Luzzasco Luzzaschi and Alexandre Milleville, both, like himself, natives of Ferrara. Luzzaschi was one of those artists, who undertook towards the end of the 16th century to rehabilitate the three primary *genera* of the Greeks, and to adapt them to the practice of their own time; like Willaert's above-named pupils Vincentio and Zarlino, he therefore had a clavier built, on which the diatonic, chromatic, and enharmonic modes could be played —a fact which exercised most lasting influence upon the training of the pupils committed to his charge. **Giròlamo Frescobaldi** was one of those highly gifted, epoch-making minds, of whom the history of an art can boast but few at any time. Unsurpassed as a virtuoso on the organ and clavier, and enthusiastically revered by all his contemporaries, he also stands forth as a composer for these instruments of solid, acute, and in the highest degree inventive genius. Though few details of his career are known to us, the greater is the number of the compositions preserved; these exhibit throughout an artist familiar with the laws of his art, but standing high above them, receptive of everything new, and fearing no difficulty. He was born in Ferrara in 1587 or 1588, studied there under the above-named distinguished musicians and organists, then paid a visit of several years to the Netherlands, returned in 1608 from Antwerp to Milan, and went to Rome in 1614 with his teacher Milleville. Such brilliant renown already preceded him thither, that according to report his first performance as an organ-player at St. Peter's attracted an audience of 30,000. As early as the following year, from the title of one of his collections of Toccatas and Partitas for the clavier, he was installed as *organista di San Pietro*, which office he appears to have held until his death. His most celebrated pupil, **Johann Jacob Froberger,** was accounted a marvel as a child, sent to Rome by Kaiser Ferdinand III., and returned thence after a stay of three years as the greatest German clavier-player and organ-player of his time. The numerous published works of Frescobaldi embrace Ricercari, Canzoni, Fantasie, Toccate, Capricci and Partite for the clavier and for the organ. Though in all these compositions we find mainly fugued movements, only the **Ricercari** show the strict and regular working-out of a distinct principal motive; whereas the fugal melodies of the **Canzoni** are sometimes introduced and interrupted by a few measures in chorale style. The leading melody of the Canzone, which already bears a distinct character, remains recognizable even at a change of time in the same. Before Frescobaldi, the **Capriccio** frequently consisted of a movement in binary (common) time, in which two different motives were worked out. This was followed by a short, animated movement in ternary time, like a dance air; and a new, fugued motive then closed the composition. The Capricci of Frescobaldi, on the contrary, are invariably founded on some strange motive, a bizarre subject; and more particularly in this does this composer reveal himself as a genius far outrivalling his contemporaries through wealth of invention, and an easy, skilful mastery of his material. Thus we find, in his *Capriccio di durezze,* harmonic roughnesses intentionally sought; in the *Capriccio cromatico con ligature al contrario,* passages chromatically worked out, with ascending resolutions of all ligatures occurring therein — then an unheard-of licence! Another of his compositions follows the compulsory rule *(obbligo)* that none of its four parts shall progress by steps; and the player of another four-part movement must sing to the same throughout a melody consisting of 8 tones. While in the fugues (Ricercari) of the elder and younger contemporaries of Frescobaldi, moreover, the ecclesiastical modes are still retained, in his own the endeavor is already often apparent, to approach our modern keys with the leading-note peculiar to the same. To this active spirit we likewise chiefly owe the introduction of a more perspicuous notation of compositions designed for keyed instruments. Thus in the works engraved on copper by Nicolo Borboni at Rome in 1615, "Toccate e partite *d'intavolatura di Cembalo* di Girolamo Frescobaldi, organista di San Pietro in Roma", as well as in several similar compositions published later, the notes for the right hand are written on six lines, and those for the left on eight. Of other compositions by him still extant we mention: Il primo libro di Fantasie a 2, 3 e 4. In Milano, 1608; Ricercari et Canzoni francesi, fatti sopra diversi oblighi, in partitura. In Roma, 1615; Il secondo libro di Toccate, Canzoni, Versi d'inni, Magnificat, Gagliarde, Correnti ed altre partite d'intavolatura di cembalo ed organo. In Roma, 1616; Capricci sopra diversi sogetti (with likeness of Frescobaldi). In Roma, 1624; Il primo libro di Capricci, Canzoni francesi e Ricercari, fatti sopra diversi sogetti et Arie: in Partitura. In Venetia, 1626; Il primo libro delle Canzoni a 1, 2, 3, 4 voci, per sonare, o per cantare con ogni sorte di stromenti. In Roma, 1628 (in separate parts; later set in score by Frescobaldi's pupil Bartolomeo Grassi); Fiori musicali di Toccate, Kyrie, Canzoni, Capricci, e Ricercari in Partitura per sonatori con basso per organo. In Roma, 1635; Toccate d'intavolatura di Cembalo ed Organo, Partite di diverse Arie, Correnti, Balletti, Ciacone, Passacagli, etc. In Roma, 1637.

While Frescobaldi was the greatest organist and clavierist of the first half of the 17th century, in its second half the same rank was taken by a native of Tuscany, **Bernardo Pasquini** (b. 1637), a pupil of the noted composer of cantatas and operas Antonio Cesti. While yet a youth, Pasquini came to Rome, and was engaged as organist at the church of Santa Maria maggiore. But his remarkable performances soon rendered him so famous, that Kaiser Leopold entrusted the education of several pupils to his charge, and presented him his portrait hung on a gold chain. In Florence and Rome he was overwhelmed with honors, and also in Paris, where Cardinal Chigi presented him to Louis XIV.; and upon his monument at Rome in the church of S. Lorenzo in Lucina is inscribed the lofty title: "S. P. Q. R. organœdus", Organist to the Senate and the Roman Nation. In the year 1679 he wrote the opera "Dov' è amore e pietà" for the opening of the Caprànica theatre, in which he was engaged as clavierist; the no less famous Corelli holding the position of leader of the violins. He died at Rome in 1710. One of his pupils was **Francesco Gasparini**, later highly esteemed in Italy as a teacher and composer, and the author of a text-book on thorough-bass for clavierists, "L'armonico prattico al cembalo, etc.", which ran through seven editions from its first appearance in Venice, 1683, to the year 1802. Of Pasquini's compositions but few have been printed; among these we find "Toccates et suites pour le Clavecin de MM. Pasquini

Paglietti, et Gaspard Kerle. Amsterdam, Roger, 1704;" yet in them the endeavor is still more apparent than in Frescobaldi's, to abandon the earlier, strict style, and to substitute therefor one more free and pleasing, and better suited to the clavier. His **Toccatas**, therefore, no longer appear as pieces contrapuntally elaborated for a regular number of parts, but he follows in the same the more buoyant flight of his fancy, now in broad, sweeping arpeggios, and again by strengthening through prolonged trills the unsustained clavier-tone; here one part appears alone, there two or more conjoined; flowing passages are now taken up in the right hand, now in the left; then one or several motives are fugued in a movement held more strictly in hand, the second division of which resumes the livelier runs of the first movement, and winds up the composition with the same.

Our modern major and minor keys having supplanted, since the beginning of the 18th century, the ancient modes, and the finally established equal temperament of the clavier permitting compositions to be written for the same in all these keys (whereby a new and wide field was opened for modulation as well), a genius was still wanting, who should be capable of employing the art-forms and effects developed by the masters hitherto named not only for the sensuous enjoyment of the ear, but rather for the expression of inner feelings and emotional phases, and thus at length to inspire the compositions intended for this instrument with a living spirit. The seed so abundantly strewn by the earlier composers required fecundation, the form so artistically constructed needed the inpiration of emotion, if compositions designed of the clavier should answer, like others, the higher ends of music, by giving intelligible expression to all feelings and moods of the soul.

In Naples, where the melodious element, as best suited to the hot-blooded Italian temperament, had from the earliest times been specially fostered and cultivated, the great reformer and inspirer of the opera, **Alessandro Scarlatti,** had labored since 1709 by word and deed; and the Neapolitan school, which finally united the pure Roman style with the freer form-development of the Venetian school, took precedence of all other schools in Italy, especially when its renowned representative Francesco Durante stood at its head. His son Domenico was in his time as active an inventor and reformer, in the field of clavier-literature, as Alessandro Scarlatti in dramatic matters, and his performances were received with the greatest enthusiasm not only by his own countrymen, but also by the German musicians who met him, among others the equally eminent composer and clavier-player **Johann Adolph Hasse** (il Sassone, 1699—1783). **Dominico Scarlatti,** born in Naples, 1683, began his musical studies under his father, and finished the same under the guidance of the above-mentioned Gasparini. In the year 1709 he met Handel in Venice, and accompanied this master, whom he deeply revered, to Rome, to benefit by longer study of his works and his performances as an organist and clavierist. The German school, then in full vigor, thus appears to have exercised thenceforward its beneficial influence on the Italian; so that the wearer of Scarlatti's mantle, Clementi, who was gifted with an equally glowing imagination, was enabled to take rank among the heads of the newer, universal school of clavier-playing. In 1715 Dominico Scarlatti was appointed *maestro di cappella* to the Vatican at Rome, went in 1719 to London, to bring out one of his musical dramas in that city and to assume the position of harpsichord player at the Italian opera; thence he journeyed to Lisbon, where the king attached him to his court under the most flattering conditions. We again find him in 1726 at Naples, later at Rome, and finally (1729) at the Spanish court in Madrid, where he lived in the fullest prosperity, and died in 1757 as the greatest virtuoso of his time and most influential composer for his instrument. The personal influence exercised by this gifted master in the places enumerated was of lasting effect, and his highly artistic and effective compositions, of which Abbot Santini of Rome possessed 349 for organ and clavier alone, insure remembrance of his name in the history of music. They all reveal an extraordinary inventive talent, contain pleasing, though not long-breathed melodies, striking rhythms, and flowing passages practicable in the swiftest tempo, in which the hands are frequently to be passed over each other. These are no longer the art-forms of the Netherlanders, products of pure mental skill, but the heart-outpourings of an Italian inspired by his art. His compositions, whose worth has by no means been fully recognized, contain effects of style and tone not again employed until long after, and then with immense success. Thus we already find in his *Sonatas* (usually *sound-pieces* consisting of a single movement) running passages in thirds and sixths; the rapid repetition on one key of various fingers; leaps wider than an octave with one hand; broken chords for both hands in contrary motion; and other effects quite novel at that time. To be sure, his works commonly hold fast to a selected, characteristic principal motive; but at the same time the accompanying parts, especially the bass, are always interestingly and effectively worked out. A collection of his clavier-works has been published under the title of "Œuvres complettes de D. Scarlatti", Cah. 1—8, Vienna, chez Riedl; another, edited by Carl Czerny, bearing the title "Sämmtliche Werke für das Pianoforte (?) von D. Scarlatti", 15 Parts (120 pieces), Vienna, Haslinger; and published separately, Fugues, Paris, Janet et Cie.; Sonata con fuga, Vienna, Cappi.

The term "for the **Pianoforte**" on the edition of his works edited by Czerny, is evidently erroneous. For although **Bartolomei Christofori** had built in Italy, as early as 1711, claviers whose strings could be struck by hammers *piano* or *forte*, we nevertheless owe the production of the first practically useful Pianofortes to the unremitting experiments and improvements of **Gottfried Silbermann,** begun in 1726; whose instruments, however, as the History of the Pianoforte at the end of this book shows, were not widely employed until after Scarlatti's death.

In Scarlatti's compositions the first movement of the modern Sonata, i. e. the proper sonata-form, is already established in its fundamental outlines. These pieces usually consist of two parts, each of which is to be repeated. The first contains the exposition of the piece; it begins with the principal theme or motive in the principal key, effects a transition through the passages and runs following to a related secondary key, and closes in the latter with an extended cadence. In major, the modulatory contrast usually chosen is the key of the dominant; in minor, either the relative major, or the minor or major key of the dominant. The second part then works up the material of the first, modulating back into the principal key; now takes up the *beginning* of the piece, or *some later passage* in the exposition, repeats the motives of the first part, this time in the principal key, and closes in the latter, generally with a cadence similar to that of the first part. Sometimes there enters, with the modulatory contrast of the first part, a thought essentially different from the principal motive—a most striking reminder of our modern sonata-form. In his rhythms and modulations Scarlatti is often bold and original. E. g. the fifth Sonata in the first number of Czerny's edition begins with a clear-cut musical thought of five measures in *A*-major, which is repeated, and to which episodes are added, modulating through *D*-minor and *A*-minor to *E*-minor, in which key the author dwells, and closes the first part. The second passes through the *E*-major triad to *A*-major, touching *D*-major on the way, and a sustained tone, *E*, leads us to *A*-minor. In this key the motives of the first part are now repeated, and the Sonata closes in the same, as did the first part.

The above-mentioned **Francesco Durante** is another of the composers, to whom we owe the expansion of the clavier-sonata through the combination of several movements outwardly different, but inwardly in harmonious affinity. In his six "Sonate per Cembalo, divise in studii e divertimenti", published in Naples, each *Studio*—a lively, freely fugued movement, relieved by flowing passages and variously broken chords, wherein to two parts a third or fourth is occasionally added—is followed by a short *Divertimento* in the same key, consisting of two parts, and less artificially elaborated, but pleasingly animated. This uniting of two pieces of different character as one sonata was practiced thereafter by various influential Italian composers, and fully developed or completely transformed. Thus the "VIII Sonate per Cembalo, opera primo da **Dominico Alberti**" (before me lies the edition printed by J. Walsh, London), at first disseminated in MS, and later printed in London and Paris, were for a time much sought after and liked. Each consists of a rather long Allegro or Andante of two parts, in the sonata-form just described, followed by a more or less extended movement in the key of that preceding, and in the form of an Andante, Allegro, Minuet, Giga-Presto, Tempo di Minuetto with variations, or Presto assai. The principal theme and the other divisions of the Sonata are not, however, accompanied by a contrapuntally independent bass, like the works previously discussed, but the bass serves here merely as a subordinate support to the leading highest part, and often breaks the full harmony of a chord in the following manner:

Sonata VI.

For dilettanti, in particular, this style of accompaniment was more convenient than the contrapuntal bass-passages of Durante and other workmanlike writers. It was dubbed the "Alberti bass". and the abuse of the same by later composers is the reason, that the development of the pianist's left hand is often less carefully attended to, than was formerly thought necessary. In 1737 Dominico Alberti, then twenty years of age, was among the suite of the Venetian ambassador at Rome, and was in high estimation there on account of his musical gifts as a singer and clavier-player. The twelve "Sonate di Gravicembalo da **Pier Domenico Paradies,** Napolitano", no longer show the fuguing style of earlier contrapuntists, but their working-up, both musically and technically, is by far more artistic than that of Alberti's, in which the strict style is also abandoned. Domenico Paradies was born in Naples about 1710, and finished his musical studies there. After several of his operas had been given in Lucca and Venice, he proceeded to London in 1747, brought out a new tragic opera of his own composing, and then settled down as a clavier-teacher in that city, which extends a friendly welcome to all foreign musicians of repute. In the year 1754 he published, through J. Blundell of London, the 12 Sonates before mentioned. Like Durante's Sonatas, those by Paradies consist of two movements alike in key but differing in tempo. The first and more extended movement has two parts, the first of which closes regularly in the dominant of the principal key. The tempo of the same is either allegro, the second, shorter movement being a Vivace or Presto, sometimes a soft, melodious aria;—or the Sonata begins with an Andante, followed by a grave Minuetto or a lively Giga. The two-part style, which was best adapted to the tone and touch of the clavichords, spinets, and virginals of the period, still forms the basis of these pieces, but is handled so boldly and brilliantly that they served as studies even for Clementi himself.

Of the masters named as yet, the following works have been published by Bartholf Senff, Leipzig, in the collection entitled "Alte Claviermusik", edited by E. Pauer: Frescobaldi, Corrente and Canzona; Alessandro Scarlatti, Fugue; Domenico Scarlatti, 3 Studii; Durante, Studio; Pietro Domenico Paradisi, Sonata. The correct name of the last is Pier Domenico Paradies. A similar, very carefully edited collection by H. M. Schletterer has been published by J. Rieter-Biedermann, Leipzig, with the following title: "Classische Claviercompositionen aus älterer Zeit" (classic Clavier Comp. of Earlier Times) containing 3 Studii e Divertimenti by F. Durante, and 18 Sonatas by Scarlatti, all in one movement. Breitkopf & Härtel have also issued 60 Sonatas by Scarlatti, either separate, in 6 Numbers, or in 1 Volume.

To judge of the music of earlier times impartially and justly, one should not set it in direct contrast with that of to-day, and compare it with this latter, but regard it as a necessary intermediate link in the historical development of our art, at the same time going back in thought and feeling to the period which gave it birth and to the genius and bent of the people in whose midst it arose.

The now frequent modernizing of earlier compositions by striking out certain apparent harshnesses in melody, harmony, or rhythm, by adding more full-sounding chords, more brilliant figuration, etc., robs the original work of its true character, clothes the worthy composer of the olden time in a garb unsuited to him and his age, and often disfigured, and is to be utterly eschewed under all circumstances.

The Earlier English Clavier School.

As early as the 7th century the Gregorian church-song was propagated by papal singers in England; in the 15th century lived **John Dunstable** (d. 1458), who won renown not only as a musician, but as an astronomer as well. He is often cited as a musical authority, together with Binchoys and Dufay, by Tinctoris, Gaforius, and other earlier theoreticians, under the name of Dunstaple and Donstable.* Among the court musicians of Eduard VI. we find, besides the singers, lutists, harpers, flutists, rebec and bagpipe-players, trumpeters and drummers, three virginal players; and in 1575 **Thomas Tallis** and

* Burney (History of Music, Vol. II, p. 339) mentions a treatise by Dunstable "De mensurabile musica" as lost. Since then, however, it has been found, and is at present, an ancient paper manuscript written in Latin, in the British Museum, "Add. Mss. 10, 336", sheet 6 to 18, among various musical essays. As the treatise has not yet been described, and can in any event be understood only by a musician who is also familiar with paleography, I will state in brief the contents of this unique document. The author treats of the various kinds of notes, shows the black shapes of the maxima, longa, brevis, semibrevis, and minima, discusses their value under certain conditions, and gives seven rules for their length when any one of the same stands before, between, or after notes of a kind differing from itself. Further, he treats of the rests, prolation, perfection, of the dot beside a note, which may be either a *punctus perfectionis* or *punctus divisionis;* of the red and black, full and empty notes: lays down eight rules for the value of the figures in the ligatures, discusses the syncopes, and illustrates all points by numerous examples in notes. The very distinctly written signature is *"Dunstable"*.

his celebrated pupil, **William Bird,** were appointed organists to Queen Elizabeth. In a MS still extant, known to us under the name of "Queen Elizabeth's Virginal Book", are preserved clavier-compositions of the two musicians just mentioned, and also by **Giles, Farnaby, Dr. Bull,** and others. Among these we find the **Fancie** or **Fantasie,** which imitates and fugues various motives following each other; further, the **Pavane** in common (binary) time, whose theme is repeated by a **Galliarde** following in triple (ternary) time, and the **Variations,** whose air (usually that of a popular folk-song) is played throughout in one part, while the other parts accompany it with imitating runs and passages. For each hand a staff of six lines is employed. But even the seventy compositions found in this clavier-book which were written by Bird, whom the English praise so highly, are heavy and wanting in grace, though often ingeniously and artistically wrought out. Dr. Bull, on the other hand, already sets the clavier-player the most difficult tasks; in a suite of Variations he writes, to a *cantus firmus* in the highest part, now two notes against three, and again gives the left hand comparatively rapid passages in thirds and sixths to play, etc. In Burney's History of Music, Vol. III, p. 89, 115, etc. are to be found various compositions taken from this Virginal Book of Queen Elizabeth. The first printed clavier-compositions appeared in England under her successor, James I. (1603—1625), bearing the following title: "Parthenia or The Maydenhead of the first musicke that euer was printed for the Virginalls composed by three famous Masters William Byrde, Dr. John Bull and Orlando Gibbons, Gentilmen of his Ma[ties] most Illustrious Chappell. Ingrauen by William Hole". Although the most eminent English composers of the 17th century, Orlando Gibbons (1583—1625), Pelham Humphry (1647—1674), and Henry Purcell (1658—1695), wrote mainly for the voice, the last-named being also an extremely admired opera-composer, compositions by them for the organ are still extant; and **Henry Purcell** had a collection of clavier sonatas printed in London, 1683. The characteristic expression of this earlier English clavier school is a wearisome monotony of melody, rhythm, and modulation; it has therefore had no influence whatever on the further development of the art of clavier-playing, which latter could attain to a higher degree of perfection in England only under the fostering care of masters from abroad, who have ever met with flattering recognition in that country.

In his collection of "Alte Claviermusik" E. Pauer gives the following compositions of the earlier English masters here mentioned:

W. Bird, Prelude and The Carman's Whistle; Dr. John Bull, The King's Hunting Jigg; O. Gibbons, Prelude and Galliarde. The first collection of English Clavier-music cited above, the "Parthenia", has been re-issued by the London Antiq. Mus. Soc., edited and furnished with an introduction on the earliest epoch of Clavier-playing by the musical scientist Edw. F. Rimbault. The latter is also the author of an excellent work (Robt. Cocks: London, 1860) entitled "The History of the Pianoforte", which treats in detail of the origin, development, and construction of this instrument, contains notes on its precursors, such as the clavichord, virginal, spinet, and harpsichord, and to which specimens of the earlier clavier-pieces of the best masters are appended.

The Earlier French Clavier School.

A lasting influence was exercised on the perfecting of our art by an Organ and Clavier School which arose in France toward the middle of the 17th century, more particularly through the evolution of a more elegant, rhythmically defined, and richly embellished clavier style. Its last distinguished élève, Jean Phillipe Rameau, (d. 1764) was likewise the reformer of the French opera and the founder of a system of harmony still current in part to this day. **André Champion**, (commonly called **de Chambonnières** after an estate belonging to his wife), a highly esteemed court clavier-player to Louis XIV., is to be regarded as the head of this earlier French school. According to the report of a contemporary, Le Gallois, he is said to have drawn such an unusually full tone from the Clavecin (harpsichord) through his peculiar style of touch, that only his pupil **Hardelle** was able partially to approach him in this art. Most distinguished among his pupils after the latter are the following: Buret, Gautier, le Bègue, d'Anglebert, Louis Couperin, and François Couperin. In the two books of clavier-pieces by Chambonnières published in Paris, the first of which bears the date of his death, 1670, we already find the groundwork of that brightly embellished clavier style, which continued down to Rameau's time. Fétis, who had before him these compositions, now extant in but rare copies, finds their style naïve and graceful, and their pure harmonic structure worthy of the closest attention.

The above-named **Jean Henry d'Anglebert** was also a clavier-player at the court of Louis XIV., whose luxurious splendor and punctilious etiquette is distinctly called to mind by the compositions of this old school still in existence. In the year 1689 he published a work under the following title: "Pièces de clavecin avec la manière de les jouer, diverses chaconnes, ouvertures, et autres airs de M. de Lully, mis sur cet instrument, quelques fugues pour l'orgue, et les principes de l'accompagnement. Livre premier". Among the clavier pieces of this collection we find 22 Variations on the theme of "Folies d'Espagne", already treated in like manner by Corelli and later by Scarlatti; and the fugues for organ are strict and carefully wrought out.

In the two Couperins also named as pupils of Chambonnières we were introduced to a family, whose members upheld its renown as remarkable musicians down to the 19th century. **Louis Couperin,** born in 1630 in Chaume, was, like his two younger brothers, gifted with eminent musical talent. In the flower of his youth he went to Paris, and obtained there the position of organist at the church of St. Gervais. Of his compositions, only three suites of clavier-pieces, in MS, have come down to us. **François Couperin** was appointed, after his brother's death, to his office at the church of St. Gervais. He attained to high repute as a clavier-teacher; indeed, the strictness of the style of his organ compositions was reached by no other subsequent French composer. The youngest of the three, **Charles Couperin,** followed his brother as organist at the same church, retaining this position until his decease in 1669. The son of the latter, named, like his uncle, **François Couperin,** not without reason received the surname of "le Grand". For by his fine playing on the organ and clavier, and also by his pleasing compositions, he surpassed by far the majority of his immediate rivals in these branches of music. In 1701 he became court clavier-player, and at the same time organist of the royal chapelle, and died at the age of 63 in the year 1733. By him are still extant four books of clavier-pieces published in Paris (1713 etc.); further "Les gouts réunies, ou nouveaux concerts, augmentés de l'apothéose de Corelli en Trio. Paris, 1717", and finally "L'apothéose de l'incomparable L(ully)". Besides these, Couperin published in Paris, 1717, a **Harpsichord Method** entitled: "L'art de toucher du clavecin", wherein, as Türk remarks in a similar work in 1789, "he appears as a pioneer, opening the way for others". Couperin retains, throughout the great number of his published works an individual, artistic, and brilliant style of composition. His clavier-pieces are mainly in two parts, seldom provided with a third or a full chord; almost all are in contrapuntal style, but the highest part generally bears the principal melody, and this latter, like the inner parts and bass, is so overladen with appoggiaturas, trills, and other graces, that the melody, often in itself really elegant and graceful, appears, as it were, like a high-frizzed beauty hidden by a richly wrought lace veil. He modulates to the keys related to the tonic by the third and fifth; and in his works the peculiarity of that method is strongly prominent, through which greater fulness was lent to the weak tone of the harpsichord by keeping down the keys with all the fingers engaged even in the most variously broken chords, thus continuing the vibration of the strings.

As renowned an organist and clavier-player as François Couperin, though by no means so estimable a composer, was his contemporary **Louis Marchand.** He was born in Lyons in 1669, and received the appointment of organist at the cathedral of Nevers when not quite 14. He remained there ten years, went thence to Auxerre and then to Paris, where he was at first engaged as organist at the Jesuit church, but was later appointed to a like position at several other churches together. Subsequently the king made him court organist at Versailles, and dubbed him knight of the Order of St. Michael. But with his growing fame also grew his pride and recklessness, and while revelling in pleasures of every kind, he often left his universally honored wife without the bare necessaries of life. The king, having gained intelligence of this, gave the order, that half of Marchand's salary should be withheld from him, and paid to his wife instead. Soon after this order went into effect, Marchand was to play the mass at Versailles before the entire court. In the Agnus Dei the organ suddenly stopped; Marchand left the church, and everybody supposed him to be taken seriously ill. At the close of the services, however, the king found him promenading in the best of health hard by the palace. On asking the reason of the foregoing disturbance of the holy office, Marchand answered: "Sire, as my wife draws half my salary, she may also play half the mass!" The king received this impertinent reply so ungraciously, that Marchand was banished for a considerable time from France. The meeting occurring thereafter between this organist, once so highly honored in France, with Sebastian Bach, is related by Marpurg according to Bach's own account as follows: "Marchand, during his banishment from France, came in 1717 to Dresden, played before the king of Poland with great applause, and was so fortunate as to have offered him a position in the royal service worth some thousands of thalers. To the orchestra of this prince was attached at the time a French leader by the name of Volumier, who either regarded his countryman's prospective good fortune with envious eyes, or had been incidentally aggrieved by him. He represented to the court musicians, how Marchand scoffed at all German clavierists, and held council with them, how the pride of this Goliath might be at least humbled in some measure, even should it not be possible to rid the court of his presence. Receiving assurance that the "Kammer- und Hoforganist" at Weimar, Sebastian Bach, was a man at any rate a match for the French court organist, if not able to surpass him, Volumier immediately wrote to Weimar and invited Herr Bach to come to Dresden without delay, and break a lance with the celebrated M. Marchand. Bach came, and with the king's consent, without Marchand's knowledge, he was admitted to the next court concert as an auditor. After Marchand had played, among other matters, a French air with numerous variations, and had been loudly applauded for the skill displayed in the variations, and likewise for his neat and fiery execution, Bach, who was standing near him, was invited to try the Harpsichord. He acceded to the request, beginning with a short though masterly prelude; then quite unexpectedly repeated the air played by Marchand, and added a dozen variations with new art in a style never heard before. Marchand, who till then had outrivalled all other organists, doubtless recognized the superiority of his present opponent; for when Bach took the liberty of inviting him to a friendly trial of skill on the organ, handing him to that end a theme, sketched on a sheet of paper, to be worked out at sight, and requesting a similar theme from him, Marchand never appeared on the appointed field of battle, but thought it more prudent to leave Dresden by extra-post." — Marchand returned to Paris, and soon succeeded in re-establishing his former fame, so that it became the fashion to take clavier lessons of him; indeed, to meet the wishes of pupils dwelling at a great distance from each other, he hired lodgings simultaneously in different quarters of the city, staying now in one, and now in another. Although at this time, as Marpurg relates, he had to give nine or ten lessons daily, the price of which had risen to a louisd'or, he was unable to cover his prodigal expenses with this income, and died in 1732 in extreme poverty.

Soon after his return from Germany, Marchand again assumed the position of organist in several churches, and his remarkable playing always attracted throngs of listeners. Even **Rameau**, later so renowned as a theoretician and opera composer, came to Paris from his native city Dijon, to make the acquaintance of this fêted organ-player. Marchand welcomed him in a friendly manner, gave him some lessons, and soon entrusted several of his places as organist to his charge. But after Rameau had shown his teacher some of his own artistically elaborated compositions, the jealousy of Marchand was thereby awakened so strongly, that he tried every means to get his then unknown and quite penniless pupil away from Paris.

The post of organist at the church of St. Paul became vacant in 1727, and Rameau, together with **Louis Claude Daquin**, admired from his eighth year onward as a clavier-player, applied for the same. Marchand, being appointed umpire of the trial of skill ensuing, awarded the prize to Daquin for the reasons before alluded to; the latter held his office with honor, it is true, up to his 78th year, but as a composer was assuredly not the equal of his rival Rameau; for his very insignificant organ and clavier compositions cannot in the least bear comparison with the artistic works of Rameau. — Ballard of Paris published in 1705 a book of pieces for the clavecin, and in 1717 two similar collections dedicated to the king. Among Rameau's compositions, on the other hand, we must mention: "Nouvelles suites de pièces de clavecin, avec des remarques sur les différens genres de musique." Furthermore, he published in Paris: Premier livre de pièces de clavecin, 1706; Deuxième livre, 1721; Pièces de clavecin avec une table pour les agrémens; and finally, "Trois concertos pour clavecin, violon et basse de viole", Paris 1741, Leclerc. His clavier style is freer, and often fuller, than that of his predecessors; for he more frequently employs three parts, and occasionally even supports his melodies by a series of chord-tones struck successively or together. The popular dance-airs were already used in France, as elsewhere, in clavier-pieces of strongly marked rhythm; and the desire, to lend the compositions a definite character, is shown in the titles given below as examples, such being frequently bestowed. Rameau, who died in Paris, 1764, was the last of the more eminent clavierists and organists of this earlier French school; and the sequel will show, that since that time the German school, which had meanwhile reached vigorous maturity, began to exercise a lasting influence in France as well. There, too, true musicians both of native and foreign origin were now confronted by the problem, constantly to extend and enhance the resources and effects of the clavier, in order that it might give most truthful expression to all phases of emotion.

In E. Pauer's "Alte Claviermusik" we find, among other things, an Allemande, Courante, and Sarabande by J. Champion de Chambonnières; also several clavier-pieces by François Couperin, e. g. "La tendre Nanette" and "La Ténébreuse". The collection contains by J. P. Rameau: Deux Gigues en Rondeau, Le rappel des oiseaux, Les tendres plaintes, and Deux Menuets. H. M. Schletterer gives, in his "Classic Clavier Compositions from earlier times", 12 pieces by Couperin, among which are three Preludes, an Allemande, Marche, Sarabande (les Sentiments), and La Voluptueuse; further 12 pieces by Rameau, as Allemande, Gigue, Tambourin, Rigaudon, Sarabande, Menuet, and the humoresque "La Poule", in which the cry of a cackling hen is imitated and worked out.

The Earlier German Clavier School.

In Germany, as in Italy, England, and France, a more highly artistic clavier style was first developed from a cultivated organ style. The clavier merely reproduced the compositions intended for the organ in another and weaker color; not until these compositions had gained a more dignified form, could the clavier style attain to an independence corresponding to its character and resources. As early as the year 1445 we found Bernhard the German settled in Venice as the organist of San Marco, and in the same century **Conrad Paulmann,** blind from birth, created such a sensation by his playing on the organ and other instruments, that he was invited to the courts of various princes, and rewarded with rich presents. A manuscript of 1452, described and elucidated in Vol. 2 of Chrysander's "Jahrbücher für musikalische Wissenschaft", bears the title: "Fundamentum organisandi Magistri Conradi Paumann's (sic) ceci de Nurenberga", etc. The examples in notes therein begin with two-part contrapuntal exercises to a *cantus firmus* in the bass, which ascends and descends by steps, or by thirds, fourths, fifths, or sixths. Then follow two-part examples of closes in the diatonic keys of *C*-major, *D*-minor minus *b*♭, *E*-minor minus *f*♯, *F*-major minus *b*♭, *G*-major minus *f*♯ in the signature, and *A*-minor. Though the counterpoint is melodically flowing, these and the following three-part examples are tiresomely monotonous, and full of ill-sounding parallel fifths and octaves. Paulmann died in 1473 at Munich; in the parish church of Unsere liebe Frau (Our blessed

Lady) is found his tombstone, on which he is depicted playing the organ, with the following inscription: "Anno MCCCCLXXIII an St. Paul Bekehrungs Abent, ist gestorben und hie begraben der Kunstreichest aller Instrumenten und der Musika Maister Conrad Paulmann, Ritterbürtig von Nürnberg und blinter geboren" etc.* According to this the name given in the title of the above-mentioned manuscript, *Paumann*, is a slip of the pen, which has been copied by modern musical writers.

The first *printed* work designed for instrumental music appeared in 1512 at Mayence (Peter Schöffer) with the title: "Tabulaturen etlicher lobgesang vnd lidlein vff die orgeln vn̄ lauten, ein theil mit zweien stimmen zu zwicken vn̄ die drit dartzu singē, etlich on gesangk mit dreien, vō **Arnold Schlicken,** Pfaltzgrauischen Churfürstlichem Organistē Tabulirt vn̄ in den truck in d'ursprūglichen stat der truckerei zu Meintz wie hie nach volgt verordent" etc. In 1869 Robert Eitner republished this work in the "Monatshefte für Musikgeschichte", Vol. 1. It contains 14 organ-pieces in three parts, sometimes with a fourth added, and a number of tabulatures for the lute. The several parts occasionally follow in imitation, the harmony is purer and more euphonious than with Paulmann; yet the highest aim of counterpoint at that period was correctness of progression. It did not take on life and warmth until the Italian vocal and instrumental music, developing in animation and emotion under Willaert and the two Gabrielis, began to exert a salutary influence upon German musical art.

Arnold Schlick, in his book for the organ and lute, did not write counterpoint to original melodies, but, as the titles of the compositions indicate, always to sacred or profane melodies then in vogue. Neither did **Paul Hofhaimer** (d. 1537), who for 25 years was court organist to Kaiser Maximilian I., and who was lauded by his contemporaries as a most eminent composer, organist, and music teacher, leave any original compositions for the organ, but only a few vocal pieces, and several written in tabulature for the favorite instrument of the time, the lute.

In the second half of the 16th century, the clavier already outrivals the lute. The clavier now assumes, beside the various house-organs, its rightful place as an instrument more easily constructed and managed; compositions even are published exclusively for the

* S. Gerber, N. Lex., under *Paulmann*.

clavier. E. g. 1560 in Lyons, by S. Gorlier: "Premier livre de tablature d'Espinette, Chansons, Madrigales et Galliardes". The books of Tabulatures published by Ammerbach in 1575 and B. Schmid in 1577, are intended for "Organ and *Instrument*". But under the latter universal term was understood (in Germany) then, as at times to-day, a Clavier (now Pianoforte) in particular.* Ammerbach, organist at the church of St. Thomas at Leipzig, gives, in his "Orgel oder Instrument Tabulatur", no compositions of his own, but chorales set in 4 parts, secular songs, and dance-tunes accompanied by chords. The German dances are in binary time, and repeat their melody in the following Afterdance "Proportio" in livelier ternary time. After several Galliardes, and southern Passamezzi and Saltarelli, we also come upon some 5-part songs arranged for keyed instruments. Neither do the "Zwei Bücher einer neuen künstlichen Tabulatur auff Orgel und Instrument" by Bernhard Schmid, organist at Strassburg, contain any original compositions, but "selected Motets and Pieces in 6, 5, and 4 Parts, taken from the (works of the) most artful and world-renowned Musicians and composers of this our time". Like his predecessor Ammerbach, Schmid followed the theoretical rules then obtaining; their counterpoint is flowing and melodious, without pretending to higher claims, and the German and foreign dance-airs arranged by both are supported by simple chords, and seldom ornamented by passing notes.

The German masters Heinrich Isaac and Ludwig Senfl had won renown, as early as the beginning of the 16th century, by their highly artistic vocal works, as rivals of the most eminent Dutch and Italian composers. Toward the end of the same century Germany, too, could show independent writers of instrumental music, the first of note being **Hans Leo Hasler.** He was born in 1564 in Nuremberg, and displayed early such a marked talent for music, that his father, the Nuremberg town-musician Isaac Hasler, decided to send him, for the purpose of finishing the studies begun under himself, to Andrea Gabrieli of Venice, justly celebrated as an eminent teacher of music. The latter was able at the end of but one year to dismiss his gifted pupil, who was immediately engaged as organist by

---

* S. Prætorius Syntagma Tom. II, of the year 1620, cap. 37, pag. 62. "A Symphony (and likewise a Clavicymbalum, Virginal, Spinett) is commonly named by most, without distinction, with the word Instrument (although very wrongly)."

a member of the art-loving Fugger family of Augsburg. Here he remained till the year 1601, when he went to Vienna, and entered the service of Kaiser Rudolf II. Hasler won universal love and respect, and the Kaiser sought to confer a special mark of his favor upon the admired artist by giving him a patent of nobility. In 1608 he proceeded to the court of Saxony, and accompanied the Elector to Frankfort on the Main, where he died in the year 1612. Hans Leo Hasler won enduring fame not only as an organist, but still more as a composer; for he may be regarded as the first to lay the foundation of the melodically and harmonically developed German style of composition, which was to ripen to perfection in Sebastian Bach. Of his numerous compositions we mention "Lustgarten newer teutscher Gesäng, Balletti, Gailliarden, vnd Intraden mit 4, 5, 6 vnd 8 Stimmen" (Pleasure-garden of new German Songs, Ballets, Galliardes, and Intradas in 4—8 Parts); Nuremberg, Kauffmann, 1601. The first two parts of the following work by Johann Woltz also contain several compositions by him: "Nova Musices Organicæ Tabvlatvra, das ist: Ein newe art teutscher Tabulatur", etc. Basel, Genath, 1617. The striving to develop such a style, suited to the more serious temper and earnest spirit of the Germans, was likewise exhibited by the Augsburg organist **Christian Erbach**, the Hamburg organist **Hieronymus Pratorius** (Schulz), the two distinguished composers **Adam Gumpelzhaimer** and **Melchior Franck**, and the ingenious composer and organist **Samuel Scheidt** (1587—1654) of Halle,—all worthy contemporaries of Hasler and sharers of his renown. They flourished from about 1600 to the time when the outbreak of the fateful 30-years' War (1618—1648) put a stop for long to the exercise of the liberal arts in Germany. Still, in the midst of this war, there appeared in 1624 the following work by one of the last-named masters in Hamburg: "Tabulatura nova, continens variationes aliquot Psalmorum, Fantasiarum, Cantilenarum, Passamezzo et Canones aliquot. In gratiam Organistarum adornata a Samuele Scheidt, Hallense, etc.; Pars secunda Tabulaturæ, continens Fugarum, Psalmorum, Cantionum et Echus, Toccatæ, etc. Variationes varias et omnimodas. Pro quorumvis Organistarum captu et modulo."

Soon after the re-establishment of peace in Germany, the Swedish ambassador passed through Halle, and was so moved by the clavier-playing and the singing of the young **Johann Jakob Froberger**, son of a cantor in that place, that he took the talented boy with him to Vienna, to present him to Kaiser Ferdinand III. This prince took him under his protection, and sent him to Rome, to be educated as a musician by the renowned Frescobaldi. In three years Froberger finished his studies with this distinguished master, and proceeded at first to Paris, where he played in public with brilliant success as the first German clavierist of eminence. Hence he turned to Dresden, played there before the court several of his Toccatas, Cappriccios, and Ricercare, and presented the manuscript of the same to the Elector, who sent him in recompense a rich golden chain and a letter to the Kaiser, to whom he then returned. The latter received his protégé, now a finished master, with marks of favor of all kinds, and appointed him his Court Organist. Froberger, the most brilliant clavier-player and learned organist of his time, soon became famous throughout Europe, and in the year 1662 he determined to win new laurels on further journeys. He therefore obtained leave of absence from the Kaiser, proposing to go to England via France. But in France, as he himself narrates, he was attacked by robbers, who plundered him so thoroughly that he saved but a few ducats which he carried next his skin, and reached Calais in rags, where he took ship for London. The gifted artist already laughed at his misadventure, when the ship on which he was a passenger, was attacked and seized by pirates not far from the English coast. To escape capture, Froberger threw himself desperately into the sea, and being a skilful swimmer, gained the land. Compassionate fishermen received him here, and gave him a poor suit of clothing, in which he set out to London, begging on the way. A stranger and destitute he arrived there, and roved about seeking shelter. He thus came to Westminster Abbey, and entered the sublime cathedral to offer thanks to the Lord for his wonderful deliverance from all danger. The last organ-tones die away, and the forsaken one still kneels lost in prayer—until a harsh voice interrupts his devotions with the words: "Friend, it is time to leave!"—"You seem very unfortunate?" asked the old man engaged in closing the doors. "I am indeed no child of Fortune", answered Froberger; "robbers and pirates have brought me to such a pass, that I neither know where to find food nor to lay my head!" "Aye, if one might believe it!" replied the old man; "but listen to me. I am the organist of this church and to the court; if you will serve me as organ-blower, I will furnish you with food and clothing." Froberger, filled with joyful hopes, accepted the well-meant proposition, and while fulfilling his humble task awaited with impatience the moment, when, without forfeiting his patron's favor, he might again emerge from his obscurity. Now it happened, while King Charles II. was celebrating his nuptials with Catharine of Portugal, that Froberger went to the palace to perform his humiliating duty. But, dazzled by the splendor and magnificence outspread before him, and quite lost in reflection, he forgot to blow the organ, and the tones suddenly died away under the organist's fingers in the midst of his loftiest strains. The unexpected pause occasioned general wonderment. The enraged organist (Christopher Gibbons) rushed upon Froberger, overwhelmed him with abuse, even striking him, and finally withdrew into a side-room. Froberger now seized a sudden resolve; he filled the bellows with wind, and then sat down at the organ, drawing the attention of all present by a few strikingly dissonant and boldly resolved harmonies. One of the court ladies, who had formerly been in Vienna, thought that she recognized the style of her former teacher, Froberger, in the playing of the new organist so unexpectedly appearing. He was immediately sent for, fell at the King's feet, and in a few words recounted his strange adventures. The King graciously commanded him to rise; a harpsichord was brought, and for over an hour the entire court listened to the fiery improvisations of the artist who appeared, in such miraculous wise, to add lustre to the festival. Charles II. rewarded him with his own royal neck-chain; thenceforward he was the hero of the day and favorite of the grandees of the realm. Laden with costly gifts, Froberger at last left England to return to the Viennese court. But here, on account of his long absence and slanders of all kinds, he had fallen into such disgrace, that he was not permitted to approach the Emperor's throne. Distressed and angered at this, he sought his dismissal, which was granted immediately, though couched in the most flattering terms. He then went to Mayence, where, though in outward prosperity, yet dissatisfied with himself and all the world, he led a sad life, and died in 1695 at the age of sixty. Of his compositions, excepting a Fantasia for the harpsichord printed in Kircher's Musurgia (Rome, 1650, pag. 466 etc.) in four-part score, only the following have been published: "Diverse curiose e rarissime partite di toccate, ricercate, capricci e fantasie dall' Eccellentissimo e Famosissimo organista Giovanni Giacomo Froberger, per gli amatori di Cimbali, Organi e Instrumenti". Mayence, Burgeat, 1695; and a second, similar collection, same publ., 1714. Mattheson, in his Critica Musica, pag. 103, Note, gives the following account of the youthful humor of this first

German clavier-virtuoso: "I possess an Allemande, by the formerly celebrated Froberger, intended to depict his perilous voyage on the Rhine. Therein is represented, how one person hands the boatman his sword, and falls thereby into the water; there are 26 special notes, among them being a *casus* where the boatman gives the sufferer a shocking blow with his long pole, etc."

Yet more eminent as an organist and composer appears Froberger's countryman and contemporary **Johann Kaspar Kerl.** He was also sent to Rome by Kaiser Ferdinand III., to be instructed in music by the excellent composer Giacomo Carissimi; and when the following Kaiser Leopold was to be crowned at Frankfort in 1658, he went thither to be presented to the new sovereign. The latter received him graciously, and sent him a theme, which be desired to hear worked out on the organ next day. Kerl declined it with the petition, that a theme should not be handed him until he was already seated before the organ. When the Kaiser and the illustrious guests at the coronation were gathered in the church at the time appointed, Kaspar Kerl began with a majestic prelude on the organ, then took up the given theme, worked it out in two parts, then in three and four, and finally with the pedal in five parts, adding thereto, to the great admiration of all hearers, a counter-subject, and closing the whole with a grand and masterly double-fugue. Following this, he had performed an artistically wrought Mass of his own composition, after which he received an ovation from the entire assemblage. The Kaiser ennobled him, and the Elector of Bavaria appointed him his Kapellmeister. He occupied this post in Munich for several years, until, disgusted at the continual cabals of the Italian singers engaged at the same court, he quitted the town, and accepted the position of organist at the Church of St. Stephen in Vienna, 1677, where he was also held in high estimation as a clavier-teacher. He returned to Munich later, and died there about 1690. His compositions, "Modulatio organica super Magnificat, octo tonis ecclesiasticis respondens", Munich, 1686, and many others, although still based upon the ecclesiastical modes, exhibit all the characteristics of our modern tonalities, and approach more and more to the German style, as distinguished from the Italian.

At the time of Kaspar Kerl's sojourn in Vienna, the talented **Johann Pachelbel** of Nuremberg, born in 1653, was the assistant organist at St. Stephen's. In his chief he had likewise such an excellent model, that he also succeeded, through untiring zeal, in winning an honorable name as a player on the clavier and organ. He was engaged successively as organist in Eisenach, Erfurt, Stuttgart, and Gotha, and finally in the church of St. Sebaldus at Nuremberg (1695). Here he died in 1706, attempting to sing in his last moments, with faltering breath, his favorite chorale "Herr Jesu Christ, meines Lebens Licht". Of his published compositions we mention "Musikalische Sterbens-Gedanken aus vier variirten Chorälen bestehend" (Musical Dying Thoughts, consisting of four Chorales with variations), Erfurt, 1683; "Choräle zum Präambuliren" (Chorales for Preluding), Nuremberg, 1693; and "Hexachordum Apollinis, aus VI sechsmal variirten Arien" (Apollo's Hexachord, in 6 Arias with sixfold variation), Nuremberg, 1699. Pachelbel's name especially deserves to be linked with that of Froberger as a composer able to arouse and promote, in Germany, the universal love for the clavier by means of works more pleasing and better suited in style for this instrument, in particular by his artistic variations. Most of his compositions, however, like those of his older and younger contemporaries, were never printed, but were spread far and wide, within and without Germany, in innumerable manuscript copies.

Georg Muffat, Kapellmeister to the Prince of Passau, has still to be mentioned as an excellent organist, clavier-player, and composer toward the end of the 17th century. However, of his compositions relevant to our subject, but one has been printed—an "Apparatus Musico-Organisticus" containing 12 Toccatas, in Augsburg, 1690, in which place he had played before Kaiser Leopold I. in the same year. In his youth he dwelt six years in Paris, in order to study the then epoch-making compositions of Lully. There he could not fail to become acquainted with the works of the above-mentioned Couperin, and thus transplanted many of the **agrémens** of the latter to Germany. **Gottlieb Muffat,** his highly gifted son, studied counterpoint thoroughly in Vienna under J. J. Fux, became Court Organist to Kaiser Karl VI., and clavier teacher in the imperial family. There were published in Vienna, 1727, of his clavier compositions: "Componimenti musicali per il Cembalo", and later LXXII Versettes and XII Toccatas. He left many equally valuable compositions in MS.

Under the domination of the Chromaticists, which had been continually gaining ground since the beginning of the 16th century, the pure diatonic Modes had been so altered and popularized by added chromatic tones quite foreign to their serious character, that they were present in the works of the 17th century only in name, and not in their essential power. Thus even theoreticians were finally forced to take note of the **Keys of the "New Music"**, so entirely different from the old. And thus Dr. **Conrad Matthäi** (in his paper published in 1652 "by favor of the honorable philosophical Faculty of the Electoral University at Königsberg", and entitled "A brief, though detailed Report on the Modis musicis" etc.) declares the Ionian Mode, our modern key of *C*-major, which until then had been termed merely an irregular key, to be the first and pre-eminent one. The organist **Andreas Werckmeister** of Halberstadt, a most deserving theoretician of this period, has a still more distinct conception of the tonality of his time. In his essay, printed at Aschersleben in 1698 (the edition before me is undated), on "Die nothwendigsten Anmerkungen und Regeln, wie der Bassus continuus oder General-Bass wohl könne tractiret werden" (The most needful Remarks and Rules for the Treatment of the Basso continuo or Thorough-bass) he observes (p. 50): "*In our present* (style of) *composition one could get along very well with two modes,* if the same were applied to the tempered clavier, and then to each key were tuned one mode, namely *major* for all, and then to each another mode, namely *minor* for all; whereupon one would have 24 *triades harmonicas,* and the clavier could be played through the circle [of fourths or fifths]: as was observed above". — And by **Mattheson,** in his "Beschützten Orchestre" (Hamburg, 1717), Solmisation was finally "carried to the grave, under distinguished escort of the twelve Grecian *modorum,* as respectable relatives and mourners". In the compositions of the now beginning *brilliant epoch of this earlier German organ and clavier school,* our modern keys therefore already display themselves clearly and distinctly, with their definite leading-note; these works still show the serious dignity of those founded on the ecclesiastical modes, but are now also able to lend animated expression to the more sensuous emotions of the heart and the more agitated moods, by the aid of their richer modulations and the prepared and free dissonances oftener occurring.

Through the numerous pupils of the German masters already mentioned, and by their meritorious compositions, which always spread over the entire musical world in thousands of copies, our art, which at first had found its chief fosterers in the South, was in time transplanted to the North of Germany as well. Here **Dietrich Buxtehude,** organist at the Marienkirche in Lübeck from 1699 to his death in 1707, won so brilliant renown through his spirited and effective performances, that Sebastian Bach, at nineteen (1704) organist in Arnstadt, felt impelled to journey several times to Lübeck on foot, to hear the masterly playing of Buxtehude and to study his ingenious compositions for an extended period. For though the liberal arts, after the frightful devastation of the 30-years' war, again began to put forth glorious blooms in Germany, the general commercial depression was especially felt in the **music trade** throughout the whole 17th century, so that extremely few of his many fine works, or of his contemporaries', became generally known through publication. Gerber, in his "Neues Lexikon der Tonkünstler" (New Lexicon of Musicians), notes only the following works by Buxtehude pertinent to our subject: "Opera 1, a V., Viola da gamba e Cembalo", Hamburg; "Opera 2", a similar Clavier Trio, Hamburg, 1696; and "VII Clavier Suites, wherein the Nature and Properties of the 7 Planets are depicted". When Buxtehude, toward the close of his life, proposed giving up his position as organist, the place was applied for by two young musicians and friends, Handel and Mattheson, who came to Lübeck for this purpose from the city of Hamburg near by. Now, although these already highly esteemed artists might assuredly have urged well-founded claims to this generously salaried office, they nevertheless beat a hurried retreat upon learning that Buxtehude was willing to resign the same only in favor of a candidate, who should first agree to espouse a daughter of his, no longer in the first flush of youth.

The above-mentioned **George Frederick Handel** (properly Georg Friedrich Händel), born in Halle in 1685 and educated as a musician by the notable organist **Friedrich Wilhelm Zachau** (d. 1712), not only lifted the protestant Oratorio to world-wide fame of yet undimmed lustre, but was surpassed, both in his fiery organ-playing and in his artistic and elegant clavier compositions, by Sebastian Bach alone, the greatest of all masters of that classic epoch. Handel spent the last forty-seven years of his restlessly active life almost without interruption in London; he it was, therefore, who carried the German style of composition of that period to England, and there his memory is still celebrated with the greatest enthusiasm. He died in that commercial metropolis in 1759, and his eighteen organ Concertos, which however do not stand in so high esteem as his other works, like his remaining organ and clavier compositions, were first published in England, and thereafter in France, Germany, and Switzerland. Among the editions of the same issued latterly, the following are specially noteworthy: "Händel's Clavierstücke" (Clavier Pieces) in No. 2, V. 1 of the *Deutsche Handelsgesellschaft,* Leipzig, Breitkopf & Härtel, 1858; 16 Suites, 12 Fugues, and other compositions, in one volume or separate, H. Litolff, Braunschweig (Brunswick); "Compositions de G. F. Handel, édit. nouvelle, revue et corrigée critiquement". 8 Parts, Leipzig, Peters.

Handel's **Clavier Suites** sometimes contain, instead of the series of dance-forms usually found in similar compositions, other fugued and freer pieces, and so-called "galante" variations, in which the endeavor, to create pleasing and brilliant pieces especially for the clavier, is distinctly apparent; yet in artistic workmanship, power, and loftier flights, they rank decidedly below the fine Suites by Sebastian Bach; and even in his purely and fluently wrought Fugues he can hardly bear comparison, in this province, with his great rival in renown.

Johann Mattheson, named together with Handel, chiefly owes his celebrity to his theoretical, critical, and musico-historical writings. Of his compositions were published: "XII Suites pour le Clavecin", London, 1714; a "Sonata per il Cembalo", Hamburg; and a volume of Fugues, in two Parts, entitled "Die Fingersprache" (Finger-speech).

We now come to the renowned contemporary of Handel, Dominico Scarlatti, and Rameau, who in all future time will be deemed a model for the classic organ and clavier style and for most artistic composition — to the perfecter of the art of Counterpoint, **Johann Sebastian Bach.** He was born in Eisenach on May 16, 1685, lost his parents when but ten years of age, and therefore was taken in charge by his elder brother Johann Christoph, organist in Ordruff, to be instructed by him in clavier-playing. Herein he soon acquired such skill, that he begged to be allowed to study a book of music belonging to his brother, which contained written copies of a large number of clavier-pieces by Froberger, Kerl, and Pachelbel. But as his brother denied his urgent entreaty, he secretly carried the coveted treasure to his chamber at night, and not only copied the clavier pieces by moonlight in six months, but studied them with equal secrecy and untiring zeal. His brother, however, having once overheard this secret practice to his no small astonishment, cruelly took away the copies so laboriously made; nor were they restored until after the latter's death, which occurred shortly after. Sebastian Bach then went with a friend to Lüneburg, where both were placed as choir-boys in the church of St. Michael, likewise attending the gymnasium of the town. Hence Sebastian undertook frequent trips to Hamburg, to listen to the playing of the eminent organist **Johann Adam Reinken** (1623—1722). In his eighteenth year he obtained a position as violinist in the court band at Weimar, but exchanged it in the following year for the post of organist in Arnstadt, better suited to his taste. It was here that he entirely devoted himself to the theoretical and practical study of the compositions of Nicolaus Bruhn (1666—1697), Reinken, Buxtehude, and other German masters; his study and practice, continued with the utmost diligence, united with his most delicate native musical sensibility and inexhaustible inventive faculty, soon raised him to such a degree of mastership, that when he was appointed organist of the court at Weimar, in 1708, both his finished playing and ingenious compositions found universal recognition in that town. Innumerable organ pieces were called forth here by the art-loving court, and in the year 1714 the Duke appointed the productive Sebastian Kapellmeister, as which he now had to write and to conduct the larger compositions intended for the church. Shortly after the victory already mentioned over the then so highly extolled French organist Marchand, in the year 1717, Bach was called to Anhalt-Köthen as Court Kapellmeister. Here he stayed for six years, during which time he made a second trip to Hamburg to visit the organist Reinken, the model of his youthful ambition. Reinken, then in his hundredth year, accompanied Sebastian to the church of St. Catharine, to hear the playing of his disciple returning to him covered with glory. Bach seated himself at the organ, and improvised for nearly two hours on the favorite chorale of the aged master, "An Wasserflüssen Babylons, da sassen wir und weinten", with such skill and feeling that the latter, deeply moved, cried out: "I had thought that this art would be buried with me, but now I hear that it will live on!"— In 1723 Bach was called to Leipzig as Cantor of the Thomasschule, and held this position till his death in 1750. Soon after his arrival at Leipzig, the Duke of Weissenfels bestowed upon him the title of Kapellmeister, the King of Saxony appointed him Court Composer, and the far-sounding name of this unexcelled musician attracted many pupils and admirers to the town. Sebastian Bach was revered not only as an artist, but also as a true friend and faithful, affectionate husband. He left nine daughters, and eleven sons gifted with the happiest musical talent, among whom are to be named, as conspicuously eminent, first of all the eldest, **Wilhelm Friedemann,** also called the "Hallische Bach" (Bach of Halle, 1710—

1784); likewise the second, **Karl Philipp Emanuel,** the Berlin or Hamburg Bach, (1714—1788); further, **Johann Christoph Friedrich,** Concertmeister at Buckeburg; and the youngest, **Johann Christian** the Milanese or London Bach. After his second son, Philipp Emanuel, had entered the service of Frederick the Great, the monarch repeatedly expressed the wish to become personally acquainted with Sebastian, the father. The latter finally acceded to the urgent invitation of his son, and in the year 1747 journeyed to Potsdam with his most dearly loved eldest son Wilhelm Friedemann. The King had just arranged a concert in his palace, and was about to begin playing a composition for the flute, when an officer entered, and handed him a list of the strangers arrived at Potsdam. Scarcely had he cast a glance over the list, when he turned to the assembled musicians, and cried: "Gentlemen, old Bach has come!" He laid the flute aside, and gave orders that the long looked-for master should be brought thither immediately. Sebastian, who had not been allowed time to doff his travelling dress, soon appeared, and the King affably requested him to try the lately invented Fortepiano, made by Silbermann, in his concert room (the Berlin "Haude und Spener'sche Zeitung" of May of that year styles it "the so-called Forte and Piano"). Bach improvised for some time on the same, and finally begged Frederick the Great for a fugue-theme, and wrought it out on the spot in such masterly fashion, that the musicians surrounding applauded him most loudly. After his return to Leipzig, Bach dedicated to the King a work entitled "Musikalisches Opfer" (A Musical Offering, Breitkopf & Härtel), in which he treats this theme by Frederick the Great in the most various styles, developing in a masterly manner most ingenious canons, a three-part fugue, a six-part ricercare, and a sonata for flute, violin, and basso continuo. Bach, an enthusiast for everything grand and beautiful, was not permitted to make the personal acquaintance of his illustrious contemporary Handel. On hearing that the latter had come from England to Halle, he immediately journeyed thither, but learned to his sorrow that Handel had already left his birth-place again on the same day. When he revisited Germany for the second time, Bach was sick in bed; indeed, the trip to Potsdam was likewise his last excursion from Leipzig. Oft-continued night-work, coupled with the necessity of engraving his compositions himself on copper, aided by his son Friedemann, in order to secure their publication despite the lack of a publisher, told on his eyesight for several years, and finished by totally blinding him. This wonderful musician, who possessed in so high measure the gift of clothing his inexhaustible, profound thoughts at pleasure in the choicest and most artistic forms, died in the year 1750. With Sebastian Bach the classic organ and clavier style attained to its supreme height, and contrapuntal composition to its fullest perfection.

The instruments already spoken of, made by **Gottfried Silbermann** under the name of *Fortepiano,* were wing-shaped (in grand-piano form). **C. E. Friederici** of Gera, the first to employ the square form (1758), called his instrument, to distinguish it from that of Silbermann, Fortebien. According to Gerber, in the old *Lexikon der Tonkünstler* (1792), Silbermann made two instruments during Bach's lifetime, and the latter, having tried one of them, praised its tone, but found the treble too weak and the touch altogether too heavy. Silbermann thereupon offered no more of these instruments for sale, and labored incessantly to improve the defects censured by Bach. Thus "many years" passed by, without further news of the invention. At last, after manifold experiments, he so far improved the touch, that he was able to sell one of his instruments to the Prince of Schwarzburg-Rudolstadt, and a second in a short time to the King of Prussia. Silbermann now had one of these new, improved instruments tested by Bach, who then approved of the same in all respects. But all the clavier compositions of Sebastian Bach, most of which were not published till after his death, as well as those of his son Karl Philipp Emanuel, *still belong to the literature of the Clavichord.*

In view of the totally different methods for tuning the clavier, after abandoning the ecclesiastical modes, our modern keys could not all be used with even measurably bearable purity. To attain this end, they were finally (from the beginning of the 18th century) founded on the system of **equal temperament,** which latter obtained full recognition more especially from the fact, that Sebastian Bach wrote a series of 24 Preludes and an equal number of Fugues, followed later by a second similar collection, for the first time in all our modern major and minor keys, and gave it the title of "*The Well-tempered Clavichord*", although both parts were not printed for publication under the same until after his death. They were first announced in the year 1800 by N. Simrock of Bonn and G. Nägeli of Zurich; according to the Leipzig "Handbuch der musikalischen Literatur" of 1817 they had up to that date been issued complete by the above publishers, and also by Peters in Leipzig and Sieber in

Paris (none of these editions mentioning, however, the manuscripts followed). **Franz Kroll**, well-known as an excellent and thoroughly educated musician, has rendered art the service of comparing all autographs and other contemporary manuscript copies still extant of the Well-tempered Clavichord, and likewise the earliest printed editions, and has published the result of his investigations in a critical edition of this highly important clavier-work (Leipzig, C. F. Peters).

The same active firm has also published a "Gesammtausgabe" (Complete Edition) of the works of Johann Sebastian Bach, which contains the following clavier-works: Parts I and II, the Well-tempered Clavichord; III, Art of Fugue, with explanations by M. Hauptmann; IV and IX, Preludes, Toccatas, Fantasias, and Fugues; V, six Clavier-exercises or Suites; Op 1; VI, Italian Concerto, French Overture, and Aria con 30 Variazioni; VII, The six French Suites, and other minor compositions; VIII, the six great English Suites; X, six Grand Sonatas for Clavier and Violin; XI and XIV, Concertos for three Claviers with accompaniment of String Quartet, in *D*-minor and *C*-major; XII and XIII, Concertos for two Claviers with String Quartet, in *C*-major and *C*-minor; XV, 16 Violin Concertos by A. Vivaldi, arr. by Bach for Clavier; XIV, Concerto for Clavier and two Flutes with String Quartet, in *F*-major; XVII to II, Clavier Concertos with String Quartet, in *G*-minor, *F*-minor, *D*- and *A*-major, *E*-major, and *D*-minor; XXIII, Concerto for Clavier, Flute and Violin, with String Quartet. A "Collection of the Clavier Compositions of J. S. Bach" has also been issued, in four volumes, by L. Holle, Wolfenbüttel. The edition of the Bach-Gesellschaft (Breitkopf & Härtel) contains Clavier works by Bach in Vol. 3, 9, 13 (second Part), 14, 15, 17, and 21 (second Part). The same publishers have issued "Clavier Works of J. S. Bach, furnished with Fingering and Marks of Expression, for Use in the Conservatory at Leipzig by Carl Reinecke". 7 Volumes, boards, red. The "Collection Litolff" contains Bach's Clavier Works in two volumes, or in 41 separate numbers.

Bach's **Concertos** and **Sonatas** exhibit only in isolated cases the combination, at present in vogue, of a more fully developed movement in the "sonata-form" before described, with a calmer Andante following and a Finale in "rondo-form"; they are, on the contrary, either two, three, four, or even more distinct pieces, of which only the first, and occasionally the last, is worked out with broader development, but which are united to a greater Whole by similarity or relationship in key, by their mutual resemblance in mood or style; so that the so-called **Suites** are distinguished from such Sonatas only through the circumstance, that in the same distinct dance-forms—though sometimes worked out in sonata-form—like the Allemande, Corrente, Sarabande, Giga, etc., often preceded by way of introduction by an Overture, Prelude, or Capriccio, are united in a similar manner to form a whole. Thus the great "English Suites" by Bach possess no less musical worth than his "Sonatas for Clavier and Violin", developed with such consummate skill, or than his valuable Clavier Concertos. Neither in the truly monumental work: "Aria con 30 Variationi", nor in any of his compositions, does Bach appear merely as a most facile contrapuntist, by his employment of the varied principal theme for canons in all intervals and other fugal work, but also gives the player an opportunity of exhibiting his virtuosity in an extremely effective style. But it is the form of the fugue, more especially, which attained to highest and final perfection through Bach's master-hand. Their subjects always contain a distinctly outspoken musical idea, whose character is maintained throughout the entire composition. And not only in the ever-new melodic and rhythmic pregnancy of the themes, but in the diversified development of the same, does Bach display the full wealth of his astounding inventive genius. All his numerous fugues show, together with the strictest unity of conception, the greatest diversity in their modulations, episodes, developments, and stretti. The theme now appears in melodic contrary motion, now in augmentation, and enters in canon-form or the most amazing stretti in all parts carrying out the fugue. In the Well-tempered Clavichord we find fugues in 2, 3, 4, and 5 parts, among them several worked out as double or triple fugues.

Bach was the first to develop the entire build of a fugue out of its subject and counter-subject and the motives derived from them, and produced thereby the fullest unity in its organic form.

For the performance of his oftentimes very complicated works, whose individual parts preserve their entire independence, the fingering till then customary for keyed instruments no longer sufficed; he therefore invented a new one, in which the hitherto quite neglected thumbs and little fingers of both hands could co-operate as required, and the key of a sustained tone was frequently held down not only by one finger, but by several in alternation. Bach executed the most difficult of his own compositions with the utmost ease and delicacy, and usually in very lively tempo; for practicing the same he often worked during the night. His organ-playing was as finished as his clavier style, his feet even imitating any appoggiatura, mordent, or other grace played by the fingers; he actually executed long double trills on the pedals, while both hands were also fully employed. He is said to have used and combined the organ-registers, too, so ingeniously, that a very ordinary instrument, under his hands, could exercise a most potent influence over the hearers. But Sebastian Bach not only promoted, by his compositions and his performances at Hamburg, Weimar, Dresden, Anhalt-Köthen, Leipzig, and Berlin, the refinement and exaltation of his art, but transmitted his influence with the happiest results through his numerous pupils. Among these, besides his sons Wilhelm Friedemann and Karl Philipp Emanuel, we also find the following distinguished musicians: Johann Ludwig Krebs, Johann Christian Kittel, Johann Friedrich Agricola, and Johann Philipp Kirnberger.

Besides the later editions already mentioned of earlier German masters, the following, have been published by J. Rieter-Biedermann, Leipzig: *Georg Muffat,* two Suites and a Ciacona (Schletterer);—by Bartholf Senff, *J. C. Kerl,* Toccata; *J. J. Froberger,* Toccata; *Gottlieb Muffat,* two Minuets and Courante; *J. L. Krebs,* Fugue in *F*-major (Pauer);—by Breitkopf & Härtel, *J. L. Krebs,* two Partite; *Froberger,* Toccata; *G. Muffat,* Gigue and Allegro spirituoso (Pauer);—by G. W. Körner in Erfurt, Complete Editions of the Organ and Clavier compositions of *Pachelbel, Buxtehude, J. L. Krebs, F. W. Zachau,* and *Handel,* all to be had in separate Parts;—by Peters in Leipzig, 14 Chorale-variations by *D. Buxtehude,* edited by S. W. Dehn;—by Breitkopf & Härtel, *Buxtehude,* Organ compositions, Vol. 1 and 2, edited by Philipp Spitta.

In this connection the following modern biographical works require special mention: *G. F. Handel,* by F. Chrysander, Vol. 1 to 3, first half. Breitkopf & Härtel, 1867, etc.—*Johann Sebastian Bach,* by C. H. Ritter; Berlin, Ferd. Schneider, 1865, 2 Vols.—*Johann Sebastian Bach,* by Philipp Spitta; Breitkopf & Härtel, Vol. 1 and 2, 1873 and 1878.

II. The Clavier Style resulting from the new System of Harmony.

The Science of Accompaniment or **Thorough-bass,** which at first proposed only the harmonic support of the solo singer, or of certain polyphonic compositions, soon found so many friends and adherents everywhere, that between the years 1620 and 1800 a great number of treatises on the same were published. The earliest of these appeared in Italy by G. Sabbatini and Gasparini; in Germany by Heinrich Albert (in the 1st Part of his poetico-musical *Lustwäldlein*), Werckmeister, Niedt, Heinichen and Mattheson; in France by Michel de Saint Lambert and J. F. Dandrieu; in England by Matthew Lock, etc. A method of Harmony going more thoroughly into the derivation and progression of the chords did not, however, appear until 1722 in Paris, entitled: "Traité de l'Harmonie reduite à ses principes naturels", by **Rameau.** This acute theoretician now first presented, together with the triads, the various chords of the seventh likewise, with their transpositions and inversions, as independent harmonic bodies, and classified the frequent progressions of the same in the works of practical musicians under distinct rules. This new science of harmony, which soon became the foundation of many similar works following, now often found practical application in the composition of clavier pieces; a bass part being set to a principal melody, and the above fuller chords being added in appropriate places as a filling. Thus the independence of the inner parts in such compositions quite disappeared; *the strict and ecclesiastically serious contrapuntal organ style was abandoned in the same, and replaced by a freer and secularly more pleasing style, better suited to the character of the clavier.*

The first musician in Germany who attempted to free **clavier compositions** from the fetters of counterpoint, was Sebastian Bach's immediate predecessor as Cantor of the Thomasschule, **Johann Kuhnau** (1667—1722), of whose compositions the following should be noted here. "Neue Clavierübung" (New clavier-practice), Part. I, "consisting of seven Suites in the Ut, Re, Mi, or Tertia majore of each Mode", etc., Leipzig, 1689 and 1695; "Neue Clavierübung", Part. II. "That is, seven Suites in the Re, Mi, Fa, or Tertia minore of each mode, together with a Sonata in the *B♭*" etc. Leipzig, 1695; "Frische Clavierfrüchte" (Fresh Clavier-fruits) "or seven Sonatas of good Invention and Style, to be played on the Clavier", Leipzig, 1696; and "Musikalische Vorstellung einiger biblischen Historien" (Musical Presentation of certain biblical Narrations) "in VI Sonatas, to be played on the Clavier" etc., Leipzig, J. Tietzen, 1700. In the Preface to the second Part of his *Neue Clavierübung* Kuhnau makes the following observations: "I have also added a Sonata in *B*♭, which will likewise afford pleasure to amateurs. For why should one not be able to perform such pieces on the Clavier, as well as on other instruments? seeing that no instrument whatever could yet pretend to take precedence of the Clavier in point of perfection. I call it perfect compared with others, but not in comparison with a Sonata or Concerto artistically written for many parts (different instruments); because one cannot always continue that, which has otherwise to be executed by many persons, in such a way as to drop no single part. Or, if it were desired to execute each single part strictly, much would appear constrained, and agreeableness would often be sacrificed. For which reason I too, following celebrated masters, have sometimes intentionally shown myself somewhat negligent in the Allemandes, Courantes, and Sarabandes, here leaving out one part, or in another place adding a new one. But the fugues in four parts are strictly worked out."—In the **Sonata** in *B*♭ here mentioned, especially interesting as one of the earliest attempts in this form, Kuhnau, despite his evident striving to create a lighter and more appropriate style for the Clavier, is unable to shake off the customary contrapuntal forms. An Allegro in *B*♭, whose monotonous rhythm in $^4/_4$ time is kept up by an uninterrupted movement in eighth-notes, is followed by a free fugued movement in sixteenth-notes in the same key. A short Adagio in *E*♭, in $^3/_4$ time, then modulates to *C*-major, immediately followed by an Allegro in the same measure, going over to and closing in *B*♭-major. The direction "Da Capo" indicates, that the piece is then to be repeated again up to the Adagio. The entire Sonata shows as yet not one characteristic thought, but only separate phrases, motives, and passages, monotonously elaborated in Imitations and Sequences melodically connected. In the *Frische Clavierfrüchte,* however, seven Sonatas of 1696, such an important advance is shown as compared with the earlier work, as to justify the conjecture that Kuhnau had in the meantime gained acquaintance with the better Italian compositions in this field, although in his Preface he inveighs against the practice of estimating foreign productions above native ones; for in

Germany one might find *almost as good* musical fruits as those which grow in foreign climes, "not to mention, that Nature has blessed our fields with many fruits which foreigners lack".—These new Sonatas have either four or five movements in different tempi; the motives already oftener grow to intelligible melodies; sections in song-form, with a subordinate harmonic accompaniment, alternate with figurate passages more strictly developed; a Ciacona is built up upon a *basso ostinata*, an interesting double-fugue is carried out; it is therefore easily explainable, that new editions of these Sonatas were issued in 1710 and 1724. In Kuhnau's *Biblical Narratives* of the year 1700, which were also reprinted in Leipzig in 1725, there are Sonatas having from three to eight movements, in which the Fugue, the figurate Chorale, Songs, Dances, and other free forms, alternate in motley succession. A Sonata in *G*-major by **J. Mattheson,** published in Hamburg in the year 1713, from the form and richer passages of which an acquaintance with the earlier-named contemporary Italians may be conjectured, still exhibits the conception of the Sonata in the general sense of "Sound-piece", as it consists of a single movement of considerable length; therefore this musician, who was uncommonly active as a theorist and critic, was quite justified in writing as late as 1739, in his "Vollkommener Kapellmeister" (Complete Conductor), (page 233): "Some years ago they began writing **Sonatas** for the Clavier, with good success; hitherto the same have no proper form, and would be rather moved than moving, that is, they aim more at the motion of the fingers than the emotion of the heart."—"In the Sonatas," he remarks further (p. 137) "a certain *complaisance* must obtain, which adapts itself to all, and wherewith every hearer may be gratified. In the various changes of the Sonata a sad person will meet with something plaintive and sympathetic, an angry one something vehement, a sensualist something exquisite, etc. The composer, too, must bear this aim in mind for his Adagio, Andante, Presto, etc.; then his work will find success." It is apparent from this, that Mattheson also strove to endow the Clavier Sonata with a more distinctively marked, pregnant meaning, together with a more generally pleasing form.

The Silesian campaigns of Frederick the Great, which held Germany in almost continual suspense and agitation from 1740 to 1763, necessarily retarded the growth of such "frische Clavierfrüchte" not a little. Yet even in these stirring times attempts were made to keep alive the love for music, especially by means of **weekly** or

monthly Periodicals, which gave the leading composers an opportunity to publish compositions of all descriptions, for which latter, under existing conditions, they could hardly have found any other publishers. Among the most noteworthy of these collections, in which clavier works were also included, or which were specially intended for the latter, the publication of the same continuing through the Seven Years' War until about 30 years thereafter, we name the following: "Musikalisches Allerley" (Musical Salmagundi) by various Composers (its editor was F. W. Marpurg), Berlin, Birnstiel, 1760—1763, nine collections; "Musikalisches Mancherley", (Musical Miscellany), four pieces, Berlin, Winter, 1762—1765; "Musikalisches Vielerley" (Musical Olio), edited by C. Ph. Em. Bach. Hamburg, Bock, 1770; "Blumenlese für Clavierliebhaber" (Selected Clavier-pieces for Amateurs) 5 Vols., Spire, Bossler, 1782—1787; "Claviermagazin für Kenner und Liebhaber" (—for Connoisseurs and Amateurs), edited by Rellstab, four collections, 1787—1788; "Neue musik. Zeitschrift" (New Music Journal) "for Encouragement and Entertainment in Solitude at the Clavier for the Skilled and Unskilled", Halle, Hendel, 1792; further we should mention the "Sammlung vermischter Tonstücke" (Collection of miscellaneous Pieces) by various authors, in two Parts, Hanover, Schmidt, 1782 and 1783; the following collections, published by Breitkopf & Härtel of Leipzig: "Raccolta delle più nuove composizioni di Clavicembalo, 2 Tomi", 1756 and 1757, edited by F. W. Marpurg; "Wöchentlicher musikalischer Zeitvertreib" (Weekly musical Pastime), four Parts, 1760 and 1761; and "Musikalisches Magazin", eight pieces, 1763; and finally, the excellent collection "Œuvres mêlées, contenant VI Sonates pour le clavessin d'autant de plus célèbres compositeurs, rangés en ordre alphabétique", Nuremberg, J. U. Haffner, which contains 36 Clavier Sonatas in 12 Parts, and appears to have been issued from 1755 to 1765.

The **Forms of Art** cultivated both in these Collections, and in the Clavier compositions published separately up to 1790, and not yet mentioned here, include Fugues, and other contrapuntally written pieces which gradually grow rarer and at last quite disappear; separate Marches, Polonaises, Minuets, etc., or Suites uniting several such dance-forms; so-called "galante Variationen" (free variations) or "Veränderungen" (Variations), calculated solely for outward effect, and affording little of interest besides; shorter Salon pieces in song-form or rondo-form; and Clavier Sonatas, of peculiar interest to us, and now appearing in ever-increasing numbers. The strict contrapuntal style of clavier composition having been gradually given up, as remarked before, as the science of harmony or thorough-bass became known, most of these compositions are written in two parts; a predominant higher part is accompanied by a more or less interesting bass, sometimes in broken chords, at others with full harmonies. Occasionally fuller harmonies are written for both hands; but even in the rarer compositions written on the whole in three or four parts, the inner parts lack contrapuntal independence, being treated only as an harmonic filling. Among the authors of these compositions, the following are most prominent:

Gottfried Heinrich Stölzel (1690—1749), Court Kapellmeister in Saxe-Gotha, by whom an original *Enharmonic Clavier Sonata* was printed, though not until after his death, in the "Musikalisches Allerley", 1761 p. 48. This consists of a Largo of arpeggio'd four-part chords in *C*-minor, $^4/_4$ time, a three-part enharmonic Fugue in $^2/_4$ time, whose episodes are at times strengthened by fuller chords, and a movement in $^3/_8$ time, in the two-part style described above, with the direction *dolce*, closing the interesting composition in *C*-minor with enharmonic plaintiveness. Its enharmonic form lies in transforming a chord, e. g. *f♯-a-c-e♭*, which is made to modulate by the succeeding harmonies into *g♭-b♭-d♭-e*, the tone *f♯* being thus enharmonically changed to *g♭*, etc.

Stölzel's successor in Gotha was **Georg Benda** (1721—1795); by him were published in 1757 (Berlin, Winter): "Sei Sonate per il Cembalo solo"; further six collections of miscellaneous clavier-pieces and songs (Gotha, Ettinger, 1781); and "2 Concerti per il Cembalo", with accompaniment by string quartet (Leipzig, Schwickert, 1779). These clavier-works already reveal in the most gratifying manner the striving of the renowned creator of the Monodrama and Melodrama in Germany, to lend instrumental works distinctive and intelligible expression.

Ernst Wilhelm Wolf (1735—1762), Court Kapellmeister in Saxe-Weimar, is likewise mentioned in Gerber's old "Tonkünstlerlexikon" as one of our classic and most original composers; besides several Clavier Concertos, he published various numbers containing six Clavier Sonatas each at Leipzig, in the years 1774, 1775, and 1779; further, a "Sonatina and four effective Sonatas for the Clavier", Leipzig, 1785; and finally, one of the earliest **Clavier Sonatas for four hands** printed in Germany (Leipzig, 1784).—A year before, there appeared a volume of carefully and skilfully wrought compositions of the same kind, by the Cathedral Organist at Halberstadt, **Christian Heinrich Müller,** entitled "Three Sonatas for the Clavier as a double piece for two Persons with four hands (sic), Dessau, 1783".

Carl Philipp Emanuel Bach, the son of the great Sebastian, must be regarded as the head of this earlier Clavier School, under whose influence all the more vigorous compositions during the period from 1750 to 1790 were produced, and whose thorough reform of Clavier-playing first opened the way for the development of a fine Clavier-style. He was born in Weimar in 1714, and his father himself gave him early instruction in Clavier-playing and composition. Although gifted with a teeming fancy, and thoroughly imbued with these highly valuable teachings, he clearly perceived that in his father's works the art of counterpoint had reached the highest pitch of perfection, and that he himself must open a new path, above all lead the compositions intended for the clavier into new channels, in order to awaken fresh interest for the same. He therefore busied himself foremostly with the principles of "accompanying", according to which a leading melody, though harmonically supported, should not be surrounded by equally prominent independent parts; he investigated the character of the swiftly vanishing tones of the Clavichord, and brings out, in his compositions of a style adapted to the same, melodies rhythmically and melodically agreeable, sounds chords broken or arpeggio'd in the most varied manner, pours out passages of effective though easy execution, reinforces the coy tone of the clavichord by frequent appoggiaturas, mordents, and trills; and strives above all things to influence the hearts of his hearers, both by his compositions and his rendering. The form chiefly and most happily developed by him in his numerous clavier-works, which were in part published at his own expense, was the **Sonata;** and it was he, who by unwearying perseverance at length wrought it out into a composition consisting of three movements, the first of which, in the sonata-form already mentioned, makes the hearer the confidant of an emotional state warmly and vividly portrayed; — while the second, the Adagio or Andante, illumines this mood, in contrast to the other two movements, in a more tranquil frame of mind; and the third, the Finale or Rondo, expresses the same urgently and repeatedly with intensified impetus. One characteristic leading idea in the principal key is the subject of the first movement; but a contrasting second theme is not yet found in the same, a substitute being given therefor in the *modulatory contrast*, the more rapid passages in the first part of the sonata passing over into the key of the dominant, or, in movements in minor, into the relative major, and closing in this new key; the second part, after a thematic development of the foregoing theme and after the repetition of the principal idea, is then carried on in the same way as the first, but closes this time in the principal key. In like manner, Emanuel Bach gave to the Rondo, where the principal theme is repeated thrice or oftener in the principal key after various modulatory episodes, for the first time the breadth and independence of an intelligible movement complete in itself. We find such in his six collections of Clavier Sonatas, Rondos, and free Fantasias. Sometimes he employs a two-part movement, sometimes one in three or four parts, to carry out his ideas, occasionally supporting a principal melody by the bass alone, but often giving the clavier fuller and stronger chords for effective execution.

At the court of Frederick II. music was then extraordinarily valued and fostered, and the royal capital thus raised to a rallying-point for the most eminent native and foreign musicians. Emanuel Bach, too, proceeded to Berlin in the year 1738 as a finished artist; but not until two years later did he obtain an appointment as *Kammermusikus* and *Hofcembalist,* in which capacity he also had to accompany the king's own performances on the flute. Although he reverently acknowledged the great qualities of the monarch, he nevertheless had no mind to submit to his dictates in artistic matters. As he expressed himself, an artist favored by Heaven is a freeman born, and needs to recognize no other laws than his own. Such views naturally came into frequent collision with those of a monarch governing according to other principles; yet the latter respected the extraordinary talent of his *Kammervirtuos,* whose ingenious compositions, however, won no approbation whatever in Berlin at that time. In 1745 **Christoph Nichelmann** (1717—1762), a pupil of Sebastian Bach and his son Friedemann, was engaged as a second Court Harpsichordist. Several of his compositions were printed in the "Musikalisches Allerley" of 1761 and 1762 in Berlin; also, 12 Sonatas in two Parts, in Nuremberg. Upon his resigning this office in 1756, he was succeeded by **Carl Fasch** (1736—1800), later the founder of the Berlin *Singakademie,* who proved a more compliant accompanist for the king's flute-practice, wherein the strictest tempo was not always observed, than Emanuel Bach. The meritorious composer of a sixteen-part Mass, Carl Fasch, was also one of the most tasteful clavier composers of that time, as is shown by the Sonatas printed in the "Musikalisches Vielerley" of 1770, and the "Musikalisches Mancherley" of 1762, as well as in the four Sonatas published after his death by Rellstab (Berlin, 1805). The two Sonatas of 1770 already have three movements, like those previously mentioned, and exhibit, together with a brilliant clavier-style, an attractive and intelligible conception.—The distinguished theoretician and musical historian **Friedrich Wilhelm Marpurg** also dwelt in Berlin from 1749 till his death in 1795; besides various contrapuntal works he also attempted freer clavier composition, though not with the happiest success. His published compositions are "Fughe e Capricci" for Clavier or Organ, Berlin, Hummel, 1777; "6 Sonate per il Cembalo", Nuremberg, 1756; "Clavierstücke für Anfänger und Geübtere, mit einem praktischen Unterricht" (Clavier-pieces for Beginners and Advanced Players, with a Practical Course), Berlin, Haude & Spener, 1762, in three Parts.—In the year 1758 **Johann Philipp Kirnberger** (1721—1783), a pupil of Sebastian Bach, entered the service of Princess Amalie of Prussia as Court Musician and Harpsichordist; in the collections mentioned we likewise find, by this celebrated theoretician, numerous Minuets, Polonaises, and similar dances, together with Variations, figurate Chorales, and other compositions designed for the clavier. However, contrapuntal work suited him better than the freer clavier style; among his compositions, therefore, only the "Four Collections of Clavier-exercises after Bach's Method of Fingering, arranged in a Series from the easiest up to the most difficult Pieces" (Berlin, 1762—1764), are still of value, on account of the fingering given therein.—Finally, Sebastian's eldest son, **Wilhelm Friedemann Bach** (1710—1784), also came to Berlin, after living for twenty years in Halle as an organist. Emanuel extols him as the only organist on a par with his father in organ-playing; he must be named here, not only as a fine clavier-player, but also as a clavier composer of bold harmonic invention. In 1778 he dedicated to Princess Amalie *Eight Fugues*, which, like twelve of his Polonaises for Clavier, did not appear in print until lately (Peters, Leipzig). During his lifetime extremely few of his compositions were published: "Sonate pour le clavecin", Halle, 1739; and No. 1 of "Sei sonate per il Cembalo", Dresden, 1745; but the Royal Library at Berlin still possesses a great number of the same in manuscript. Friedemann Bach died in Berlin in extreme destitution; for his brother Emanuel had turned his back upon that city, in which he had labored for twenty-nine years and which so little recognized his high deserts, as early as

1767, to accept a position as Music Director in Hamburg vacated by Telemann's decease. Here the mentally vigorous artist labored for twenty-one years longer, dying in 1788. He was one of our most fruitful, inventive, and influential composers, leaving over 300 works for Clavier, including 52 Concertos, whose effect, however, seems to have been calculated for the general public, and but 9 of which have been published; among these the last, entitled: "Sei Concerti per il Cembalo concertato accompagnato da due Violini, Violetta e Basso; con due Corni e due Flauti per rinforza" etc., Hamburg, 1772, at the author's expense. His first VI Sonatas, dedicated to the King of Prussia, were published in 1742 by Schmidt, Nuremberg; "Sei Sonate per Cembalo, opera IIda", dedicated to Duke Carl Eugen of Württemberg, Nuremberg, 1744, at the expense of the Engraver, J. W. Winter; 10 Sonatas, in the above-mentioned *Œuvres mêlées,* Nuremberg, Haffner, 1755 *et seq.;* Six Sonatas for Clavier, with varied *Reprises,* dedicated to Princess Amalie of Prussia, Winter, Berlin, 1759; Two Continuations to the same, 1761 and 1763; "Una Sonata per il Cembalo solo" in *C*-minor, Breitkopf, Leipzig and Dresden, 1785; "Sei Sonate per il Cembalo solo all' uso delle donne", Hartknoch, Riga, 1786; Six Collections of Clavier Sonatas, free Fantasias, and Rondos, "for Connoisseurs and Amateurs", Author's subscription edition, Leipzig, 1779—1787. The second of these Collections (1781) bears the title; "Clavier-Sonaten nebst einigen Rondos für's Fortepiano". His Clavier-compositions consist besides of Quartets, Trios, and Duos for Clavier and various other instruments, but only a small part has been printed; further, of Sonatas, Variations, and shorter Pieces, scattered among the Collections of the period. For example, Nos. 25, 26, and 27 of the Musikalisches Allerley for 1761 contain a "Claviersonate von Herrn Carl Philipp Emanuel Bach", which consists of an Allemande, Courante, Sarabande, Minuet with two Trios and a Gigue, thus forming a Suite which ranks with his most powerful compositions, and correspondingly develops the more free and flowing clavier style inaugurated by him, in contrast to the strict contrapuntal work of his father in pieces of like form.

Fully as lasting as in his vigorous compositions was Emanuel's influence in his theoretico-practical work, published in 1753 in Berlin: "Versuch über die wahre Art das Clavier zu spielen" (Essay on the true Method of playing the Clavier). In it he treats of the correct *fingering* according to his father's principles, settles the execution of the many *Agrémens* or Graces then in vogue, particularly as copied from French masters, and closes with sagacious observations on a good rendering. First, he explains the proper *position of the hands and fingers*, advises training the left hand to equal skill with the right, and aims at attaining, through his systematic method, a finished, clear, natural, and singing style. He then recommends practice not only on the light action of the clavichord, but also on the harpsichord, with its heavier touch; treats the hitherto neglected thumb as the principal finger, which by reason of its shortness, however, like the little finger, should be used only "in case of necessity on the black keys intended for the longer middle fingers." Of the **Appoggiaturas** he says, among other things, that they must always be played stronger than the following note, and *drawn up* or *bound* to the latter; they usually occupy half the time of a following note consisting of two equal parts, but two thirds of such a note consisting of unequal parts. The short appoggiaturas take one or more tails, and are so executed, that the following note loses as little as possible in value. Occasionally, he proceeds, the long appoggiatura may for the sake of effect take more than half of the following note; the harmony, too, often decides the length of the appoggiaturas, for the same must cause neither parallel fifths nor other discords. The **Trills,** of which he mentions very many kinds, are all indicated by *tr* or a simple cross (dagger) †; but the regular trill, he remarks, properly takes the sign of a short or long ~ ~~. This latter always begins on the second above the main note which it embellishes. When the trill is "rather long", or followed by a leap, it always takes an after-beat (after-turn); only when the note having the trill falls by a second, does it take no after-beat. Even a fairly good ear, Emanuel observes, will in all cases perceive when an after-beat is required or not. Chromatic notes not indicated in the trill or its after-beat, must be divined from what follows, or from the modulation; in general, the interval of an augmented second must be formed neither in the trill nor the after-beat; thus a trill on the note *f*♯, in *G*-minor, would not take *e*♭ in the after-beat, but *e*♮, etc. The following fingerings given by Bach for certain trills (p. 54 of the Third Edition, 1787) are peculiar:—When the higher tone of a trill falls on a black key (e. g. on *e*♭), and the lower tone on a white one (e. g. on *d*), it is not wrong to play the trill, in the left hand, with the second finger on *e*♭ and the thumb on *d*. "Some persons, for the sake of convenience, especially if the touch is heavy, have the habit of playing trills in the right hand with the third and fifth fingers, or the second and fourth." The **Rendering,** he says further on, consists in the delivery of musical ideas to the ear according to their true meaning and feeling; for through it, one and the same idea may be made to take on very various significance. An Adagio should therefore not be taken too fast, or an Allegro too slowly; all notes must have their due force, and the expression altogether must be clean, flowing, and clear. "But one should play from the heart, not like a trained bird", for a musician cannot move others unless he himself be moved, and he must himself feel all those emotions which he would awaken in his hearers.—A second Part of this work, published in Berlin, 1762, contains the *Science of Accompaniment* and of *Free Improvisation.* In the Introduction Emanuel remarks: "The taste of to-day has brought into vogue a style of harmony quite different from that formerly in use. Our melodies, graces, and delivery therefore often demand unusual harmonies. These are now weak, now strong, and consequently the duties of an accompanist have far wider scope now-a-days (2nd Edition, 1797) than formerly, and the familiar **Rules of Thorough-bass** are no longer adequate, and undergo frequent modifications." Then in the sequel he gives the boldest resolutions of dissonant chords, up to that time used occasionally only by himself; but treats neither these nor the consonant chords in their connection as a fundamental chord with its transpositions or inversions; he likewise still treats suspensions before triads or chords of the seventh as individual harmonic forms, under the names of "chords of the second and fifth, second and third, sixth and seventh, fourth and seventh", etc. The **Free Improvisations,** he observes further on, are either Preludes, which prepare for the subject of a following piece, and must therefore bear the character of the same, or pieces invented on the spur of the moment, containing no definite mensural divisions, in which modulations may be effected not only to related keys, but also to any others. By means of a thorough knowledge and bold employment of harmony, he remarks, one becomes master of all keys, and can then invent modulations, even in the free style, quite unknown before. The trained musician can then modulate in an agreeable and striking fashion whither he will, even in developed compositions; for "*Wisdom, Science, and Courage put up with no such confined transitions as our forefathers laid down*".

The most notable and influential **German Clavier Methods,** and works treating of the Art of Clavier-playing, belonging to this earlier period, were issued as first editions in the following succession:

(Only the shorter titles are given in full in German).

1738. **Franz Anton Maichelbeck,** Music Director in Freiburg: "Die auf dem Clavier lehrende Cäcilia" (Cecilia teaching at the Clavier) "giving good instruction, not only how to play from scores with three or four parts, but also how such pieces may be written out in score, and for inventing all kinds of runs. Likewise the rules of composition both in counterpoint and in the Church and Theatre Styles at present in vogue, with the addition of many examples, including the eight Chorale Modes, provided with illustrative pieces, and divided into three parts, viz: I. de clavibus, mensuris et notarum valore; II. de fundamentis partituræ; III. *mit* exemplis tonorum et versuum. op. II, Augsburg, Lotter."

1750. **Friedrich Wilhelm Marpurg,** War Councillor and musical writer of Berlin: "Die Kunst, das Clavier zu spielen" (The Art of playing the Clavier). First Part; Second Part, "On Thorough-bass", 1755, Berlin. Published "unter dem Namen des kritischen Musicus an der Spree".

1753. **Carl Philipp Emanuel Bach,** *Kammervirtuose* in Berlin: "Versuch über die wahre Art das Clavier zu spielen" (Essay on the true Method of playing the Clavier), "illustrated by Examples and eight Specimen Pieces in six Sonatas. First Part, Berlin; Second Part, treating of the Science of Accompaniment and of Free Improvisation. Berlin, Winter, 1762.

1755. **Friedrich Wilhelm Marpurg:** "Method of Clavier-playing, devised in accordance with the elegant Practice of the Present Time". Berlin, Haude & Spener.

1765. **Georg Simon Löhlein,** Kapellmeister at Danzig: Clavier Method, or short and thorough Instruction in Melody and Harmony, illustrated throughout with practical Examples." Leipzig; Vol. II, 1781.

1767. **Johann Samuel Petri,** Cantor at Bautzen: "Anleitung zur praktischen Musik" (Introduction to practical Music). Lauban, Wirthgen. Treats in lucid and thorough style of music in general, of Thorough-bass, of the Organ, of the Clavier and all other keyed instruments and their treatment, and of other instruments.

1789. **Daniel Gottlob Türk,** Music Director in Halle: "Clavierschule oder Anweisung zum Clavierspielen für Lehrer und Lernende" (Clavier Method, or Instructor in Clavier-playing for Teachers and Learners). Leipzig and Halle, at the Author's expense; sold on commission by Schwickert, Leipzig.

The next work on the same subject, by **A. E. Müller** (Jena, 1804), already bears the title of *"Clavier* and *Fortepiano Method"*. But Türk, who was also acquainted with the Fortepiano, still gives decided preference to the Clavichord, or Clavier proper, "for on no other keyed instrument can a delicate execution be so well acquired as on this. A good Clavichord", he observes, "must possess a strong, full, but at the same time pleasing and singing tone, which does not vanish instantly after the key is struck, but sounds on in the deepest and medium register for at least four to six eighth-notes in a moderately slow Adagio, letting the **Bebung** (balancement) be distinctly audible". — This Bebung, however, is a touch impracticable of execution on our modern Fortepiano.* For in the Clavichord, a metallic pin (or similar tangent) was pressed against the string on striking the key, causing the string to sound, and not quitting the same until the finger was lifted from the key. *Marpurg,* in his "Art of playing the Clavier" (4th Edition, 1762) gives the sign .... for the Bebung over a Half-note, and as an "effectus" he exhibits four separate eighth-notes on the same degree, with the same sign over them. This style of touch is somewhat more definitely explained by **Georg Friedrich Wolf,** in his treatise: "Short but plain Instruction in Clavier-playing", Göttingen, 1783; — "The *Bebung* (which is indicated by dots .... written over a half-note or whole note) is executed by balancing the tone, so to speak, with the finger holding the same down; that this should be done gently, is self-evident".

Perhaps the earliest composition, mentioning in its title the **Fortepiano** then coming slowly, step by step, into use, is the following: "Duetto für zwey (two) Claviere, zwey Fortepiano oder zwey Flügel", by **Johann Gottfried Müthel;** Riga, Hartknoch, 1771. The author of this work, a pupil of Sebastian Bach, was the organist of the First Church at Riga; he also published "3 Sonates et 2 Ariosi avec 12 Variations pour le Clavessin", (Nuremberg, Haffner), and "2 Concerti per il Cembalo" (Riga, 1767). In style Müthel somewhat resembles his friend Emanuel Bach, but wrote "less gently and more noisily". Burney found his works, though more difficult than those of Handel, Scarlatti, Schobert, and Emanuel Bach, so teeming with

* On Pianofortes furnished with a sensitive Érard action, not only the *Bebung,* but the still more delicate effect of a continued singing tone, can be brought out. To obtain this effect, the vibration of the key must be very short and rapid, the finger never leaving the key nor allowing the latter to rise quite to its usual level. In no style of touch is perfect looseness and yieldingness more requisite, than in this. **Transl. Note.**

new ideas, grace, and artistic skill, that he ranked them among the greatest productions of his time.

To the day of his death, Emanuel Bach used a Silbermann clavichord. The Harpsichords then likewise very popular, with their rasping *(rauschenden)* tone, he thought ill-suited for more delicate clavier-playing; and regarding the **Fortepiano** he makes, in the third edition of his "Versuch über die wahre Art das Clavier zu spielen" (1787), the following observations: "The newer Fortepianos, when they are well and durably made, possess many advantages, although their management must be studied as a special art, and not without difficulty. They sound well either when played alone, or with a not too powerful orchestra; but still I think that a good Clavichord, saving its weaker tone, has all the beauties of the other, and has the further advantage of the *Bebung* and the sustained tone; because, after striking, I can press down on any note. The clavichord is therefore the instrument, on which one can most accurately test a clavierist." Emanuel Bach had to suffer many vexations from the critics of the period; they upbraided him on the score of a light, unscholarly style—though the same that such masters as Haydn and Mozart took as a model—and also the daring harmonies, which then were held to be harshnesses, and which our science of harmony and modulation later multiplied and extended. In 1773 Dr. Burney met him in Hamburg, and was of the opinion that even his enemies would have been reconciled with those freer compositions, could they have heard them executed by their author on his Silbermann Clavichord, with the tenderness and vivacity peculiar to himself. Emanuel himself said, that he had always striven to write melodiously *("singingly")* for the clavier, and to touch the heart by his delivery. At that time, the attacks alluded to no longer troubled him; for—he observes—since I was fifty I have given up all ambition, and wish to live in peace, as I do not know how near my end may be.

The following musicians, who will find mention later, were among Emanuel's most distinguished pupils:—**Johann Wilhelm Hässler** (1747—1822), **Nicolaus Joseph Hüllmandel** (1751—1823), and his younger brother **Johann Christian Bach,** the latter requiring special notice here. — He was born in Leipzig, 1735, and went after his father's death to his brother Emanuel in Berlin, to be taught by him in clavier-playing and composition. In the year 1754 he journeyed to Milan, where he became organist of the principal church, proceeded thence in 1759 to London, on receiving an appointment as

Director of Concerts, and died there in 1782. His clavier-works, which were printed in London, Berlin, Amsterdam, and Paris, embrace 18 Clavier Concertos, 28 Clavier Trios, a Sonata for 2 Harpsichords, another for four hands, and 12 Sonatas for Clavier solo. To him Gerber chiefly ascribes, in 1790, the greater increase of clavier amateurs of both sexes in his time; for "the naïve playfulness, the vivacious joyfulness, which mark all his clavier-works, have won him the favor of both sexes of every nationality, and one of his works was hardly out, when the hands of all the amateurs were busied with it". — An edition of his Sonatas lies before me without place of publication, entitled: "Six Sonates pour le Clavecin ou le Pianoforte, dédiées à S. A. le Duc Ernest de Mecklenbourg etc., Major général des armées de S. M. Britannique; comp. par Jean Chrétien Bach, maître de musique de S. M. la reine d'Angleterre. Œuvre V." From the dedication, and also from the costly title-page, drawn by Cipriani and engraved by Bartolozzi (both these celebrated artists had lived in London since 1764), it is apparent that these **Sonatas** were published during his stay in London. They not only justify the favorable reception accorded to his compositions whenever published, but are, besides, remarkable for the fact, that here the **first theme** of the Sonatas is followed, perhaps for the first time, by a distinctly marked **second theme.** E. g. the second Sonata begins with an *Allegro molto* in *D*. The first theme of four measures is repeated, and the bass then stands out in relief against a more animated accompaniment in the right hand, modulates through the dominant chord of the seventh *B-d♯-f♯-a* to *E*-major, forming an episode, after which the second theme, entirely different from the first, begins in *A*-major; it ends in the same key after sixteen measures, and a distinctly marked coda of four measures, which are repeated, closes the first division in the abovenamed key of the dominant. The short developments of the second division touch *B*-minor in particular, and the first theme of the Sonata again appears after a modulation to the principal key; the second theme and the coda are then repeated again, as in the first division, but now in *D*-major. Immanuel Faisst, in his excellent "Beiträge zur Geschichte der Claviersonate" (Cäcilia, Vol. 26, p. 21), mentions various composers of that time, in particular Emanuel Bach, in whose sonatas a second theme likewise seems to be recognizable at times; but in Johann Christian Bach's sonatas this latter is introduced and brought to a close with such distinctness, that they already exhibit *precisely the form later consistently adopted by Mozart* for the same. The combination of the movements in the Sonata still varies greatly in the "London Bach's" works; for instance, the first of the above sonatas consists of an *Allegretto* and a *Tempo di Minuetto,* both in *B*-major; the second, of an *Allegro di molto* in *D*-major, an *Andante* in *G*-major, and a *Minuetto* in *D*-major; the third unites an *Allegro* in *G*-major to an *Allegretto* with variations, in the same key; the fourth gives an *Allegro* and a *Rondo* in *E♭*-major; the fifth, an *Allegro assai* in *E*-major, an *Adagio* in *A*-major, and a *Prestissimo* in *E*-major; and the sixth, a *Grave,* a fugued *Allegro moderato,* and an *Allegretto* in *C*-minor.

We close the first Section, devoted to the Clavichord, of this historical sketch with a glance at that city, which was soon to rise to the position of a focus for all the musical life of Europe. Like Sebastian Bach and, in particular, his two sons Friedemann and Emanuel in North Germany, there labored in Vienna the eminent theoretician, and composer for the church and opera, **Johann Joseph Fux** (1660—1741), whose teachings and works systematized and propagated the Art of Counterpoint committed by the Netherlanders to the hands of the Italians, and further developed by the latter and the Germans. One of his most talented pupils was **Gottlieb Muffat,** whose "Componimenti musicali per il cembalo" (Vienna, 1727) and other Suites, Toccatas, and Fugues left in manuscript, are among the most valuable clavier-pieces of that period; and also **Georg Christoph Wagenseil** (1688—1779), then in high estimation, more especially on account of his "Sinfonien fürs Clavier mit zwei Violinen und Bass", printed in Vienna as Op. 4, etc., who is said still to have played on the clavichord with great fire when in his eighty-fourth year, and to have still given lessons on the same. Besides the above works there were published by him "Suavis artificiose elaboratus concentus musicus, continens VI parthias selectas ad clavicymbalum compositas", Bamberg, about 1740; "VI Divertimenti da Cembalo", Op. 1, Vienna; similar pieces as Op. 2 and 3; and further, Six Clavier Sonatas with Violin, Op. 5, Paris, where several of his "Sinfonies" were also engraved. **Johann Wanhal** (1739—1813) also lived in Vienna at this time, and from about 1760 to 1780 was accounted one of the most favorite fashionable composers, as in his compositions he employed scales, broken chords, and other exercises, familiar even to mediocre players, for passages, which sounded brilliant and bold in the ears of dilettanti. His numerous compositions, among which are found some contrapuntal works in clavier style and several text-books much prized at the time, include the following: 3 Caprices, Op. 14, Amsterdam, Hummel; ditto Op. 31, 35, etc., Vienna, publ. by Cappi, Artaria, and Steiner; 36 Progressive Clavier-pieces, Op. 41, Leipzig, Peters; 3 Congratulatory Sonatas, Bonn, Simrock; 12 Fugues, ditto; Sonate militaire, Offenbach, André; "Die Friedensfeier" (Celebration of Peace), characteristic Sonata, Bonn, Simrock; and some 70 books of Variations. His compositions issued after 1790, however, show at least in form, if not in spirit, the influence of the masters of the following period of clavier-playing. — The Sonatas and other clavier-pieces of the Prussian Kapellmeister **Johann Friedrich Reichardt** (1752—1814), celebrated for his compositions and musical writings, plainly exhibit the endeavor to endow the pieces with a definite character. Their style is pure, and suited to the clavier, and they already reach over, like those of the composers named above, into the later history of clavier-playing.

New editions of clavier-works pertinent to our subject have been issued by the following publishers:

BREITKOPF & HÄRTEL:—*Benda, G.*, Largo and Presto; *Hässler, J. W.*, Op. 13, 14, each having 3 Sonatas, Op. 17, Fantasia and Sonata in *G*-minor; Easy Sonatas, books 1, 2 3, and 4, each having 3 Sonatas; *Kirnberger*, Fugue in two and three parts; *Kuhnau, Joh.*, Sonata; *Marpurg*, Capriccio; *Mattheson*, Double Fugues with two and three subjects.—BARTHOLF SENFF:—*Kuhnau, Joh.*, Suite in *E*-minor; *Mattheson*, Suite in *A*-major.—LEUCKART (Leipzig):—*C. Ph. Em. Bach*, 6 series of Clavier Sonatas, Rondos, and Free Fantasias for Connoisseurs and Amateurs.—RIETER-BIEDERMANN:—*Reichardt, J. Friedr.*, 3 Sonatas, Rondo, "naiver Scherz", and Andantino.—Further we should mention the Collections "Classische Studien" (Fischhof, continued by Zellner) publ. by HASLINGER; "Alte Claviermusik" (Roitsch) publ. by PETERS; and "Les maîtres du clavecin" (Louis Köhler) in Collection LITOLFF, which contain valuable compositions by all the Masters hitherto named.

C. H. BITTER, already mentioned as the author of a biographical work on Joh. Seb. Bach, had published by W. Müller in Berlin, 1868: "Carl Philipp Emanuel und Wilhelm Friedemann Bach und deren Brüder", 2 Vols.

As an Appendix to this first Section we now subjoin a brief account of the Dance-melodies in vogue during the 16th, 17th, and 18th centuries, several of which have been named already. The observations on the character of these earlier folk-tunes apply to the primitive, original compositions, which were really danced to, and also occasionally sung. Later composers, who employed such forms for execution on the clavier or any other instrument, gave free rein to their imagination, lengthened out the short dance-tunes, lent them greater variety of rhythm, and thus changed their character to one no longer corresponding to the original. Wandering minstrels carried the ancient folk-songs from one land to another; but these airs were differently apprehended by different nations, and reproduced, when imitated or arranged, in a style which probably no longer showed the original features of the prototype. This circumstance explains the contradictions with which we meet in modern writings occupying themselves with this topic; and at the same time furnishes an excuse for the divergence between later arrangements of such earlier forms.

The earlier Dance-forms.

In Germany, as in Italy and France, the first instrumental compositions were mere echoes of sacred or secular vocal works. Folk-dances harmonically arranged, and designed for instrumental music alone, then followed, the melodies of which had long been familiar to the fiddlers of all countries, often reinforced by singing, especially when the dance tunes were founded on popular folk-songs. The compositions contained in the earliest collections of such harmonically accompanied dance-melodies were intended for playing as dance-tunes. In an extended form, however, they had found favor since the 17th century simply as instrumental pieces, and cultivated until toward the end of the 18th, particularly as choice combinations in the so-called *Suites* or *Partite*. The finest among the dance-forms occurring in them are characterized as follows by earlier writers:

The **Allemande** portrays a contented mind; its harmonies are serious, well-chosen, and carefully developed; it has two reprises of nearly equal length, usually with an *auftakt* of varying proportion, and its rhythm is a $^4/_4$ measure in Tempo moderato. The **Corrente** or *Courante*, in $^3/_2$ or moderate $^3/_4$ time, disports itself in pleasing and delicate runs, and its melody expresses hope, yearning, and desire; it consists of a shorter and a longer reprise, begins with a short *auftakt*, and closes on the thesis. The **Sarabande** comes forward full of earnestness and *grandezza*, in ternary (triple) time, and has two divisions of eight measures each. Its melody always begins on the full measure, but as a rule closes on the third beat. Its short, expressive melody, with a range of but few tones, is well adapted for variations, to which end one old melody of this dance, "Folies d'Espagne", was later used, in particular, again and again, e. g. by Dominico Scarlatti. The French **Gigue** or **Gique** sometimes appears in $^3/_4$ time, with an auftakt and following dotted quarter-note, or in $^6/_8$ time, with an auftakt and following dotted eighth-note on the arsis. The Italian **Giga**, now beginning with the full measure, now with a short or long auftakt, has a well-sustained rhythm and rapid tempo, affecting the following times: $^6/_8$, or $^9/_8$, or $^{12}/_8$. The dances here described formed, in the above or a similar succession, a so-called **Suite.** To these a *Prelude,* an *Overture,* a *Symphony* (at that time an harmonic prelude), an *Intrada,* a *Toccata,* a *Capriccio,* or some other piece was subsequently prefixed as an Introduction, the choice of the dances being left to the pleasure of the composer, except the lively Giga, which usually formed the close. In this extended shape the Suites were also called **Sonatas,** or more definitely **Sonate da camera,** to distinguish them from the more serious instrumental pieces called **Sonate da chiesa.** However, the several movements of a Suite or Partita showed not only an *external connection,* in that they all moved within one and the same key and exhibited, in their simple or more artistic working out, a certain mutual resemblance; they were likewise bound together in intelligible *internal unity* by a definite character assumed and maintained throughout, and by a tranquil, joyous, agitated, or passionate mood attaining to expression in all these various forms. Hereby the Suite was first raised to a significant work of art, finally developed by Sebastian Bach to perfect beauty.

Other earlier Dances, sometimes appearing separately, sometimes in the Suites or Clavier-exercises, or even as elements of a Sonata for the Clavier, are the following: The **Minuet.** It was a dignified and refined movement in $^3/_4$ time. The melody of the same, always beginning and closing on the metrical climax of the full measure (thesis), at first consisted of two reprises, each of four or eight measures, the four-measure grouping being strongly marked. The first division sometimes closed in the principal key, and was repeated after the second, which closed in a key related to the first. The principal melody was often followed by a *second Minuet* in a related key, after which the first was repeated. Sometimes a *third Minuet* in a related key followed, the principal theme then being finally repeated. Such secondary divisions were either termed *Minuetto* 2 and 3, or a *single* second minuet was named *Alternativo,* and in the latter half of the 18th century *Trio* as well, because, as many examples at hand prove, this movement was worked out strictly in three parts; a circumstance not always taken into account even then, despite which the second movement was called, as to-day, a Trio. Instead of Alternativo, *Double* was written, when the second theme formed merely a variation of the first, retaining the harmony of the same. Brossard observes: The original Minuet which came to us from Poitou, is a very rapid and merry dance in $^3/_8$ or $^6/_8$ time; it consisted of two parts that were repeated, and always closed on the first beat.—The term *Tempo di Minuetto,* however, meant the tranquilly measured movement characteristic of the first-mentioned dance of this name as performed in social festivities; whereas the instrumental minuet afterwards introduced into the sonata, and not used in dancing, usually bore the gay character of the dance derived from Poitou. The **Entrée** is a short introduction to the following dance. The **March** *(la marche)* should be given, according to its design, now with solemn gravity, now pointedly marked, rustically frolicsome, or lightly and rapidly, but never toyingly or frivolously. The **Loure,** beginning with an auftakt or on a dotted first note of a measure, is danced very seriously and slowly. The rhythm of the **Gavotte,** usually in *alla breve* time ($^2/_2$), is to be distinctly marked in the moderate tempo. The melody begins on the second half of the measure, i. e. with two quarter-notes, and consists of a reprise, closing on the first beat in a related key, and a following reprise of eight measures, closing in the principal key. The **Bourrée,** in $^4/_4$ time and with two reprises, each of four measures, always begins with an auftakt of a quarter-note, usually followed by a rhythm of a quarter-note and two eighths sustained throughout. The **Rigaudon** (Riggadoon) is a merry or grotesque dance set in $^4/_4$ time and beginning on the last quarter, having 3 or 4 reprises, whose shorter and most singular third part falls in as if by chance, often appearing in a lower register and without proper close, so that the more regular part following may have a more surprising effect. The **Passepied** (Paspy), in $^3/_8$ or $^6/_8$ time, generally begins with an eighth-note in the auftakt, and has three or four reprises in an even number of measures, the third, as in the Rigaudon, being short and toying or dallying. The form of the **Ronde,** a rustic round dance, is employed in binary or ternary measure in pieces for dancing, playing, or singing. Its lively principal theme ends in the principal key. This is followed by 2, 3, 4, or more *"Couplets"* in related keys, after each of which the first melody, which also closes the piece, is repeated as a refrain. Among other dances in this form is the **Branle,** a joyous, rural round dance, the short melody of which serves as a close to each of the succeeding different couplets. The **Canarie,** in $^3/_8$ time, is a Gigue of a very vivacious and skipping character, whose first measure-note is almost invariably dotted.

The **Pastorale** in $^6/_8$ time, and the **Villanella,** are jocund rural dances with an airy, pleasing melody, as are likewise the **Musette** (bagpipe) and the **Tambourin.** The last two have the tonic, or else the tonic and dominant, as sustained tone(s) in the bass; but while the Musette runs on easily in $^6/_8$ time, the Tambourin (accompanied by the instrument of that name) is executed in very lively $^4/_4$ time, with an auftakt of two quarter notes or two eighth-notes. The **Ciacona** or **Chaconne** is a longer dance-piece, almost always in major and in $^4/_4$ time of moderate progression, in which a *basso obbligato* usually consisting of four measures, and beginning the piece alone, is continually repeated as a **basso ostinato,** to which variations of all kinds are executed. The **Passacaglia** or **Passecaille** *(Germ. Gassenhauer)* is a similar dance of gentler character and slower movement, invariably in minor and in $^3/_4$ time, which is likewise founded on a *basso ostinato,* whose *volksthümliche** melody may, however, be taken up by the soprano or a middle part during the course of the piece. The **Pavane** or **Paduane** was a stately dance moving seriously and deliberately in *alla breve* time, often followed in sharp contrast by the **Gagliarda** or **Gaillarde** (formerly called **Romanesca,** acc. to Brossard and Rousseau)—romping, with dotted notes, and strongly marked, beginning with the full tripartite measure. The **Volta** was a sort of Gagliarda in $^3/_4$ time, and, like this latter, a very lively dance. The easy, tranquil strain of the **Passamezzo** was frequently followed by the **Furia,** with fiery accentuation and sometimes sharply dissonant tones. The **Siciliano,** in $^6/_8$ time with dotted initial measure-notes, displayed a rural, unaffected style; whereas the Venetian **Forlana,** having the same rhythm and similar dotted notes, was always performed in a brisk movement. The hot blood of Southern Italy is strikingly manifested in the native dances.

* A *volksthümliches Lied* is a product of art in the style of the folk-song. Transl. Note.

The **Saltarello** in $^3/_4$ time, with its reckless leaps, begins on the full measure, and progresses, with few exceptions, in the rhythm of a half-note followed by a quarter. The earlier examples in my possession were, however, probably performed in very quick tempo, so that their rhythm would be more plainly expressed by 𝅘𝅥 𝅘𝅥𝅮 | 𝅘𝅥 𝅘𝅥𝅮 or by 𝅘𝅥𝅮 𝄾 𝅘𝅥𝅮 | 𝅘𝅥𝅮 𝄾 𝅘𝅥𝅮. The wild **Tarantella** in minor, in $^6/_8$ time, with an auftakt of three eighth-notes, was danced by a youthful pair. It commences in agitated, yearning strains. But the movement grows more and more animated, increasing in rapidity toward the end until the dancers are quite exhausted. The effect of this dance is further enhanced by the sweeping accompaniment of the guitar (chitarra) and the booming, jingling tambourin. Sometimes the tarantella is also sung and danced in Italy by young girls, when its Bacchantic character is changed to youthful joyousness and mischievousness.

An interesting example of the **Moresca** (Moorish dance) often alluded to in the 16th century and later, is given by Kiesewetter ("Schicksale des weltlichen Gesanges", p. 104 of the Appendices); the same forms, as a dance-number, the close of the opera "Orfea" by Monteverde. The highest part takes the principal melody, while four accompanying parts support the same with simple chords:

The repeat indicated here is not, however, executed in unison, but in sequences. The melody is first repeated a fourth higher (d″—g″ etc.), then a second higher than at first (b′—e″ etc.), and finally a fifth higher than the piece began (e″—a″ etc.), whereupon the entire piece is repeated. Quite different from this appears "*La Morisque,* basse danse" in the work by Tielmann Susato, printed at Antwerp in 1551: "Het derde musyck boexken — — daer inne begrepen alderhande danserye" etc. Here the melody runs:

Tielman Susato's dances are arranged in four parts, and the soprano is accompanied harmonically or "note against note" in just the same simple style as in most collections of dances of the 16th and 17th centuries.

About the middle of the 18th century, the **Polonaises** attained to high favor in Germany. The original dance-melodies of this kind always begin on the full measure in $^{3}/_{4}$ time, often dot and accent the second quarter, progress with a strong, majestic movement, and form the close of each division, with rare exceptions, by an eighth-note and two sixteenth-notes, or four sixteenths and a marked quarter-note, which progresses as leading-note or second to the closing tonic then following:

or

At nearly the same period, short pieces for clavier and voice, usually in $^{2}/_{4}$ time, were transiently in vogue under the name of **Murky.** Their peculiarity resided in a persistent bass in broken octaves (16th-notes), which accompanied the whole insignificant trifle. The term "murky bass" is still used to designate basses of a like sprawling progression.

A. Czerwinski has an interesting chapter on the dances of the Germans in his "Geschichte der Tanzkunst" (History of the Art of Dancing), Leipzig, J. J. Weber, 1862. He describes the mediæval *Schreittänze* or *Schleiftänze*, whose slow steps were necessitated by the long trains then worn by the ladies, and the rustic *Springtänze* or *Reihen*, wherein the dancers of both sexes sought to outvie each other in the height and length of their leaps. The author finds the origin of the waltz in the opera "Una cosa rara", by Vincenz Martin, performed at Vienna in 1787, in which four ladies executed a dance with such great applause, that it was speedily introduced into the higher social circles, and received the name of "cosa rara". Later it was called *Langaus*, *Ländler*, *Viennese Waltz*, or "*Deutscher*".

The German dances contained in the earliest German "Orgel- und Instrument-Tabulaturbüchern" (Tabulatur Books for Organ and Clavier) by Ammerbach (1571), B. Schmid (1577), and J. Paix (1583), viz. "*Herzog Moritz Tanz*" ($^{4}/_{4}$), with a *Nachtanz* (Proportio, $^{3}/_{4}$), "*Hupfauf*" ($^{3}/_{4}$), "*Bruder Cunrad Tanzmaass*" ($^{4}/_{4}$) with *Nachtanz* ($^{3}/_{4}$), *Hoppeltanz*, etc., seem to be merely isolated examples, and not to have come into general use.

The more serious **Allemande,** however, already appears in the above book by Tielman Susato (Amsterdam, 1551), and was elaborated with peculiar care in the Suites down to the middle of the 18th century. The artistic Allemandes of Sebastian Bach and his contemporaries, like all the dance-forms found in their Suites, had for a long time not been intended as accompaniments to actual dances, the proper destination of the dance-melodies of the 16th and 17th centuries, harmonized with simple chords. A specimen from Susato's collection described above will illustrate this:

The Germans have never been prominent as inventors or reformers in the field of dance-music; they had a higher mission. In like manner as the counterpoint of the Netherlanders and Italians was first suffused with life and warmth by the Germans, Sebastian Bach elevated it in his master-piece, the Fugue, to a height which will hardly be again attainable in future. Through the Germans the Sonata, too, first gained living expression, and attained to fullest perfection at the hands of Beethoven. In this Master's works, all phases of emotion find idealization and tranquilization; they make us forget the dark side of every-day life, and discover the bright regions of an ideal world filled with love, where longing is unknown —thus grasping the mission of Music in its fullest meaning, and affording the only satisfactory solution possible of the same.

THE MODERN HISTORY OF CLAVIER-PLAYING.

The Fortepiano.

III. The Lyrical Clavier Style.

Joseph Haydn and Wolfgang Mozart.

The Fugue, progressing according to strict rule and in monochromatic seriousness, combining within itself the whole art of counterpoint, was opposed, through the efforts of EMANUEL BACH, the head of the Earlier German Clavier school, by the more brilliantly hued and freer form of the Sonata. With masterful energy he committed nearly 80 such compositions for the clavier alone to the press; and the peculiar mission of the masters following him consisted in developing the Sonata-form—which was soon accepted for all compositions of larger scope, like the Symphony, the Concerto, the Quartet, etc.—to a form perfectly in accord with the universal laws of beauty, and thus to raise it to a master-piece of the freer style of composition. Like every reformer, Emanuel Bach did not escape vexatious attacks from his contemporaries, but in amends he had the satisfaction of numbering the most liberal-minded of the same among his intimate friends and admirers. For instance, the celebrated writer of musical history, Forkel, in his "Musikalischer Almanach" for 1783, notices the first three Collections of Clavier Sonatas for Connoisseurs and Amateurs by C. P. E. Bach as follows: "The author is noted as a man, cujus gloriæ neque profuit quisquam laudando, nec vituperando quisquam nocuit"; and in the following yearly volume (pp. 22—38) Forkel furnishes a profound paper on the *F*-minor Sonata in the third of these Collections. Joseph Haydn, the musician whose work we next have to consider, also confesses: "Whatever I know, I owe to Carl Philipp Emanuel Bach!"—and Mozart, too, renders him his due in the words: "He is the father, we are the boys; whichever of us can do anything well, learned it of him!" When Emanuel Bach died at Hamburg in his 74th year, his younger contemporaries Haydn, Mozart, and Beethoven were 56, 32, and 18 years old respectively. The circumstance, that these three musicians, revered both in their time and ours, made Vienna their permanent residence—Haydn from 1740, Beethoven from 1770, and Mozart from 1781—explains to us, how this capital, rendered so attractive by its art-loving nobility and the graceful ease of its society, and so favored by its agreeable situation, should have become the cradle of all the reforms of the following period in the history of our art.

Joseph Haydn was born on March 31, 1732, at Rohrau in Lower Austria, and on account of his remarkable musical talent was already engaged as a choir-boy, in his eighth year, in the principal church at Vienna. Here he enjoyed thorough instruction in singing, and on the clavier and violin, besides which he learned, in his solitary chamber, the laws of counterpoint from Fux's *Gradus ad Parnassum.* The first clavier-works of importance with which he became acquainted, and which were likewise destined to give his exercises a new direction, were 6 sonatas by C. P. E. Bach. He played them unwearyingly again and again, and remarked later, that he had most zealously studied this master's style and striven to imitate it. In Vienna he was early occupied in giving music lessons, and the first clavier sonatas, which he wrote for his pupils, were soon spread abroad in innumerable copies, and were even published in print without his knowledge, an author's proprietorship then being protected in no way. But through these so favorably received compositions he gained access as a teacher to the highest circles, and likewise, through the very numerous violin-quartets composed by him, which attracted no less attention, to the best musical societies of the capital. After 1760 his compositions also became known beyond the limits of Vienna; the freshness and vivacity of their naïve style gave pleasure everywhere, though loud complaints were not wanting, that music was thereby debased to comic trifling and that they contained many incorrectnesses and forbidden octaves (doublings of a melody, now long ago "permitted"). In the year 1773 Emanuel Bach observed, referring to the character of the then rising tide of new music, which even his liberality thought dangerous to the dignity of musical art: "Who does not know the time, at which music and its performance entered into a new phase and rose to a height which, as I feel it, was productive of harm. I hold, with many clear-sighted men", he cries, "that the comic feature now in such vogue bears most blame in this". It is also apparent, that we owe to our

Haydn the introduction of the **fancifully humorous style**, unknown before, from a characterization of this master in the "Musikalisches Handbuch" for 1782, where we read, on pag. 19 etc.: **Haydn**, "Musical jester, but not, like Yorik (sic), for pathos, but for broad comedy; and this is desperately hard in music.—Even his Adagio's, where one should properly weep, often bear the stamp of broad comedy. Haydn once was chidden by the Berlinese for the incorrectnesses of his style; but these people must have forgotten—that one ought either not to laugh at all, or must needs often laugh in defiance of the rules of propriety, following the ebb and flow of the mood". In the year 1761 Haydn entered the service of Prince Nicolaus Joseph Esterházy as Kapellmeister, and dwelt until 1790 at Eisenstadt, the seat of the latter, though sojourning yearly for some three winter months in Vienna. Down to 1789 he had already written 175 Symphonies for the private band of this prince, besides equally numerous clavier-pieces and other compositions. Concerning this important period of his life, Haydn himself speaks as follows: "My Prince was satisfied with all my works; I was applauded; as the master of an orchestra I could make experiments, observe what produces the effect and what weakens it,—could improve, add, strike out, venture; I was cut off from the world; no one near me could make me doubt myself—thus I necessarily became original." In 1770 a countryman of his, **Ignaz Pleyel** (1757—1831) came to Vienna, to take lessons in clavier-playing of the already mentioned Wanhal. Pleyel's happy musical gifts occasioned Count Erdoedy to send him to live with Haydn, that he might study violin-playing and composition with the latter. He quickly became the master's favorite pupil, stayed in his house until 1777, then went to Naples, thence to Rome, and in 1783 was appointed music director at the cathedral of Strassburg. It was in this city, especially, that Pleyel composed a great number of String Quartets and Clavier-pieces, which attained to extraordinary favor at the time, although they reproduced in pale reflection only the popular features of Haydn's compositions, without the ideality of the same. They were printed at Paris, London, Vienna, Berlin, Leipzig, etc.; of his Clavier-pieces we mention the following: 6 Grandes Sonates, Op. 15, Leipzig, Hofmeister; 3 Easy Clavier Sonatas, Nouvelles Sonatines progressives, and 4 Rondeaux favoris, Leipzig, Peters.

Prince Esterhazy died in 1790, bequeathing to Haydn a life-pension of 1000 florins, which was increased by his son and successor by seniority to 1400 florins. Haydn now moved to Vienna, intending to live there in peace and free from care; but toward the end of the year 1790 he received a visit from Peter Salomon, a celebrated violinist of Bonn, then living in England, who was commissioned by the manager of the Haymarket Theatre in London to engage him under the most favorable terms as a composer for 12 concerts to be given there. Mozart, then living in Vienna on the most friendly footing with Haydn, said to him on this occasion: "Papa! you have had no education for the great 'world', and speak too few languages!" But Haydn answered: "O, my language is understood all over the world!" and the 15th of December was fixed as the day of departure for London. That day Mozart was constantly with him; and at the leave-taking, which filled the eyes of both with tears, he said: "This is probably our last farewell in this life!"—and not a year had passed when Haydn, who was still in London, received the tidings of the death of his friend, younger by 24 years than himself, and wrote to Vienna: "The world will not see such another talent in 100 years!"—Haydn was enthusiastically received in London, and his compositions met with extraordinary success in the concerts which he directed at the harpsichord. But a society of professional musicians, who were likewise about to give a series of concerts, strained every nerve to dim his lustre. Among other masters Muzio Clementi, then staying in London, composed a symphony for the Professional Concerts, which had a very flattering reception. In the second part of the soirée one of Haydn's earlier symphonies was then performed, with the intention of letting it serve as a foil to the brilliancy of the other. But the audience received it with such demonstrative applause, that Clementi never again cared to attempt a similar contest in this field.—In the summer of the same year Haydn journeyed to Oxford with Dr. Burney, to take the honorary degree of Doctor (of Music); after returning to London he remained there till the following year (1792), in order to bring out 12 new Symphonies in a series of as many concerts. The Society already named now stated publicly that Haydn was too old to write anything new, and that therefore his celebrated pupil, Ignaz Pleyel, had been called to London to produce his fresher compositions in 12 Professional Concerts. Pleyel conducted himself so amiably in London toward his old master, that the latter wrote: "Pleyel behaved so modestly toward me on his arrival, that he has won my love anew. We are very often together, which is an honor for him, and he can appreciate his father. We shall divide the honors between us, and each go home pleased."— —"Last year I found great approval, but at present still more. Pleyel's boldness is much criticized. Nevertheless I love him still. I never miss his concerts, and am the first to applaud him." Pleyel, however, shared the fate of all imitators barren of invention; on his decease at Paris in 1831 as a music publisher and pianoforte maker, his compositions, formerly in so high favor, had long been consigned to oblivion, whereas Haydn's Oratorios and instrumental works are still applauded as models of a healthy and unaffected style. In Germany Haydn's renown first began, as he himself often said, with his return from England. His compositions, among them a large number of clavier-pieces of all kinds, were printed at Vienna, Leipzig, Berlin, London, Paris, Amsterdam, etc., and were issued later in Complete Editions by Breitkopf & Härtel of Leipzig, and L. Holle of Wolfenbüttel. There were published: — A *Concerto* in *D,* Op. 37, Mainz, Schott; *a second* in *G,* Amsterdam, Hummel; *2 Sonatas for 4 hands,* Op. 81 and 86, Leipzig, Breitkopf & Härtel; *Il maestro e lo scolare,* Variations for 4 hands, same publ.; *34 Clavier Sonatas,* ditto, also in Wolfenbüttel by L. Holle; *8 Sonatas for Clavier and Violin,* new edition in score, Breitkopf & Härtel; *31 Sonatas for Clavier, Violin, and Violincello,* ditto; and various numbers of *Variations, Caprices* (Vienna, Artaria), and minor pieces. In 1794 Haydn once more went to London, brought back thence the text for his Oratorio "The Creation", to Germany, had the same done into German at Vienna by Van Switen, and in 1799, already in his sixty-seventh year, he completed and brought out this admirable work in the latter place. In the year 1801 the venerable master finished his "Seasons", a work of youthful freshness, and died in 1809, amid the tumult of the French war, as one of our most active and influential composers, who, in all his compositions, preserved and lent most natural expression to the true German character of heartiness and easy good nature *(Gemüthlichkeit).*

Latterly the following editions of Haydn's Clavier-works have appeared: — *Ausgewählte Sonaten und Solostücke* (Selected Sonatas and Solo Pieces). Edited, with the co-operation of J. Faisst and L. Lachner, by S. Lebert. 2 Vols. Stuttgart, J. G. Cotta. — *Sonatas for the Pianoforte.* 2 Vols. (Dörffel), Breitkopf & Härtel. — *Sonatas,* complete edition (Köhler). 4 Vols. Edition Peters. — All 34 *Sonatas* (Köhler & Winkler) 1 Vol., Collection Litolff.

The following works should also be mentioned here:—"J. Hadyn in London, 1791 and 1792", by Th. G. Karajan. Vienna, Carl Gerold's Sohn, 1861.—"Mozart and Haydn in London", by C. F. Pohl. 2 Parts. Vienna, same publ., 1867.—"Joseph Haydn", by C. F. Pohl. First half-volume. Breitkopf & Härtel, 1878.

Haydn introduced the Minuet into his Symphonies, usually giving it a gay and lively turn, whereby Beethoven was later occasioned to insert a similar Scherzo or Allegretto in the Clavier Sonata at times, in which the mood of the entire composition is reviewed under as cheerful an aspect as possible. While Haydn was the first who had the faculty of stamping his compositions with humor and the most wanton mirthfulness, we must, on the other hand, concede to his younger contemporary and the sharer of his fame, Mozart, who was active not only as a composer, but also as a clavier virtuoso, that he gave his works, together with an expanded and more noble form, a more exhilarating beauty of tone, while lending to his performances the tenderest and warmest expression. The elder master first visited foreign lands at an advanced age, and therefore expressed his amiable individuality foremostly in his *genuinely German style of composition.* Mozart, on the contrary, during the professional tours of his childhood and youth, had already met the leading musicians in the capitals of Germany, France, England, Holland, and Italy; his youthful mind was impressed by the peculiarities of each, and his native wealth of imagination and exquisite sense of the Beautiful made it possible for him to become the creator of a *universal style of composition* finding equal favor everywhere.

Wolfgang Amadeus Mozart was born at Salzburg on January 27, 1756. His father, Leopold Mozart, noted as the author of the first thorough German violin method and of several practical compositions, gave early instruction in music to him and his sister Maria Anna, his senior by five years, and both soon displayed the happiest talents for this art. Nissen, in his biography of Mozart, gives several clavier-pieces already composed by Wolfgang in his sixth and seventh years. The happy father was encouraged thereby to undertake a *Kunstreise* to Munich as early as 1762 with his children, and a second later to Vienna; in both places they were admitted to the highest circles, and their performances rewarded by unanimous applause. Even Emperor Francis I. frequently invited the young virtuosi to his palace, sometimes put Wolfgang's musical abilities to the proof, and enjoyed his frank, child-like speeches. For instance, the latter was once to play before a brilliant assemblage at court. But before beginning, he looked about him, and cried: "Is not Herr Wagenseil here? He must come — he understands it!" — missing the then highly esteemed clavier-player and composer. The latter thereupon approaching the harpsichord, Mozart said to him: "I am to play one of your Concertos; you must turn over for me!" — Among the compositions which Wolfgang chose somewhat later for performance, were the Sonatas by Johann Christian Bach already mentioned, and as studies the brother and sister used, among others, the Sonatas by Domenico Paradies and a Concerto by Andrea Lucchesi — a thoroughly trained musician appointed in 1771 Kapellmeister to the Elector at Bonn. In Vienna a little violin was presented to Wolfgang, who soon learned to play on it without instruction; in like manner, he needed only a suggestion as to the treatment of the pedal of the organ, to become fully familiar with this instrument. His great successes in Vienna encouraged his father to venture on a longer trip in the year 1763, this time to Paris. On their way thither the children were everywhere admired, and in Frankfort they gave several successful concerts. Here Wolfgang played, according to an advertisement of August 30, 1763 (s. Jahn, Life of Mozart, Vol. I, pag. 45, etc.), not only Concertos on the *clavecin* or harpsichord, but also on the violin; he accompanied the symphonies on the harpsichord, and finally improvised "as long as one cared to listen" in any, even the most difficult keys that one could name, "from his head". In Paris the brother and sister were introduced to Madame de Pompadour, played thereafter before the royal family at Versailles, and finally gave two brilliant concerts at Paris. The most eminent clavier-players then in that city were Schobert of Strassburg and Johann Gottfried Eckart of Augsburg. They both brought the children the engraved editions of their clavier-works, and Maria Mozart in particular, won, by her exact execution of these difficult compositions, the plaudits of all the musicians assembled at the concerts. Mozart the father now had four clavier-compositions with violin accompaniment, by Wolfgang, engraved in Paris as op. 1 and 2, whose dedication was most graciously received by the ladies named on the title-pages: "II Sonates pour le Clavecin qui peuvent se jouer avec l'accompagnement de Violon, dédiées à Madame Victoire de France par J. G. Mozart de Salzbourg, âgé de sept ans. Œuvre premier." The second work, with a similar title, was dedicated to the Comtesse de Tesse; Nissen gives a movement in *B*♭-major from the same. In 1764 the family journeyed to England, where they met with such an extremely kind reception that they remained there some fifteen months. Johann Christian Bach was at that time Director of Concerts, and took special delight in Wolfgang's rare musical gifts. The King, too, admired his playing on the organ and harpsichord, and set before him compositions by Wagenseil, Bach, Handel, Paradies, and the Chorus Master to the Queen, Carl Friedrich Abel, which he had to play *prima vista.* From this time onward the free improvisations on given themes, which later formed the climax of his concerts, find special commendation. In London, Wolfgang composed six more Sonatas for harpsichord with accompaniment of violin or flute, which he dedicated to Queen Charlotte; they may be found in Cah. XV of the edition of Mozart's Works, Leipzig, Breitkopf & Härtel, as Sonatas 1—6. In England, too, he wrote his first Symphonies for orchestra, and altogether made such marvellous mental progress, that his father could write home: "Our high and mighty (grossmächtiger) Wolfgang knows everything in this, his eighth year, that one can require of a man of forty."—On his return to Salzburg, he continued his serious theoretical and practical studies, and wrote several Oratorios, besides other compositions. During his twelfth year he also wrote at the Emperor's request, while in Vienna, his first Opera: "La finta semplice", in three acts, which could not be brought out, however, on account of numberless cabals; although Hasse and Metastasio declared that thirty operas had been given in Vienna, not one of which was in any way equal to that of the boy, which they both admired greatly.

To establish his son's renown still more firmly, and at the same time to insure a most diversified development of his musical talent, Leopold Mozart decided to go with him to Italy, the land of promise for all artists. Wolfgang's concerts were received with the liveliest enthusiasm in Verona, Mantua, Milan, Florence, Rome, and Naples, and on the way back to Germany the Pope conferred upon the youthful musician at Rome the Order of the Golden Spur. The program of a concert given at Mantua by Amadeo Mozart on Jan. 16, 1770, contains the following numbers: — A Symphony of his own composition; a Clavier-concerto, which will be handed to him, and which he will immediately play *prima vista;* a Sonata handed him in like manner, which he will provide with variations, and afterwards repeat in another key; an Aria, the words for which will be handed to him, and which he will immediately set to music and sing himself, accompanying himself on the harpsichord; a Sonata for Clavichord on a subject given him by the leader of the violins; a Strict Fugue on a theme to be selected, which he will improvise on the harpsichord; a Trio, in which he will execute a violin-part *all' improvviso;* and finally, the latest Symphony composed by himself.—In that same year Wolfgang composed the Opera "Mitridate", in three acts, for Milan; it was performed on December 26, 1770, under his direction, and was received with such extraordinary favor that it had to be repeated twenty times during that season.

Wolfgang had heard the spirited delivery of the most eminent Italian singers, and the expressive melodies, by which the general public was chiefly roused to enthusiasm; he now endeavored to write himself in an equally vocal and universally appreciated style, and had acquired, through his constant practice in improvising entire compositions, the then so necessary art of writing, rehearsing, and bringing out an Italian opera "in a short month". The remarkable success of his first opera speedily brought him new commissions for similar compositions; and a *Festspiel* (serenata drammatica), written in 1771, and also the opera "Lucio Silla", written in 1772 for Milan, were received there with equal applause. With the Comic Opera "La finta giardiniera", which he wrote in 1775 for Munich, now begin his successful labors for his native country, which he does not again leave, excepting for a second short trip to Paris. In the year 1770 Archbishop Sigismund of Salzburg, and later his successor Hieronymus, had appointed Mozart Concertmeister, at first without salary, and afterwards at 150 florins annually. The unworthy treatment experienced at the hands of the latter occasioned Mozart, however, to leave his service, and to undertake a new journey in 1777, to find a sphere of activity better adapted to his abilities.

Provided with a great number of compositions which he had finished in Salzburg, he first went to Munich and thence to Augsburg, accompanied by his mother. In the latter town he immediately sought out the celebrated builder of organs and claviers, GEORG ANDREAS STEIN, and was so greatly delighted with his **Pianofortes,** on which the tone was easily and precisely produced and promptly dampened, and whose hammers played in brass sockets (a contrivance later called the "Viennese Action"), *that he thenceforward adopted this instrument, with its more powerful and fuller tone, for the performance of his clavier compositions.* Thus he writes from Augsburg in October, 1771: "Here and in Munich I have already often played all my sonatas by heart ——the last, in *D,* comes out inimitably on the Stein pianoforte."

After a concert, the returns from which were unhappily very scanty, Mozart proceeded to Mannheim, whence his mother wrote (Dec. 28, 1777): "Wolfgang stands in high estimation everywhere; but he plays quite otherwise than when in Salzburg, for here there are only pianofortes, and these he can manage so inimitably, that the like was never heard before; in a word, everybody who hears him says, that his match is not to be found. Although both **Beecke** and **Schubert***[*] have been here, everyone says that he far surpasses them in beauty, and taste, and delicacy (Feinigkeit); and all are astounded, too, that he plays by heart, and whatever is put before him." The Abbé **Georg Joseph Vogler** (1749—1814), celebrated both as an organist and clavier-player and as a composer and theoretician, who had opened a *Tonschule* (music school) at Mannheim in 1776, also felt a lively interest in the gifted Mozart; but the latter could take no liking to him, and wrote his father (Mannheim, Jan. 17, 1778): "Herr Vogler desires *absolument* to become well acquainted with me, having often importuned me to visit him, and now he has finally put his pride in his pocket, and paid me the first visit.——After dinner he had two of his claviers brought, which are tuned together, and also his tiresome engraved sonatas. I had to play them, he accompanying me on the other clavier. At his urgent request, I likewise had to send for my sonatas. N.B. Before dinner he had—murdered my Concerto *prima vista.* The first movement went *prestissimo*, the Andante *allegro*, and the Rondo, *prestissimo* indeed.—You may easily imagine, that it was not to be borne, because I could not venture to say to him: Much too fast. Besides, it is far easier to play a piece fast than slowly; in passages one can leave some few notes in the lurch, without its being noticed by anyone; but is it well done? —And wherein does the art lie, of reading prima vista? In this: To play the piece in the right tempo, as it ought to be, and to execute all the notes, appoggiaturas, etc., with proper expression and taste, as they stand, so that the hearer may think that he who is playing it composed it himself." The Abbé **Johann Franz Xaver Sterkel** (1750—1817), who attracted attention through several Clavier Con-

---

[*] Ignaz von Beecke (d. 1803), Major, and afterwards music director to the Prince of Oetting-Wallerstein, was a clavier-player and composer highly esteemed at his time; the clavier performances of our popular poet Christian Friedrich Daniel Schubart (d. 1791) "in the Bach style", were also much praised at that period.

certos (Vienna, Artaria, and Offenbach, André), Clavier Sonatas (Mainz, Schott, and Offenbach, André), Sonatas for 4 hands (ditto), and other easily executed, "galante" pieces, was also staying in Mannheim at that time, and his clavier performances were likewise censured by Mozart: "He played so fast, that it was quite unintelligible, and not at all clearly or in time!" From these remarks, as well as from abundant contemporary testimony, it is evident that Mozart played, and wished to have his compositions performed, in a not too rapid tempo, but always with the warmest expression and most exquisite taste. He was also invariably "*accurat* in time, and nevertheless played expressively", and did not allow the regular course of the left hand to be disturbed even by a *tempo rubato* in the right in an Adagio (see Nissen, pag. 318, etc.) In Mannheim Mozart played often, and always with success before the Electoral court, but his desire of an appointment there remained unfulfilled. He therefore proceeded in 1778 to Paris, where he had been so flatteringly received as a boy. Here, however, a most vehement strife was in progress between the adherents of Gluck and their opponents, the admirers of Piccini; the entire interest of musical circles was concentrated on the outcome of the musical dramas of these rival composers; thus little hope was left for Mozart of finding proper appreciation in Paris at such an agitated time. The death of his faithful mother having made Paris repugnant to him, he hastened back to Salzburg, in order to re-enter, at his father's desire, the service of the Archbishop so cordially detested by him, as *Concertmeister* and *Hoforganist* at a salary of 400 florins. He now composed, in particular, several masses, and the opera "Zaide", which however was not performed. He at last received the flattering commission, to write a grand serious opera, "Idomeneo", for the Carnival of 1781 at Munich. The opera had extraordinary success, and Mozart reluctantly left Munich in response to the command of the Archbishop to follow him to Vienna. But here he was repeatedly treated by the latter in such an outrageous manner, that he finally felt compelled to break with him for good. At this time **Leopold Kozeluch** (1753—1814) was one of the most popular composers and fashionable clavier-teachers in Vienna, and had already written fifty Clavier Concertos, three Concertos for 4 hands, a Concerto for two pianofortes, and over sixty Sonatas for two and four hands, which have been published in part by Artaria of Vienna, André of Offenbach, Peters of Leipzig, and Schott of Mainz. The Archbishop now approached him, in order to persuade him to accept the position in Salzburg given up by Mozart, offering him a salary of 1000 florins. But Kozeluch declined the offer, and remarked: "If he lets such a man go, how would he act towards me!"

In the year 1787 Gluck died, who, as Imperial Kammerkomponist (composer for the Emperor's private band), had drawn a salary of 2000 florins, and Mozart then entered the Emperor's service, but only as Kammermusikus, at a salary of but 800 florins. But Kozeluch, whose compositions now appear dry and quite unenjoyable to us, received the position of Kammerkomponist after Mozart's death with a salary of 1500 florins!—A year subsequent to his arrival in Vienna, Mozart married Constance Weber; and though he wrote from this time down to his death nine years later his finest musical dramas and other vocal and instrumental compositions, and celebrated the most brilliant triumphs as a pianoforte virtuoso, he was never able, despite untiring assiduity, to banish the cares attendant upon the support of his family. The cause of this was, that the theatre managers and music publishers, with few exceptions, paid comparatively insignificant sums for his manuscripts; and further, that the receipts from his concerts did not always correspond to the applause which was showered upon his performances.

The first Opera composed by Mozart during this period for Vienna, was "Belmonte und Constanze" (1782); it was given there, and in Prague, Leipzig, Hamburg, and other places, with great success. It was followed by the "Schauspieldirector" and "Le nozze di Figaro" (1786); the latter opera, which was written and composed within six weeks, met with extraordinary success, especially in Prague. Mozart, who gave concerts there in 1787, was greeted with enthusiasm, and after a free improvisation which he executed at the close, he was thrice recalled to the pianoforte. His Opera "Don Giovanni", written for Prague in 1787, was received with overwhelming applause from overture to close. But Mozart's pecuniary circumstances remained embarrassed. To improve them, he undertook a professional tour to Berlin in 1789, touching Dresden and Leipzig on the way. In Berlin he met with a most flattering reception, both at Court and in private circles, but abandoned the idea of giving a concert, as his friends considered it doubtful if the receipts would be sufficient. King Frederick William II., with the benevolent intention of rescuing him from his petty cares, offered him an appointment as Kapellmeister with a salary of 3000 thalers; but Mozart felt bound to decline the same, "as he did not wish quite to forsake his good Kaiser". After his return to Vienna he acquainted the Kaiser with this brilliant offer, but the latter was not moved thereby to increase his paltry income, though he commissioned him (in December, 1789) to write a new opera, "Così fan tutte". The same was brought out on January 26 of the following year; yet we do not learn that the Viennese noticed any difference between Mozart's master-works and the then fashionable operas by Sarti, Salieri, Guglielmi, Cimarosa, Paisielli, Martin, and Weigl. In 1790 he determined to make another journey to Frankfort, to the coronation of Kaiser Leopold II., and wrote thence to his "darling wifey" (Herzensweibchen): "Now I am firmly resolved to do my work here as well as possible, and then joyfully back to you.—What a magnificent life we shall lead, I will work—work, so that I may not again be placed in such a disagreeable position through unforeseen accidents."— In a concert given there, only compositions of his own were performed; he played among other things the Piano Concerto in *F*, Op. 44, and the "Coronation Concerto" in *D*, Op. 46. The presence of the above-mentioned J. v. Beecke also induced him to perform a Pianoforte Concerto for 4 hands with his assistance. On the return trip he stopped at Mainz, Mannheim, and Munich, but he did not succeed in improving his pecuniary condition by this journey. Soon after his arrival at Vienna, Salomon also came thither, to engage his fatherly friend Haydn for London. To Mozart he also held out the prospect of going to London, after Haydn's return, under similar favorable terms. But we know, that Mozart was never again to behold the one contemporary, who seems to have fully recognized his greatness. In the Spring of 1791 the theatre manager Schikaneder entreated Mozart to set to music an opera, the Magic Flute, for which he himself had written the libretto, for performance in his theatre, hardly more than a mere wooden booth. Mozart, good-natured and ever ready to help, had not yet finished the same, when he received the honorable commission to write a festival opera for Prague, for the coronation of the Kaiser as King of Bohemia. In 18 days the opera intended for this purpose, "La clemenza di Tito", was finished, rehearsed, and performed in Prague, in spite of Mozart's continued indisposition. The success of the same did not answer his expectations; indeed, his happy star was not to rise until the last months of his life. The Magic Flute, given for the first time shortly after his return to Vienna, was then received with such unexampled applause, that it had to be repeated one hundred times, with like tremendous ovations, from Sept. 30, 1791, the day of its first performance, up to Nov. 23 of the following year. Mozart, though suffering seriously both physically and mentally from unremitting work and various excitements, was still laboring zealously on his requiem, in defiance of growing indisposition, when stricken by death on December 5, 1791.

Despite the almost miraculous ease and rapidity with which Mozart sketched and completed the majority of his compositions, he nevertheless endowed them all with the purest euphony, the most soulful meaning, and the most artistic form. To his earliest clavier compositions, which he performed at his concerts, belong the **Variations** on a Minuet by Fischer, in *C*-major. In 1774 he had them sent him while in Munich, and also played them in 1778 in Paris. The theme, thoroughly appropriate to the graceful dance, appears in 4-measure rhythm. But the fourth measure of the second strain is repeated, whereby a peculiar 5-measure phrase is formed, which Mozart retains in all twelve variations. These, like the variations on "Je suis Lindor", which he played in public at Leipzig and Vienna, are by far more flowing in their runs and passages than the earlier "galante" variations *(Veränderungen)* by Emanuel Bach, Kirnberger, and others; yet they offer no difficulty whatever to a modern pianist, and are intended, like all similar compositions of Mozart's, to affect the hearers mainly through the expressive delivery of their pleasing melodies. The **"free improvisation"**, always greeted with demonstrative applause, consisted for the most part of such variations, in which the audience was treated to familiar themes, now varied in melody, harmony, or rhythm, and now ornamented with pearling and brilliant figures and passages.

One of the most prolific authors of this style of clavier pieces was the Abbé **Joseph Gelinek** (1757—1825). When Mozart went to Prague in 1787 to bring out his Don Giovanni, he heard the Abbé extemporize on one of his melodies, and was so favorably impressed by this performance, that he recommended him to the family of Count Kinsky as *Claviermeister*. Gelinek soon after accompanied the family to Vienna, continued in most friendly relations with Mozart, and published his first variations on the theme from Don Giovanni "Reich mir die Hand, mein Leben" (Vienna, Artaria; Mainz, Schott, etc.), gradually followed by various similar ones on melodies by Mozart and others, which soon became so generally popular, that down to 1815 more than 125 Numbers had appeared, printed in

Vienna, Leipzig, Berlin, Mainz, Paris, London, etc. These Variations, like the similar fashionable pieces by his contemporaries J. Wanhal, F. J. Kirmair, D. Steibelt, J. W. Wilms, and others, can lay no claims to artistic value, but have only the aim, while easy of execution, of sounding brilliantly to the non-professional, and to set in motion, at best, the pupil's fingers. Far more valuable and original both in form and in the development of their melodies, are the Variations of the inconstant and original **Johann Wilhelm Hässler** (1747—1822), a pupil of the excellent organist J. Ch. Kittel of Erfurt. His "Fantaisie et chanson russe variée, op. 19, gravée et imprimée chez Reinsdorp et Kaestner" (place not given), still strikes us as a piquant piano-piece. The Variations form a connected series, and the player is already confronted by passages in thirds and sixths for the right hand, chords stretching a tenth (e. g. *f♯-c-e♭-a*) for the left, and for both the rapid change of fingers on the same key, later so much employed. Hässler is said to have played the clavier with genuine and animated expression, which he also maintained in *prestissimo*. He once gave a performance on the organ in the *Garnisonkirche* at Berlin, where he played, according to the testimony of a musician present, "like an angel with his hands, and like a devil with his feet". Of his Clavier Sonatas were published: 3 Sonates, op. 13, 14, and 16, Leipzig, Breitkopf & Härtel; Fantaisie et Sonate, op. 17, same publ.; 6 Easy Sonatas (ditto); Grande Sonate pour 3 mains sur un Pianoforte, Riga, Hartknoch, 1793; etc. In the year 1789 Mozart met Hässler in Dresden. But Mozart, in the musical match there contested, so far outrivalled his opponent, that even the latter could not withhold the full tribute of his admiration.

With the same consistency shown by Emanuel Bach in clinging to the 3 movements of the Clavier Sonata, Mozart developed the first movement in the sonata-form still retained to-day, in which—as in similar compositions by Johann Christian Bach, with whom he became acquainted in his childhood in London and whose compositions he studied later — a first and second theme appear and are developed. Among Mozart's 31 Pianoforte Sonatas we notice especially that in *A*-minor (Œuvres compl. de Mozart, Leipzig, Breitkopf & Härtel; Cah. 1, No. 6), the Fantaisie and Sonate in *C*-minor, and the Sonate in *F* (Cah. 6, Nos. 1, 2, and 13). The **Pianoforte Sonatas for 4 hands** (Cah. 7, Nos. 1—4) also first received from Mozart a really interesting conception and an extended form; he sought to occupy both players in an equally interesting manner, and to his pattern-work we owe the fine sonatas for 4 hands by G. ONSLOW (Op. 7 in *E*-minor and Op. 22 in *F*-minor), J. N. HUMMEL (Op. 92 in *A♭*-minor), and I. MOSCHELES (Op. 47 in *E♭*). But in the **Pianoforte Concertos**, which he designed for his own performances, and of which he composed seventeen during his last stay in Vienna, Mozart so far surpasses his predecessors, that we have almost to regard him as the *inventor of this species of composition.* Through their interpretation he aimed at affecting his hearers not only as a virtuoso, but more, and rather, as a tone-poet and declaimer. His Concertos are Symphonies, in which the pianoforte takes a leading part in accordance with its character, and the orchestra has not merely a subordinate accompaniment, but displays its full volume and splendor of tone independently, to form a due contrast to the harder tone and brilliantly animated passages of the pianoforte. Of these the Breitkopf & Härtel edition contains 20, among them one (No. 17) in *E♭* for two pianofortes; an edition of the same in score has also been issued by André of Offenbach. We call special attention to No. 5 of the Score Edition in *B♭*, of 1784; No. 2 in *G*, of same year; No. 3 in *D*-minor of the year 1785; No. 6 in *C*-major, same year; No. 7 in *C*-minor, of 1786; No. 8 in *C*-major, ditto; and the "Coronation Concerto" in *D*, of 1790 (No. 20 in Breitkopf & Härtel Edit.), which as Mozart reports made a "great stir" in Vienna, he having to repeat the Rondo as an encore. Among his other Pianoforte Works are to be noted the pleasing *Sonatas for Pianoforte and Violin* (Œuvres, Breitkopf & Härtel; Cah. 4, 6 Son.; Cah. 9, 5 Son.; Cah. 11, 5 Son.; Cah. 17, 4 Son.), for whose composition he in many instances showed peculiar fondness; further, *2 Quartets* for Pianoforte, Violin, Viola, and Violincello, in *G*-minor and *E♭*-major (Cah. 13); and finally, a *Quintet* for Pianoforte, Oboe, Clarinette, Horn, and Bassoon in *E♭* (Cah. 14), in which he exhibits remarkable skill in the interesting and effective employment of the various qualities of tone, both individually and collectively, afforded by the several instruments. Two *Trios*, in *B♭*-major and *E*-major, for Pianoforte Violin, and Violoncello (Cah. 10, Nos. 1 and 3) are also markedly prominent among his compositions of a similar kind. A cheap edition of Mozart's Complete Pianoforte Works has been published by L. Holle of Wolfenbüttel.

Mozart, like Emanuel Bach, was far in advance of the theoreticians of his time as a harmonist. Both in his symphonies and pianoforte works are found harmonies, chord-progressions, and modulations sometimes considered of doubtful propriety even now. E. g. the

Fantasia set before the Sonata mentioned above (Op. 11) begins in an Adagio in $^4/_4$ time with the melodically broken chord *c-e♭-f♯-(g)-a♭*, resolving to the *G*-major triad, and a following sequence leads in like manner through *b♭-d♭-e-(f)-g* to *F*-major. The motive of the first measure is then developed in the harmonies given below, in uninterrupted succession: — *A♭-c-e♭-g♭*, *D♭*-major; *a-c-e♭-g♭*, *E♭*-major; *B*-major, *f♯-a♯-c♯-e*, *A-c♯-e-g*, *F*-minor, *G-b-d-f*, *E♭*-minor, etc. Further on, the *F♯*-major triad is followed by a more developed middle division in *D*-major, and the latter by an Allegro in *A*-minor, whose middle division touches the following keys: *F*-major, *F*-minor, *D♭*-major, *E♭*-major, *C♯*-minor, etc. Now, after the chord of the dominant seventh *F-a-c-e♭*, there enters an Andantino in *B♭*-major and $^3/_4$ time, the more animated second half of which leads back to the Adagio of the beginning, in which tempo the so richly harmonized piece closes (*C*-minor). Chord-progressions, modulations, and enharmonic transitions like those here described, were quite as harshly censured at that time as are to-day the similar licences of modern, free-thinking composers; and nevertheless they are the very things which led to a broadening of our science of harmony.*

In 1781 Mozart was invited by the Kaiser to a contest of skill with the Roman MUZIO CLEMENTI, who was then in Vienna, and who had already caused a great sensation in London and Paris by his extraordinary virtuosity on the Fortepiano. At the meeting of the two artists arranged for this purpose Clementi played first, choosing his Sonata in *B♭*-major, the first two measures of which resemble those in the Allegro of the Overture to the Magic Flute, composed later by Mozart. The latter thereupon performed variations, and both then improvised on two pianofortes on a theme given by the Kaiser. Regarding Mozart's playing, Clementi afterwards remarked: "Until then I had never heard anyone play with such spirit and grace. I was chiefly surprised by an Adagio and several of his extemporized variations, the theme of which had been chosen by the Kaiser, we having to vary the same, accompanying each other alternately." But Mozart, who had a decided aversion for all Italians, describes Clementi as a mere "Mechanicus", possessing great skill in passages of thirds, but for the rest not a Kreutzer's worth of feeling or taste. Sub-

* A theoretical justification of these licences is contained in the following treatises by the Author: "Harmoniesystem", Leipzig, Kahnt, and "Die neue Harmonielehre im Streit mit der alten", same publ.

sequently, too, when discussing the passages in sixths and octaves in Clementi's sonatas, he advises his sister not to take too much pains with them, so as not to spoil her quiet and steady hand, and thus to lose her natural lightness, suppleness, and flowing velocity. The German Opera-composer then preferred above all others in Vienna and Berlin, Carl Ditters von Dittersdorf, gave the Kaiser, who had ennobled him and lavished all sorts of favors upon him, the following opinion on these two, the greatest pianoforte-players of the period: "In Clementi's style, art (skill) alone prevails; but in Mozart's, art and taste."

In the spiritualization and vivifying of the pianoforte style Mozart has rendered great services not only through his genial compositions and their spirited interpretation, but through direct teaching as well. Further on we shall notice, at greater length, JOHANN NEPOMUK HUMMEL, who in his seventh year took lessons of and lived with Mozart. The general propagation and cultivation of pianoforte-playing first begins with Mozart's appearance, and under his influence arose, in Vienna, that Pianoforte School, whose élèves were distinguished for precision, taste, and warmth in their playing, and for engaging perspicuity and euphony in their compositions. We must regard Hummel, in particular, as the later leader of this school; and Beethoven as at once the perfecter and the reformer of the same.

Latterly the following editions of Mozart's compositions have appeared: *Mozart's Works,* Complete Edition, critically revised. Containing, in various series, all his Pianoforte Works. Breitkopf & Härtel. — *Selected Sonatas,* and other Pieces. Edited, with assistance of J. Faisst and J. Lachner, by S. Lebert. Vol. 1, 2, and 3, the latter for 4 hands. Stuttgart, J. G. Cotta. — *Complete Sonatas* (L. Köhler), *Complete Variations* (Winkler), *7 Concertos,* Collection Litolff. — *Complete Sonatas, Variations, and Concertos,* Edition Peters.—

On Mozart and his Works we have the following: *O. Jahn,* "W. A. Mozart", 4 Vols., 1856—1859. New edition in 2 Vols. Breitkopf & Härtel.—*G. N. von Nissen,* "Mozart's Biography", 2 Vols. and Supplement, 1828, same publ. — *C. F. Pohl,* "Mozart and Haydn in London", first Part, Vienna, Carl Gerold's Sohn, 1867.—*L. v. Köchel,* "Chronologico-thematic List of all Compositions by W. A. Mozart". Breitkopf & Härtel, 1862.

The enterprising publishing house of Breitkopf & Härtel has also issued the following, by masters previously named: *Wagenseil,* Sonate, op. 4 (alte Meister No. 19); *Kozeluch,* Symphonies pour Piano Nos.

1 and 2; *Abbé Vogler*, "Der eheliche Zwist" (Conjugal Dispute), Sonata for Pianoforte with 2 Violins, Viola, and Bass; *Gelinek*, 21 books of Variations; *Schobert*, Minuetto and Allegro molto (alte Meister No. 39).—

Muzio Clementi.

Contemporaneously with the German School of Pianoforte-playing, the Italian School, at whose head Clementi had placed himself, had attained to a high degree of development in another direction. While Mozart's playing and style of composition were chiefly instrumental in introducing a warmer delivery, easier fluency, and a more perfect finish of the passages, Clementi's services consisted mainly in greatly extending the resources of the virtuoso, and in facilitating the acquisition of the higher skill demanded thereby through excellent Studies. Muzio Clementi was born in Rome (1752), and educated as a musician. As early as his ninth year his unusual talents for this art procured him a position as organist in that city, and at the age of fourteen his clavier-playing so enchanted a wealthy Englishman by the name of Beckford, that the latter engaged to provide for him in future, and took him to England. We learn that he studied here the sonatas of the Neapolitans D. Scarlatti and P. D. Paradies, and at the same time became acquainted with the works of German masters, such as Handel and Bach, through whose salutary influence his own compositions were first endowed with enduring value. The Sonatas published by him as op. 2 (Offenbach, André) created a general sensation; even the actual originator of this species of serious clavier-music, Emanuel Bach, did not withhold his praise. Soon after their publication he was appointed cembalist of the Italian Opera in London; in the year 1780 he began his professional tours to Paris, Strassburg, Munich, and Vienna, on which both his brilliant delivery and artistically wrought compositions everywhere aroused the greatest enthusiasm. In 1785 he again settled in England, where he was quickly surrounded by a throng of pupils, who revered in him a teacher full of vigorous and stimulating life. In 1800 he became partner in an extensive Pianoforte Manufactory, and did valuable work in improving the tone and touch of the instruments produced by the same. To his pupil Ludwig Berger he remarked later, that at a former period he had taken pleasure chiefly in powerful and brilliant execution, especially in the pa sages in doubled notes (thirds sixths, etc.) not previously attempted, and in extemporized performances, not having until later acquired, by attentively listening to renowned singers, a more singing and chaste style of rendering, to which the gradual perfecting of the tone of the English grand pianofortes added a highly important stimulus. In 1802 Clementi undertook, with his favorite pupil, **John Field,** another professional tour to Paris, where, in particular, the fine interpretation of Bach's and Handel's fugues by Field received high praise. Both then proceeded to Vienna, and later to St. Petersburg; in this latter place the reception accorded to Field was so cordial, that he decided to make it his permanent abode. Louis Spohr, who also visited St. Petersburg at the time, describes Clementi as a man of a very jovial disposition and engaging manners; Field, on the other hand, as a pale tall youth, whose romantically melancholy style of playing he found peculiarly moving. In the years next-following Clementi continued his successful tours; in Dresden he was joined by **Alexander Klengel,** and in Berlin by **Ludwig Berger,** who desired to profit by his masterly teaching and his instructive performances. They accompanied him on his second journey to St. Petersburg in 1805, and found Field already the most popular teacher in the City of the Czars, and in the full tide of prosperity. His example determined both Klengel and Berger to take up their residence in Russia, far from the disturbances of war then beginning in Germany. Clementi afterwards made a protracted stay in Vienna, where his teaching and playing exercised a most salutary influence; as, to name one instance, on Kalkbrenner's pianoforte style. He then revisited Italy, and finally returned to England in 1810, where he closed his active life in 1832 at the age of eighty, having edified but a few days before a gathering of his pupils and admirers — among whom J. B. Cramer and I. Moscheles were also present—by his playing on the pianoforte.

Clementi left more than 200 Sonatas for the Pianoforte, 35 of which are arranged with accompaniment of Violin or Flute, and 48 with accompaniment of Violin or Flute and the Violoncello; also a Duo for 2 Pianofortes; 6 Duos for 4 hands; "Caprices, Préludes et Point-d'orgue composés dans le goût de Haydn, Mozart, Kozeluch, Sterkel, Wanhal et Clementi", Op. 19, Mainz, Schott; "Introduction à l'art de toucher le Pianoforte, avec 50 leçons", Leipzig, Peters; several Fugues, Toccatas, Variations, etc.; and finally the volume of Studies, still indispensable to every pianist, entitled "*Gradus ad Parnassum,* oder die Kunst des Pianofortespiels durch 100 Beispiele gelehrt".

3 Parts. Wolfenbüttel, Holle.—A Collection of his Pianoforte Works has been issued by Breitkopf & Härtel, Leipzig; a cheaper edition of the same, in 5 Vols., by L. Holle, Wolfenbüttel.

Of his **Sonatas,** which have in part a pedagogic aim, we note especially the one already alluded to in *B♭*-major, which is followed by a brilliant Toccata in the same key, to be executed *prestissimo;* also a plaintively agitated Sonata in *B*-minor, Stuttgart, Hallberger, in the *Edition de luxe* of the Classics Beethoven, Clementi, Haydn, Mozart, No. 12; and "Trois Sonates dédiées à Cherubini", Op. 50, Leipzig, Breitkopf & Härtel.—In these last compositions Clementi shows himself not only an able contrapuntist, but also a harmonist far surpassing those of the earlier Italian school. The third of the same, in *G*-minor, bears the title "Didone abbandonata, Scena tragica"; it is peculiarly distinguished by its rich volume of tone and bold harmonic development, the expression of its passionate meaning being intensified by the stronger effects employed.

Clementi's most important pianoforte work, written with peculiar and loving care, is the **Gradus ad Parnassum.** The entire pianoforte technique of that period, so materially extended by himself, is represented therein by eminently practical **Studies.** The fingers are made independent of each other, their equalization in strength and endurance promoted, and both hands trained in runs of thirds and sixths, in rolling and undulating passages, in broken chords, and in octave-playing. In the *Stravaganza,* Ex. 94, three notes against two are given; in the *Bizzarria,* Ex. 95, the Quintuplet runs on throughout; the **Canon** affords an opportunity of occupying both hands in full equality; and by **Fugues** written in true pianoforte style the player's attention is fixed on the significance of the inner parts; the changing of fingers for repeated notes, the crossing of the hands, the scales, triplets, appoggiaturas, turns and trills are all studied in the interesting compositions, several of which often form a connected Suite, and whose form sometimes even touches the dramatic as in the *Scena patetica,* Ex. 39. The movement at times occupies two, three, or four parts, at others the greatest possible number, and all of the hundred studies are distinguished by the most brilliant and natural pianoforte style of the skilfullest contrapuntist.

Late editions of Clementi's Pianoforte Works have been published by *Breitkopf & Härtel,* 64 Sonatas in 3 Vols., boards, red;—*J. G. Cotta,* Sonatas and other works (Lebert), 2 Vols.;—*Collection Litolff* contains 61 Sonatas in 3 Vols., and the Gradus ad Parnassum I, II, III;—*Edition Peters* contains 4 Vols. of Sonatas, and the Grad. ad Parn. in 3 Vols.;—*Carl Tausig* has furnished selected Études from the Grad. ad Parn. with fingerings and Notes, which serve as an excellent preparation for modern demands on pianoforte virtuosity (publ. by T. Trautwein, Berlin).

Among the pupils of Clementi finding special mention further on, J. B. Cramer and L. Berger chiefly propagated the solid virtuosity of their master; whereas A. A. Klengel cultivated almost exclusively the art of counterpoint, and John Field was wholly plunged in the deeps of emotional life.

Contemporaries of Emanuel Bach, Haydn, Mozart, and Clementi.

The brilliant performances of illustrious virtuosi, and the successful representations of the works of creative tone-poets, always call into being a swarm of parasites in every sense of the term. Such press in, in order to participate in the opulent banquets of the former, and to distribute thereafter to the numberless throng of dilettanti the stale and diluted scraps of their booty; not forgetting, however, to revile and disparage those mighty ones to whom they owe their existence. Such are they who disgustingly ape certain externalities and effects, forced out of their true connection, of eminent artists, and also the brainless scribblers who flood the market with their fashionable articles, in which they have stupidly set the stolen and dismembered gems.—But disciples and admirers also draw near, seeking to fathom the spirit capable of producing such imposing effects, to gain enlightenment from their master regarding revelations of art, and to spread the same further and further in his sense;—these are the only parasites of merit, the priests of the same divinity, who are *called*, in the primitive meaning of the term, *to enjoy the feast of sacrifice together with the High Priest.* The former kind, who produce their countless fabrications after certain easily handled patterns, have sometimes exercised a mischievous influence on the taste of the great mass of dilettanti during considerable periods, and can therefore be no more left out of this historical sketch than the latter class, who have often been the first to spread the more peculiar and original style of their models in composition, and to render the same intelligible, in wider circles, through their attractive performances and compositions.

One of the earliest of the voluminous spoilers of taste, whose witless "Fantasias and Variations, Storm and Battle Pieces, Potpourris, Rondeaux, and Bacchanales" encumbered all pianoforte racks for a season, was **Daniel Steibelt.** He was born about 1765 in Berlin, and had instruction from Kirnberger in clavier-playing and composition. After various professional trips undertaken through Germany from his fifteenth year, he settled down in Paris in 1790, where he behaved with the greatest arrogance, and vanquished as a virtuoso both the German clavierist **Johann David Herrmann** then living there, who enjoyed the special favor of the Queen Marie Antoinette, and **Ignaz Pleyel,** who had gained great popularity as a composer. In 1793 he composed in Paris the opera "Romeo et Juliette", the brilliant success of which made him the lion of the day. Ladies from the highest circles became his pupils, and often looked upon his extremely unbecoming behavior as eccentricity, until more serious faults obliged him to leave Paris in 1798. In London, where he then dwelt for a considerable time, he married a charming Englishwoman, who now accompanied him on the tambourine to noisy pieces specially written for that purpose. Steibelt was, altogether, a hero of effect, as the following titles of his clavier-pieces, for instance, testify: *Combat naval,* op. 41; *Sonate martiale,* op. 82; *Bataille de Gemappe et de Neerwinde;* "*The Destruction of Moscow*", Leipzig, Peters; etc. etc. Of all these *tone-paintings,* "l'Orage, précédé d'un Rondeau pastorale" (Leipzig, Breitkopf & Härtel), the Finale of his third Concerto, met with the greatest success, making the rounds through the hands of all dilettanti of the time. Steibelt later visited Hamburg, Dresden, Prague, Berlin, and Vienna, gave brilliant concerts everywhere, and always found as many admirers as condemners of his tactless and affected style and his shallow compositions. Gerber reports, that on his return to Germany he was ashamed of his mother-tongue, and acted sometimes the haughty Englishman, at others the arrogant Frenchman. One grand effect he sought to produce with the but meagerly artistic and frequently employed *tremolando* in both hands, by which style of playing he could likewise conceal the weakness of his left hand. The form of the "Fantasia with Variations", which he brought especially into vogue, had been employed before, as we saw, by Hässler; it was at the same time the favorite style in the "free Fantasia". But he was the inventor of the prosaic "Bacchanales" just mentioned, to which his spouse beat the tambourine with her own hand, "most artistically and gracefully", in the concerts given at Prague, Berlin, and Vienna, and of which 10 series, each containing 6 of the same for Pianoforte and Tambourine, sometimes with Triangle as well, were published in Paris by Pleyel, Érard, and others, in Offenbach by André, and in Leipzig by Breitkopf & Härtel. In 1808 Steibelt became Kapellmeister of the French Opera at St. Petersburg, where he died in the year 1823. He left his family in very straightened circumstances; but a concert arranged for their relief yielded 40,000 rubels. This fact, together with the host of compositions for which he everywhere found generously paying publishers, testifies to the great popularity which he enjoyed during some twenty years, though hardly more than a talented naturalistic player and composer. He left 7 *Pianoforte Concertos* (among them a *Grand Concerto militaire* in *E*-minor with accompaniment of *two* orchestras), of which Nos. 1 to 5 were published by Breitkopf & Härtel; also several *Quintets, Quartets,* and *Trios, 65 Pianoforte Sonatas with Violin or Flute, 46 Sonatas for Pianoforte solo,* and countless *Fantasias, Rondos, Études, Dances,* etc.

Emanuel Bach was already 69 years of age, when the young, amiable, and versatile **Johann Ludwig Dussek** (b. 1760 in Czaslau, Bohemia) paid him a visit in Hamburg. The latter had previously found most flattering approval in Amsterdam, whither he had followed his eminent patron, and also at the Hague (where his first compositions, "Trois Concertos pour le Pianoforte, deux Violons, Alto et Basse, Op. 1", were printed) by reason of the pleasing melodies, supported by rich harmonies, of his works, and likewise through his clean and melodious pianoforte style; nevertheless, he did not wish to pursue an artistic career without the approbation of the revered master named above. Emanuel Bach immediately recognized the eminent talent of the young virtuoso and composer, encouraged him to follow the path already entered on, and aided him with his advice and efficient recommendations. Dussek first proceeded to Berlin and thence to St. Petersburg, winning fullest applause as a virtuoso on the pianoforte and also on the "Glasharmonica" newly invented by Hessel in that city. He then visited Paris and Milan with like favorable results, went to France for a second time in 1788, and settled in London in 1792. Here he contracted a friendship for Clementi, but unluckily became a partner in a music business, the failure of which necessitated his flight to Hamburg in 1800. In London he had published a *Pianoforte Method,* issued later both in Paris and Leipzig; also a Sonata belonging to the same period, "Les adieux de Clementi", in *E♭*, op. 44, and further, the earlier 6 Sonatas op. 9 and 10 (Leipzig, Breitkopf & Härtel), and "3 Grandes Sonates", op. 35 (Offenbach, André), all of which he ranked with his most successful works. At Magdeburg in 1802 he was presented to Prince **Louis Ferdinand of Prussia** (1772—1806), who induced him to accompany him as teacher and friend. The Prince was himself an excellent pianoforte virtuoso and composer. Beethoven, who met him at Berlin in 1796, lauded his playing, which, he said, was not at all princely, but that of a good musician. Louis Ferdinand's compositions—among which the Quartet in *F*-minor for Pianoforte, Violin, Viola, and Violoncello (op. 6, Leipzig, Breitkopf & Härtel) deserves special mention on account of its heartfelt, mournfully elegiac expression—are full of original touches and characteristic motives, though frequently disfigured by amateurish incorrectnesses of style. Dussek remained with the Prince until the heroic death of the latter on the ill-starred field of Saalfeld, in 1806. To his memory Dussek dedicated a valuable Sonata in *F♯*-minor, entitled "Élégie harmonique sur la mort de Louis Ferdinand, Prince de Prusse", op. 61, Leipzig, Breitkopf & Härtel, and an Andante, extraordinarily popular at the time, in *B♭*, "La Consolation", op. 62, same publ. In the year 1808 he again visited Paris, where he now remained until his death in 1812. When he arrived there, the violinists Rode and Baillot, and the violoncellist Lamare, were giving brilliant concerts in the Odéon. But Dussek, who also gave performances in the same place, not only threw these famous artists into the shade by his brilliant playing, but celebrated triumphs outrivalling by far the successes of the pianoforte virtuosi Steibelt and Woelfl, who had played there shortly before. His *12 Pianoforte Concertos* (Leipzig, Breitkopf & Härtel), the tenth of which in *B♭* is written for two pianofortes, and also his *Sonatas* (33 have been issued by same publ.), *Rondos, Fantasias,* and *Variations*, formed on their appearance the study of all ambitious pianoforte players. One of the most valuable and best-developed sonatas is op. 70, "Le retour à Paris", in *A♭*. The pianoforte setting of the same is richer and fuller than that of any of his predecessors; chords in the compass of a ninth or tenth are frequently employed for either hand, and enharmonics are applied in various passages; e. g. after the first movement closing in *A♭*-major, there begins an Adagio in *E*-major, followed by a Scherzo—then in any event a rare intermezzo in the pianoforte sonata—which begins with the *F♯*-minor triad and ends in *A♭*-major. In equally surprising fashion the Finale, shortly before the close, makes a sharp transition to *A*-major, but returns directly to the principal key *A♭*-major through the chords *a-c♯-e* and *g-b♭-d♭-e♭*. Dussek's *Pianoforte Works* have been issued in *12 cahiers* by Breitkopf & Härtel; newer and cheaper editions are in Collection Litolff, *Complete Sonatas and Sonatinas*, 2 Vols. (Köhler & Winkler), and Edition Peters, *Sonatas and Pieces*, 1 Vol.

Virtuosity was valued by this meritorious artist solely in so far as it is adapted to give to a peculiarly agitated and elevated mood a yet more animated expression by means extraordinarily enhanced. Another contemporary, however, **Joseph Woelfl**, eleven years his junior, chiefly calculated his compositions, in which a loftier vein was often lacking, to exhibit a technique acquired by untiring application in a style the more dazzling by contrast; but was able to awaken only a passing interest in exhibitions of virtuosity otherwise quite empty. He was born in Salzburg in 1772, still early enough to enjoy the instruction of the aged Leopold Mozart, and of the excellent composer Michael Haydn, in clavier-playing and composition. In 1793 he commenced his professional tours to Warsaw and Vienna, stayed in the latter place until 1798, and journeyed then to Prague, Dresden, Leipzig, Berlin, and Hamburg, his brilliant performances being everywhere received with astonishment and admiration. He vanquished the greatest difficulties in his compositions with playful ease, and the "Leipziger musikalische Zeitung" relates as a specimen the following occurrence in Prague: "The orchestra had already assembled for the rehearsal of his concert, and the parts of a pianoforte concerto in *C*, written by himself, were already distributed; but his pianoforte had not yet come. At length the porters bring it, and behold! it is tuned a semitone too low. The tuner demands an hour for tuning it to pitch.—You don't mean it!—says Woelfl quite coolly;—please have the kindness to begin; I must transpose!—And he actually played, in *C♯*-major, one of the most difficult concertos that had ever been heard in Dresden, and that with an ease, readiness, accuracy, and precision, which astounded the entire orchestra."—Woelfl having written but one *Grand Concerto militaire* in *C*-major (Offenbach, André), the same is probably identical with that so transposed by him. Woelfl was later received in London with the same enthusiasm as in the German capitals. But in Paris, where he arrived in 1801, he was unable to dim the memory of Steibelt, so celebrated there only a short time before, and could obtain only a small, though highly appreciative audience for his performances. His evil star pursued him on his journey to Brussels; he therefore returned to London in 1805, but could not succeed in regaining his former brilliant position there; and the virtuoso, who could measure himself with a Beethoven during his stay in Vienna, died in London so unnoticed, that even the year of his death (1811 or 1814) cannot be ascertained positively.—His published compositions include *6 Pianoforte Concertos* (Leipzig, Breitkopf & Härtel, and Offenbach, André), *18 Trios*, *35 Duos*, and more than *40 Sonatas for Pianoforte solo*, besides a great number of *Fantasias*, *Fugues*, *Rondos*, *Variations*. A work published by him under the title of "Méthode de Piano, op. 56, 2 Parties" (Offenbach, André), contains 100 Exercises, among which are found valuable compositions with interesting technique and pianoforte effects. Of his Sonatas he seems, from their titles, to have considered the following as the boldest: "Le diable à quatre" (op. 50, Offenbach, André), and "Non plus ultra" (op. 41, Leipzig, Peters). The latter, in *F*-major, begins with a short Adagio in $^{3}/_{4}$ time, serving as an introduction to the following Allegro moderato in $^{4}/_{4}$ time. This movement is founded on a prosaic, étude-like passage in thirds, performed by both hands alternately or together in octaves, and accompanied by a commonplace counter-theme. The second and equally insignificant theme is intertwined in the episodes by similar passages in thirds, and the coda is likewise formed in part by the same. Then follows an Andante in *C*-major, in the simplest two-phrase song-form; and as a Finale appears a series of variations on "Life let us cherish". In these Woelfl evidently aimed at displaying his then unheard-of technique as brilliantly as possible; though they offer the modern pianist merely the following difficulties, hardly calculated to elicit applause:—In Var. 4 the right hand plays the theme to broken chords in the left, at the same time crossing over the latter several times in each measure to strike the fundamental bass of the harmony; Var. 6 carries out octave passages, now in the right hand and now in the left; in Var. 7 each hand is required to execute a continuous trill, as it were, between bass and soprano; Var. 8 has the theme in the alto, from the tones of which continuous leaps are made in sixteenth-notes to the tonic or dominant sometimes two octaves higher. None of these Variations are provide with richer harmonies than the theme itself, and would therefore be of only historical interest to our modern concert-going public.

August Eberhard Müller (b. 1767 in Nordheim) devoted his powers in another way, and with more quiet thoughtfulness, to developing and popularizing genuine skill by various excellent textbooks for the pianoforte. In his youth he travelled in North Germany, sojourned during 1792 in Berlin, and especially charmed his hearers by performances of Mozart's Pianoforte Concertos. This approbation induced him in 1797 to publish in Leipzig an "Anleitung zum genauen und richtigen Vortrage der Mozart'schen Clavierconcerte in Absicht richtiger Applicatur" (Guide to the exact and correct Rendering of Mozart's Pianoforte Concertos with a View to a correct Fingering). In 1804 he also published in Jena a "Clavier- und Fortepiano-Schule (Clavichord and Pianoforte Method) or a Guide to a correct and tasteful Execution on both Instruments, with an Appendix on Thoroughbass" (the Appendix is taken from the earlier *Clavierschule* by G. S. Löhlein), which in particular treats exhaustively, both theoretically and practically, of practical Fingering. From 1794 A. E. Müller acted as organist of the two principal churches in Leipzig, went to Weimar as Hofkapellmeister in 1809, and died there in the year 1817. As a Supplement to his *Clavierschule* he published several *cahiers* of "Pièces instructives" and "Sonates progressives"; among his larger compositions, which are peculiarly euphonious and practically arranged, the following are prominent: *Caprice*, op. 4, Offenbach, André; *Grands Caprices*, op. 29, 31, 34, and 41, in 5 *cahiers*, Leipzig, Peters; and the posthumous work "Cadenzas to the eight finest Pianoforte Concertos of Mozart", same publ.

We have already remarked that in Vienna, after Mozart had taken up his abode there, pianoforte-playing was cultivated with peculiar fondness. Two composers mentioned before, **J. B. Wanhal** (1739—1813) and **L. Kozeluch** (1753—1814), who survived him and whose later works clearly show the beneficial influence* of that "High Priest", were at the same time active teachers; and a pupil of the latter, **Marie Therese Paradies** (1759—1824), stricken with blindness in her third year, won a name not only in her native city, Vienna, but also in Paris, London, Berlin, etc., as a distinguished pianist, often moving the hearers to tears by her affecting interpretations. For her Mozart wrote one of his Pianoforte Concertos, and

* Compare *Wanhal*, Sonata in *F*, *opera ultima*, Leipzig, Hofmeister; and also *Kozeluch*, 3 Sonates, op. 51, Leipzig, Peters, with earlier similar Pianoforte works by these composers.

his heart-stirring style of playing cannot but have had an influence on her own, and on that of her numerous pupils. The gifted **Anton Eberl** (1766—1807) of Vienna also early became enthusiastic for the art of music. As his wealthy parents had, however, forced him to become a lawyer, he published his first attempts at composition—Pianoforte Variations on "Zu Steffen sprach im Traume", on the Savoyarde song "Ascoulta Jeannette", and on "Bei Männern, welche Liebe fühlen"—in 1792, under the name of his late friend Mozart. In like manner one of his Sonatas in *C*-minor was published as Mozart's op. 47 at Vienna and Offenbach, and by Pleyel in Paris as the "Dernière grande Sonate de Mozart", not appearing until 1798 under the name of its real author (Vienna, Artaria). Mozart would scarcely have consented to this exchange of names, for Eberl's pianoforte works, though displaying and striving toward definiteness and unity of conception, have by no means the inventive genius and purity of style of his model. His parents subsequently losing their property through unfortunate accidents, Eberl devoted himself exclusively to music; among his later compositions the following deserve mention: *Grande Sonate charactéristique* in *F*-minor dedicated to Haydn, op. 12, Peters, Leipzig; and his last work, written for Maria Pawlowna, *Erbprinzessin* of Weimar, who wished to possess a composition in pathetic style by him, which was issued after his death as *Grande Sonate* op. 39, in Leipzig, Peters. The first Allegro appassionato of this composition closes on the full *G*-minor triad, and the following Adagio then modulates to *E*-major in the harshest manner through the sustained tones *B*, *G*♯, *E*. The 7th measure of this second movement has a held tone in the outer parts, such as we find again later in Beethoven's works, for example; in the 8th and 9th measures a sustained soprano accompanied by staccato chords appears, a style later employed so effectively by C. M. von Weber and others. Generally speaking, Eberl's pianoforte style sometimes even attains to the full wealth of tone, but not to the purity and fresh *élan*, of his contemporary Dussek; whose works are wrongfully almost forgotten, for they oftentimes develop an opulence of ideas not found in equal measure in the compositions of **Friedrich Kuhlau** (b. 1786 in Lüneburg), who is still in high favor in Denmark. This composer, also much esteemed in Germany for a time, died at Copenhagen in 1832 as Hofkapellmeister. His numerous published compositions afford, it is true, no fresh creative ideas, but are written throughout in a serious and elevated style. We mention the following: *Trois Sonates,* op. 52, Leipzig, Kistner; *Gr. Sonate brilliante,* op. 127; *Trois Sonates faciles et brill. à 4 mains,* op. 66; *Allegro pathétique à 4 mains,* op. 123; and a great number of *Duos* for Pianoforte with Violin or Flute, four-handed *Sonatas, Rondos,* and *Variations,* publ. in Leipzig by Peters, Breitkopf & Härtel, and Hofmeister.

Kuhlau's instructive Pianoforte Pieces have been issued in new, cheap editions:—*Edition Peters,* Sonatinas, 2 Vols.; Rondos and Variations, 1 Vol.—*Collection Litolff,* Sonatinas, 2 Vols; Rondos and Variations, 1 Vol.—*Breitkopf & Härtel,* Sonatinas, boards, red.

Clementi's Pupils.

Before taking up a new period of Pianoforte-playing, we must more closely consider the influence of the pupils of Clementi and Mozart, who strove to maintain and develop the lyrical and contrapuntal pianoforte style foremostly cherished by their masters.

We first name **Johann Baptist Cramer** (1771—1858), Clementi's most zealous pupil from 1783 to 1784. In London he became acquainted with Haydn, who afterwards received him very cordially in Vienna, where Cramer, as in several other German cities, gave successful concerts, distinguishing himself in particular by his tender and singing delivery of the *adagio.* He dwelt from 1832 to 1845 in Paris, though otherwise living chiefly in England, where he died in the year 1858. Cramer left 105 *Pianoforte Sonatas,* 7 *Concertos,* 3 *Duos for 4 hands,* a *Quintet* and a *Quartet* (both for Pianoforte and strings), 2 numbers of *Nocturnes,* op. 32 and 54, and innumerable insignificant Fantasias, Rondos, etc. His once very popular Pianoforte Method was published in Offenbach (André), and other places; but in greater detail as op. 98 in four parts, Berlin, Schlesinger. His excellent Text-books "Étude en 42 Exercices doigtés", and also the "Suite de l'Étude en 42 Exercices", have likewise been published in various places; in conception and form they belong to classic Pianoforte Literature, and form fitting companion pieces and supplements to the Studies of his teacher.

Among the many editions of Cramer's text-books, one is of such pre-eminent importance, that teachers and students of the pianoforte will be grateful to me for calling their attention to it. It was published in Munich by Jos. Aibl, and bears the title: "50 ausgewählte Klavieretüden von J. B. Cramer" (50 Selected Pianoforte

Études by J. B. Cramer). "In systematic progression, with a thorough, critical revision of the fingering, and marks of expression, together with instructive Notes, for Use in the Pianoforte Classes of the Royal Music School at Munich. Edited by Dr. Hans von Bülow." The Editor, equally pre-eminent as an interpreter of classic pianoforte works and as a *maestro* of the loftier pianoforte style, has furnished each of these Études with such classical annotations, that the latter alone are a sufficient inducement to begin and carry out the study of the Études as therein directed. For the benefit of my book I cannot deny myself the pleasure of quoting the general technical course of study approved by Bülow in his practice as a teacher. "It embraces all stages, from Beginner to Virtuoso."

"After the first 'rudiments' have been conquered, to which end the first Part of the Lebert-Stark Pianoforte Method (Stuttgart, Cotta, new edition) is most recommendable, as being to the best of our knowledge the most reliable aid, there may follow:

(I.) a. The Études by *Aloys Schmitt,* op. 16 (Bonn, Simrock), in connection with the 'Exercices préparatoires' introducing the first number—always to be practiced in all 12 keys. It is worthy of note, that the master Felix Mendelssohn-Bartholdy, also eminent as a pianist, laid with this work the foundation of his classical technique.

b. To counteract Schmitt's relative dryness, secondary employment of *Stephen Heller,* op. 45.

(II.) a. *J. B. Cramer's* Études. Perhaps at same time, as introduction to Bach's style, the latter's Preludes and Inventions.

b. *St. Heller,* op. 46, 47.

c. *C. Czerny,* Daily Studies, with his collection of Études, hitherto strangely not noticed according to desert, entitled 'The School of the Legato and Staccato'.

(III.) a. *Clementi,* Gradus ad Parnassum (selected and edited by Carl Tausig).

b. *Moscheles,* op. 70, 24 Études; a work better known in North than in South Germany, to which the epithet "classical" applies unqualifiedly.

(IV.) a. *Henselt,* Selected Études from op. 2 and 5.

b. Together with and as preparation for the latter: *Haberbier,* "Études-poésies" (Hamburg, Cranz), a sort of sequel to Stephen Heller.

c. Selected pieces by *Moscheles:* "Charakteristische Etüden", op. 75.

(V.) *Chopin,* op. 10 and op. 25, in conjunction with the study of separate Preludes (special style of technique) in his op. 28.

(VI.) *Liszt,* 6 Études after Paganini (Leipzig, Breitkopf & Härtel); 3 Concert Études (Leipzig, Kistner); the 12 grand Études "d'exécution transcendante" (Leipzig, Breitkopf & Härtel).

(VII.) *Rubinstein,* Selected Études and Preludes; *V. C. Alkan,* 12 grandes Etudes (selected); *Theodor Kullak's* School of Octave-playing; and other useful specialties of a subordinate nature, for purely technical ends.

J. B. Cramer's accomplished fellow-pupil **Ludwig Berger** (1777—1839), whom we left in St. Petersburg, returned to his native land after the full restoration of peace, living from 1815 onward in Berlin as a thorough and popular music teacher. He dedicated to Clementi a *Grande Sonate pathétique* in *C*-minor (op. 7, Leipzig, Peters); other of his well-written and full-sounding Pianoforte Works, published by Schlesinger of Berlin, are *Alla turca,* op. 8; *Préludes et Fugues,* op. 5; *3 Pièces caractéristiques,* op. 24; by Hofmeister in Leipzig *Air norvégien varié, Toccata* in *F, Concerto* in *C, Études,* op. 12, 22, 30, and 41; and *Bagatelles,* op. 39 and 40. It is mainly the following pupils of L. Berger who, taking him as their model, have adhered to the style of playing and composition of the Clementi school, and continued the same to the present day: **Carl Wilhelm Greulich** (1796—1837), the following of whose compositions belong here: *Grosse Sonate,* op. 12 (Berlin, Schlesinger); *Sonate,* op. 21 (ditto). — **Heinrich Dorn** (b. 1804), among whose published compositions is an interesting elementary work entitled "Surprise du jeune Pianiste, Romance à 4 mains", in which the first player touches only the black keys (Berlin, Jul. Weiss); also an original pianoforte piece, "*The Sphinx*", in $^5/_4$ time (Stuttgart, Hallberger). — **Wilhelm Taubert** (b. 1811) dedicated to his teacher Berger a thoughtfully written *Sonate* (op. 4, Leipzig, Hofmeister), and published among numerous other pianoforte compositions the often-played "*Campanella, Étude de Concert*", (op. 41, Berlin, Schlesinger); the cleanly written and pleasing salon pieces *Minnelieder ohne Worte* (op. 16 and 45, Berlin, Bote & Bock), *Camera obscura, 10 Bagatelles aux jeunes élèves* (op. 38, Berlin, Bahn), *Silvana* (op. 60, ditto), *Tanz der Meerfräulein* (Mermaids' Dance, op. 98, Berlin, Bote & Bock), *Lied und Reigen* (op. 119, Stuttgart, Hallberger), *Trüber Mai, Mondnacht, Heimliche Fahrt, Unter Rosen* (op. 121, Leipzig, Siegel), and a *Trio* for Pianoforte, Violin, and Violoncello (op. 32, Berlin, Bote & Bock).—**Albert Loeschhorn** (b. 1819), also a pupil of Berger, published a series of easily executable salon pieces, and the following very useful Études: *30 Études mélodieuses, progressives et doigtées* (op. 38 and 52, Leipzig, Peters), *Études* progressively arranged (op. 65, 66, and 67, Berlin, J. Weiss). His op. 25, *La belle Amazone* (Bote & Bock), was very popular for a time, like his brilliant Galop op. 50, *Le diable à quatre.*— The works of **Felix Mendelssohn,** who first-studied pianoforte playing under Berger and later under Moscheles, are specially mentioned further on.—The compositions of Greulich's talented pupil **Carl Eckert** (b. 1820) must still be noticed; a *Trio* for Pianoforte, Violin, and Violoncello in *B*-minor, op. 18, and twelve *Charakterstücke,* op. 17, Leipzig, Breitkopf & Härtel.

August Alexander Klengel (1783—1852), who, as we have seen, accompanied his teacher Clementi to St. Petersburg, went in 1811 to Paris, later visiting Italy and England, and finally took up his permanent abode in Dresden in 1816 as Hoforganist. Before this time he had published two *Pianoforte Concertos*, a *Trio* for Pianoforte, Violin, and Violoncello, a *Fantasia* for 4 hands, a *Rondo* in *A*♭, op. 5; further, *Promenade sur mer, interrompue par une tempête* (op. 19, Leipzig, Peters), and other salon pieces; but subsequently won an enduring name in the annals of music, by carrying the **art of the canon** to a perfection unattained in the compositions of his most renowned predecessors. Among his finest contrapuntal works may be mentioned *Les Avant-Coureurs, exercices, contenant 24 canons dans tous les tons, calculés pour servir d'étude préparatoire au grand recueil de Canons et de Fugues.* En deux Suites (Mainz, Schott). This principal work, however, on which he labored untiringly during the last decades of his life, did not appear until after his death, under the title "Canons et Fugues dans tous les tons majeurs et mineurs pour le Piano, en deux parties" (48 Canons and 48 Fugues), Leipzig, Breitkopf & Härtel, 1854.

The more rarely such strict contrapuntal works are published in our time, the greater are the thanks due to their authors. For since the Science of Chords has gained more and more ground, the Art of Counterpoint, being no longer regarded as absolutely essential for composing, and also as decidedly more difficult in practice, has no longer been generally taught and studied. But a composition which merely appeals to the hearer's feeling, without calling into play his mental faculties by contrapuntal imitations, developments, involutions and resolutions, cannot hold the attention for any length of time.

Those theoreticians, during and after the time of Sebastian Bach and his pupils, who were foremost in the endeavor to spread the Science of Counterpoint through their writings and pupils, were J. J. FUX and J. G. ALBRECHTSBERGER in Vienna, MARPURG (Treatise on the Fugue), FÉTIS (Traité de Contrepoint et de Fugue), and the Italians F. GIUS. PAOLUCCI and F. GIAMBATTISTA MARTINI in their works on the subject, which are furnished with numerous excellent examples. Latterly, counterpoint has been successfully taught, more particularly by oral instruction, by MORITZ HAUPTMANN (1792—1868), first at Cassel and thereafter at Leipzig; S. W. DEHN (1799—1858) at Berlin; E. F. RICHTER (1808—1879) at Leipzig; and IMMANUEL FAISST (b. 1823) at Stuttgart.

Friedrich Kiel (b. 1821) studied the freer style of counterpoint under S. W. Dehn, and published as op. 1 *Fifteen Canons in Chamber-style*, as op. 10 *Four two-part Fugues* (Breitkopf & Härtel); also, among many other compositions, a *Trio* for Pianoforte, Violin, and Violoncello, op. 24; *2 Trios*, op. 65; and *12 Fantasiestücke*, op. 8, 3 Parts (all issued by Bote & Bock). Under the influence of Moritz Hauptmann's strict method of counterpoint

C. F. Weitzmann (1808—1880) published in Leipzig (J. Schuberth & Co.) two numbers of a new species of Pianoforte Pieces, entitled *"Musikalische Räthsel"* (Musical Puzzles), in which the freer forms of the Prelude, Cavatina, Rondo, etc., are performed in the shape of canons by two players executing the same part, beginning at different times. The *"Contrapunkt-Studien"* published later by the same firm, in 2 Parts, contain similar pieces set in score, likewise solve the most difficult problems of simple and double counterpoint, and give, besides canons and fugues of every description, examples of the latterly neglected *basso ostinato.*

John Field, born in Dublin 1782, who travelled with Clementi to Russia and lived from 1804 in St. Petersburg, went in 1822 to Moscow, where he remained till 1832, highly esteemed both as a virtuoso and a teacher. He then undertook a second professional journey to Paris; and his unpretentious, singing style, for exhibiting which he chose no concert grand, but only a simple pianoforte, again found warm appreciation. Field always played with remarkably quiet hands, and had adopted an original fingering, peculiarly favorable to the binding of the tones, which he taught to his pupils. His further travels led him through Belgium and Switzerland to Italy. But here his simple, tender melodies were unappreciated. In 1835 he was found in Naples, sick and in the utmost destitution, by a Russian family, and taken back to Moscow, where he died in 1837. Among his pianoforte compositions were published, by Breitkopf & Härtel, Peters, and Kistner of Leipzig, and Schlesinger of Berlin, *7 Concertos,* including No. 5, *l'Incendi par l'orage* in *C; 4 Sonatas,* various *Exercises, Romances, Rondeaux, Fantasias, Variations,* and *Dances.* The Nocturnes, musico-lyrical poems of a style of composition created by him, and occupying the first place among his works, were published as follows: Nos. 1—6 by Kistner, 7—8 by Peters, 9—10 by Hofmeister, 11 by Schlesinger, and 12—13 by Breitkopf & Härtel. J. Schuberth, Leipzig, has published a selection of the same, in an introduction to which Franz Liszt raised a highly poetic memorial to his fellow-artist. From it we quote the following, admirably characterizing the artist and his works: "Field's Nocturnes retain their newness beside much long since grown antiquated; thirty years have passed since their first appearance, and still they exhale a balsamic freshness, a sweet fragrance. Where else do we find such perfection of inimitable naïveté?——No one else has succeeded in seizing these intangible harmonies of the Aeolian harp, these half-sighs floating away in air, gentle plaints dissolving in sweet pain. No one has dared — especially none of those who themselves have heard Field play or rather dream away his songs in moments when, quite lost in inspiration, he turned aside from the first sketch of the piece as it lived in his imagination, to invent new groups in unbroken succession, winding them like flower-wreaths about his melodies, to which he added ever-new adornments by this shower of fragrant blossoms, yet always so choosing their garb, that their tremulous languor and charmful meanders should not be hidden, but only overspread with a transparent veil." — Liszt tells us further, that Field enchanted his auditors without either willing or knowing it. "The wellnigh motionless attitude of his hands, and his expressionless mien, aroused no curiosity. — But just to this avoidance of all calculation of effect do we owe the first so fortunate endeavor to free the pianoforte style from the constraint exercised upon the same by the standard last, on which all pieces had regularly and prescriptively to be stretched. ——Formerly a composition had necessarily to be a Sonata, a Rondo, or something of the kind. Field was the first to introduce a style deriving its origin from none of the existing forms; in which feeling and melody exclusively prevailed, liberated from the fetters and dross of an enforced form. He cleared the way for all subsequent efforts appearing under the names of "Songs without Words", "Impromptus", "Ballades", etc.; and up to him can be traced the origin of those pieces which are designed to express through tones particular phases of emotion and warm feeling".

Carl Mayer (b. 1802, d. 1862), a gifted pupil of Field, who in his first period distinguished himself by a *Concerto symphonique,* op. 88, several brilliant *Études* like op. 61, and other serious compositions, preferred later to assume the function of a fashionable composer, and to write according to certain convenient formulas for the taste of the herd of dilettanti. He dwelt for a length of time in Dresden, and published over 300 pianoforte numbers, among which are found the following *Exercises* and *Caprices:* op. 31, 40, 55, 61, 62, 73, 85—87, 91—93, 97, 100, 119, 180, 200, 226 271, and 305. His remaining compositions include *Fantasias, Variations,* brilliant *Dances,* and shorter pieces, belonging to the lightest "entertaining reading for amateurs", and contained in the following Collections: *Myrten,* op. 106; *Mosaique,* op. 166; *Immortellen,* op. 140; *kleine Tonbilder,* op. 172; *Frühlingsblüthen,* op. 174; *Schattenspiele,* op. 198; and *Rosenblüthen,* op. 202.

The sterling school of Clementi was perhaps still recognizable in Carl Mayer's smooth and fluent playing, but no longer so in his later for the most part superficially wrought compositions.

We now turn to Hummel, Mozart's most eminent pupil, to follow in like manner the course of the Vienna Pianoforte School down to the present time.

A pupil of Mozart.

Johann Nepomuk Hummel was born in Pressburg, in 1778, and educated as a musician. In 1785 his father became conductor of the orchestra in Schikaneder's theater at Vienna; and it was here that Mozart's interest was awakened for the rarely talented boy, whose finished clavier-playing already created a stir. Mozart took him to his home, in which the quick-witted Nepomuk remained for two years, gaining instruction not only from the spirited performances of his teacher, but also having to play to the latter all novelties appearing in pianoforte literature. To such stimulating studies he owed the *precision of his touch* later so much admired, *the finish of his passages, his readiness in free improvisations and variations, and the clearness and grace of his compositions.* In the year 1787 he gave his first concert as a pupil of Mozart at Dresden, performing in the same the variations on "Lison dormait" and the Second Concerto in *C* by Mozart, to the admiration of all present. He then proceeded to Berlin, where he also arranged a concert; while playing, he suddenly perceived Mozart among the audience, and hardly had he finished the piece, when he hastened through the hall to his revered master, embracing him amid mutual heartfelt greetings. Thence he journeyed on to Edinburgh, where he published his first work, a set of *Variations*, which he dedicated to the Queen of England. During 1791 and 1792 he sojourned in London to be near Clementi; and the boy, endowed as he was with the most active receptivity, untiring endurance, and a teeming imagination, comprehended the weighty teachings of his two masters so thoroughly, and was able to combine and apply them so aptly, *that in later years he attained to the high position of the perfecter of the euphonious, lyrical pianoforte style, both as a player and composer.* After a brief stay in Holland he returned to Vienna. Here he studied, over and above the severest piano-practice, composition under Albrechtsberger and Salieri, and his first Mass was received by Haydn with approval. In Germany Hummel's compositions speedily found general approbation; in Paris, too, Cherubini had his great *Fantasia* in *E♭* (op. 18, Offenbach, André) performed at the *concours* in the Conservatory, in 1806. Thenceforward his valuable pianoforte works were everywhere sought and studied by all earnest pianists. From 1811 to 1816 he was occupied in Vienna exclusively with pianoforte teaching and composing; he then became Kapellmeister to the King of Württemberg, and four years later accepted a similar position with the Grandduke of Saxe-Weimar. Hummel remained in Weimar until his decease in 1837, though at various times employing extended leave of absence for highly successful professional tours through Germany, Russia, Belgium, and France. In the inspired interpretation of his pianoforte concertos he showed himself a finished artist; his free improvisations also everywhere aroused the greatest enthusiasm. Whenever he stayed in a place for a time, he was immediately surrounded by numerous pupils, several of whom afterwards became distinguished both as players and composers. He left 7 *Pianoforte Concertos*, of which op. 85 in *A*-minor, op. 89 in *B*-minor, and op. 113 in *A♭*-major are especially noteworthy; furthermore, a grand *Fantasia* with orchestral accompaniment, *"Oberon's Zauberhorn"*, op. 116; and vario u brilliant *Rondos* for Pianoforte and Orchestra, the finest of which are op. 56 in *A*, op. 98 in *B*♭, and op. 127 in *F*; a grand *Septuor* in *D*-minor for Pianoforte, Flute, Oboe, Horn, Alto, Violoncello, and Double Bass, later performed with brilliant effect by the eminent *pianiste* **Marie Camille Pleyel** (1811—1875) on her concert tournées; a *Quintet,* op. 87, for Pianoforte and Strings; a grand *Septette militaire* for Pianoforte, Flute, Violin, Clarinet, Trumpet, Violoncello, and Double Bass; 7 *Trios* for Pianoforte, Violin, and Violoncello; 5 *Sonatas* for Pianoforte solo, including op. 81 in *F*♯-minor, and a grand *Sonata* in A♭, op. 92, for 4 hands, both specially noteworthy; the much-played *Polacca "La bella Capricciosa"*, op. 55; besides various *Fantasias, Variations, Rondos, Caprices, Études, Amusements,* and *Bagatelles.* Hummel was also the author of an extended *Pianoforte Method* (Vienna, Haslinger), which surpasses in completeness all earlier works of its class, and in which the fingering is ordered by definite laws. The work lacks, however, a practical arrangement; the author was neither capable of sifting the mass of material, nor of keeping the student's interest alive in the least. In his compositions, on the other hand, Hummel not only broadeneed the form of the Concerto, the concert and salon Rondo, and the Sonata, and furnished the same with new, difficult, yet still proper pianoforte passages according to his school, but always endowed them with an interesting meaning, and developed them in a style refined throughout, sometimes even trespassing on the dramatic.

Ferdinand Hiller (b. 1811 in Frankfort, d. 1885 in Cologne), Hummel's most distinguished pupil; although later, influenced by his intimate intercourse with Chopin and Liszt at Paris, he exchanged the chiefly lyrical style of his teacher for the romantic. His first instructor in piano-playing and composition was G. J. VOLLWEILER, who will be mentioned further on; at thirteen years of age he entered Hummel's school at Weimar. In 1828, a thoroughly trained musician, he went to Paris, finding here most remunerative appreciation and diversified educational stimulus in the circles of his fellow-artists. In concerts of his own given in 1830 and 1831 he received the warmest applause both as a virtuoso and composer; his fame was most firmly established, however, by his soirées arranged in company with the celebrated violinist Baillot in 1835, only earlier classical pieces being performed at the same. Hiller returned to Germany soon after, and acted since 1853 as Director of the Conservatory of Music at Cologne. Among his Pianoforte Compositions the *Caprices* and *Études* are particularly noteworthy, e. g. the following: *Trois Caprices ou études caractéristiques,* op. 4, Bonn, Simrock, 2 livres; *ditto* op. 14 and 20, Leipzig, Hofmeister; 24 *Études,* op. 15, same publ.; *Capriccio,* op. 88, Breitkopf & Härtel; *6 Capriccetti*, op. 35; *34 Rhythmische Studien*, op. 56, Berlin, Schlesinger; *Caprice fantastique*, op. 10. Liszt praises the *6 cahiers* of the Études dedicated to Meyerbeer, op. 15, as follows: "These Études are vigorous sketches of finished design, reminding of those forest studies in which the landscapist has succeeded, with a single tree, a single twig, a single happily and exhaustively developed *motif,* in creating a charming poem of light and shade." Besides the above, Hiller published a *Pianoforte Concerto*, op. 5; several *Quartets* and *Trios* for the Strings; a *Sonata,* op. 47; *La danse des fées,* op. 9, Leipzig, Hofmeister; *La danse des fantômes,* Berlin, Schlesinger; 3 *Ghazèles,* op. 54, same publ.; *Rêveries,* op. 17, 21, and 33; *Impromptus,* op. 30 and 40; *Sérénade,* op. 11; and other salon pieces and dances.

Julius Benedict (b. 1804 in Stuttgart, d. 1885 in London) became Hummel's pupil in 1819; but went to Dresden in the following year to study composition under C. M. von Weber. From 1839 he lived in London, where he became one of the most popular music teachers of that city. Among other things, he published the following pianoforte works: *3 Concertos*, op. 13, 29, and 45; a *Concertino,* op. 18, Leipzig, Hofmeister; 3 *Sonatas*, op. 1, 2, and 3; *Caprices*, op. 33, Paris, Brandus; *Souvenir de Naples,* op. 11; *Souvenir d'Ecosse,* op. 34; *Rêveries,* op. 39; *Idyls,* op. 41; and various *Fantasias, Variations, Rondos,* etc.—Hummel's pupil **Rudolph Willmers** (b. 1821 in Copenhagen, d. 1878 in Vienna) also deserves mention as an esteemed virtuoso and a composer of brilliant salon pieces. In 1853 he settled in Vienna, and published, among many others, the following pianoforte pieces: *Un jour d'été en Norvège,* op. 27; *2 Études de Concert, La pompa di festa,* and *Danza delle Baccanti*, op. 28; *Mazeppa, Capriccio de concert,* op. 97, all issued by Bote & Bock of Berlin; *Sérénade pour la main gauche seule*, op. 5, Leipzig, Hofmeister; *Klänge der Minne,* op. 57, same publ.; *Lyrische Tonbilder,* op. 88, Leipzig, Breitkopf & Härtel; *Wintermärchen*, op. 92, same publ.; *Trillerketten* (Chains of Trills), *Caprice-Étude*, op. 69, Leipzig, Kistner.—

The "pianist and eminent teacher of the piano" **Ernst Pauer** (born 1826 in Vienna) was taught by Mozart's second son Wolfgang Amadeus, and pursues the tendency of the Hummel school. The historical concerts originated by him in 1861 and given in London have materially furthered his renown; the same embraced a series of six performances, illustrating the foundation and development of pianoforte playing from about the year 1600 down to the present time. He is also well known as a lecturer on the composers for the harpsichord and pianoforte.—A further disciple of the Hummel school is **Johann Peter Pixis** (1788—1874), who labored at Mannheim, Munich, Vienna, and Paris, as a thorough teacher, and of whose numerous pianoforte works with or without accompaniment of other instruments we notice the following; *Grandes Variations militaires* pour 2 Pianos avec orchestre, op. 66, Leipzig, Kistner; *Trios* for Pianoforte, Violin and Violoncello, op. 75, 86, and 95, same publ.; *Grosse Sonate*, op. 3, Leipzig, Breitkopf & Härtel; *Exercices en forme de valses*, op. 80, Leipzig, Kistner; *Les trois clochettes*, op. 120, Leipzig, Hofmeister; *Scène populaire de Rome*, op. 145, same publ.

In 1829 Hummel undertook a last professional tour, its chief objective points being London and Paris. But his once so highly lauded performances now remained almost unnoticed. For Beethoven, on whose coffin Hummel had in 1827 laid the laurel at Vienna, had created in the pianoforte works of his last period—which, understood at first by but few, had gradually been comprehended everywhere in their full grandeur—a *new, more vigorous, and moving style — the dramatic pianoforte style.* Hummel and his epigones regarded this new style of composition, with its more powerful melodic, rhythmic, and harmonic resources of expression, better adapted for the orchestra than the pianoforte. But Beethoven's utterances, which found the truest expression for every phase of emotion, and soon were apprehended, taken up, and fostered by the widest circles, likewise led to a complete reform of the earlier grammar—to a complete revolution in the style of pianoforte-playing.

IV. The dramatic Pianoforte Style.

Ludwig van Beethoven.

This reformer of instrumental music was in all probability born on Dec. 16, 1770. His father, on the contrary, always gave 1772 as the birth-year of the son distinguished, like Mozart, by great musical talent in his earliest youth. This circumstance explains many contradictions in the dates given for occurrences in Beethoven's earlier life and compositions. He received his first instruction in music from his father, who was a tenor singer in the *Kapelle* of the Archbishop of Cologne; from 1782 he studied under **Christian Gottlieb Neefe** (1748—1798), then much esteemed as a piano composer and organist. In a short time the latter not only so developed the gifted boy, that he could perform the preludes and fugues in Bach's Well-tempered Clavichord and similar works by Handel in the liveliest tempo, but also had published as early as 1783 his pupil's first attempts at composition, "*9 Variationen über einen Marsch*" (one by E. Ch. Dressler), and *3 Claviersonaten* (in *E*♭, *F*-minor, and *D*), together with a few Songs, at Spire & Mannheim. Both the performances of the young virtuoso and his first compositions soon created a sensation. He once played some variations of his own on Righini's theme "Vieni, amore" to the Vicar Sterkel, then in high standing as a musician, and as the latter expressed doubts as to his authorship of the same, he improvised to the connoisseur's astonishment an entire series of new variations on the same melody (comp. "24 Variations on 'Vieni, amore' in *D*, dedicated to the Countess of Hatzfeld", Bonn, Simrock). In the winter of 1786 Beethoven went to Vienna, to hear the playing of Mozart, whom he revered, and to show him a sample of his talent. At first Mozart bestowed rather cool praise on his playing; but when Beethoven requested a theme for free development, and began with its working-out, Mozart grew more and more interested, and in high excitement he exclaimed in a low voice to friends in the next room: "Take note of him! he will make a stir the world later!" This time Beethoven's stay in Vienna was of brief duration; not until 1793, after his father's death, did he choose that city as his permanent abode. He was so fortunate as to find an eminent protector in Mozart's pupil, Prince Lichnowsky, who not only took him into his house, but allowed him a pension of 600 florins. This assistance rendered it possible for him to begin serious studies in composition under Haydn, to continue them under Albrechtsberger, and to profit by the teachings of Salieri, who was well-versed in particular in the dramatic style. The unceasingly active disciple of art expressed his gratitude to the Prince by dedicating to him the *Three Trios for Pianoforte, Violin, and Violoncello* (in *E*♭, *G*♭, and *C*-minor; Vienna, Artaria) which he now marked op. 1. On their very first performance at a soirée given by the Prince, at which Haydn was also present, they made an extraordinary sensation. They were not printed until 1795, and when they reached London and were played at a gathering of musicians, J. B. Cramer, who executed the piano-part, exclaimed prophetically: "That is the man, who will console us for the loss of Mozart!"

In 1796 Beethoven dedicated to his teacher Haydn, as op. 2: *Trois Sonates pour le Clavecin ou Pianoforte* (*F*-minor, *A*, and *C*; Vienna, Artaria & Comp.); and to Kapellmeistor Salieri, in 1799: *Tre Sonate per il Clavicembalo o Fortepiano con un Violiño*, op. 12 (in *D*, *A*, and *E*♭; same publ.).

Beethoven studied counterpoint under Albrechtsberger *con amore*, with zeal, as proved by the *Studien* (not those published in 1832 by J. v. Seyfried, and falsified throughout) which he left, and shown convincingly by his numerous works. Familiar with all the rules of ancient counterpoint, he quickly recognized the enduring laws, as well as what was untenable, in the same. He ventured upon bolder progressions and modulations, and thus became the efficient reformer of the science of modulation practiced until then. For it was he, who exhibited in his practical works that the affinity of keys is not to be determined according to degrees (e. g. *C*-major — *G*-major — *D*-major, or *C*-major—*F*-major—*B*♭-major) but must be sought in the connection of the tones of their fundamental chords; thus the key of *C*-major, for instance, is connected through the Third not only with *A*-minor and *E*-minor, but also with *A*-major and *E*-major, and likewise, through the mediation of the like-named key of *C*-minor, with *A*♭-major and *E*♭-major.

Beethoven, now a musician complete in himself, went in 1796 to Berlin, where he played several times before King Frederick Wilhelm II.— a rare protector of German music, and at the same time a good violoncello player. To him Beethoven dedicated "*Deux grandes Sonates pour le Clavecin ou Pianoforte avec un Violoncelle obligé"*, op. 5 (*F*-major and *G*-minor, Vienna, Artaria & Comp.), which he played for the King with his first violoncellist, Duport. On his departure, a magnificent golden box filled with louisd'ors was presented to him. In Berlin he met the Kapellmeister **Friedrich Heinrich Himmel** (1765—1814), a pianist and composer of the highest standing, whose *Sonatas* for Pianoforte, Violin, and Violoncello (Leipzig, Breitkopf & Härtel, and Peters) were much played for a time. Beethoven having once improvised on the pianoforte in his presence, Himmel was also invited to extemporize. He immediately complied, and had played for a considerable time, when Beethoven turned to him with the question: "Are you not going to begin soon?" The offended Kapellmeister never forgave Beethoven this laconic characterization of his improvisation; the latter afterwards said of him, that he possessed a very pretty talent and was an agreeable pianist, but that Prince Louis Ferdinand, whose acquaintance he also made at Berlin, excelled him in every way.—Beethoven likewise gave this latter eminent patron of art a signal token of his high consideration, by dedicating to him in 1805 the delightful *Pianoforte Concerto* in *C*-minor, op. 37 (Offenbach, André, and Vienna, Haslinger).

At Vienna Beethoven at first excited more attention by his spirited pianoforte-playing than by his compositions, although he already appears, in the *Trios* published as op. 1, as the head of the Vienna School of Music founded by Haydn and so grandly extended by Mozart. Thus Seyfried tells us, that Beethoven, during the closing years of the last century, found in **Woelfl** "a rival fully his peer", (?) and that opinion was divided in Vienna regarding the excellences of the playing of these two masters. They sometimes met (1798) at the charmingly situated villa of Freiherr v. Wetzlar. "There", Seyfried relates, "the highly interesting rivalry of the two athletes not seldom supplied the numerous and very exclusive gathering with indescribable enjoyment of art; each performed the latest product of his Muse; now the one or the other would give free, unchecked course to the sudden inspiration of his glowing imagination; now both would sit down at two pianofortes, improvise alternately on themes mutually proposed, and thus produce many a four-hand Capriccio which, could it have been brought to paper at the instant of its birth, would surely have bade defiance to time and decay.— It would have been difficult, perhaps impossible, to award the palm of victory to either champion by preference for his mechanical skill; Woelfl, indeed, had been the more kindly treated by Mother Nature, who had furnished him with a gigantic hand capable of stretching tenths as easily as other mortals take octaves, thus enabling him to execute with lightning-like rapidity continuous double note passages in the intervals named. — In improvisation Beethoven at that time already discovered his bent toward gloomy weirdness; once revelling in the illimitable world of tones, he was quite lost to earth; the soul had burst asunder all cramping fetters, thrown off the yoke of servitude, and soared, victoriously jubilant, into bright ethereal space; now the tones rushed onward like a wildly foaming cataract, the exorcist sometimes forcing his instrument to yield a power which the strongest build was hardly capable of obeying; now he sank back, exhausted, breathing low plaints, melting away in melancholy; — and anon the soul would rise up, triumphing over transient earthly woe, lifted on high in devotional harmonies, and finding tranquilizing consolation on the innocent breast of Nature". — Woelfl's compositions could in no respect bear comparison with those of Beethoven at that period; the partisans of the former could therefore have been captivated only by his surprising virtuosity, and not by the profundity of his ideas. The incapacity of the Viennese amateurs to form a judgment was still more glaringly exposed, when they thought a favorite pianist who appeared somewhat later likewise fit to enter the lists with Beethoven. This was **Steibelt,** who touched Vienna on his professional tour in 1800, and met Beethoven at a party given by the Count v. Fries. Besides Beethoven's *Trio for pianoforte, violin, and violoncello* in *B*♭, op. 11, a *Quintet* by Steibelt for pianoforte, two violins, viola, and violoncello was performed. The latter being thereafter again urged to play, he employed the *tremolando* breaking of the chords which he in particular had brought into vogue, winning loud applause thereby. Beethoven, however, could not be prevailed on to touch the pianoforte again that evening. A week later Steibelt surprised the same company, after a second of his pianoforte Quintets, with a series of brilliant variations on a theme (Pria ch'io l'impegno) which Beethoven had varied the week previous in the Finale of his *B*♭-major Trio, and aroused unprecedented enthusiasm. Beethoven was now besieged by his friends to pick up the gauntlet thus thrown down; he immediately sat down at the pianoforte, reached for the bass part of Steibelt's quintet, set it up before him, and played the notes of the opening measures carelessly with one finger. But he then developed, from the apparently insignificant motive, a Fantasia so artistic and heart-stirring, that Steibelt left the room before he had finished, and never again showed himself in at a party where Beethoven was expected. — We gain a clear idea of this improvised master-piece from the later published *Fifteen Variations with a Fugue** in *E*♭ (op. 35, Breitkopf & Härtel), dedicated to Count Moritz Lichnowsky. To the simple theme of the bass part are added, first one, then two, three, and more parts; the soprano now added to the bass is varied, and the whole finally ends with a brilliantly fugued movement, of which the original bass motive forms the foundation. The theme of these variations, with the added soprano, was also used by Beethoven for the ballet, first performed at Vienna in 1801, "*Die Geschöpfe des Prometheus*", and in the Finale of his *Sinfonia eroica*, sketched in 1804. Thenceforward, indeed, Beethoven's peculiarity of beginning the exposition of a composition with the most simple motive, from which a momentous musical idea is only developed further on, appears more and more markedly. Beethoven and Steibelt each gave a concert at Vienna in 1800, but the latter was only able to win the applause of dilettanti, whereas the former filled his authors with the highest admiration. Here Beethoven first played his second *Concerto* in *B*♭ (published in 1801, Leipzig, Peters), executed a free improvisation, and at the same time brought out his first *Symphony*, and the *Septet* in *E*♭, op. 20.

In the course of the year 1800 **Ferdinand Ries** came to Vienna; and he and Archduke Rudolf are to be noted as the only pupils trained by Beethoven. Ries, born at Bonn in 1784, was sent to Vienna by his father, a musician and Beethoven's friend, with a letter of recommendation to the latter. The talented youth remained four years under the guidance of his great master, then visited the European capitals on various professional tours, his masterly playing and refined style of composition everywhere meeting warm approbation. He then stayed for two years in Paris, and later for ten years in London, where he was an esteemed and popular teacher and composer. He died in the year 1838 in Frankfort.—Ries wrote *9 Pianoforte Concertos*, among which the third in *C*♯-minor (Bonn, Simrock) is especially noteworthy; also an agreeable *Concertstück*, "*Airs suédois*

* The Note, "On a theme from the Ballet, *Die Geschöpfe des Prometheus*", is not found on the title-page of the original edition published in 1803, but was added later by certain publishers.

variés", op. 52, with orchestral accompaniment, same publ.; an *Octet*, a *Septet*, and several other large works in which the pianoforte figures; *50 Sonatas* for Pianoforte solo and with accompaniment of other instruments, including op. 49, *"Le songe"*, and op. 160 *for 4 hands*, Leipzig, Kistner; also Polonaises, Variations, Rondos, and other salon pieces. His larger compositions are filled with earnest musicianly feeling, but are all modelled after Beethoven's masterful creations, without displaying new, original thoughts.

Beethoven, on the contrary, who in the sonatas dedicated to Haydn, op. 2, still reminds us of the latter, then his teacher, and in some later works of Mozart, so deeply reverenced by him, already reveals originality in the Sonate pathétique, op. 13, the *A*♭-major Sonata, op. 26, the two Sonatas "quasi una fantasia" in *E*♭-major and *C*♯-minor, op. 27, in the three Sonatas for Pianoforte and Violin dedicated to Czar Alexander, op. 30; likewise in the *D*-minor Sonata in op. 31, the above-mentioned Variations, op. 35, the third Concerto in *C*-minor, op. 37, the grand Sonata for Pianoforte and Violin dedicated to R. Kreutzer, op. 47, the Sonata dedicated to Count Waldstein, op. 53, and still more in the Sonata appassionata in *F*-minor, op. 57, in the Concertos in *G*, op. 58, and *E*♭, op. 73, and the two Trios in *D* and *E*♭, op. 70. Through these works and those following, equally eminent both in conception and form, displaying the fullest wealth of invention and conceived in fiery inspiration, he ushered in another new period—that of dramatically animated pianoforte composition. His last, most pregnant creations, the Trio in *B*♭, op. 97, and the five Sonatas op. 101, 106, 109, 110, and 111, long remained uncomprehended; and as Sebastian Bach in the work "Aria con 30 Variazioni", had formerly displayed the full opulence of his contrapuntal art, Beethoven at the close of his career likewise once more exhibited his extraordinary faculty for developing, from the simplest motives, the most artistic forms of most diversified rhythm and harmony, in his *33 Variations* on a waltz by **Anton Diabelli** (1781—1858), a considerable music-publisher and inconsiderable composer in Vienna. Beethoven died in Vienna on March 26, 1827; with him fell the last pillar of that renowned School of music, wherein Vienna had elevated and illumined the entire musical world.

Beethoven, whom the loss of his hearing had caused wholly to withdraw from the outer world during the last twenty years of his life, possessed the faculty of portraying all the feelings and passions of the human breast with the aptest touches. To this end, however, the resources of expression employed until then were inadequate, and his inventive genius often augmented the same to a height, which sometimes even yet dizzies weak-nerved critics. The works of his last period, in particular, abound in surprisingly new and characteristic rhythms and harmonic transitions. Whenever a criticism fell into his hands in which harsh harmonies and grammatical faults in his compositions were blamed, he laughed aloud, and cried out: "Yes, yes! they stare and lay their heads together, because they have never seen it in any book on thorough-bass!"

Beethoven's longer compositions in some cases bring before us a complete drama, and his Sonatas form, as it were, a connected Trilogy or Tetralogy, in which latter the satyric drama, the Scherzo, likewise occupies a place, though usually not as final link, but in the middle. The exposition, the first part of the **first movement,** is clear and intelligible, and the various motives of the same soon excite our full interest. Here we distinctly recognize a first subject, followed by one or more episodes or subsidiary themes, which are connected with each other by passages or transitions organically developed, and in perfect harmony with the mood of the whole. The episodes, or the middle and closing sections of the exposition, formerly always began in the key of the dominant, or with a minor key, in the relative major as well; but Beethoven freely chose other related keys for modulatory contrasts. The second division begins with the intertwining, the struggle, or the development of the various elements of the first division; here Beethoven ventures upon the boldest modulations, often touches the remotest keys, delaying the *reprise* of the first subject to excite the greater suspense. It then appears, well prepared or even quite unexpectedly, in the principal key, in which the several episodes of the first division are now gathered together. In an epilogue or conclusion, however, which once more restates the main features of the musical poem concisely and intensified, another striking modulation often enters suddenly, whereafter the final unraveling is the more satisfactorily brought about.—Thus in his Sonata op. 53, whose principal key is *C*-major, Beethoven does not select the dominant for a modulatory contrast, but the key of *E*, related through the third; and while developing the various motives in the second division, he touches among others the keys of *G*-minor, *C*-minor, *F*-minor, *C♭*-major, and *A♭*-major; and, further on, *F*-major, *B♭*-major, *E♭*-minor, *B*-minor, *C*-minor, and *G*-major. After the first subject in *C*, in the second division, the second subject begins in *A*-major, then passing over into *C*-major, and in the conclusion the first subject suddenly recommences—this time in *D*♭-major. In the course of the further modulations a new counter-theme starts up; the second subject again appears, but in *C*-major, and the following suggestion of the first subject is succeeded by a short, animated passage, then winding up the composition. Like each and every one of Beethoven's works, this Sonata breathes an exhilarating natural freshness, and its contrasts, melodically and rhythmically differing from each other, yet in harmonious agreement with the whole, keep our interest constantly on the alert. By unusual resolutions of dissonances and deceptive progressions Beethoven at times excites expectation to the utmost, and the rhythms wherewith he conceals the measure also hold us in breathless suspense; but broad plains, mental resting-places, are likewise not wanting in his ofttimes rugged paintings; and never does the genial master weary or exhaust us, or make us provoked with his work, by too long-continued deceptions, by a constant hiding and holding back of what is expected.—Beethoven also devoted special care to the **development of his melodies**; they invariably contain a thought of distinct and finished character, given out in a form readily grasped, often popular, whereby they not only engage the interest of a wider circle of hearers, but enable the latter to follow the artistic evolution of the same.—With Beethoven the **Adagio** or **Andante** takes either the broader form of the sonata, having an episode repeated in the second division, or the song-form with one or more counter-themes appearing but once; or it forms merely an introduction to the following movement.—The gay or humorous movement, in livelier tempo or more striking colors, which had at an earlier time found room in the Sonata as the **Minuet** or **Scherzo,** was first fashioned by Beethoven to a form corresponding to the style of the whole piece; compare in this connection the various forms specially invented by him to this end, e. g. the march-like movement in the *A*-major Sonata, op. 101, the Scherzo in the *B*♭-major Sonata op. 106, and the *Allegro molto* in the *A*♭-major Sonata op. 110.—The **Finale,** in which the idea first finding expression is treated as the chief theme, is written either in Rondo-form—in which this chief theme appears three or four times, or even oftener, together with various episodes, interludes, and developments,—or follows the Sonata-form of the first movement; the chief theme is sometimes treated as a very free fugue, or worked out in the shape of variations, whose mood, however, does not vary, but is only diversely illumined, darkened, or elevated, as in op. 109 and op. 111.

Beethoven gave no lessons in composition. When Ries came to Vienna, a lad of sixteen, he therefore commended him to the aged Albrechtsberger, but taught him pianoforte-playing himself. Ries relates that Beethoven, contrary to his wont, was remarkably patient as a teacher. Occasionally he would have a passage repeated ten times or more, e. g. the *Adagio molto* forming the close of the Variations dedicated to Princess Odescalchi, op. 34*, because the expression of the same, and the rendering of the short closing cadence, did not please him. "When I", Ries relates, "missed anything in a passage, or struck wrongly certain notes and leaps which he desired *brought out prominently,* he seldom said anything; but if I neglected any matter of expression, the crescendos, etc., or in the character of the piece, he was exasperated, because, as he said, the former was accidental, while the latter showed want of knowledge, feeling, or attention." Schindler, too, states that Beethoven laid most stress on the musical declamation in the interpretation of his pianoforte works. "For just as the poet", he observed, "carries on his monologue or dialogue in steadily progressing rhythm, while the declaimer, to insure intelligibility of the sense, must supply cesuras and pauses even in places where the poet cannot indicate them by punctuation, this style of declamation is applicable to music, and is modified only by the number of executants."

With Beethoven, therefore, begins the endeavor, so peculiarly marked at the present time, first of all to fathom the character of the composition to be performed and to execute it accordingly furthermore, to render distinctly prominent the main features in the same, and to reproduce the entire work, free from the constraint of the metronome, with dramatic vividness, according to its true nature and meaning.

The complete list of Beethoven's pianoforte works contains *5 Concertos for Pianoforte and Orchestra* and a sixth for *Pianoforte, Violin, and Violoncello*, op. 56; *1 Fantasia with Chorus and Orchestra,* op 80; *1 Quintet for Pianoforte, Oboe, Clarinet, Horn and Bassoon,* op. 16 in *E♭*; *3 Quartets* for Pianoforte, Violin, Viola, and Violon-

---

*) Their theme is in the key of *F;* Var. 1, in *D;* Var. 2, in *B♭*; Var. 3, *G;* Var. 4, *E♭*; Var. 5, *C*-minor; Var. 6 and the closing Adagio, *F*-major. Comp. above Beethoven's key-relationship by the third.

cello; *8 Trios* for Pianoforte, Violin, and Violoncello; *1 Trio* with Clarinet and Violoncello, op. 11 in *B♭*; *14 Variations*, op. 44, and also the *Adagio, Rondo, and Variations,* op. 121, with Violin and Violoncello; *10 Sonatas* with Violin; *1 Rondo* in *G* and *12 Variations* in *F*, with Violin; *5 Sonatas* with Violoncello; 3 books of *Variations* with Violoncello; *1 Sonata* in *F* with Horn; 7 books of *Variations* with Flute or Violin; *1 Sonata,* 3 *Marches,* and 2 books of *Variations for 4 hands; 38 Sonatas for Pianoforte solo;* 21 sets of *Variations for Pianoforte solo;* and 20 books of *Bagatelles, Rondos, Preludes,* and *Dances* for Pianoforte. A handsomely got-up, uniform edition of Beethoven's *Complete Works* has been published by Breitkopf & Härtel, Leipzig; his *Pianoforte Concertos,* in score, by Peters, Leipzig; a cheap and correct edition of his *Pianoforte Sonatas,* revised by Franz Liszt, has been issued by Holle, Wolfenbüttel; and another, revised by Moscheles, by E. Hallberger, Stuttgart.

Among late editions of Beethoven's works, the following may be mentioned:—J. G. COTTA, Sonatas and other Works, 5 Vols. (Faisst & Lebert), the last two volumes being edited by Hans von Bülow, who has furnished them with excellent introductions, analyses, and notes;—COLLECTION LITOLFF, Complete Concertos, Sonatas, Variations, Quartets, Trios, Duos, etc.;—EDITION PETERS, contains cheap editions similar to those of Litolff.

Franz Schubert.

Separated from Beethoven by only one grave, lies the true German, warm-hearted song-writer **Franz Schubert.** He was born at Vienna in 1797, and survived Beethoven but one year. His compositions display uncommon productive vigor, and extraordinary ease in developing the motives; and the same sympathetic reception immediately accorded in Germany, and beyond her borders, to his melodies sung to German poems, was also given to his Pianoforte Compositions, which breathe the same true-hearted tone. We mention here the *4 Impromptus,* op. 90, the *Moments musicals,* op. 94, and the *4 Impromptus,* op. 142. Of more earnest and weighty meaning is the *Fantasia,* op. 78, with the soul-stirring opening movement and the agitated Minuet. Of yet more pregnant significance is the grand *Fantasia*, op. 15, with the melancholy Wanderer melody of the Adagio, and the fugued, fiery Finale. It is wrong, that Schubert's Sonatas should be almost forgotten; for most of them have an attractive, often dramatically interesting meaning—for instance, the first in *A*-minor, op. 42—and will always, like all his compositions, afford to musicians refined entertainment. Robert Schumann recommends the same with the following words: "Schubert will always be the favorite of youth; he displays what youth desires—an overflowing heart, bold thoughts, swift deeds; tells it what it most loves to hear—romantic tales, knights, maidens, and adventures; mingled with wit and humor, too, but not enough to interfere with the tenderer general mood".

We have the following Pianoforte Compositions by him:—*Grand Quintet* for Pianoforte and Strings, op. 114; *2 grand Trios* in *B♭* and *E♭*, op. 99 and 100, and also *1 Nocturne*, op. 148, for Pianoforte, Violin, and Violoncello; *1 Rondo brilliant* in *B*-minor, op. 70; and *3 Sonatinas*, op. 137, for Pianoforte and Violin. Furthermore, *for 4 hands:—Grand Sonata*, op. 30; *grand Duo*, op. 140; *Fantasia*, op. 103; *Lebensstürme*, op. 144; *Fugue*, op. 152; *Marches*, op. 27, 40, 51, 55, 66, 121; *Divertissements*, op. 54, 63, 84; *Polonaises*, op. 61, 75; *Rondos*, op. 107, 138; *Variations*, op. 10, 35, 82; and various *Dances*, op. 33. For pianoforte solo: —*2 Fantasias*, op. 15 and 78; *2 Impromptus*, op. 90 and 142; *Moments musicals*, op. 94; *Adagio and Rondo*, op. 145; *"5 Posthumous Pianoforte Pieces"*; *7 Sonatas*, op. 42, 53, 120, 122, 143, 147, 164; and finally *3 grand Sonatas*, "Allerletzte Compositionen", in *C*-minor, *A*-major, and *B♭*-major.—Among these we call special attention to the two *Trios* for Pianoforte, Violin, and Violoncello; the *grand Fantasia* in *C*, op. 15, which in Franz Liszt's arrangement has become a highly effective concert piece for Pianoforte and Orchestra; the second *Fantasia* in *G*, op. 78, consisting of an Andante, Minuet, and Allegro; the *Duo* for 4 hands, op. 140; the *3 Marches héroïques*, op. 27, for 4 hands; and the *3 grand Sonatas* left by him.—A Collection of his Pianoforte Works has been published by Holle, Wolfenbüttel.—The greater number of his Songs were first made popular in Germany by Liszt, through his noble pianoforte transcriptions, which set the deep intensity of these tone-poems in the strongest light; and in similar arrangements, by the same master, of Schubert's cheery Dances in the "Soirées de Vienne" (Vienna, Spina, 9 books), the brightness, the gaiety, and the youthful joyousness of a Viennese *Volksball* is smilingly portrayed.

Late editions of Schubert's Pianoforte Works are "*Selected Sonatas and Solo Pieces*", arranged by Franz Liszt, 2 Vols. (J. G. Cotta);—

"Complete Pianoforte Works" (Breitkopf & Härtel); — *"Pianoforte Compositions"*, complete or separately (Edition Peters and Collection Litolff).

V. The brilliant Style.

a. Germany and Italy.

All epoch-making, creative masters not only bring the prevailing tendency of their art to a close, but also lay the foundation for the period immediately following them. Thus the shorter Suites, some of the "30 Variations", and other works of Sebastian Bach, although still maintaining with contrapuntal strictness the independence of all parts engaged, already contain the fundamental traits of a lighter pianoforte style; and Emanuel Bach often plainly shows the endeavor, to endow his subjective mood with distinct expression. In like manner we already find, in the lyric writers Mozart, Clementi, Hummel, etc. following, transitions to the dramatic instrumental style brought to perfection by Beethoven; and Beethoven's last works already contain the groundwork for the romantico-fantastic style especially cultivated after him.

At the beginning of a new period, two parties always form. The adherents of the one bend all their energies to keeping art within the limits of the foregoing period. Familiar only with the rules and forms of the earlier tendency, their slow comprehension sees only arbitrariness and formlessness in the creations of inventive minds. On the other hand, the party of progress battles with fresher youthful vigor for the legitimacy and general acceptance of the licences adopted by their models; and to their enduring energy alone do we owe the gradual expansion and enrichment of our science of harmony and form. When Beethoven sometimes ventures on his boldest modulations, until then untried, this is not to be viewed as arbitrariness, but as a deeper understanding of the natural affinities of a key. And only most arrogant ignorance can term his last grand compositions, in their visibly organic arrangement, "formless". Only the still undeveloped, uninspired raw material, or the irrational and unconnected, unintelligible work of a brainless bungler, can appear "formless" to us. But Beethoven mastered and formed his material as did none of his predecessors. For the ideal intent of his thoughts he always found the outer form best suited to the same, and when instead of one episode in his instrumental dramas he sometimes employs several, these latter preserve throughout the necessary mutual inner connection; they often call forth the sharpest and most surprising contrasts, yet never efface the harmonious, characteristic grounding of his moving tone-pictures.

It likewise happens, that the contemporaries of a great master ruling his time do not dare follow on the path which he has constructed to such dizzy heights; and it is left to later disciples of art, who have grown up with his works and gained full familiarity with them, to succeed him as epigones. His contemporaries then attempt the cultivation of some branch of art left unnoticed by him, to win favor for their works in another way. Thus Sebastian Bach's immediate successors forsook the strict contrapuntal style which he had brought to perfection, to bring into vogue a lighter and freer style of writing; and in Vienna, too, where Beethoven carried the school of ideal pianoforte-playing to final perfection, we note a transition of the latter into one striving to develop externals and technique only. The period of the brilliant pianoforte style so brought about already begins, therefore, in that preceding it,—a relation which is everywhere observable.

As the most active head of the later Viennese Pianoforte School, in whose illustrious élèves virtuosity was raised to its extreme height, **Carl Czerny** stands forth. He was born at Vienna in 1791, early devoted himself to music, and even began giving piano-lessons in his fourteenth year. He later became such a popular teacher that he often had to give more than twelve lessons daily; and to his ability testify the following pupils, to be spoken of further on:—Franz Liszt, Fräulein von Belleville (afterwards Madame Oury), Theodor Döhler, Theodor Kullak, etc. In teaching, his great facility in composing was an extraordinary aid to him; he invented on the spur of the moment the most suitable and helpful exercises for his various pupils, and was able to keep alive their interest in playing by pieces specially calculated for their powers, and of elegant and brilliant effect. From 1810 he began to publish such compositions, and they soon attained to so general popularity that Czerny, besides giving his numerous lessons, found time up to his death in 1857 to bring out some 900 larger and smaller pianoforte works for two, four, and eight hands, with or without accompaniment by other instruments. Among them we find a set of shorter pieces for piano, *for 6 hands,* entitled: "*Les trois soeurs*", op. 609; furthermore, *for 4 hands,* besides many *Rondos, Fantasias, Variations,* and *Marches,* the following larger compositions: *Presto caratteristico,* op. 24; *Grande Sonate brillante,* op. 10; *Sonate militaire,* op. 119; *Sonate sentimentale,* op. 120; *Sonate pastorale,* op. 121. Prominent among his works for 2 hands as eminently practical, are the Text-books; e. g. the *100 Progressive Studies,* op. 139; the *School of Velocity,* op. 299, in 40 Exercises; the *School of the Embellishments,* op. 355, in 70 Studies; the *School of the Left Hand,* op. 399, in 10 Exercises; the *School of the Virtuoso*, op. 365; the "*Kunst der Fingerfertigkeit*" (Art of Finger-expertness), op. 740, in 50 brilliant Studies; *Étude in Thirds,* op. 735, No. 1; *2 Études for the Left Hand alone,* op. 735, No. 2; and many others. The "*Complete theoretico-practical Pianoforte Method,* progressively arranged from the first Rudiments up to the highest Development", op. 500, in 3 Parts, contains a great number of interesting and practically selected exercises; but it labors under the disadvantage of the same disproportionate length and wearisome monotony as the similar work by Hummel, and has therefore found little favor.

Czerny's Pianoforte works, and the school founded by him, aimed at effect through *sound* rather than *sense,* and sought to win applause and appreciation less for the composer than for the virtuoso. It was consequently the object of this later Viennese Pianoforte School, like the similar one in Paris mentioned further on, to write in the most brilliant pianoforte style possible, without regard to distinctive characterization, to flatter the ear in the chief divisions and episodes, to embellish the melodious passages with bright figures and graces, and to flourish with pearling passages in the transitions and conclusions. Thus outward show, painted luxury, superseded warm-hearted simplicity and noble sincerity in composition, until the Romanticists following Beethoven again raised the inner meaning to the place of honor, and awarded the palm only to that virtuoso having the power of expressing the poetical idea of the composer most clearly and intelligently.

Madame de Belleville-Oury (1808—1880), a finished and tasteful pianiste, appeared in Vienna as a pupil of Czerny, and thereafter in other European capitals, with great success.—**Theodor Döhler**

(1814—1856), after concluding his studies under Czerny, also undertook successful professional tours, and in 1839 his playing, though not always accurate and occasionally weak, even created a sensation in Holland. His elegant pianoforte compositions were quite in vogue for a time, e. g. the following:—*Nocturne* in *D*♭, op. 24; *Tarantelle* in *G*-minor, op. 39; *Études de Salon*, op. 42; *Romances sans Paroles*, op. 57; *Promenade en gondole*, op. 65; *Veder Napoli, e poi morir*, op. 74; and many others.—More tasteful in his salon pieces, and more thorough in works devoted to technique, was **Theodor Kullak** (1818—1882). This distinguished pianoforte virtuoso began his musical studies with the deserving Albrecht Agthe in Posen, and finished the same at Vienna with Czerny in 1842, under the influence of the performances and compositions of two masters highly revered by him, Liszt and Henselt. From 1843 he lived in Berlin as a much-sought teacher, and Manager of the "Neue Akademie der Tonkunst". In a vigorous *Trio* for Pianoforte, Violin, and Violoncello in *E*-minor (Leipzig, Peters, 1852), Kullak proves himself a master of broader forms, and his brilliant pianoforte compositions, everywhere favorites for playing, are animated by a grateful and attractive youthful freshness. We note the following among many:—*La danse des Sylphides*, op. 5 (Berlin, Schlesinger); *La gazelle*, op. 22, (Berlin, Trautwein); *Perles d'écume, Fantaisie-étude*, op. 37 (Dresden, Paul); *4 Salon pieces*, op. 104 (Leipzig, Kistner). Among his instruction books are: *Kinderleben*, short pieces, op. 62 and 81 (Berlin, Trautwein); *Sheherezade*, 6 petits morceaux, op. 78 (Leipzig, Peters); the *School of Finger-practice*, op. 61 (Berlin, Schlesinger); the excellent *School of Octave-playing*, op. 8 (same publ.); and, as a *Sequel to the same*, op. 48 (same publ.); and op. 59 (Leipzig, Peters).

As the leader of this Vienna school of brilliant pianoforte playing figures **Sigismund Thalberg,** whose aristocratically refined, clean, and sonorous style aroused the greatest enthusiasm in all the capitals of Europe. He was born at Geneva in 1812, early began his musical education at Vienna under a *Hofmusicus* of that city, and in 1828 published there his first work. "*Mélange sur des thèmes d'Euryanthe*"; also a "*Fantaisie sur un air écossais*", op. 2, and an "*Impromptu sur des motifs du siège de Corinthe*", op. 3. In 1834 he was appointed Imperial Hofpianist, and began in 1835 his professional tours to Paris, Brussels, London, St. Petersburg, and all the German capitals. His bravura pieces, Fantasias on melodies from "Moses" and "La Donna del lago" by Rossini, on motives from Bellini's "Norma", and on Russian folk-songs, gained extraordinary popularity through his own brilliant performance; but their themes are always treated in one and the same fashion, and the ever-recurring grand effect is, to play the melody-notes in the middle octaves of the keyboard now with the thumb of the right hand, now with that of the left, the other fingers executing thereto arpeggios covering the entire range of the keyboard. But such stencil-work does not please even dilettanti for long; and while Thalberg was still winning great applause in America in 1857 and 1858, his once so popular compositions were in Europe already consigned to oblivion. Several of his richly ornamented, vigorous, and effective *Studies* have, however, justly remained in favor with pianists; among others the following: —*Caprice* No. 1, op. 15; No. 2, op. 19; *12 Études,* op. 26 (Leipzig, Breitkopf & Härtel); *Grand Caprice sur la marche de l'apothéose de Berlioz,* op. 58 (same publ.); *La cadence,* op. 36, No. 1; *Étude de perfection,* op. 36, No. 2 (Berlin, Schlesinger).

The style of playing alluded to, and so often used by Thalberg, of executing wide-spreading arpeggios to a melody of medium pitch, was first brought out in Germany, as it appears, by the pre-eminent harper **Parish-Alvars** (b. 1816 in London, d. 1839 in Vienna), who performed them most effectively on his instrument. According to Dehn, however, the inventor of the same was the Italian **Giuseppe Francesco Pollini,** an adherent of the Clementi school. Being in Paris in 1801, he published there three *Sonatas* for the Pianoforte (Érard), and a "Fantaisie sur un thème de Viotti" (Pleyel; also published later by Breitkopf & Härtel). On returning to his native country he became honorary member of the Conservatory of Music at Milan, where he wrote the instruction book "Metodo per Clavicembalo" (Milan, G. Ricordi), which the professors of the above institute, at a general meeting on Nov. 16, 1811, extolled by saying, "that it is founded on definite, clear, and unshakable rules, and is worthy to be used exclusively as the basis of pianoforte instruction in the Milan Conservatory, and in all other educational institutions of Italy".—This Pianoforte Method, of peculiar importance from such a recommendation, is dedicated to the Viceroy of Italy, "Eugenio Napoleone". In the first section it treats of the attitude of body and hands in piano-playing, and of the fingering of all the scales; gives exercises for making the fingers independent of each other, for skilfully passing the second, third, fourth, and fifth fingers over the thumb, and the latter under all the other fingers; treats theoretically and practically of changing the fingers in rapid repetitions on one and the same key, of passages in broken thirds, sixths, and arpeggio'd full chords, and the various passages in octaves, thirds, and sixths. All exercises are first to be played with the right and left hand alone, then with both together, finally in melodic contrary motion of both hands and in different keys. The second section treats of the various appoggiaturas, turns, mordents, trills, double trills, and trills executed to melodious passages; he gives practical rules for the fingering in the legato style, and for varying the touch for the different marks of expression; and finally teaches the effective employment of the pedals. The third and last section contains exercises in full chords, scales, etc., carried out in sequences through all the keys. As diversions, Pollini recommends the Sonatinas by Ferrari, Steibelt, and Dussek, together with Clementi's Waltzes in rondo-form. As a second Part to his Method, *3 Sonatas* (op. 26, liv. 1 and 2) were published by Riccordi, Milan. Of his remaining pianoforte compositions we mention the following: —*Introduction et Rondeau pastoral à 4 mains* (same publ.); *2 grand Sonatas* (Vienna, Artaria); *Fantasia* on themes from Rossini's "Gazza ladra" (Berlin, Schlesinger); *Variations and Rondo* (Zürich, Nägeli); *Capriccio*, op. 28; *Toccata*, op. 31; *Esercizj per Clavicembalo*, op. 42; *Introduction et Toccato*, op. 50 (Leipzig, Breitkopf & Härtel); *Scherzo, Variations, and Fantasia* in *B* (same publ.); and a *Toccata* noted on three staves, op. 56, (Milan, Ricordi). Pollini's compositions at times augment the difficulties of the Clementi school, and contain interesting modulations, figures, and pianoforte effects; but their influence, aside from the effect borrowed by Thalberg, has not reached beyond the borders of Italy, as they in great measure lacked the novel and generally attractive subjects necessary for a wider dissemination, and that alluring external elegance with which Thalberg later graced his compositions.—**Adolf Fumagalli** (born 1828 at Inzago, d. 1856 in Florence), who was trained by Angeleri in the Milan Conservatory according to Pollini's principles, undertook brilliant professional tours through Italy, France, and Belgium, as a pianoforte virtuoso, and excited great admiration, in particular, by his masterfully developed left hand. Besides many brilliant salon pieces, e. g. the *Luisella Tarantella*, the *Nenna Tarantella*, op. 29, *1 Sérénade napolitaine*, op. 50, *1 Nocturne*, and *1 Sogno d'amore* (all publ. by Schlesinger, Berlin), he published a fantastic *Pianoforte Concerto* "Les clochettes", op. 21 (Milan, Ricordi).

Tomaschek, Dionys Weber, and Proksch in Prague.

In Prague, where Mozart first found just appreciation of his high importance as a composer and pianoforte virtuoso, pianoforte-playing was taken up with remarkable zeal and zest after the stimulus afforded by his presence. Simultaneously with Czerny in Vienna, great services were rendered in thoroughly teaching and further spreading this art by Tomaschek and Dionys Weber, seconded later by Joseph Proksch. From the beginning of the year 1801 till 1803 Abbé Vogler, a man of high merit, was also engaged at the University of Prague to deliver public lectures on the theory of music. The beneficial influence of such an advanced musician on musical matters in that city was soon felt, although he complains bitterly, in the Preface to a Manual of Harmony published there in 1802, of the spiteful attacks to which his writings and even his person were subjected at that period.

Johann Wenzel Tomaschek, born in 1774 at Skutsch in Bohemia, had by untiring industry educated himself according to Türk's then much-esteemed Clavier Method to be an able player. Though he completed a law course at Prague in 1799, he devoted himself wholly to music when his pupil, Count Georg Bouquoy, hospitably invited him to his house and at the same time allowed him a regular salary. Thenceforward down to his death in 1850 he was unweariedly occupied as a teacher of composition and pianoforte-playing; and to the thoroughness with which he fulfilled his duties, a succession of distinguished pupils testifies. Tomaschek's compositions found such favor upon their appearance, that he was lauded in his native country as "the Schiller of music".* Concerning his **12 Eclogues** and **12 Rhapsodies,** published in 1812 by Kühnel (later by Peters, Leipzig), E. L. Gerber remarked in 1814: "The former sweet, naïve, with the spellful charm of Gessner's Muse; the latter the most daring flight of a fiery fancy, bold in leading and captivating in vividness". Of the Eclogues 4 books of 6 each were published by Peters in Leipzig as op. 35, 39, 47, and 51, and their continuation by Hofmeister in Leipzig as op. 63, 66, and 83, the last "en forme de danses pastorales". The first book of 6 Rhapsodies was published by Haas in

---

* See "Hesperus" for the year 1811, acc. to Gerber in the new Tonkünstler-Lexikon.

Vienna, op. 40; the second by Peters, op. 41; the third by Hofmeister, op. 110; also *1 grand Sonata* in *G*, op. 15, Peters; *Sonata* in *A*, op. 48, Hofmeister; *Sonata* in *C*, op. 14, Zürich, Nägeli; *Sonata* in *F*, op. 21, Vienna, Steiner; *Sonata* in *B♭* and *Rondo* in *G*, Zürich, Nägeli; *Gr. Rondeau*, op. 11, Bonn, Simrock; and *6 Allegri capricciosi di bravura*, op. 52 and 84, Hofmeister.

On the foundation of a Conservatory of Music at Prague in 1810 the then highly esteemed theoretician **Dyonis Weber** (1771—1842) was appointed Director of the same; and under his management a large number of fine musicians were trained in this institute, which later attained to high standing, though pianoforte-playing and organ-playing were not cultivated at the same. Of his private pupils, too, several won distinction as pianists and composers, among them Ignaz Moscheles, Carl Maria von Bocklet, Sigismund Goldschmidt, and others. The first of these three will find special mention elsewhere. **Carl Maria von Bocklet** (b. 1801 in Prague, d. 1881 in Vienna), finished his studies under Dionys Weber, went to Vienna in 1821, created a great stir there through his interesting free fantasias on the pianoforte, and became one of the most popular music teachers. His fellow-pupil **Sigismund Goldschmidt** (b. 1815) was styled while sojourning in Paris "le roi des sixtes", and has won a good name not only as a virtuoso, but also as the composer of the following works: *Études de concert*, op. 4 and op. 13, dedicated to Clara Schumann and Moscheles; *2 Sonatas*, op. 5 and op. 8; *Rêverie au bord de la mer*, op. 10; *Nocturne*, op. 18; all publ. by J. Schuberth & Co. of Leipzig.

A lasting influence on the welfare of musical matters in Prague was also exerted by Carl Maria von Weber, who at the beginning of his artistic career was chiefly admired as a spirited pianist, and from 1813 to 1816 acted as Kapellmeister at the City Theatre in Prague.—After the death of Dionys Weber in 1842, **Johann Friedrich Kittel** (1809—1868) a pupil of Tomaschek, became Director of the Prague Conservatory, and attracted favorable notice by the publication of several pleasing pianoforte compositions. Among them we notice the following: *Grand Septet* for Pianoforte, Flute, Oboe, Clarinet, Horn, Bassoon, and Double Bass, op. 25, (Leipzig, Kistner); and various sets of lyrical *Impromptus* — op. 17 (Berlin, Schlesinger), op. 26 (Leipzig, Peters), op. 18 and op. 30 (Leipzig, Hofmeister). His rarely gifted fellow-pupil **Alexander Dreyschock** (1818—1869) shone in extended professional tours more particularly by his brilliant execution with the left hand alone — *Variations pour la main gauche seule,* op. 22, Leipzig, Hofmeister — and with the bravura piece "*La campanella*", op. 10; but likewise proved himself a player of true worth in his rendering of Mendelssohn's *G*-minor Concerto and other serious compositions. His numerous "drawing-room" pieces include, among others, *Rhapsodies,* op. 37, 38, and 39 (Leipzig, Kistner); op. 40 (Berlin, Bote & Bock); op. 98 (Breitkopf & Härtel); and the descriptive pieces "*Le naufrage*", op. 68, and "*Le festin de noces vénitiens*", op. 69. — Among Tomaschek's remaining pupils, **Ignaz Tedesco** (1817—1882), the "Hannibal of Octaves", and **Julius Schulhoff** (born 1825), became favorites more especially in ladies' circles through their elegant execution and the publication of various graceful dances and other charming trifles. Schulhoff made himself known, among other things, by *Two Polkas,* op. 4; *Valse brilliante,* op. 6; *2 Mazurkas,* op. 9; *12 Études,* op. 13; and *Idyls,* op. 23, 27, and 36; — Tedesco by the following pieces: *Bohemian National Songs,* op. 22; *Caprice de concert sur des airs de Czikos,* op. 24; *Rastlose Liebe,* op. 34; *In einsamen Stunden,* op. 98; etc.

In the year 1831 **Joseph Proksch** (1794—1864), blind since his seventeenth year, but of keen mental vision, opened a Music Institute in Prague, which speedily attracted general interest, and for which he elaborated the following extremely practical works: Attempt at a Rational Method of teaching Pianoforte-playing, in 6 Parts; *Variations* on Mozart's Spring-song, for 4 Pianofortes, each taking 4 hands; The Art of the Ensemble in Pianoforte-playing, 12 books.—As a thoughtful and stimulating teacher we still have to name **Louis Köhler** (1820—1886), a pupil of C. M. v. Bocklet. He settled in Königsberg in 1847, and has attracted favorable attention by the publication of a work which exhaustively presents its subject: —"A Systematic Method for teaching Pianoforte-playing and Music", in 2 Parts (Leipzig, Breitkopf & Härtel); also Mechanical and Technical *Pianoforte Studies,* op. 70 (same publ.); *Studies in Thirds, Sixths, and Octaves,* op. 60; *Folk-songs* of all Peoples, (Braunschweig, Litolff); "Festgaben, den Kindern zur Freude am Clavierspiel dargeboten" (Festival Gifts for the Children's delight in playing the Pianoforte), op. 24; and many other instruction books.

G. J. Vollweiler and A. Schmitt in Frankfort on the Main.

G. J. Vollweiler (1770—1847) in Heidelberg, and of **Aloys Schmitt** (1788—1866) in Frankfort, had like success as able pianists and thorough teachers as Tomaschek, D. Weber, and Proksch in Prague. The son and pupil of the former, **Carl Vollweiler** (1813—1848), a highly gifted virtuoso and composer, settled in 1835, after several tours through Denmark, Sweden, and Russia, in St. Petersburg, rose to be one of the most respected piano-teachers, and published a series of compositions distinguished both by their pleasing melodies and refined harmonies, and also by their good pianoforte style. Of these we note especially a *Prize Sonata; Six Études mélodiques,* op. 4; *Études lyriques,* op. 9 and op. 10, romantically inspired, delightful counterparts to Mendelssohn's Songs without Words; a *Tarantelle* in *G*-minor, wherein all the effects of the tambourine accompanyinng this fiery dance are reproduced by interesting pianoforte touches; — all publ. by J. Schuberth & Co., Leipzig; *3 Pensées fugitives,* op. 16, Leipzig, Hofmeister; *2 Impromptus,* op. 18, same publ.; *Nocturne, Barcarolle, and Gigue,* op. 12, 22, 23, Leipzig, Kistner; and *1 Grand Caprice sur des motifs de Russlan et Ludmilla,* J. Schuberth & Co. — a bravura piece performed by Franz Liszt in his concerts at St. Petersburg. Vollweiler brought the manuscript of this last, which was difficult to decipher on account of being written in small notes and with pale ink, to Liszt with the request that he would try it at his leisure. But Liszt immediately placed it upon the piano, played it at sight to the composer's astonishment in the proper tempo and with the most fiery delivery, from time to time letting fall pertinent remarks on the original melodic turns and daring harmonies of the brilliant Capriccio, without interrupting his performance. By giving music-lessons, Vollweiler had amassed a considerable property, and in 1847 departed from St. Petersburg to surprise his aged father in Germany by an unexpected return, full of joyful plans for the future. On arriving at Leipzig, he takes up a Frankfort newspaper, and reads therein — the notice of his father's death. Leaving all his effects at the hotel, he hastens on to Heidelberg by post, to his sister, in whose arms he expires.

Aloys Schmitt labored as a teacher, chiefly in Frankfort, from 1816, and published a series of compositions resembling in form and substance those of the Clementi school. Among them we find *6 Pianoforte Concertos* (Offenbach, André, and Vienna, Artaria); several *Sonatas*, with and without accompaniment of other instruments, for 2 and 4 hands; and various books of extremely practical *Studies for Pianoforte*, e. g. *Études en deux parties*, op. 16, Bonn, Simrock; *Nouvelles Études*, dediées à J. B. Cramer, 2 Livr. op. 55, Leipzig, Kistner; *Rhapsodies* in 2 books, op. 62, and *18 Studies*, op. 67, Leipzig, Hofmeister; *8 Études*, liv. 12, Leipzig, Peters; and as op. 114, *Method of Pianoforte-playing*, a systematically arranged Collection of Pieces for progressively developing the Fingers and the Taste. His younger brother and pupil, **Jacob Schmitt** (1803—1853) likewise published a complete practical School of Pianoforte-playing, op. 301, Leipzig, J. Schuberth & Co.; and, together with many unimportant dilettantish pieces, several well-sounding *Studies*, e. g. *4 Études brilliantes*, op. 271, and *4 Études de concert*, op. 330, same publisher. — Aloys Schmitt also trained his son **Georg Aloys Schmitt** (b. 1828) as an able musician and finished pianist, who published among other things 3 Pianoforte Pieces, *Caprice, Impromptu*, and *Nocturne*, op. 10.

The first to endow the Studies, as well as the Concert and Salon Pieces with subjects more spiritually animated, was Ignaz Moscheles, who combined the dramatic with the brilliant instrumental style, and through his signally successful concert tours likewise rendering enduring services in the ennoblement and propagation of his art.

Ignaz Moscheles,

born in Prague on May 30, 1794, studied from his tenth year onward, under the guidance of Dionys Weber, the works of Seb. Bach, Handel, Mozart, and Clementi, and as early as 1804 published a *Fantasia* for Pianoforte on the Jewish funeral lament "Potem mitzwo!" In 1808 his fine pianoforte performances were received with the loudest applause at a concert given by him in his native city; encouraged by this, he resolved to go to Vienna, then the capital of the musical world, with the special aim of completing his studies in composition under Albrechtsberger, the teacher of Beethoven. In Vienna, too, his audacious and brilliant playing found universal favor. Here he made the acquaintance of **J. Meyerbeer**, at that period also celebrated as a pianist; after uninterrupted, zealous study, he in 1816 began his professional travels through Germany, and was everywhere received with the greatest enthusiasm not simply as a finished virtuoso, but as an original composer as well. In 1820 he also created a general sensation at Paris, and his masterly playing met with no less favor in London, where he sojourned for a considerable time as the worthiest representative of the meritorious Clementi, to whom, a septuagenarian then living in retirement, though still robust, Moscheles paid his respects. From London Moscheles again visited the German capitals in 1823 and 1824, Brussels in 1835, and Paris in 1839, and displayed his lofty mastership foremostly in the interpretation of his *G*-minor *Concerto* op. 58, a work of chastest conception, and in the sparkling *Bravura Variations* on the Alexander March, op. 32; likewise in the performance of free fantasias, the choice of whose motives he left to his audience. In the year 1846 he followed a call to Leipzig, where he worked as one of the most revered professors in the Conservatory of Music. Among his numerous Pianoforte compositions, eight masterly and effective *Concertos* are prominent, of which that already mentioned, in *G*-minor, and the *Concerto fantastique*, op. 90, are peculiarly esteemed; furthermore, *Souvenirs d'Irlande* with orchestral accompaniment, op. 69; *1 Sextet* for Pianoforte, Violin, Flute, 2 Horns, and Violoncello, op. 35; *1 Sonata for 4 hands* in *E*♭, op. 47, *1 Sonate symphonique*, op. 112, and *Les Contrastes*, op. 115, also for 4 hands; *Hommage à Handel*, op. 92, a grand Duo for 2 pianofortes; *Humoristic Variations*, *Scherzo*, and *Festival March*, op. 128; and *Cadenzas* to Beethoven's Pianoforte Concertos. To his finest works, and supplied with a wealth of novel figures and pianoforte effects, also belong the "STUDIES for the higher finish of already advanced pianists, consisting of 24 characteristic compositions in the various major and minor keys, provided with fingering, and with explanatory notes on the aim and performance of the same", op. 70, Leipzig, Kistner; also NEW CHARACTERISTIC STUDIES for the Pianoforte, op. 95, and Quatre grandes *Études de concert* pour Piano, op. 111, same publ. The last two works reveal, through titles like *Zorn*, *Widerspruch*, *Versöhnung*, *Kindermärchen*, *Volksscenen*, etc., the striving of the composer to imbue his creations with distinct meaning; and in this he really met with happier success than any of his predecessors in the same field. In like manner Moscheles attained, by the frequent but well-calculated use of the pedal (which Hummel quite neglected), and by the greater strength and diversity of his touch, effects unknown to the master just named and so much resembling him. We must therefore regard him as one of the most influential amplifiers of the art of Pianoforte-playing. He died at Leipzig, universally mourned, in the year 1870.

To the most distinguished of the many pupils trained by Moscheles belong the following: Leopoldine **Blahetka** (b. 1811); her first teachers of music were Frau von Cibbini, *née* Kozeluch, and Joseph Czerny; she early exhibited uncommon talent for this art, and from her eighth year attracted much notice in Viennese musical circles by her neat pianoforte-playing. Under Moscheles' tuition her talent later developed so rapidly, that her concert tours through Germany, Holland, France, and England were attended by most flattering success. From 1840 she resided at Boulogne as an esteemed teacher. As the pupil of Simon Sechter she also became known through the following compositions:—*Souvenir d'Angleterre,* with orchestral accompaniment, op. 38, Leipzig, Hofmeister; *3 Rondeaux élégants* (Amour à la Bouteille, Hommage à l'Amour, and Rage de Danse), op. 37, same publ. —Also **Henry Litolff** (b. London, 1818); in 1846 he settled in Brunswick, moved to Paris in 1860, and is noted as a pianist of the first rank. Of his compositions we name *6 Études de concert,* op. 18; *Tarantelle infernale,* op. 79; *Grand Caprice de concert,* op. 37, Berlin, Bote & Bock;—and call special attention to his *5 Symphonic Concertos,* the second of which, *Concerto-Sinfonie* pour Piano et Orchestre in *B*-minor, op. 22, has been published in Berlin by Schlesinger.—**Robert Radecke** (b. 1830), also a pupil of Moscheles, settled in Berlin in 1854, where he became a popular pianoforte teacher, and was appointed in 1863 to the office of Kapellmeister of the Royal Opera, which he held until 1887.

Moscheles and **Fétis** published (Berlin, Schlesinger) a "Method of Methods" bearing the following title: "The most Complete School, or the Art of Pianoforte-playing", resulting from a searching examination of the best works of this kind, more particularly the Textbooks of Bach, Marpurg, Türk, Müller, Dussek, Clementi, Schmitt, Adam, Czerny, Hummel, and Kalkbrenner. The second and third parts of the same contain Rudimentary Exercises, Progressive Études, and Studies for the higher development, by Cramer, Czerny, Moscheles, Mendelssohn, Henselt, Chopin, Liszt, etc. A fellow-worker of Moscheles in the Leipzig Conservatory of Music was the acute theoretician and contrapuntist **Moritz Hauptmann,** whose six fine *Sonatas* for the Pianoforte and Violin, op. 5 and op. 23, Leipzig, Peters, by reason of their thoughtful conception and finished form, will remain of enduring value in musical literature.—Among the similar works of the sterling composer **George Onslow** (1784—1853), two extremely valuable *Grand Duos* for Pianoforte and Violin, op. 29, in *E*, and op. 31 in *G*-minor, are deserving of special mention.

Carl Maria von Weber.

The development of modern pianoforte technique, the wider extension of the chords, and the more sonorous passages, we owe after Moscheles in no small degree to **Carl Maria von Weber**, whose soulful compositions immediately won the sympathies of his nation and made him its favorite. He was born on Dec. 18, 1786, at Eutin in Holstein, busied himself at an early age with music, and was taken by his father for education in this art to Michael Haydn, then already sixty years old, in Salzburg. The fruits of his study were *six Fughettas*, which were published in 1798. He then proceeded with his father to Munich, where he continued his theoretical work under the organist Kalcher, and had printed *6 Variations* in *C*, No. 1, for Pianoforte. In 1803 he visited Vienna, and became acquainted there with the ABBÉ VOGLER, who stood in high estimation alike as a theoretician and as an organist and pianist, and whose more rational principles of harmony decided him to devote two further years to theoretical study under the Abbé's guidance, while also training himself to virtuosity on the pianoforte. In response to an invitation from Duke Eugene of Württemberg he visited this patron of art in Silesia (1806), where he composed, besides other pieces, his first *Pianoforte Concerto* in *C*, op. 11, Offenbach, André. Two years later he gave at Leipzig, and in 1810 at Munich and Berlin, concerts universally well received; once more returned to the Abbé Vogler, and lived in intimate friendship with his fellow-pupil Meyerbeer until called to Prague in 1813 as Music Director, in which city he remained till 1816. These were the stirring times of Germany's uprising against the foreign conqueror; and Weber, too, was inspired by them to pen the songs of freedom soon echoing throughout the land. We may consider his *Concertstück* in *F*, so important for the further development of the animated dramatic pianoforte style, as an echo of that glorious period; it was issued as op. 79 by Peters, Leipzig. The orchestra begins in the same with a *Larghetto* in *F*-minor full of anxious expectancy, whose sustained melody is then taken up by the pianoforte and accompanied by evanescent harmonies. In the succeeding *Allegro passionato* the mood becomes more unquiet and agitated; a consoling ray of hope—the middle movement in *A*♭—breaks through, but dark clouds soon gather densely and rapidly, and the movement is brought to a close in passionate agitation. Now there sounds, as from a distance, a march gently intoned by the wind instruments. The pianoforte strikes boldly in, and the grand *tutti* of the orchestra finally brings it out as an energetically marked march of triumph. Now the pianoforte again begins, softly and tentatively; its passages grow stronger and faster, until, after constantly rising intensification, it storms in full ecstacy into the last movement, *Presto assai,* in *F*-major. The glowing, brilliant passages express most fervent rapture and jubilation, and stamp this *Concertstück* altogether as the most effective and powerful of all compositions of its class issued up to that time. Prominent among the other pianoforte works of Weber are also several books of easy *Pièces à 4 mains,* op. 3, 10, and 60; four *grand Sonatas,* op. 24, 39, 49, and 70; *Momento capriccioso,* op. 12; *Aufforderung zum Tanz,* op. 65; *Polonaise* in *E*♭, op. 21; *Variations* on "Vien qua, Dorina bella", op. 12; and a *Polacca brillante* in *E*♭, op. 72, Berlin, Schlesinger, also issued by the latter in a brilliant arrangement for Piano and Orchestra by Liszt. Weber, from 1817 Hofkapellmeister of the German opera at Dresden, wrote "Der Freischütz" for Berlin in 1821, "Euryanthe" for Vienna in 1823, and "Oberon" for London in 1826, in which latter city he succumbed to a disease of the lungs, soon after the opera had been successfully brought out. But his naïvely fresh melodies still live among his countrymen, and the combination of dramatic animation with brilliant effect in the pianoforte style, so powerfully employed both by him and Moscheles, found countless imitators; — the most gifted of whom, able at the same time ingeniously to apprehend and elaborate the rarest features in the epochs preceding him, was FELIX MENDELSSOHN.

As a pianoforte virtuoso, Weber had the *Crescendo,* swelling from the softest *piano* through all degrees of intensification up to the mightiest *forte,* so completely at command, that he always exerted an electrifying effect therewith upon his hearers. In his written works this effect is most clearly illustrated in the *Concertstück* already described, measure 68—84, where it leads up powerfully to the stormy *Allegro passionato.*

The following late editions of his Pianoforte Works must be mentioned: — *Sonatas* and *Salon Pieces,* arr. by Franz Liszt, 2 Vols.

(J. G. Cotta); *Pianoforte Works*, compl., Reinecke (Breitkopf & Härtel); *Complete Compositions*, 3 Vols. (Edition Peters); the same, 1 Vol. (Collection Litolff).

The following works on his life and labors are well worthy of notice—"Carl Maria von Weber. Ein Lebensbild von Max Maria von Weber." 3 Vols., Leipzig, Keil, 1864.—"C. M. v. Weber in seinen Werken." A chronological thematic list of his complete compositions, by F. W. Jähns. Berlin, 1871, Schlesinger (Robt. Lienau).

The pianist and composer Ludwig Böhner (1817—1861), in his last period quite run wild, was an original character, whom E. T. A. Hoffmann portrayed in so interesting a manner, in his *Fantasiestücke*, as "Johannes Kreisler". From 1808 to 1820 he travelled about Germany giving concerts, playing his own compositions, but afterwards led a nomadic life in his native province of Thuringia, in very restricted circumstances. Among other things he had printed *5 Pianoforte Concertos*, op. 7, 8, 11, 13, and 14, and *1 Sonata*, op. 15; *1 Capriccio* in *A*, and a great number of *Dances* (principally in Leipzig, Hofmeister or Breitkopf & Härtel); and his assertion that C. M. v. Weber had taken the loveliest passages of his "Freischütz" from his pianoforte concerto in *D*, op. 8, created a great sensation for a time. One sees, however, on closer examination, that this pretended theft concerns only two measures, which occur in the above opera in the part sung by Agathe, to the words: *"Süss entzückt entge——"* (N. B. only to the first note of this syllable), and consist of the tones of a broken triad embellished with turns. But Weber frequently begins his most popular melodies with the broken tones of a triad, which even occur without melodic embellishment; e. g. in the following: "Was glänzt dort vom Walde im Sonnenschein"; "Einsam bin ich nicht alleine"; the middle theme of the *Preciosa* overture, etc.; so that the term theft no more applies to this case than to the motive mentioned before, first employed by Clementi, from the overture to the *Magic Flute*.

Weber's successor to the post of Hofkapellmeister at Dresden, and at the same time his warm admirer, was **Carl Gottlieb Reissiger** (1798—1859). He produced a series of elegant and easily executed Pianoforte Compositions, which are distinguished rather by the natural flow of their melodies than through profundity. Special favorites for a time were his *Trios* for Pianoforte, Violin, and Violoncello, of which he published 22, and which belong to the better class of entertaining musical literature. We notice the following: the *2 Trios*, op. 164 and op. 175, "faciles et brillants", Berlin, Schlesinger; also the larger *Trios*, op. 25 in *D*-minor, op. 77 in *E*♭, op. 85 in *E*, op. 125 in *A*-minor, and op. 192 in *D*, the last one in full score, all published by Peters in Leipzig.

Heinrich Marschner, too (1795—1861), Hofkapellmeister at Hanover, and renowned from his true German operas conceived in Weber's spirit, left a few interesting Pianoforte Compositions of the same class, among which the following are to be specially recommended:—*2 Trios* for Pianoforte, Violin, and Violoncello, op. 29 in *A*-minor, Leipzig, Kistner, and op. 111 in *G*-minor, Leipzig, Hofmeister; also *1 Quartet* for Pianoforte, Violin, Viola, and Violoncello in *B*♭, op. 36, same publisher.

Finally we should not neglect to notice the following compositions by Hofkapellmeister **Louis Spohr** of Cassel (1784—1859):—*Quintet* for Pianoforte, 2 Violins, Viola, and Violoncello in *D*, op. 130, Leipzig, J. Schuberth & Co.; *5 Trios concertants* for Pianoforte, Violin, and Violoncello, op. 119 in *E*-minor, op. 123 in *F*, op. 124 in *A*-minor, op. 133 in *B*♭, and op. 142 in *G*-minor, all editions in score, same publ.; *3 Duos concertants* for Pianoforte and Violin, op. 113 in *E*♭, op. 114 in *E*♭, and op. 115 in *A*♭, same publ.—In these the pianoforte part appears as original as is this admirable writer's style of composition throughout; and in these works, wrought with loving care, Spohr likewise charms his many admirers with noble and well-chosen melodies and harmonies.

Felix Mendelssohn.

Mendelssohn, inspired by the beauties of Beethoven, Bach, and Mozart, and in his youth a witness of Carl-Maria von Weber's epoch-making triumphs, sought to combine the warmth and outward brilliancy of the latter with the more artistic work of the earlier masters; and to this endeavor we owe a series of pianoforte-works, whose appearance was joyfully greeted by all pianists, and in which, though lacking the spirit of originality, the well-schooled and impressionable musician is always recognizable.

Felix Mendelssohn-Bartholdy, a grandson of the philosopher Moses Mendelssohn, was born in Hamburg on February 3, 1809, but in his fourth year removed with his parents to Berlin, where he early received instruction in piano-playing from Ludwig Berger. In his tenth year the talented boy already played the *Concert militaire* by Dussek with applause in public; in the theory of music he quickly became the favorite pupil of Zelter, then Director of the Berlin Singakademie. The latter presented him in 1821 to his friend Goethe at Weimar, in which town Mendelssohn had an opportunity of listening to Hummel's fine playing, and in particular to his much-lauded free fantasias. Felix, then twelve, had already finished his first *Quartet* for Pianoforte, violin, viola, and violoncello, played by heart fugues by Seb. Bach and sonatas by Beethoven, and won the hearts of all by his frank and merry temper. In 1825 his father took him to Paris, to hear Cherubini's opinion on the intention of the youthful Felix, to devote himself wholly to music. The Master tested him, and expressed an extremely favorable judgment on his abilities. Moscheles, too, who at that time paid several visits to Berlin on the tours undertaken by him from London, took great delight in the gifted young artist, becoming not only a helpful teacher, but a faithful and appreciative friend until his untimely death. Mendelssohn visited him in 1829 at London, where he won great applause as a composer and pianist. In the following year Felix journeyed by way of Weimar, Munich, and Vienna to Italy, and in that country composed the counterpart of the above-described *Concertstück* by Weber, his *Capriccio with orchestra* in *B*. During an extended stay in Rome he wrote, in 1831, the first book of his *Songs without Words*, a series of melodically attractive pieces of a simpler form, with an often finely elaborated harmonic accompaniment, which found such general favor that he gradually composed, at the desire of the publisher (Simrock of Bonn), seven books of six numbers each. In the year 1832 he once more travelled to London *via* Paris, meeting with a most cordial reception in both places. In the following year he was appointed Music Director at Düsseldorf, and in 1835 Conductor of the Gewandhaus Concerts at Leipzig, in which latter place he now settled permanently, till called away by death in 1847. His first *Quartet* for pianoforte, violin, viola, and violoncello in *E*-minor, op. 1, is dedicated to Prince Anton of Radziwill, appearing in 1824; the second, op. 2, in *F*-minor, is dedicated to Zelter, the third, op. 3, in *B*-minor, to Goethe. Of his other Pianoforte Works the following require special mention:—*Concerto* in *G*-minor, op. 25, Leipzig, Breitkopf & Härtel, 1833; *Concerto* in *D*-minor, op. 30, same publ., 1836; *Capriccio brillant* with Orchestra, op. 22, same publ.; *2 Trios* for Pianoforte, Violin, and Violoncello, op. 49 and op. 66, same publ.; *Sonata* for Pianoforte and Violin, in *A♭*, op. 4, Leipzig, Hofmeister,

1825; *2 Sonatas* for Pianoforte and Violoncello, op. 45 and op. 58, Leipzig, Kistner; *Songs without Words,* op. 19, 30, 38, 53, 62, 67, 87, Bonn, Simrock; *Capriccio* in *F*♯-minor, op. 5, Berlin, Schlesinger; *3 Capriccios* in *A*-minor, *E*-major, and *B*♭-minor, op. 33, Breitkopf & Härtel; *6 Études* and *six Fugues,* op. 35, same publ.; *Sonata* in *E,* op. 6, Leipzig, Hofmeister; *Fantasias,* op. 14 and 15, Vienna, Mechetti: *Fantasia* in *F*♯-minor, op. 28, Bonn, Simrock; *Rondeau brillant* in *E*♭, op. 29, same publ.; *Serenade* and *Allegro giocoso,* op. 43, same publ.; *Variations* in *D* for Piano and Violoncello, op. 17, Vienna, Mechetti; *Variations sérieuses* in *F,* op. 54, same publ.; and with Moscheles' collaboration, *Duo and Variations* on a theme from *Preciosa,* for 2 Pianofortes with Orchestra.

A critical Edition of Mendelssohn's Complete Works (folio), whose several Parts are also purchasable separately, has been published by Breitkopf & Härtel; also the Pianoforte Works in cheap editions.— Edition Peters and Collection Litolff likewise contain the pianoforte works complete or separately.

Information concerning his life and labors is given by August Reissmann, "Felix Mendelssohn-Bartholdy". Berlin, Guttentag, 1867. — Highly interesting and instructive are Mendelssohn's own "Reisebriefe" of the years 1830 to 1832; also of the years 1833 to 1847 (Leipzig, H. Mendelssohn, 1864).—The Letters (Reisebriefe) have been publ. in English by Longmans & Co., London. Some other biographical works are: —

Benedict. "A Sketch of the Life and Works of the late Felix Mendelssohn-Bartholdy". 2nd ed. London, 1853; — Lampadius. "F. M. B., ein Denkmal", Engl. editions New York 1866, London 1878; — Hiller. "Mendelssohn, Letters and Recollections", etc., London, 1874, Macmillan & Co.; — Devrient. "Meine Erinnerungen an F. M. B.", English ed. London, 1869; and many others. — A study (Essay) on Mendelssohn's pianoforte style, which Hans von Bülow prefixed to his edition of Mendelssohn's Rondo capriccioso op. 14 as a Preface, is also of the highest interest.

Mendelssohn shares with Moscheles and Weber the merit of having given a more ideal tendency to **Concert and Salon Music,** earlier calculated merely for outward effect, *by endowing his attractive compositions, written in the purest pianoforte style, with a depth of meaning which everywhere reveals the amiable and well-schooled musician.* We have to name, as musicians educated directly through his teachings and intercourse with him, his sister **Fanny Hensel,** *née*

Mendelssohn-Bartholdy, whose published pianoforte compositions include the following:—3 books of *Songs without Words,* op. 2 and 6, Berlin, Bote & Bock; op. 8, Breitkopf & Härtel; and 2 books of *Mélodies pour le Piano*, op. 4 and 5, Berlin, Schlesinger. Also **J. J. H. Verhulst** (b. 1816), a talented Dutchman, down to 1886 Hofmusikdirector at the Hague;—and the Englishman **William Sterndale Bennett** (1816—1875), who began his musical studies in London under Moscheles. Having become acquainted there with Mendelssohn, he followed the latter to Germany, and until his death remained his faithful pupil and friend. He lived in London as a piano teacher in the highest circles, and in 1841 published a *Pianoforte Method* under the following title: "Classical Practice for Pianoforte Students." Of his Pianoforte Compositions, all of which show refined taste, may be mentioned *Four Concertos*, Leipzig, Kistner; *Fantasia* with Orchestra, op. 22, same publ.; *Trio* for Pianoforte, Violin, and Violoncello, op. 36, London, Cramer, Beale & Co.; *Sonata* in *F*-minor, same publ.—**Carl Reinecke** (b. 1824) was engaged in 1851 as piano teacher at the Conservatory at Cologne, went in 1854 to Barmen as Musikdirector, in 1859 to Breslau, and in 1860 was appointed Kapellmeister of the Gewandhaus Concerts, and at the same time teacher at the Conservatory. "He is an excellent conductor, an eminent composer, and an extremely fine pianist; as a Mozart player he hardly has a rival; his pianistic individuality is quietness, clearness, cleanness; he always meets with a most enthusiastic welcome on his almost yearly concert tours, especially in Scandinavia, England, the Netherlands, and Switzerland..... Of his many pianoforte pupils we need mention only Louis Maas, J. Quast, A. Winding, R. Joseffy, Dora Schirmacher, and Jeanne Becker. Reinecke's pianoforte compositions reveal throughout the refined pianist; he has published *4 Pianoforte Concertos, 1 Quintet, 1 Quartet, 6 Trios, 2 'Cello Sonatas, 4 Violin Sonatas, 1 Fantasia* for Pianoforte and Violin (op. 160), *1 Flute Sonata* (op. 167), *1 Pianoforte Sonata for 4 hands,* several *Sonatas* and *Sonatinas*, together with many minor piano works". [RIEMANN, Musik-Lexikon].—**Carl Lührs** (1824—1882) who likewise profited by Mendelssohn's instruction, has published (Berlin, Trautwein) very graceful "*Märchen*", little pieces for the pianoforte, op. 2, in two books, dedicated to the distinguished *pianiste* **Wilhelmine Clauss-Szarvady** (b. 1833).

Adolf Henselt.

As a composer nearly related to Mendelssohn, yet pursuing his own path, we must name **Adolf Henselt,** likewise noted as a highly accomplished pianoforte virtuoso. He was born at Schwabach on May 12, 1814, and received his first teaching in music from *Geheimräthin* von Flad in Munich, she having been a fellow-pupil of Weber's under the Abbé Vogler. In his seventeenth year King Ludwig of Bavaria sent him to Weimar, to continue his studies under Hummel's eye; with this master he remained, however, but eight months, travelling in 1832 to Vienna, where he studied composition under Sechter, at the same time training himself to finished virtuosity through the most assiduous practice. In 1836 at Berlin, and later at Dresden and Weimar, he awakened the admiration of his hearers in private circles, and is said to have played Weber's sonatas, in particular, with wonderful charm. In the year 1837 he played a few times in public at Berlin, Leipzig, and Dresden, and then journeyed to St. Petersburg, where he has resided since 1838 as a teacher of high standing and Court pianist. Among his carefully elaborated compositions, which are teeming with novel and characteristic pianoforte effects, the following are prominent: — two books of euphonious and melodious *Concert Études*, op. 2, Leipzig, Hofmeister, including the oft-played "Wenn ich ein Vöglein wär" in *F*♯; *12 Études de Salon,* op. 5, Breitkopf & Härtel; *Poëme d'amour,* op. 3, Berlin, Schlesinger; *Rhapsodie,* op. 4; *2 Nocturnes*, op. 6; *Pensée fugitive,* and *Scherzo*, op. 8 and 9, Breitkopf & Härtel; *Romance,* op. 10, same publ.; *Variations de concert,* op. 11, same publ.; *Frühlingslied,* op. 15; *Tableau musical,* op. 16; *2 Impromptus*, op. 7 and 17; *Romances sans paroles*, op. 18; *Toccatina*, op. 25; *Valse,* op. 30; *Ballade, Nocturne,* and *Chant sans paroles*, op. 31, 32, 33; *1 Trio* for Pianoforte, Violin, and Violoncello, op. 24; and a grandly developed, impassioned *Concerto* in *F*-minor, op. 16, Breitkopf & Härtel, which must be regarded as belonging to the most valuable works of pianoforte literature. We must also notice his *Exercices préparatoires,* Berlin, Schlesinger: *Illusion perdue,* op. 34, same publ.; *Valse mélancolique*, op. 36, Breslau, Hainauer; *Souvenir de Varsovie,* Valse bril lante, Leipzig, Hofmeister; *Chant sans paroles,* Leipzig, Stoll; *Lullaby* (*G*♭), Vienna, Mechetti.

b. France.

The last eminent clavier-player and organist of the earlier French school was the distinguished theoretician **J. P. Rameau** (b. 1685 in Dijon, d. 1764 in Paris). Under his pupil **Claude Balbastre** (1729 to 1799) the former serious clavier style degenerated into complete shallowness. The compositions published by the latter at Paris — *Pièces de clavecin;* Quatre suites de Noëls avec variations et Quatuors pour le clavecin avec accompagnement de deux violons, une basse et deux cors ad libitum — are full of incorrect and trashy phrases. But his organ-playing, in particular the *Noëls,* Christmas pieces with all manner of variations, always drew such crowds to St. Roch, and later to the cathedral of Paris, at which churches he was engaged as organist, that the Archbishop was several times obliged (1762—1766) to prohibit his performing the midnight masses.

When Mozart and his sister visited Paris in the year 1763, the two most prominent clavier-players there were **Schobert** (1720—1768) and **Eckard** (1734—1809). The former, a native of Strassburg, in 1760 entered the service of the Prince of Conti at Paris as harpsichordist. In France, Holland, and England he was extolled as the most original composer of his time; he is said, in particular, to have been the first to endow the orchestral accompaniment of his Concertos with a peculiar charm, and also to have introduced a style of clavier-playing quite different from that before in vogue. Schobert, whose given name cannot now be ascertained (on the title-pages of his works only the family name is to be found), seems to have been little known in Germany, although it must be said in praise of his compositions that they were supplied with the most graceful melodies, and that their expression reveals now romantic melancholy, and now animated and attractive brilliancy. He left *17 Sonatas* for Clavier and Violin; *11 Sonatas* for Clavier, Violin, and Violoncello; *3 Quartets* for Clavier, 2 Violins, and Violoncello; *6 Symphonies* for Clavier with Violin and 2 Horns; *6 Clavier Concertos;* and 4 books of *Sonatas for Clavier Solo;* they were printed as op. 1 to 18, first at Paris, then at Amsterdam by Hummel, and in London after his death. One of the clavier sonatas was published by Haffner in Nuremberg in the *Œuvres mêlées,* Partie XII. — His contemporary **Johann Gottfried Eckard** was born of poor parents at Augsburg, and early displayed a great fondness for music. Without instruction from a teacher, he fitted himself through unremitting industry to execute the most difficult pieces in Bach's Well-tempered Clavichord. The talented Eckard was induced by a friend, the organ and clavier-maker **Johann Andreas Stein** of later celebrity, to bear him company on a journey to Paris in 1758. Eckard, who was also a skillful draughtsman, earned his living there at first by portrait-painting, and employed the nighttime for the prosecution of his musical studies. This untiring zeal did not fail of reward; his clavier-playing soon found such favor that he decided upon remaining permanently in Paris. Andreas Stein returned to Augsburg; his pianoforte was subsequently (1777) preferred by Mozart to all other instruments of its class. Eckard published in Paris *6 Clavier Sonatas* (1765), also two *Sonatas,* op. 2, and "Menuet d'Exaudet, varié pour le clavecin", and died there in 1809 as one of the first clavier-players of his time. Schubart, in his "Ideen zu einer Aesthetik der Tonkunst", devotes an extended article to him, writing among other things: "Eckard does not write with the fire of a Schobert, but makes amends for this by greater profundity. Rousseau, the profound thinker and musician, ranks Eckard with the foremost clavier-players of the world. — The way in which Eckard attained perfection is well deserving of notice. He first selected a harpsichord, in order to practice the simple contours and to strengthen his hand: for the hand tires much sooner on a fortepiano or clavichord. Only after some years did Eckard play on a fortepiano, and finally on the clavichord, in order to endow his sketch with body, tone, and life. Thus Eckard has become the great man, whom France and Germany admire in him."

The modern French Pianoforte school, however, which teaches according to a fixed method, and in which a certain style in compositions and interpretations is set up as a traditionary model, owes its origin to a pupil of C. Ph. E. Bach, its founder being **Nicolaus Joseph Hüllmandel** (b. in Strassburg, 1751, d. in London, 1823), an artist, like the preceding, but little known in Germany. After travels in Italy, this distinguished clavier-player, who is likewise described as an extremely amiable person, came in 1776 to Paris, where the way was paved for his favorable reception by several compositions of his, already published there (*6 Sonatas* pour Clavecin, Violon, et Basse, op. 1, 1760). In a short time he rose to be one of the leading and most popular clavier-teachers; he was invited into the highest circles, published several clavier-works (op. 1 to 11, Boyer-Nadermann & Sieber; *Petits airs faciles et progressifs,* op. 5, Offenbach, André), and in 1787 married a wealthy heiress, who prevailed upon him to withdraw completely from the world of artists.

The Conservatory of Music at Paris was opened in the year 1792, and one of the finest of the pupils trained by Hüllmandel, **Hyacinthe Jadin** (b. 1769 at Versailles), was chosen as head of the department of piano-playing. Among his compositions some *Pianoforte Concertos* (Paris, Michel Ozy, Erard & Pleyel) were very popular at the time; but they were already written under the influence of Ignaz Pleyel's works, which made an unprecedented sensation from 1785 to 1795. Hyacinthe Jadin died in 1802, and in the same year his brother and pupil **Louis Emanuel Jadin** entered the Conservatory as professor. This latter, the composer of 39 operas and other considerable works, was also the first to bring into vogue those abominable botches, the **Mélanges** and **Potpourris**, wherein "favorite melodies" are senselessly linked together by some few inane measures for the purpose of tickling the ears of dilettanti.

The pianoforte school of the Paris Conservatory received its most important impetus from **Louis Adam.** He was born near Strassburg in 1758, early developed himself to an able pianist through the study of the works of Sebastian and Emanuel Bach, Scarlatti, and Schobert, and came to Paris in 1775 as a music teacher. Here he also became familiar with Mozart's and Clementi's compositions, and exercised a highly beneficial influence in developing the taste of his numerous pupils by his preference for the substantial works of the above masters. In 1797 he was appointed professor of the Conservatory, where he turned out a goodly number of noted pianists, among whom F. Kalkbrenner, F. Chaulieu, Henri Le Moine, and Hérold are especially prominent. After a service of forty-five years he was pensioned in 1843, and died in 1848 at the age of 90. Of his compositions, the variations on "Le Roi Dagobert" were for some time a special favorite with pianists. Adam rendered a great service *through a more definite regulation of the fingering,* by a work written with L. W. Lachnith's co-operation: "Méthode ou principe générale du doigté pour le Forte-piano, suivie d'une collection complète de tous les traits possibles avec le doigté", Paris, Sieber, 1798, and his "Méthode nouvelle pour le Piano à l'usage des élèves du conservatoire" proved of such practical utility, that from 1802 to 1831 it ran through five editions in Paris.

To fill the position of a pianoforte teacher at the Paris Conservatory, made vacant by the decease of Hyacinthe Jadin in 1802, a competition *(concours)* was arranged, for which Cherubini, then one of the Inspectors, composed several fugues. **Louis Barthélemi Pradher** (Pradère) (b. 1781 in Paris, d. 1843 in Gray) was so fortunate as to obtain the position, as he not only played the above difficult compositions fluently at sight, but also proved himself a thorough virtuoso by performing a concerto by Dussek. After laboring 25 years at the Conservatory, he went to Toulouse, where he became Director of a similar musical institute. Among the pupils trained by him in Paris, the brothers Henri and Jacques Herz, Dubois, Rosellen, and Hünten must be mentioned as most distinguished.

The élève of the Conservatory already alluded to, **Friedrich Kalkbrenner**, was destined to spread throughout musical Europe the fame of the French Pianoforte School, which during its brief existence had attained to such encouraging results. He was born at Cassel in 1784, and received his first musical instruction from his father. The latter assumed the post of chorus-master of the grand opera at Paris in 1798, the son then continuing his studies at the Conservatory. In pianoforte-playing he was taught by Adam, in composition somewhat later by Cattel, and made so decided progress under both, that he won the first prize awarded for the two branches named as early as 1801. In 1803 his father sent him to Vienna, that his development might be promoted by the brilliant performances of Clementi, then sojourning in that place; on his return to Paris in 1806 the brilliant distinction of his playing rendered him one of the most highly esteemed teachers. The presence of Dussek, who was engaged in Paris from 1808 to 1812 as master of concerts to the Prince of Talleyrand, and whose sonorous pianoforte works found great applause, had an extremely happy influence on the further perfecting of Kalbrenner's style of playing and composing, and on the prosperity of the French pianoforte school as a whole. From 1814 to 1823 Kalkbrenner dwelt in England. His finished performances were received there with demonstrative applause, and the numerous brilliant compositions afterwards published by him were eagerly sought for and much played. At that time the so-called **chiroplast** or **hand-guide**, an apparatus* invented by **Johann Bernhard Logier** to aid

* Two parallel rails attached in front of the keyboard, between which the hands were free to move to the right and left, but were constrained to remain at a proper distance from the keys.

in gaining a correct position of the hands in piano-playing, was in great vogue in London, and in the year 1817 Logier united with Samuel Webbe and Kalkbrenner to found an Academy in which, besides piano-playing, the theory of music was also taught according to an easily comprehended method. Here, in various classes, all pupils possessed of an equal degree of skill were taught simultaneously. This method was brought to Germany by Dr. Franz Stöpel, and taught since then in the institute of Adele Dorn at Berlin, and in that of Louis Wandelt at Breslau, although not without many changes and improvements.

In 1821 Moscheles had also settled in London, and his powerful and finished style did not remain without influence on Kalkbrenner's performances. The latter, however, bent all his energies to the greatest possible perfection of his technical skill, and calculated his compositions purely for placing the same in the best light; whereas Moscheles continually strove to render the subjects of his compositions interesting, and through his virtuosity to lend them the most living expression. In 1823 and 1824 Kalkbrenner gave concerts in Frankfort, Leipzig, Dresden, Berlin, Prague, and Vienna, and was received everywhere with loud applause, even beside Moscheles, then making like professional tours. He then returned to Paris, where he became a partner in Pleyel's Fortepiano Factory, while at the same time ranking as the head of the modern French pianoforte school, whose foremost merit is the precept, *to avoid all exertion of the arm in playing, and to concentrate the entire strength in the fingers, which are to be equally developed in both hands.* Kalkbrenner not only required passages in thirds and sixths to be executed by the right or left hand, but added to the same the higher octave of the lower tone; he introduced effective double and triple trills, and was the first to write extended compositions for the left hand alone, which he played with finished ease. His op. 42 is *1 Sonate pour la main gauche principale* (Leipzig, Kistner); we also find a four-part fugue in his *Méthode pour apprendre le Piano à l'aide du Guide-mains;* contenant les principes de la musique; un système complet de doigté; des règles sur l'expression, etc., op. 108, dedicated to all conservatories of music in Europe (same publ.). Among his pupils Madame Pleyel, in particular, is distinguished as the finest French *pianiste.* On the very pinnacle of virtuosity, Kalkbrenner aroused the greatest enthusiasm in the years 1833, 1834, and 1836 on his trips to Hamburg, Berlin, Brussels, and other places. But with his compositions, the majority of which are devoted solely to outward effect, begin the series of those meaningless salon pieces, which blunt the taste for loftier music, and whose titles unhappily yet fill most pages in the catalogues of certain publishing houses. Kalkbrenner died in Enghien near Paris in 1849. Of his four *Pianoforte Concertos*, op. 61, 85, 107, and 127, the first, in *D*-minor, has found most favor. Among his other works we note *Grand Concerto* pour 2 Pianos in *C*, op. 125; *Gage d'amitié*, op. 66; *Les charmes de Berlin*, op. 70, also op. 101 and 102; *Rondeaux brillants* with orchestral accompaniment; *Fantasias* and *Variations* with Orchestra, op. 72, 83, 90, and 113; *Sonatas* for Pianoforte solo, op. 1, dedicated to L. Adam; op. 28, to J. B. Cramer; op. 48, Cherubini; also op. 4, 13, 35, and 56; *1 Grande Sonate* for 4 hands, op. 79; *Grand Duo* for 2 Pianos, op. 128; *Études, Caprices, Fugues*, etc., op. 20, 54, 88, 104, 125; a large number of pieces with accompaniment of one or more instruments, and numerous *Fantasias* and *Variations* for Pianoforte solo.

The decay of this later French school of brilliant Pianoforte-playing begins with the compositions of the above-mentioned pupils of Pradher (Herz, Rosellen, and Hünten), which are for the most part characterless, being calculated merely for the most striking pianoforte effects attainable, or for shallow prettiness, and which remained for a time in vogue. These three fashionable composers and their imitators at first tickled the already *blasé* palates of the pianists with novel and piquant difficulties, and then contented themselves with setting the sweetest tidbits before the musical gourmands, finally quite giving up the ghost at the birth of the Romantic School, on the appearance of Chopin's soul-stirring tone-poems.

The first-named, **Heinrich Herz,** was born at Vienna in 1806, came early to Coblenz, took his first piano-lessons there from the organist Daniel Hünten, and in his eighth year already executed Hummel's Variations op. 8 ("sopra una canzonetta nationale austriaca") with applause at a public concert. His father sent him in 1816 to the Conservatory at Paris, where he soon became Pradher's favorite pupil. In the very next examinations Herz was to shine as a pianist, when an attack of the measles supervened. But four days before the *concours* he gathered up his strength, began his practicing afresh, and carried off the first prize at the competition by his brilliant performance of the 12th Concerto by Dussek and an Étude by Clementi. In the year 1818 he issued his first compositions: *Air tyrolien varié*, and *Rondeau alla Cosacca*, which were at once favorably received.

A great influence on his later pianoforte works, and also on the finishing of his style of playing, was exerted by the concerts given by Moscheles at Paris in 1820 and crowned with triumphant success. Thenceforward it was Herz's ambition to surpass that master, if possible, in virtuosity, and to lend more grace and brilliancy to his own compositions; while Moscheles after that time evidently strove to endow his compositions and performances with greater dignity and deeper meaning. Herz's Pianoforte Compositions, for which the publishers paid unheard-of prices, were the reigning favorites during some 15 years; and his concerts, too, especially those undertaken in company with the eminent violin virtuoso Lafont in Germany (1831), were attended by the liveliest applause. To the co-operation of these two virtuosi the pleasing composition "Duo et Variations concertans pour Piano et Violon sur la romance *C'est une larme*, par Lafont et Henri Herz", owes its origin. In 1834 Herz visited London, Dublin and Edinburgh, his easy and elegant style of playing earning him ovations, particularly in the last two cities. One of his most effective pieces at the time was the *Variations de bravoure* sur la romance de Joseph in *C*, op. 20, in which among other things the theme is executed in leaps, the extremes of which are two octaves apart. In the year 1824 he took an interest in the pianoforte factory of Klepfer of Paris, and subsequently established one of his own, which has since then turned out excellent concert grands. His earlier compositions, like the three grand *Concertos*, op. 34, 74, and 87, also the *Rondeau brillant* dedicated to Moscheles, op. 11, often afford the player interesting and fiery passages and effective difficulties; whereas the later ones—excepting the *Études*, op. 100 (from his *Méthode de Piano)*, 119, 151, 152, and 153—consist of meagre *Fantasias*, *Variations*, and other worthless amateur-pieces.

Henri Bertini (b. 1798 in London), who made Paris his permanent residence from 1821, followed a loftier tendency in his compositions. He appears in the same as a weak reflection of Hummel; but his numerous instruction books, in particular,—*Études progressives, élémentaires et de perfection*, arranged in the Berlin edition of Schlesinger progressively according to difficulty, as op. 84, 100, 101, 86, 97, 29, 32, 66, and 94—have permanent value as *practice-pieces* and for a time were preferred to all others by thorough teachers. Bertini died in 1876.

The pianoforte works published by Hünten & Rosellen, the abovementioned fellow-pupils of Herz, under their name, sank to the merest factory work, although when issued they went off so rapidly that the publishers paid higher prices for single sheets of the same, than the complete larger works of Beethoven had brought. The inventor of such trash in Paris seems to have been **Henri Karr** (b. 1784), the father of the noted writer Alphonse Karr. N. l'Étendart, regarded as the best élève of the organist Balbâtre earlier alluded to, gave Henri Karr instruction in music and recommended him to the Brothers Érard, the celebrated pianoforte makers, as a skilful player for showing off the instruments in their ware-rooms. He was engaged by them for 2000 francs, and in the publishing house of the same firm appeared his first and better compositions (*Sonate pour Piano*, op. 1, etc.). These having gained a certain vogue, however, he gave up his position, and now supplied *to order, after given patterns and specified melodies*, over *200 Fantasias, Divertissements, Rondeaux, Bagatelles,* and similar stuff, which were eagerly taken by dilettanti in the decade from 1811 to 1821. After that time, however, a rival arose in the person of **Franz Hünten** (b. 1793 in Coblenz, died there in 1878), who entered the Paris Conservatory in 1819, and whose *Variations militaires à 4 mains*, op. 12, a childish imitation of Moscheles' variations on the Alexander March, had such extraordinary success, that in the course of time the publishers fairly besieged him with orders for similar *divertissements*, which, though easy to play, sounded brilliant in the ears of amateurs. With the great demand, the price of the article also rose; and Hünten finally received for a book of 8 or 10 printed pages the outrageous price of 1500 to 2000 francs. From 1835 he lived in Coblenz on his income, and his fellow-pupil **Henri Rosellen** (b. 1811 in Paris) then continued the same lucrative business, for which, however, several competitors had come forward, such as J. Ascher, Friedrich Burgmüller, H. Ravina, Henri Cramer, and Charles Voss, whose works are even surpassed in worthlessness by the Fantasias and Potpourris of Ferdinand Beyer, C. T. Brunner, J. B. Duvernoy, H. Martin, Theodor Oesten, etc. The occupation with such brainless productions of fashion dulls the sense of the pupil for all more serious and valuable work, without furthering his technical skill in any way whatever; an able and conscientious teacher will therefore not require the pupils committed to his charge to kill their time with the same.

Moritz Hauptmann's talented pupil **Norbert Burgmüller** (1810—1836) must not be confounded with the above-mentioned Friedrich Burgmüller; but few of the inspired compositions of the former have been published. Among his pianoforte works, op. 1, *Concerto* with orchestra in *F*♯-minor, and op. 16, *Polonaise,* were issued by Fried. Kistner, Leipzig; — op. 8, *Sonata* in *F*-minor, a Romance from the same, with portrait, and *Rhapsodie,* op. 13, by Fr. Hofmeister.

The number of those pianoforte amateurs who seek and esteem only brilliant compositions for their instrument, which promise to exhibit their skill in the strongest light, is very considerable. The way marked out by Henri Herz and Sigismund Thalberg, lying wholly within the domain of virtuosity, has therefore been trodden by many, among whom may be named **Antoine de Kontski** (b. 1817 in Cracow), well known as a brilliant player through his professional tours throughout Europe, whose pianoforte works, of a most conceited and affected style, have reached the number of 200, among them *Le reveil du lion,* op. 115; *Le trille du diable,* op 53; *Fleurs mélodiques,* op. 77; *Feuilles volantes,* op. 139; furthermore **Emile Prudent** (1820—1863), whose smooth and clean playing was much praised in Paris, and who published among other things the salon pieces *Le reveil des fées,* op. 41; *Les najades,* op. 45; *Études de genre,* op. 16.

The compositions of **Karl Wehle** (b. 1825, d. 1883), a talented pupil of J. Proksch, who lived for the most part in Paris, are of a pleasing and unassuming character, and are favorites on account of their elegant and easily mastered pianoforte style; we note *Poëme d'amour,* op. 6; *Ballade,* op. 11; *Sérénade napolitaine,* op. 31; *Marche cosaque,* op. 37.—**Wilhelm Krüger** (b. 1823 in Stuttgart, d. 1883 in that city) also held for several years a distinguished position in Paris as a pianist and composer for his instrument; of his larger pianoforte works we mention the *Concerto* in *G,* op. 42, dedicated to the King of Württemberg; a grand *Sonata* in *C,* op. 100, dedicated to Duke Ernest of Coburg-Gotha; and the interesting salon pieces *La gazelle,* op. 14; *La harpe éolienne,* op. 25; *Chanson du gondolier,* op. 40; *Ménuet symphonique,* op. 56; *Presto impromptu,* op. 57; *Marche nocturne,* op. 96; *Zigeunermarsch,* op. 104; *La coupe d'or,* op. 110; and many others. He likewise edited a Complete Edition of the Clavier Works of G. F. Handel for the publishing house of Cotta, Stuttgart.

VI. The romantic Style.

François Frédéric Chopin.

Toward the close of the year 1831, when the Polish revolution had excited all minds to feverish agitation, and the wanton carnival of the authors of the dazzling, but meaningless virtuoso-pieces just described was at its height, **Chopin**, then twenty-one, entered the gay and brilliant salons of Paris, pale and ethereal as an apparition from another world. Here, invited to try one of those Pleyel pianofortes which he later preferred to all others on account of "their veiled, silvery tone", he drew from it, in the pathetic crystal tones of the harmonica, songs of the sufferings, the stifled complaints, the high-soaring hopes of his people. In the hall reigned the silence of death. None dared breathe freely. Not till the last tones of his soul-stirring elegies died away, was he greeted with a burst of enthusiasm, which was decisive for the future position of the young Pole in Paris. He was immediately welcomed into the circles of the many high Polish families then in the French capital, and his numerous lady pupils were as extravagantly fond of their so amiable instructor as of his romantico-poetical tone-poems, that opened a new field of music. Franz Liszt, who after Chopin's untimely death dedicated such an exquisite tribute* to his memory, was one of the first to recognize his high significance for musical art. For this reason Chopin loved him in particular, choosing this friend, so congenial to him in art and by nature, before all others as the interpreter of his characteristic compositions. The leaders in art and literature did him homage, and Liszt once found assembled in his room, dimly lighted only by the candles on the piano, the *spirituelle* Mme. George Sand, the saddest of all humorists, Heine, the head of the romantic school of painting, the daring Eugène Delacroix, and the venerable Niemcewicz, together with Meyerbeer, Bellini, Adolphe Nourrit, Hiller, and the latter's best pupil and fast friend Gutmann, all intent upon listening to his marvellous playing. Chopin played unwillingly, and

---

* F. Chopin par Liszt. Paris, M. Escudier; nouvelle édition, 1877, Leipzig, Breitkopf & Härtel.

therefore but seldom, in public concerts; but in the *salon* his playing had an indescribable charm. He phrased and accented his compositions in the freest manner, and in the earlier works often indicated this by **„tempo rubato"**. The rhythm then wavered, sinking and rising "like a flame agitated by the breath". He was unwearying in the endeavor to transmit his peculiar style of rendering to his pupils — ladies, for the most part — and expected that the player of the pieces published later would in himself be able to feel and apply "the rule of this irregularity of measure" even without that indication.

François Fréderic Chopin, whose family was of French origin, was born on March 1, 1809, in Zelazowa near Warsaw. At the age of nine the boy, from childhood nervously weak and infirm, began his musical studies under an old Bohemian musician named Zwiny, who admired Sebastian Bach's works above all others. Prince Anton Radziwill later took the talented youth under his protection, and cared for the completion of his training; his tender, emotional playing rendered him a welcome guest in the first Polish families. The theory of music was taught him by Elsner, the Director of the Conservatory at Warsaw; through short excursions to Berlin, Dresden, and Prague he profited by hearing practical virtuosi, until he went to Vienna in 1831, where he made his début in concerts of his own. The correspondent of the Leipzig "Allgemeine musikalische Zeitung" (No. 46, Nov. 18, 1829) then already regarded him as one of the most remarkable meteors in the musical heavens, and emphasized as traits of true genius his masterly skill, his delicate touch, and the melancholy tinge of his finely shaded interpretations. On account of the Polish revolution breaking out meantime, he prolonged his stay in Vienna, giving his farewell concert in 1831, after which he proposed to make a brief visit to Paris, proceeding thence to London. But in Paris his playing and compositions met with such favor, that he resolved to remain there, and dwelt in that city, with but short interruptions, until his death. In the year 1837 he showed such alarming symptoms of lung-disease, that physicians advised an extended sojourn beneath softer skies. He therefore betook himself to Majorca, accompanied by George Sand, at that time his fondest admirer. He returned refreshed to Paris, but as early as 1840 the symptoms reappeared, and the disease took a highly dangerous turn in 1846 and 1847. Nevertheless, after the Paris revolution of 1848, he decided upon a trip to London, where he appeared in public several times, and arranged a final concert for the assistance of the Poles. On his return to Paris in the same year he once more played in a concert; on the 17th of October, 1849, he died there, soothed by the tones of a psalm by Marcello, sung at the request of the dying man by his favorite pupil the Countess Delphine Potocka, so distinguished for her wit, talent, and beauty.

Chopin published one *Pianoforte Concerto* in *E*-minor, op. 11, and another in *F*-minor, op. 21; the latter, the Adagio of which he was especially fond of and often played, is dedicated to the Countess Potocka just mentioned. His other compositions, in which, foremostly, the romantic tone-poet struck chords stirring the inmost soul, thus opening the way for a new style of music filled with a living spirit, are the following: *3 Sonatas* for Pianoforte solo, op. 4, 35, and 58 (the movement in the second entitled "Marche Funèbre" was performed at his funeral); *1 Sonata,* op. 65, and *1 Polonaise,* op. 3, for Pianoforte and Violoncello; *1 Trio* for Pianoforte, Violin and Violoncello, op. 8; *1 grand Polonaise,* interrupted by a *Mazurka,* in *F♯*-minor; *Polonaises,* op. 22, 26, 40, 53, and 61; *3 Rondeaux,* op. 1, 5, and 16; *4 Ballades,* op. 23, 38, 47, and 52; eight books of *Nocturnes,* op. 9, 15, 27, 32, 37, 48, 55, and 62, which in all probability owe their origin to the earlier mentioned compositions of the same class by Field, this inventor of the same being in Paris at the very time when Chopin arrived there; a set of *24 Preludes* — precious gems, in which the whole poetic nature of Chopin shines and sparkles in most diverse iridescence; two equally important series of fantastic *Études,* op. 10 and 25; *Fantasia* on Polish melodies, with orchestral accompaniment, op. 13; *Krakoviak* with Orchestra, op. 14; *Bolero,* op. 19; *3 Scherzi,* op. 20, 31, and 39; *Impromptus,* op. 29 and 36; *Tarantella,* op. 43; *Allegro de Concert,* op. 46 and 51; *Fantasia,* op. 49; *Valses,* op. 18, 31, 34, 42, and 64; *Variations,* op. 2 and 12; and finally 11 series of *Mazurkas,* op. 6, 7, 17, 24, 30, 33, 41, 50, 56, 59, and 63. — Chopin's Works have been published in a critically revised Complete Edition (folio) in 14 Volumes, which are also sold separately, by Breitkopf & Härtel. The same firm has also published his Pianoforte Compositions in 10 cheap octavo volumes, stiff paper covers, red. [Since the year 1879, on the last day of which the copyright in Chopin's works expired, a great number of complete and selected editions have appeared. As both the best and earliest of these must be mentioned the Complete Edition edited by CARL KLINDWORTH (first published in Russia and afterwards by Bote & Bock of Berlin), in which, through a careful revision and comparison of the French, German, and Polish editions, together with the aid of Liszt's personal recollections, a wellnigh perfect text, and most excellent directions for phrasing and fingering, are supplied. Other editions have appeared, edited by Hermann Scholtz (Peters), Th. Kullak, Mertke, and others. **O. L.**]

The first **Polonaises** to portray in colors both attractive and true to nature the character of that people, to whom they owe their name, were composed by Count **Michael Kleophas Oginski**; the most celebrated of the same, the so-called *Death Polonaise* in *F*,* was written in 1793. These pieces created such a general sensation, that in 1820 Oginski published a collection of the same for the benefit of the Poor-house in Wilna, which netted the sum of 10,000 rubles. A Selection of 14 of these Polonaises has been issued in Collection Litolff (L. Köhler). The *Kosciuszko Polonaise*, the peer of the Marseillaise in its exciting effect (Hamburg, Boehme), was composed in 1794 during the uprising led by that hero. Equally characteristic with these, Chopin's Polonaises also breathe, now a profound, elegiac mournfulness, a smile effacing in melancholy, and now an inflexible pride, an indomitable courage.

Chopin, however, left us the most faithful and animated pictures of his nation in the **Mazurkas**, which form finished master-pieces of their class. Here he stands forth in his full originality as the head of the romantic school of music; in them his novel and alluring melodic and harmonic progressions are even more surprising than in his larger compositions. They are strikingly described by Liszt as follows: "Some portray foolhardy gaiety in the sultry and oppressive air of a ball on the eve of a battle; one hears the low sighs of parting, whose sobs are stifled by sharp rhythms of the dance; others betray the grief of the sorely anxious soul amid the festivities, whose tumult is unable to drown the profound woe of the heart; others again show the fears, premonitions, and struggles of a broken heart devoured by jealousy, sorrowing over its loss, but repressing the curse. Now we are surrounded by a swirling frenzy, pierced by an ever-recurring, palpitating melody like the anxious beating of a rejected and breaking heart; and anon distant trumpet-calls resound, like dim memories of by-gone fame".

---

* The first of the *"Four National Polonaises"* by Oginski, Berlin, Schlesinger.

A spirited portrait of the gifted composer is given by MORITZ KARASOWSKI in the work: Friedrich Chopin. Sein Leben, seine Werke und Briefe. 2 Vols., 1877. Dresden, Ries.

Robert Schumann.

In France, Franz Liszt had come forward as the enthusiastic champion, both by word and deed, of the neo-romantic music which was to seal the doom of the loftily affected pianoforte literature then holding sway. In Germany, this fresh and luxuriant growth, exhibiting at once the freer form corresponding to its novel conception, and unprecedentedly bold harmonies and modulations, found an enthusiastic admirer and defender in **Robert Schumann.** In the year 1834 he founded, in company with Friedrich Wieck, Ludwig Schunke, and Julius Knorr, the "Neue Zeitschrift für Musik" in Leipzig, and determined to take the field most energetically against the constantly spreading *Philisterthum* (narrow and prosaic pedantry), and to reinstate the dethroned poetry of art. Through this periodical, which speedily found general favor, and was edited from 1835 to 1845 by himself, Schumann was the first to call the attention of Germany to the compositions of Chopin, to whom he felt irresistibly drawn; and under the names of Eusebius, Florestan, and Meister Raro he scourged the earlier and more recent insipid pattern-work, while elucidating the inspired compositions of the older masters and their ambitious followers in forceful phrase appropriate to the matter under discussion.

Schumann was born at Zwickau on June 8, 1810, and showed from earliest youth a decided inclination to and talent for music. At the desire of his parents he studied law at Leipzig in 1828, and at Heidelberg in 1829, but in the ensuing year already resolved to devote himself entirely to music. He proceeded to Leipzig in order to profit by the instruction of the excellent pianoforte teacher **Friedrich Wieck** (1785—1873); the latter took him into his home, and Schumann thus became the daily companion of the then eleven-year old daughter of the house, **Clara Wieck** (b. 1819 in Leipzig). At the same time he began his studies in composition under Heinrich Dorn, then likewise dwelling in Leipzig, to which he soon turned his exclusive attention, an experiment to which he had subjected his left hand, in order to widen the stretch of the same, having resulted so unfortunately, that it was crippled and rendered incapable of further piano-playing. His first compositions, *Thème sur le nom Abegg varié pour le Pianoforte*, op. 1. (Leipzig, Kistner), and *Papillons pour le Pianoforte*, op. 2 (ditto), were written in Heidelberg; after these, Fr. Hofmeister of Leipzig published *Studies for the Pianoforte* after Caprices by Paganini, op. 3; *Intermezzi per il Pianoforte*, op. 4, and somewhat later *Impromptus* on a theme by Clara Wieck, op. 5. In 1833 Schumann contracted an intimate friendship with the distinguished pianist **Ludwig Schunke** (b. 1810 at Cassel), who came to Leipzig from Stuttgart, among whose published works for the pianoforte we note an *Allegro passionato*, op. 6, and *1 Rondo brillant*, op. 11, and to whom Schumann dedicated *1 Toccata* in *C* (Leipzig, Hofmeister). But in the very next year the unhappy end of this friend, who threw himself out of a window in Paris, caused him the sharpest grief.

Schumann had styled the like-minded co-workers on his critical sheet the "Davidsbündler;" this name he also gave to his op. 6, at first issued as the work of "Florestan and Eusebius", but in later editions under his own name (publ. by J. Schuberth & Co., Leipzig). The humoristic pieces also belonging to this period, entitled *Carneval, Scènes Mignonnes sur 4 notes*, op. 9 (Leipzig, Breitkopf & Härtel), have as a Finale the playfully mocking "March of the *Davidsbündler* against the Philistines", written in $^3/_4$ time. The notes given beneath the title, *a es* (*e*♭) *c h* (*b*), and *as* (*a*♭) *c h* (*b*), spell the name of the birthplace (Asch) of his first youthful flame, to whom he dedicated his op. 8, *Allegro pour le Pianoforte* in *B*-minor (Leipzig, Rob. Friese).

In his earlier compositions Schumann had followed the ingenuously warm-hearted tone of Weber and Mendelssohn; but in the pianoforte works published from 1835 to 1840 an original vein is struck. His themes become more serious and pregnant, their development fuller and more exciting. Beethoven and Schubert had proposed a new theory of modulation, and Chopin, by a peculiar employment of chromatic intervals and the greatest diversity of suspensions and retardations, had called into being means of expression not yet assimilated in the theory of thorough-bass. Impressionable for all extensions in the theory of his art, Schumann not only used the freedom won by his predecessors, but himself added new harmonies, modulations, and rhythms to the common stock of harmony and metre. In the full flower of youth, his heart aglow with love for his Clara, he produced the following momentous Pianoforte Compositions: Three grand

Sonatas, op. 11 in *F*♯-minor, op. 14 in *F*-minor, and op. 22 in *G*-minor, which he dedicated to Clara Wieck, Moscheles, and Henriette Vogt, a gifted pupil of Ludwig Berger; the first publ. by Kistner, the second by J. Schuberth & Co., and the third by Breitkopf & Härtel of Leipzig; *Fantasiestücke,* op. 12, Breitkopf & Härtel; *Études en forme de Variations,* op. 13, a fine work dedicated to Sterndale Bennett, Leipzig, J. Schuberth & Co.; *Kreisleriana,* op. 16, Leipzig 1839, G. Heinze — adventurous scenes of soul-stirring pathos, dedicated to Chopin, and revealing the full depth of our composer's emotional life; *Fantasie,* op. 17, Breitkopf & Härtel — dedicated to Franz Liszt, and instinct with an irresistible romantic attraction and hot-glowing passion; *Novelletten,* op. 21, Breitkopf & Härtel; *Nachtstücke,* op. 23, Vienna, Spina; *Faschingsschwank,* op. 26, ditto, animated scenes and situations, ingeniously and delicately wrought out in the most manifold colors and motliest succession. Finally there still belong to this period the *Kinderscenen,* easy pieces for the pianoforte, op. 15, Leipzig, Breitkopf & Härtel, which was the first of his compositions to be understood and appreciated in wider circles.

Clara Wieck made her first professional tours through Germany in 1836 to 1838, and her spirited playing everywhere received the most flattering applause. The degree of Doctor of Philosophy having been bestowed on Schumann in 1840, she became his wife, and in 1844 they undertook a journey to St. Petersburg and Moscow, in which cities both the wife's playing and the husband's compositions met with a most favorable reception. On returning to Leipzig, Schumann entrusted the editorship of the Neue Zeitschrift für Musik to Franz Brendel's hands; it had fulfilled its mission, "it had set a dam in the way of mechanical imitation and easy frivolity, and pioneered the way for a poetically spiritualized, earnestly striving tendency of art; Schumann had no further reason for wielding his shining critical weapons against Philistines or fools". (A. W. Ambros).

From 1839 to 1849 he produced the following compositions, to be numbered among his chief works: *Quintet* for Pianoforte, 2 Violins, Viola, and Violoncello, in *E*♭, op. 44, Breitkopf & Härtel, dedicated to Clara Schumann; *Andante and Variations* for 2 Pianofortes, in *B*♭, op. 46, ditto; *Quartet* for Pianoforte, Violin, Viola, and Violoncello, op. 47, in *E*♭; *Studies and Sketches* for the Pedal-Pianoforte in canon-form, op. 56 and 58, Leipzig, F. Whistling; *6 Fugues* on the name of Bach, op. 60, Leipzig, Gustav Heinze; *Trio* for Pianoforte, Violin, and Violoncello, op. 63 in *D*-minor, Breitkopf & Härtel;

Album für die Jugend, 55 Piano-pieces for Small or Grown Players, op. 68, Leipzig, J. Schuberth & Co.; *Adagio and Allegro* for Pianoforte and Horn, op. 70, Leipzig, Kistner; *4 Fugues,* dedicated to Carl Reinecke, op. 72, Leipzig, Whistling; *Fantasiestücke* for Pianoforte and Clarinet, op. 73, Cassel, Luckhard; and four *Marches* dated 1849, op. 76, Leipzig, Whistling, which are eminently noteworthy as fiery, forceful, and sonorous pianoforte pieces.

In the year 1843 the Conservatory of Music at Leipzig was founded, and the direction of the same entrusted to Mendelssohn. At the instance of the latter, his friend Schumann accepted a position in that institution as teacher; but on Mendelssohn's departure for Berlin in the ensuing year, Schumann also left Leipzig, settling at first in Dresden, and making a professional journey in 1847 to Prague and Vienna. The post of Town Music Director at Düsseldorf, which he assumed in 1850, was given up by him in 1853, he then making a journey to Holland with his Clara, where they "were welcomed with joy, yes, with honors", and he "saw with surprise, that his music was almost better known in Holland than in the Fatherland". From 1854 symptoms, sometimes noticeable even earlier, of a disease affecting his brain, grew more and more alarming; on the 29th of July, 1856, death put an end to the sufferings caused by the disorder. He rests in the cemetery outside the Sternthor of Bonn. Ferdinand Hiller said of him: "With a golden sceptre thou reignedst over a lordly realm of harmonies, and wroughtst therein with a strong and free hand. And many of the best followed thee, gave themselves up to thee, inspired thee by their enthusiasm, and rewarded thee by faithful love".

To his last period belong the following Pianoforte Works: *Trio* for Pianoforte, Violin, and Violoncello, op. 80 in *F,* Leipzig, J. Schuberth & Co.; *Waldscenen,* 9 Piano-pieces, op. 82, Leipzig, Senff; *12 Piano-pieces* for 4 hands, for great and small children, op. 85, Leipzig, J. Schuberth & Co.; *Fantasiestücke* for Pianoforte, Violin, and Violoncello, op. 88, Leipzig, Kistner; *Concertstück* with accomp. of Orchestra, Introduction and Allegro appassionato, op. 92, Breitkopf & Härtel; *Bunte Blätter,* 14 Pieces for the Pianoforte, op. 99, Elberfeld, F. W. Arnold; two grand *Sonatas* for Pianoforte and Violin, op. 105 and 121, Leipzig, Hofmeister, also Breitkopf & Härtel; *Ballscenen,* 9 characteristic Pieces for 4 hands, op. 109, J. Schuberth & Co.; third *Trio* for Pianoforte, Violin, and Violoncello, in *G*-minor, op. 110, Breitkopf & Härtel; *3 Fantasiestücke,* op. 111, Leipzig, Peters;

Märchenbilder, 4 Pieces for Pianoforte, and Violin dedicated to his subsequent biographer J. v. Wasielewski, op. 113, Cassel, Luckhard; *3 Claviersonaten für die Jugend,* op. 118, Leipzig, J. Schuberth & Co.; *Albumblätter,* 20 Piano-pieces, op. 124, Elberfeld, Arnold; *7 Piano-pieces* in fughetta-form, op. 126, ditto; *Kinderball,* 6 Easy Dance-pieces for 4 hands, Breitkopf & Härtel; *Märchenerzählungen,* 4 Pieces for Clarinet, Viola, and Pianoforte, op. 132, ditto; *Gesänge der Frühe,* 5 Pieces for Pianoforte, dedicated to the lofty poetess Bettina, op. 133, Elberfeld, Arnold; and finally *Concert-Allegro* with *Introduction,* for Pianoforte with orchestral accomp., in *D*-minor, dedicated to Johannes Brahms, op. 134, Leipzig, B. Senff.

After the expiration of the legal thirty-years' term of copyright, a Complete Edition of Robert Schumann's works was published by Breitkopf & Härtel, under the supervision of the deceased composer's wife, Frau Dr. Clara Schumann. Earlier issues of the Pianoforte Works had been edited by Nicolas Rubinstein (Moscow, Jürgensen), this one being quite useless on account of incorrect readings; also by Dr. Hans Bischoff (Hanover, Steingräber), and Dr. O. Neitzel (Cologne, P. Tonger). While Frau Schumann has carried the reverence for her dead husband's name so far, as to leave standing mistakes evidently overseen by Schumann or erroneous corrections by "Des" (Fr. Wieck), Bischoff and Neitzel, by bringing to bear all their philological acumen and noteworthy pedagogical experience, have done in part faultless work both in critical revision and for the study of the works in technical and æsthetical regard.

In Schumann's character were blended seriousness and humor, profundity and naïveté, roughness and good nature, in a striking manner. His compositions, so teeming with sharp contrasts, did not therefore become more generally understood and appreciated until after his death, even in Germany, whereas they can hardly ever find favor in France and Italy. Moreover, Schumann often requires for the execution of his pieces the entire skill of a virtuoso, without setting that skill in a brilliant light. The Virtuoso should not find his reward as such, but as the interpreter of the art-work to which he gives life. Schumann's pianoforte style is consequently more akin to Beethoven's last great pianoforte works, than to the salon and concert compositions produced by the school of Hummel or Moscheles. The more intimately we become acquainted with such a richly gifted nature, the more attractive do we find intercourse with it; but the imitators of such a peculiar style, so closely knit with the inmost fibres of its author, fail to move us, whereas epigones like Mendelssohn, who follow no untried path, but rather one already trodden smooth, may command our respect, or even our love.

Respecting his life and labors we have the following: Robert Schumann, A Biography, by J. W. v. WASIELEWSKI. Dresden, Kuntze, 1858.—Robert Schumann, Life and Works, by AUGUST REISSMANN. Berlin, Guttentag, 1865.—Collections of Letters, and also a work entitled "Davidsbündler", by JANSEN, have recently been published by Breitkopf & Härtel.

After Schumann's death a party formed, which designated him as the climax of the "neo-romantic music", and disallowed all further progress in this direction. The disciples of the "neo-German school" on the contrary, who chose Franz Liszt as their leader, held any and every innovation and reformation of musical art-forms for justifiable. A third, the so-called "classical party", despised all music claiming originality subsequent to Haydn, Mozart, and Beethoven, and sought, like Chinese reformers, to push us back into "the good old times".

But in the realm of the liberal arts the rule of a one-sided and narrow law-giver can never be of long duration, and in music, too, the parties so struggling for sole mastery have long since been rightly consigned to oblivion. For the unprejudiced musician, acquainted with the beginnings and the growth of his art, regards with due respect not only the illustrious masters of earlier and more recent times, but likewise those of to-day, who are striving by word and deed to extend the boundaries of their art, and thus to promote its theoretical progress.

Schumann's Successors.

We find, advancing on the paths opened by Schumann, several meritorious composers, who sought foremostly to assimilate his style of developing given motives of an interesting type. Among these is **Woldemar Bargiel** (b. 1828), since 1874 teacher of composition at the Royal *Hochschule für Musik* at Berlin, who has published a number of serious and dignified pianoforte works, including the following: *Fantasia* for Pianoforte, dedicated to his sister Clara Schumann, op. 5, Elberfeld, Arnold; *Trio* for Pianoforte, Violin, and Violoncello, dedicated to Robert Schumann, op. 6, Breslau, Leuckart; *Suite* for Pianoforte, for 4 hands, op. 7, Breitkopf & Härtel;

16 Pianoforte Pieces, op. 34, and op. 41 (ditto); *Third Trio* for Pianoforte, Violin, and Violoncello, op. 37 (ditto); *Fantasia*, dedicated to Johannes Brahms, op. 19, Breslau, Leuckart.—**Theodor Kirchner** (b. 1824) greets us breezily and spiritedly in his compositions for the pianoforte, which, though for the most part set in the smaller forms, are always refreshingly attractive in their unconstrained naïveté. In Leipzig there have been published by J. Rieter-Biedermann: op. 9, two books of *Preludes;* op. 13, *Songs without Words;* op. 14, *Fantasiestücke*, 3 books; op. 24, *Still und bewegt*, Piano-pieces, 2 books; op. 33, *Ideale;*—by Fr. Hofmeister: op. 32, *Aus trüben Tagen*, 2 books; op. 26, *Album;* op. 27, *Caprices*, 2 books; op. 28, *Notturnos;* op. 29, *Aus meinem Skizzenbuche*, 2 books; op. 30, *Studies and Pieces*, 4 books; op. 31, *Im Zwielicht*, Songs and Dances, 4 books;—by Bartholf Senff: op. 5, *Gruss an meine Freunde;* op. 16, *Kleine Lust- und Trauerspiele*, 3 books.—**Johannes Brahms**, the most eminent of those following Schumann's track, has risen step by step to be one of the first composers of the present day, and will be separately noticed hereafter.

Below we add a few composers, who endeavor to keep their pianoforte works free from commonplaces, and who have often succeeded in developing their subjects in a stimulating and entertaining manner. **Carl Grädener** (1812—1883) dedicated to Hans v. Bülow a *Trio* in *E* for Pianoforte, Violin and Violoncello (Hamburg, Fritz Schuberth), which has everywhere met with a favorable reception; his brilliantly colored character pieces "*Fliegende Blättchen*" for the Pianoforte (op. 24, 27, 31, 33, and 43, same publ.) also enjoy great popularity, especially in his residence, Hamburg.—**Friedrich Robert Volkmann** (1815—1883), also first attracted attention by a *Trio* for Pianoforte, Violin, and Violoncello in *B♭*-minor, op. 5, which, though planned in Schumann's spirit, immediately stamped him as an original composer of teeming fancy. His *Pianoforte Works* without accompaniment are also full of inspired touches, as, among many others, the *Buch der Lieder*, op. 17, three books (Spina in Vienna); *Cavatina and Barcarole*, op. 19; 12 musical poems in "*Visegrad*", op. 21; *Ungarische Skizzen*, op. 24; and above all the "*Musikalisches Bilderbuch*", op. 11, 2 books (Fr. Kistner, Leipzig), and the "*Tageszeiten*", op. 39, both works for 4 hands.—Finally, the Belgian **César Auguste Franck** (b. 1822), who was trained in the Paris Conservatory of Music, came forward in his op. 1 with *3 Pianoforte Trios* in *F♯*, *B♭*, and *B*-minor (Leipzig, J. Schuberth & Co., in score and parts), followed by a fourth in *B*-major as op. 2 (ditto), all of which exhibit such an individual and attractive *colorit,* that they made a stir not only in Paris—where their author established himself as a highly esteemed teacher, being at present organist of the church of St. Clothilde—but in Germany as well, and despite their difficulty have been much played and discussed. These are compositions born of hours of self-consecration and true inspiration, for which we could only desire the finishing touch of the master-hand. Then followed, for Pianoforte solo, op. 3, *Églogue;* op. 4, *Duo* for 4 hands on "God save the King"; op. 7, *Souvenir d'Aix-la-Chapelle* (Leipzig, J. Schuberth & Co.); and *1 Sonata* (Paris chez l'auteur).

Charles Valentin Alkan, born at Paris in 1813, and known there under the name of Alkan *l'aîné,* was taught, like the musician last mentioned, by the meritorious teacher of the pianoforte and composition P. J. W. Zimmermann (1785—1853) in the Conservatory at Paris, and is more at home in his study than in the world of fashion. He has written a series of Pianoforte Works, whose originality and wealth of invention is as surprising as the boldness of their harmonies and modulations. Of his romantic compositions, which "have not yet met with the attention on the part of pianoforte virtuosi which they merit", and which he himself performs in a peculiarly free style, we note the following: *25 Preludes,* op. 31 (Berlin, Schlesinger), which, from their comparatively easy style, their diversified and interesting conception, and even their astounding parallel fifths and octaves are especially suited for gaining acquaintance with this gifted composer; further, op. 32, *l'Amitié;* op. 26, *Fantasietta alla Moresca;* op. 31, *Preludes,* 3 books; and op. 46, *Minuetto alla tedesca,* all publ. by Schlesinger;—*12 Études* in all major keys, 2 suites, Bote & Bock;—op. 17, *Le Preux,* Étude de Concert; op. 27, *Le chemin de fer;* op. 29, *Bourrée d'Auvergne;* op. 22, *Nocturne;* and op. 23, *Saltarelle,* publ. by B. Schott's Söhne of Mainz;—op. 15, *Trois grandes Études* dans le genre pathétique; op. 16, *Six morceaux caractéristiques,* 2 *Fughe di camera,* Jean qui rit et Jean qui pleure; and *Trois grandes Études* pour la main gauche seule, pour la main droite seule, et pour deux mains, publ. by Fr. Hofmeister, Leipzig.

Contemporaries of Mendelssohn, Chopin, and Schumann.

While the above successors of Schumann presented us chiefly with long and serious works, often pervaded with *Weltschmerz* (splenetic melancholy), other gifted composers, like Theodor Kirchner, followed in the more flowery paths taken by Chopin and Mendelssohn, and brought us offerings of cheerful character-pieces and Novellettes, whose worth should by no means be underrated in comparison with grander compositions. The published pianoforte works of **Gustav Flügel** (b. 1812, since 1857 *Schlossorganist* at Stettin) are full of romantically poetical, thoughtful musical motives, and are therefore well worthy of notice. We mention op. 25, *4 Fantasiestücke* (Schlesinger); op. 17, *Tagfalter,* and op. 14 and 24, *Nachtfalter* (Fr. Hofmeister); op. 18, *Mondscheinbilder;* op. 40, *Volkspoesien;* op. 44, *Humoreske;* and the *Sonatas* No. 2 and No. 5 (Breitkopf & Härtel).—**Stephen Heller** (b. 1815 in Pesth, d. 1888), who lived from 1838 in Paris, wrote a great number of works in the purest pianoforte style, which have justly attained to universal favor through their graceful melodic flow and ingenious technique. Liszt first called the attention of the musical world to this richly endowed composer, by performing in public his ballade-like, brilliant piece "*La chasse*" (op. 29, Schlesinger). Other of Heller's pianoforte works published by the same are: *Études progressives,* op. 47, 46, 45; *Blumen-, Frucht- und Dornenstücke,* op. 82, in 3 Parts, peculiarly distinguished by their poetical conception and their exqnisite workmanship;—op. 79, *Traumbilder,* and op. 92, three books of Églogen (Bote & Bock);—op. 78, *Spaziergänge eines Einsamen,* 5 books; op. 96, *Grande Étude;* and op. 119, *Albumblätter;* —by B. Schott's Söhne, *4 Fantasiestücke,* op. 99, in 2 books; *3 Bergeries,* op. 106; *4 Ländler,* op. 107; *Scherzo,* op. 108; *Herbstblätter,* op. 109; *Balletstücke,* op. 111; *Caprice humoristique,* op. 112; *Fantaisie-Caprice,* op. 113; *Préludes, Scènes d'enfants* and *Presto scherzoso,* op. 114; *Trois Ballades,* op. 115; *Deux Etudes,* op. 116; *Trois Préludes,* op. 117; and *Variétés, Boutade, Feuillet d'Album* et *Air de Ballet,* op. 118.—The eminent pianoforte virtuoso **Jacob Rosenhain** (b. 1813 at Mannheim) has become widely known and popular through various pianoforte works. Among these there have been published, by B. Schott's Söhne: *Grand Trio* pour Piano, Violon et Violoncelle, op. 33, and another, op. 50; *Grand Caprice brillant*, op. 23; *Romances sans paroles*, op. 25, 31, and 37; *Polka de concert*, op. 36; *Characterstücke* (Spanish, Polish, Oriental, etc.), op. 25, 31, and 37; *Variations humoresques* sur le Carneval de Venise, op. 46;—by Fr. Hofmeister: *12 Études caractéristiques*, op. 17, and *1 Concertino* avec quatuor, op. 30;—by Peters: *Sonata*, op. 44, and *2 Morceaux de concours*, op. 39.—**Louis Trouillon-Lacombe** (b. 1818 in Bourges, d. 1884 in St. Vaast-la-Hongue) was much esteemed in Paris as a pianist and composer of pleasing piano-pieces, such as the *Étude en Octaves*, op. 40, B. Schott's Söhne; *Chorale*, grande Étude de concert, op. 45 (ditto); also *Les Harmonies de la Nature, Deux Nocturnes, Marche turque*, etc. [Among his compositions a Pianoforte *Quintet* and two *Trios* deserve special mention. **O. L.**]

John Field was perhaps the first to present us, in his Nocturnes, with *Stimmungsbilder* (mood-pictures) of the smaller kind, whose attractive naturalness delighted even the Parisians, *blasé* though they were with the then epoch-making virtuosity. Frédéric Chopin heard him in Paris in 1832, and to these simple pieces we owe in great part the latter's six books of Nocturnes, with their more diversified character and livelier colors. The Mazurkas, too, that mirror his nation in all their sufferings and joys, and also many of his Preludes, belong to the heart-felt and therefore warmly sympathetic *Stimmungsbilder*. The purely lyrical Songs without Words of his contemporary Mendelssohn followed the Fantasiestücke, Novelletten, and Nachtstücke of Schumann, which are apt to trespass, however, upon the epic and dramatic field of art. Besides the composers already named in this section, Franz Liszt, in particular, has poured out from his glowing heart lyric and epic poems in his *Années de pelerinage*, the *Apparitions, Consolations, Harmonies poétiques*, and *Rhapsodies hongroises*. But this unexcelled master not only ushered in the present brilliant era of pianoforte-playing through his original compositions and interpretations; he also was enabled to spread and maintain the same through numerous pupils. Of these we will mention here **Franz Bendel** (1833—1874) as the author of several pregnant *Stimmungsbilder*. A few of these are accompanied by short programs, a feature frequently decried by many writers. But when after expunging such programs, which attribute definite ideas or definite feelings to the tones, intelligible music is left behind, as in this case, the latter can lose none of its value through the program. Any truly significant music whatever is interpreted by each listener in a manner most conformable to his character, his memories, hopes, and fears; in its tones he hears the mystic revelations and prophecies of an inspired singer. In 4 books of *"Schweizer Bilder"*, op. 137 (Berlin, Carl Paez), and 6 books *"Am Genfer See"*, op. 139, Bendel portrays the impressions of his journeyings in the fresh air of the valleys and heights of Switzerland; and in the *"Sechs deutsche Märchenbilder"* (op. 135, Hamburg, Hugo Pohle), illustrated with more striking colors, the dream-like, weird, and bizarre scenes of these *Fantasiestücke* pass before our inner vision with dramatic animation.

Musical Review at the Present Time.

We begin with a survey of the most prominent **Conservatories** and **Schools of Music** in which special attention is paid to pianoforte-playing. The flourishing *Royal Conservatory of Music* at Leipzig was founded in 1843 by Mendelssohn; in this institution pianoforte-playing and composition have been fostered from the start. The former branch is at present represented by Carl Reinecke, noted as an eminent virtuoso and composer; S. Jadassohn, pianist and composer; Oscar Paul, author of a noteworthy History of the Pianoforte and many other musical works; R. C. Papperitz; C. Piutti, organ virtuoso and composer; A. Richter; and several other pianists.* The Leipzig Conservatory adheres to its traditional methods, and has by consequence fallen in the scale of musical importance, or at least not risen. The exclusive tendency observable at this institution, represented as following the artistic traditions of Mendelssohn, but which is in fact unfriendly to the spirit of modern pianoforte-playing and to the modern development of music altogether, has notably strained the earlier relations of this once justly renowned school to the general musical life of the world, and in many cases quite dissolved them. Of the old Masters, to whose co-operation the former fame of the conservatory was due, but few are left. E. F. Wenzel, born on Jan. 25, 1808, at Walddorf in Saxony, died Aug. 16, 1880, in Bad Kösen; Louis Plaidy, born Nov. 28, 1810, at Hubertusburg, died on March 3, 1874, in Grimma; Ignaz Moscheles, born May 30, 1794, at Prague, died March 10, 1870, in Leipzig; Moritz Haupt-

* The remainder of this survey of the Music-schools is by the editor of he second German edition, Herr Otto Lessmann. **Transl. Note.**

mann, born Oct. 13, 1792 at Dresden, died on Jan. 3, 1868, in Leipzig; and although their places as teachers of pianoforte-playing have been taken by younger men, the latter are nevertheless obliged to accommodate themselves to the prevailing conservative spirit. That the regular academical course is still conscientiously taught, is proved by the annual examinations *(Prüfungen)* and hereby the Conservatory fulfils its mission to a certain extent. But whether it is right to narrow the intellectual horizon of the pupils in opposition to the spirit of the times, is a question hardly requiring serious consideration. —In essential points, like praise and like blame are to be bestowed upon a much younger institution, the *Berlin Royal Hochschule für ausübende Tonkunst.* The blind hatred with which prominent representatives of this institution denounce the entire modern development of music and its promotors and abettors, is but ill-suited to a school of art founded and maintained by the State. Happily, no monopoly in art can be enduringly upheld, neither can any institute, however richly endowed, check the steady march of events. In this academy the chief teachers of the pianoforte are Profs. Ernst Rudorff and Heinrich Barth.—The *Conservatory at Cologne,* since the decease of its former Director **Ferdinand von Hiller** (b. Oct. 24, 1811, at Frankfort, d. May 11, 1885, at Cologne), has prospered markedly under the management of **Franz Wüllner** (b. Jan. 28, 1832, at Münster in Westphalia). Instruction in pianoforte-playing has hitherto been in the hands of men like Prof. Ignaz Seiss, Prof. E. Mertke, Dr. Otto Neitzel, etc.—The *Neue Akademie der Tonkunst* (New Acad. of Music) was founded in 1855 by Th. Kullak (b. Sept. 12, 1818 at Krotoschin in Posen, d. March 1, 1882, in Berlin), and celebrated its 25th anniversary in 1880 with 100 teachers and 1000 pupils; since its founder's death it has been carried on by his son Franz.—The *Conservatory* founded in 1850 by *Julius Stern* is continued since his death (1883) under the artistic direction of Prof. Robt. Radecke; Profs. Heinrich Ehrlich and Ernst Franck are engaged as first teachers of the pianoforte, a position held by Prof. Franz Mannstädt until his removal to Wiesbaden.—The soil of Berlin has proved peculiarly favorable to the growth of music-schools; whether real service is rendered to art by such wholesale fabrication of pianists, is a thesis hard to maintain.—Among the numerous pianoforte schools opened in Berlin during the last decade, only two can lay claim to artistic significance in a wider sense. These are the *Conservatory of Music* of Prof. **Xaver Scharwenka** (b. Jan. 6, 1850, at Samter in Posen, and a pupil of Kullak and Wüerst), and the *"Classes in advanced Pianoforte-playing"* led by **Karl Klindworth** (b. Sept. 25, 1830, in Hanover, a pupil of Liszt). Klindworth has won a name less through public pianoforte recitals and original compositions (as Pianoforte Concerto, Pieces, and Songs), than by his editions of Chopin's Pianoforte Works, Beethoven's Sonatas, and the masterly Pianoforte Arrangements of Wagner's *Nibelungen-Tetralogie*, and also by his eminent talent as a conductor. From 1854 to 1868 Klindworth lived as teacher, pianist, and conductor in London, 1868—1884 in Moscow, in which latter year he came to Berlin, taught at first in Kullak's Academy, and in the year 1885 opened his pianoforte classes, which were led by Moritz Moszkowski in the winter of 1887/88, during Klindworth's absence in America.—Among the North German Conservatories of good repute we mention that at *Dresden* (Dir. Pudor died Oct. 9, 1887), at *Hamburg* (Dir. v. Bernuth), at *Dresden* likewise the *Rollfuss Academy for Ladies*, also the Grand-ducal *Musikschule* at *Weimar* (Dir. Prof. Müller-Hartung), and the *Conservatory* at *Sondershausen* (Dir. Ad. Schulze). In South Germany there are flourishing at present the *Conservatory* at *Stuttgart*, which has, to be sure, lost two of its most eminent teachers, Siegmund Lebert (Levy), b. Dec. 12, 1822, in Ludwigsburg, d. Dec. 8, 1884, in Stuttgart,—and Ludwig Stark, b. June 19, 1831, d. March 22, 1884; the *Royal Musikschule* at *Munich*, established by Hans v. Bülow at the instance of King Ludwig II.; the *Royal Musikschule* at *Würzburg* under the management of Dr. Kliebert; *Dr. Hoch's Conservatory* at *Frankfort* (Dir. Prof. Bernhard Scholz), first instructress of the pianoforte Frau Clara Schumann; also in the last-named city the *Raff Conservatory*, at whose head stands, as first teacher of the pianoforte, Max Schwarz (a pupil of Bendel and Bülow), and in which Hans v. Bülow himself, as honorary President, gives courses in rendering during one month in each year.

Among non-German institutions, the Conservatory of the *Gesellschaft der Musikfreunde* and the *Horak Clavierschule* at *Vienna* enjoy a high reputation; in *St. Petersburg* we find the *Imperial Conservatory*, whose management since Davidoff's retirement has been resumed by Anton Rubinstein, its founder; in *Brussels* the *Conservatory* under Dupont's direction; in *Paris* the long-renowned *Conservatory;* in *Pesth* the *National Music Academy*, whose president was Franz Liszt, and the *Conservatory;* in *Helsingfors* the *Musikschule* (Dir. Wegelius), serving as a *point d'appui* for German music in Finland.—In London flourishes the *Royal Academy of Music,* for which in honor of Liszt's last visit to London a Liszt scholarship was founded, affording to talented and industrious students means for a stay of several years in Germany and other countries. (For American Conservatories see Appendix.)

The above institutions all owe their establishment to the praiseworthy endeavor to provide places for the earnest cultivation of art, and so long as this aim is kept in view, well-founded arguments can hardly be brought forward against their continuance. But opinion on the value of music schools undergoes a change when one perceives, that the moving cause for opening such is in great part only base speculation on the ignorance of the great public, which unhappily follows the fashionable craze for playing the piano regardless of concomitant circumstances. Pianoforte-playing, once the hard-won art of musically gifted individuals, has become a public calamity—indeed, it is openly and aptly termed the *piano-nuisance*—and a large proportion of the blame for the mischief must be laid at the door of those music schools, which are conducted by mediocre or yet worse musicians and teachers, and in which too frequently wretched bunglers give cheap instruction, thus doing their best to lower the level of pianoforte-playing in particular and of artistic taste in general.

In must be admitted, on the other hand, that pianoforte-playing, as a really artistic manifestation, has on the whole won a far broader basis than formerly. Dilettanti of true artistic taste are no longer a rarity, and the demands of the public upon pianists now appearing have decidedly risen. Mere virtuosity now leads but a sorry life, since public taste has begun to require of artists to provide programs containing works of intellectual worth, for whose interpretation mental power, and not mere external finger-technique, is needed. The most astounding programs have been furnished by the two Past Masters of Pianoforte-playing, Hans v. Bülow and Anton Rubinstein, the former having first confronted the public with the five last Sonatas by Beethoven, while the latter, in a *cyclus* embracing seven evenings, gave a review, though a hasty one, of the historical evolution of pianoforte-playing. Bülow then followed with cycles of four evenings, in which, by a series of sonatas, variations, and other works, he reproduced the development of Beethoven's pianoforte style before the astonished audience. Hans v. Bülow has embalmed the fruits of his art-studies and experience in an edition of the

Sonatas, Variations, and other Pianoforte Works by Beethoven from op. 53 on (Stuttgart, Cotta), which according to Liszt's dictum excel, by reason of their extraordinary wealth of pedagogical and æsthetical material, a dozen conservatories in instructiveness; furthermore, in a series of pianoforte works by Bach, Scarlatti, Haydn, Field, Handel, Schubert, Mendelssohn, Weber, Mozart, and Beethoven again (earlier Sonatas op. 27, II; op. 26; op. 13; op. 31, III; 32 Variations in *C*-minor) published in Munich by Aibl under the general title of *"Aus den Concertprogrammen von Hans v. Bülow"*; a Selection by Bülow of Chopin's and above all Cramer's Études also merits mention here on account of its high pedagogic value.

Besides the Music Schools already noticed, others are found in nearly all considerable German towns, and the teachers engaged in the same are everywhere supplemented by pianists and composers whose name is legion. The following list of musicians still living, who are composers for or players on the pianoforte, therefore lays no claim to completeness.—Prominent among the Berlin musicians not yet named are Heinrich Ehrlich, a distinguished pianist, teacher, writer, and the composer of a characteristic *Concertstück in Ungarischer Weise*, op. 1, and various salon pieces (all publ. by Bote & Bock);—F. E. Wilsing, the composer of *4 grand Sonatas, 1 Fantasia* in *F♯*-minor, and *1 Humoreske* in canon-form (ditto);—C. Hering, composer of *1 Zigeuner-Serenade* for 4 hands (Rieter-Biedermann), *1 Sonata* (ditto), and other piano pieces;—J. Hopfe, author of *Ein Frühlingsmärchen*, Quartet for Pianoforte and Strings, op. 48; *Ein Pfingstfest auf dem Lande, Humoreske* for 4 hands, op. 37; *3 Pianoforte Trios*, op. 40, 41, and 43; *2 Easy Trios*, op. 46 and 49 (C. A. Challier & Co., Berlin);—Philipp Scharwenka has published a great number of tasteful pianoforte pieces varying in difficulty, among them *1 Cavatina* with 'Cello, op. 22, and *Three Concertstücke* with Violin, op. 17, 3 books; special gratitude is due to him for his short, melodious and finely finished pieces for instruction, such as the *Albumblätter*, op. 27 (Breitkopf & Härtel); *In bunter Reihe*, op. 32; *Aus der Jugendzeit*, op. 34, 2 books; *Festklänge für die Jugend*, op. 45 (Praeger & Meier); *Divertimenti*, 10 short piano-pieces, op. 55, 3 books (Ad. Fürstner); *Kinderspiele*, Series I—II, op. 64 and op. 68 (Breslau, Hainauer). In all these, and in others as well, is found material of instruction both stimulating and formative for the taste; —his younger brother Xaver Scharwenka played and had published *1 Concerto* with Orchestra in *B♭*-minor, op. 32, which has met with much favor; a second *Pianoforte Concerto* with Orchestra, op. 56, *C*-minor; and for Pianoforte without accomp. the *Wanderlieder*, op. 23, 2 books; *Bilder aus Ungarn*, op. 26, 2 books (all publ. by Praeger & Meier, Bremen); also, besides various salon pieces, *2 Sonatas*, op. 6 in *C*♯-minor and op. 36 in *E*♭-major; *Theme and Variations*, op. 48, *D*-minor, etc.;—C. Bürgel has issued the well-received works *Sonata* in *E*♭, op. 15; *2 Nocturnes*, op. 17 (Bote & Bock); *Mimosen*, lyric poems, 6 books, op. 24 (Fr. Hofmeister); *Walzer-Capricen*, op. 11 (Bartholf Senff), and other pieces;—Philippe Bartholomé Rüfer (b. 1844 in Liége, since 1871 in Berlin) manifests an opulent musical nature in his *Violin Sonata*, op. 1, a brilliant *Trio*, *2 Suites* for Pianoforte and 'Cello, op. 8 and 13, and various piano-pieces. Inventive originality, genuine passion, and a highly artistic style, mark his compositions. Rüfer is at present a teacher in Klindworth's Pianoforte School;—Moritz Moszkowski (b. 1854 in Breslau), a dis tinguished virtuoso, has published a large number of tastefully and ingeniously wrought salon pieces for his instrument, taking Chopin as his model. These have been issued for the most part by Hainauer, Breslau.

Dresden.—Here we find the excellent pianoforte virtuoso A. Blassmann;—the pianist and composer J. E. Leonhard (d. 1883);—the celebrated concert *pianiste* Marie Wieck;—Marie Krebs, who has played in England, France, and America with equal success;—and the gifted Laura Karer-Rappoldy. In Dresden also dwell the pianist and music-historian J. Rühlmann;—Döring, noted as a teacher and composer of practical pianoforte Études;—and Fritz Spindler, a composer of easily playable and elegant Salon Pieces, among them *Sonatinas*, 6 books, op. 136 (J. Rieter-Biedermann); 3 little *Trios*, op. 305 (S. W. Siegel, Leipzig); *Im Wald*, op. 75, 6 books; *Wanderlieder*, op. 100, 6 books; *3 Fantasiestücke*, op. 199; *Elegante Tanzweisen*, op. 294, 6 books;—Hermann Scholz has published the following interesting pianoforte works: *Sonata* in *G*-minor, op. 44 (F. E. C. Leuckart, Leipzig); *Geistertanz*, op. 21; *Traumbilder*, 4 books, op. 22; *Humoreske*, op. 23; *Saltarello and Tarantella*, 2 books, op. 24; *8 Minnelieder*, op. 25; and others;—as popular pianoforte teachers in Dresden we note Bertrand Roth, a pupil of Liszt, a fine, impressionable pianist; and Jean Louis Nicodé (b. 1853 at Jerczik in Posen), a pupil of Kullak, Wüerst, and Kiel. Nicodé is a most talented pianist of brilliant powers of development; besides a number of original orchestral works, he has arranged Chopin's *Concert-*

Allegro, op. 46 for public performance with Pianoforte and Orchestra, and has published various tasteful and interesting pianoforte works, as *Variations and Fugue* on an original theme, *Sonata* in *F*-minor, *3 Études,* and *1 Sonata* in *G* for Pianoforte and Violin. His chief orchestral work, *Symphonic Variations,* has appeared in an arrangement for Pianoforte for 4 hands (Breitkopf & Härtel).—Felix Draeseke, for 2 years a teacher of theory in the Dresden Conservatory, has also written a brilliant *Pianoforte Concerto* in *E*♭ (Leipzig, F. Kistner).—Emil Sauer, one of the most eminent among the younger pianists of the Liszt school, has also settled in Dresden.

Adolf Jensen (b. 1837 in Königsberg, d. 1879 in Baden-Baden) was a fruitful author of attractive, cleanly written, and technically "convenient" piano-pieces, all of which manifest the poetic vein of the genial composer. We name the following: *Sonata* in *F*♯-minor, op. 25 (Bartholf Senff); *Innere Stimmen,* 5 pieces, op. 2; *Fantasiestücke,* 2 books, op. 7; *Romantische Studien,* 2 Parts, op. 8; *3 Pianoforte Pieces* for 4 hands, op. 18; and *Alla Marcia, Canzonetta, Scherzo,* op. 42 (Fritz Schuberth, Hamburg); *Jagdscenen,* op. 15; *Trois Valses-Caprices,* 3 books, op. 31; *Lieder und Tänze,* 20 little *piano-pieces,* op. 33 (Fr. Kistner, Leipzig); *2 Nocturnes,* op. 38 (Robt. Forberg, Leipzig); *Wanderbilder,* 2 books, op. 17; *Études,* 3 books, op. 32; and *Erinnerungen,* op. 48 (C. F. Peters); *Idyllen,* op. 43; *Hochzeitsmusik* for 4 hands, op. 45; *Ländler aus Berchtesgaden,* op. 46; *Abendmusik* for 4 hands, op. 59; *Lebensbilder* for 4 hands, 2 books, op. 60; and *Silhouettes,* 6 piano-pieces for 4 hands (Julius Hainauer, Breslau).—Jacob Rosenhain (b. 1813), an excellent pianist of the old school, and a composer whose talent was praised by Robert Schumann, is still living at Baden-Baden; he has written 3 Pianoforte *Trios,* 1 Pianoforte *Concerto, 3 Sonatas* for Pianoforte, *1 Sonata* for 'Cello and Pianoforte, and many salon pieces.

Louis Ehlert (1825—1884) numbers among his delicately wrought compositions *Pianoforte Pieces* for 4 hands, op. 18 and 19; *Lieder und Studien,* op. 20 (Berlin, Schlesinger). As able teachers, virtuosi, and composers we may also mention Mortier de Fontaine (b. 1816 in Wisniewiec, d. 1883 in London), who was the first that ventured to perform in public one of Beethoven's last great Sonatas, op. 106, —and Julius Schäffer (b. 1823) of Breslau, whose poetically musical compositions, as the *Fantasiestücke,* op. 1, *Fantasie-Variationen,* op. 2, and *Polonaise,* op. 4, are well worthy of notice.—Alfred Jaell (1832—1882), a pianoforte virtuoso distinguished for his fine touch and delicate *pianissimo*, as well as for his large repertory, undertook very successful concert-tours. His published pianoforte pieces are effectively written, and display their composer's refined taste; we note *Caprices*, op. 104 and 105; *Nocturne sentimental*, op. 125 (Leipzig, Kistner); *Trois morceaux de salon*, op. 106 (Leipzig, Siegel); *La Sylphide*, op. 116 (B. Senff); *La Fontaine*, op. 117 (Leipzig, Leuckart); *Valse caprice*, op. 161 (Leipzig, R. Forberg).— Leopold von Meyer (b. 1816 in Vienna, d. 1883 in Dresden) extended his travels to America, where his appearance excited a furore; but neither his programs nor compositions are equal in quality to Jaell's. — Two highly talented pianistes, Anna Mehlig of Stuttgart and Sophie Menter-Popper of Munich, win applause and laurel wreaths wherever they go. The latter was for some years a piano teacher in the St. Petersburg Conservatory, but resigned this position in 1887, after Anton Rubinstein assumed the management of this institution and instituted energetic reforms.—Ignaz Brüll (b. 1846) is not only a favorite opera composer, but is also well-known as a pianist and composer of valuable pianoforte works. Of these latter we note the following: *First Concerto* with Orchestra in *F*, op. 10, and *Second Concerto* in *C*, op. 24 (Bote & Bock); *Three Piano-pieces* (Vienna, Spina); *7 Fantasiestücke*, 3 books, op. 8 (Fr. Kistner).—At Munich the highly gifted composer Rich. Strauss (b. there June 11, 1864) is at present engaged as third *Hofkapellmeister; 1 'Cello Sonata, 1 Pianoforte Sonata* in *B*-minor, op. 5, a number of smaller, characteristic pieces, and above all a prize *Pianoforte Quartet*, reveal an unusual inventive faculty, and a confidence of style remarkable in view of the composer's youth.

Outside of Germany Jul. Carl Eschmann of Zurich (1825—1882) is to be mentioned. His *Album für Pianoforte*, op. 17 (Berlin and Leipzig, Luckhardt), contains 12 strongly characteristic, cleanly written *Fantasiestücke* of a serious or cheerful nature; his numerous piano-pieces written for the young, like the *28 German Folk-songs*, op. 51, The *16 German Folk-songs* for 4 hands, etc., are interesting for the teacher and stimulating for the pupil. Among these we may also mention op. 60, *For the First Pianoforte Year*, and op. 61, *For the Second and Third Pianoforte Years*, and many instructive works issued by the same publisher.—Auguste Dupont (b. 1828) is engaged in the Conservatory of Music at Brussels, and is highly esteemed as a teacher and composer; among his published works we find the following brilliant pianoforte pieces: *Le Staccato perpétuel*, grande Etude de concert, op. 31 (Breitkopf & Härtel); *Pluie de Mai,* Étude de trilles, op. 2; *Contes du foyer,* 6 morceaux caractéristiques, op. 12; *Danse des Almées,* Étude fantastique, op. 25; *Fantaisie et fugue* pour la main droite, op. 41; *Roman en dix pages,* op. 48, dix cahiers (all publ. by Schott's Söhne, Mainz). Dupont also published with the collaboration of Gustave Sandré an *École de Piano* du Conservatoire royal de Bruxelles (Breitkopf & Härtel), a collection of early and recent classical master-works, provided for the purpose of instruction with fingerings, phrasing, notes on the rendering, etc.—The finished pianoforte virtuoso Louis Brassin (b. 1840, d. 1884) was in turn teacher in the Stern Conservatory at Berlin, the Brussels Conservatory, and the Conservatory at St. Petersburg; his published works include, besides many concert pieces, the *Grand Galop fantastique,* op. 5; *Valse-Caprice,* op. 6; *Le Ruisseau,* morceau de salon, op. 8; *Grandes Études de concert,* op. 12, en 4 suites; *6 Morceaux de fantaisie,* op. 21, 3 suites (all publ. by Schott's Söhne, Mainz). A pupil of Brassin, Franz Rummel (b. 1853 in London) an eminent pianist, lives at Berlin.—Fritz Gernsheim (b. 1839), the Director of the Conservatory at Rotterdam, is noted as a fine pianist, and has written valuable pianoforte works, among them being *1 Quartet* for Pianoforte, Violin, Viola, and Violoncello, op. 6, in *E*♭ (Breitkopf & Härtel); *Suite* in 4 movements, op. 8; *Variations* in *C*-minor, op. 22; *Fantaisies,* op. 26, 27 (Mainz, Schott's Söhne).—In his native city, Copenhagen, dwelt and died the renowned composer Niels W. Gade (b. 1817, d. 1890), whose pianoforte works are written cleanly and in the peculiar northern style; of these there have been issued by Breitkopf & Härtel, *Sonata* in *A* with Violin, op. 6, and another in *D*-minor, op. 21; *Frühlingsfantasie,* Concert piece for 4 solo voices, Orchestra, and Pianoforte, op. 23; *Arabeske,* op. 27; *Sonata* in *E*-minor, op. 28; *Volkstänze, Fantasiestücke,* op. 31; *Trio* with Violin and Violoncello in *F,* op. 42;—by Fr. Kistner, *Aquarellen,* op. 19; *der Kinder Christabend,* little piano-pieces; op. 41, *Fantasiestücke;*—by Rieter-Biedermann, *Idyllen;*—and by C. F. Peters, *Marches* for 4 hands, and *Skandinavische Volkslieder.*—Among the northern composers Edvard Hagerup Grieg, born on June 15, 1843, at Bergen in Norway, occupies a prominent place. In his Pianoforte *Concerto,* op. 16, *A*-minor, for 2 Pianofortes, *Violin Sonatas,* op. 8, *F*-major, and op. 13, *G*-major, *1 Sonata* for Pianoforte and 'Cello, op. 36, and in a number of piano-pieces and songs, Grieg displays strong original talent, and a poetic vein happily influenced by the folk-songs of his native land

—Ludwig Normann (b. 1831 at Stockholm, d. there in 1885) deserves mention as a gifted composer. Besides many pieces for 2 and 4 hands, his published works include *1 Violin Sonata, 1 Pianoforte Trio, 1 Pianoforte Quartet,* etc.—Emil Hartmann the younger is a remarkably gifted musician (b. at Copenhagen in 1836), who has written among other things *1 Pianoforte Trio, 1 Serenade* for Pianoforte, 'Cello, and Clarinet, and *salon pieces* for Pianoforte, wherein he, however, does not reach as high a plane as his father and teacher, E. Hartmann the elder (b. 1805), who is one of the first of northern composers, having written, besides operas, symphonies, overtures, cantatas, etc., some very original piano-pieces—*Novelletten.* —We also note the original Swedish composer Franz Berwald of Stockholm (1796—1868), the early and self-sustained writer of the following neo-romantic Pianoforte Works: *Two Quintets* for Pianoforte and Strings; *3 Trios* with Violin and 'Cello; and *1 Duo* with 'Cello (Leipzig, J. Schuberth & Co.)—Joseph Nowakowski, the Pole (b. 1805, d. 1865), likewise deserves mention as the composer of national *Mazurkas,* op. 10, 19, and 26, and his *Polonaises,* op. 13 and 14 (Breitkopf & Härtel).—Anton Dvořák (b. 1841 at Mühlhausen near Kralup in Bohemia) also occupies a high place among non-German composers for the pianoforte. His "*Slavic Dances*" for 4 hands, *1 Pianoforte Concerto,* op. 35, and other piano-pieces and larger works, reveal a distinguished talent, which is, to be sure, almost exclusively devoted to the national tendency. Slavic rhythms and melody-forms characterize his works wellnigh throughout.

Theodor Leschetizki (b. 1840 in Vienna), a pianist of high standing, was from 1864 to 1878 a teacher in the St. Petersburg Conservatory, and is now living with his spouse and former pupil Annette Essipoff in Vienna as a private instructor. His Pianoforte Works published by Schlesinger (Berlin) include *Romance,* op. 14; *Les Clochettes,* op. 16; *Six Méditations,* op. 19; *Perpetuum mobile,* op. 20; *Étude* for the left hand, op. 13;—by Spina (Vienna), *Gruss an die Nacht,* op. 1; *Valse cromatique,* op. 22;—by Leuckart (Leipzig), 6 books of *Improvisations,* op. 11.—His renowned pupil, Annette Essipoff (b. 1850) everywhere wins enthusiastic and well-earned applause on her frequent professional tours.—Nicolas Rubinstein (b. 1845 at Moscow, d. 1881 in Paris), a brother of Anton, founded a Conservatory of Music at Moscow; as a pianoforte virtuoso he knew no difficulties.

Turning to London, we find Arabella Goddard, "the most distinguished of English pianoforte-players" (b. 1838), a pupil of Kalkbrenner, Thalberg, and finally of J. W. Davison (d. 1885), the feared and famous musical critic of the Times, whom she married in 1860. As a classical player, especially of Beethoven's Sonatas, she is greeted with enthusiasm not only in England, but also on the continent of Europe (Leipzig, Gewandhaus, 1855), America, Australia, and India; —Charles Hallé (b. 1819) also enjoys a high reputation both in England and France. In 1836 he left Germany, his native country, for Paris, where his spirited performances, and in particular his characteristic interpretation of classical compositions, speedily gained him numerous friends and pupils. In 1848 he proceeded to London, and created a sensation there by his fine renderings of Beethoven's works. Since 1857 he has been about equally occupied in Manchester and London. Of his published compositions we note *4 Romances*, op. 1 (Schlesinger); *4 Esquisses*, op. 2, *Scherzo*, op. 4, and *Miscellanies*, op. 5 (London, Cramer, Beale & Co.). — Rudolph Schachner is the composer of several pianoforte *Concertos* and minor salon pieces, such as *La chasse*, op. 12 (Schlesinger), and *Souvenir de Deepdene* (Kistner). —G. A. Osborne, W. Kuhe, and J. Blumenthal also dwell in London, and have published a series of "easy and entertaining pianoforte pieces for amateurs".

Among Parisian pianists Saint-Saëns still takes the lead as a musician (comp. page 205); beside him shone or still shine the artists from the school of Marmontel, as Francis Planté, Th. Turner, Georges Bizet (1838—1875), Henri Ketten (1828—1883), Louis Diémer, Victor Alphons Duvernoy, Lavignac, Lack, Galeotti, Delafosse, and others.

Franz Liszt.

In the course of our survey we have seen how in Italy, during the 16th century, the instrumental style was developed under the influence of the Netherlander Adrian Willaert out of contrapuntally wrought vocal music, beginning with the stricter organ style. Further on, this instrumental style showed greater animation and flexibility in the works of Merulo and the ingenious Frescobaldi, until in the 17th century, foremostly through Pasquini's interesting performances, a freer secular clavier style was created, which reached its climax during the 18th century in the brilliant sonata movements of Dominico Scarlatti. Contemporary with this Italian school there arose, in France, another cultivating more graceful measures and motlier embellishments, which flourished from Champion (d. 1670) down to Couperin le Grand (d. 1733); while in Germany the more serious contrapuntal compositions, gradually disappearing from Italy and France, found their proper abiding-place. To Hans Leo Hasler (d. 1612), who was trained in Venice under the guidance of the meritorious Andrea Gabrieli, and to his contemporaries and successors, we owe the groundwork of an intellectually inspired German organ style, which attained to perfection in the master-fugues of Seb. Bach (d. 1750). His impressionable son Emanuel Bach then succeeded in establishing the art-form of the Sonata, written especially for the clavier and consisting of three movements, which Mozart later endowed with expressive lyrical inspiration, and Clementi with more diversified and brilliant colors. Beethoven thereafter raised the Sonata to a heart-stirring musical drama, gave it the unity necessary to every work of art by his ingenious and exhaustive working-out of its various motives, and likewise contrived the most interesting contrasts by means of spirited episodes and unexpected modulations. And while the following pure virtuoso pieces of Herz and Thalberg, calculated solely for external effect, quite gave over special characterization, Chopin and Schumann poured into their romantic compositions the inspiration of an enthusiastic, lofty poetry.

This language of souls lifted so far above the common herd, was still understood by but a narrow circle of sympathetic friends, and Schumann was still hurling his sharp arrows at the dull-witted opponents of the rising flood of R manticism, when **Franz Liszt** appeared in the arena, recalling to life the ancient myths of the spellful charm of music. Wherever he appeared, he won irresistibly the adherence of all parties, and celebrated triumphs whose like had been granted to no other conqueror in this field. His indescribably vigorous and powerful playing caused a complete revolution in pianoforte-playing, pianoforte literature, and pianoforte construction; he elevated virtuosity to a dizzy height, and has seemingly exhausted the means of expression of his instrument so far, that a further enhancement would seem hardly imaginable. He was born on Oct. 22, 1811, in Raiding near Pesth, received pianoforte lessons from his father from 1817, and was able only three years later to play in public, at Oedenburg, Ries' Concerto in *E♭* and a free fantasia. Prince Esterhazy, of whose estates his father was the overseer, attended the concert, and was much delighted at the boy's playing, rewarding him with a costly present. Soon after, his father took him to Pressburg, and here too his playing met with so favorable a reception, that Counts Amaden and Zapary were induced to allow him an annual stipend of 600 florins for six years, for his further education. The happy parents thereupon moved to Vienna, where Franz began regular music lessons under Carl Czerny. He found Clementi's sonatas uninteresting, but grasped the works of Hummel and Beethoven with such fiery zeal that the aged Salieri, having once heard him play, likewise felt drawn to him, and offered to give him his first instruction in composition. On his visits to the music shops, the compositions shown him never promised sufficient difficulty. But once he happened to meet several musicians engaged in the examination of Hummel's pianoforte concerto in *B*-minor, then fresh from the press, and was asked by them, whether this work would not put his skill to the test. The youthful Liszt placed the concerto on the piano, and played it at sight, to the astonishment of all present. In the year 1822, after the unbroken, assiduous study of 18 months, he gave his first concert in Vienna before a brilliant assemblage; after the concert was ended, the otherwise morose master, Beethoven, approached him with friendly mien, and with a kiss pressed the seal of consecration on his forehead. In the following year his father accompanied him to Paris, and the remarkable performances of the inspired romanticist, then scarce twelve years old, created a sensation even at that early day at the elegant soirées of the metropolis. In England during 1824 he found no scantier favor, and a grand concert arranged on his return to Paris called forth the liveliest enthusiasm. His strict father, however, insisted upon his continuing regular practice; among other matters he had daily to play several of Bach's fugues to his father, and to transpose them immediately into various keys. From 1826 he resumed theoretical studies under Reicha, but at this period fell into a state of gloomy religious exaltation, which took such full possession of him, that his father occasioned him to make a concert-tour through France, and in the following year sojourned for a considerable time in Switzerland and England. To invigorate his unstrung nervous system, his father took him in 1827 to the ocean resort Boulogne, but died shortly after, and Liszt returned to Paris, resolved to occupy himself there in teaching music. His chief intercourse at this time was with the able and original musician **Christian Urhan,** who was at once violinist in the Grand Opera and organist of St. Vincent de Paule, and whose liberal views on theoretical questions, together with pianoforte works correspondingly composed, had gained Liszt's liking. Of Urhan's little-known compositions, the following were published at Paris by Richault: *Elle et moi,* Duo romantique à 4 mains, op. 1; *Deuxième Duo romantique; La salutation angélique,* Duo à 4 mains; *Les regrets* and *Les lettres,* two pieces for pianoforte solo.

In the year 1828 HECTOR BERLIOZ, the gifted originator of our modern Program Music, brought out his Overtures to *Waverley* and the *Francs-juges,* and, in the year succeeding, the grand *Symphonie phantastique,* "Épisode de la vie d'un artiste". Liszt instantly recognized the extraordinary creative genius of this composer—still rightly appreciated by but a few unprejudiced musicians—and exhibited for the first time, in the *Partition de Piano* of the latter work, through what hitherto unknown means of expression (effect) the pianoforte is able to take the place of an entire orchestra in its volume and its manifold effects of tone. This pianoforte transcription, which only Liszt himself could then play, aroused the admiration of all pianists, and induced him later to undertake similar, though less difficult, arrangements, of the following instrumental works: *Cinquième et Sixième Symphonie* de Beethoven, Partition de Piano, Leipzig, Breitkopf & Härtel; *Septième Symphonie* de Beethoven, Vienna, Haslinger; *Ninth Symphony* by Beethoven, arr. for two pianofortes, Mainz, Schott; *Grand Septuor* de Beethoven, Leipzig, J. Schuberth & Co.; *Marche funèbre* de la Sinfonia eroica de Beethoven, Vienna, Mechetti; *Harold,* Symphonie de Berlioz; Weber's *Overtures* to *"Der Freischütz"* and *"Oberon"*, and the *Jubelouverture,* Berlin, Schlesinger; *Overture* to *William Tell,* by Rossini, Mainz, Schott; *Overture* to the *Francs-juges* and to *Roi Lear,* by Berlioz (ditto); *Overture* to *Tannhäuser,* by Wagner; *Kirchliche Fest-Ouverture,* by Nicolai, Leipzig, Hofmeister.

A sharp contrast to these bold transcriptions of orchestral works is formed by the deeply emotional tone-poems in which Liszt gave himself up to pious contemplation, whereby he was frequently led to keep his room for weeks together. To such original compositions belong: *Harmonies poétiques et religieuses,* 7 books, Leipzig, Kistner; *Apparitions,* Berlin, Schlesinger; and *Consolations,* Breitkopf & Härtel.

PAGANINI, the mighty master of the violin, appeared in Paris in 1831 and threw all former virtuosi into the shade by the irresistible attraction of his concerts. He not only executed the most incredible difficulties with perfect finish, but such difficulties also seemed like essential means for expressing special moods, for the manifestation of the keenest pain or wantonest humor. By these performances Liszt was stirred to his inmost soul; he reached the conviction, that a great assemblage could be thrown into such unexampled enthusiasm only through novel and unusual means;—that, the pianoforte could be made to produce musical and emotional effects rivalling in expressiveness those of the violin; and resolved to become the Paganini of the pianoforte.—For a long time nothing more was heard of Liszt; he vanished almost utterly from public notice, and people were reminded of him only through his *Grandes Études de Paganini,* transcrites pour le piano, 2 books (the first contains *La Campanella),* which appeared at that time (Breitkopf & Härtel). These Studies were supplemented later by the following original works: *Études d'exécution transcendante,* 2 books (same publ.), including *Mazeppa, Éroica, Feux follets,* etc.; *Trois grandes Études* de Concert, Leipzig, Kistner; and *Ab-Irato,* Étude de perfectionnement, Berlin, Schlesinger. Meantime he had quitted Paris, was heard from as staying by the Rhine and in Switzerland, and not until five years after the first Paganini concerts in Paris did he suddenly reappear on the scene of his earlier successes, with the announcement of a concert. But now he was no longer "le petit Liszt" who formerly enraptured the *beau monde* of the salons; he was the finished master, whom thenceforward no rival dared oppose. Under his hands the pianoforte was transformed, now to a thrilling organ, now to a soothing Æolian harp; anon his unheard-of, demonic harmonies swept on like a stormwind, and again he charmed the ear with dulcet, flute-like tones and wierd melodies, around which marvellous passages wound like arabesques twined of bright flowers and pearls.

The years from 1836 to 1848 show an unbroken series of the brilliant triumphs of this creator of the modern art of pianoforte-playing, which combines all fine traits of the earlier schools. He first proceeded to Vienna and Hungary in 1837, then travelled through Italy as far as Naples, appeared in 1840 at Leipzig, in 1842 at Berlin, visited Russia, Sweden, Denmark, Spain, and Portugal in turn, and in 1847 played even at Constantinople. In Pesth he was presented with a splendid sword, in Königsberg he was created Doctor; the Emperor of Austria conferred the order of knighthood upon him, the Pope honored him with the order of the Golden Spur, and the Grand-duke of Weimar, who had made him his Hofkapellmeister in 1848, appointed him his chamberlain. No artist has been so loaded with honors as Liszt, but as a man no one has proved himself worthier of them. Wherever help was needed to support a great undertaking, to raise a monument to the memory of a celebrated man, to encourage an ardent talent, or to succor the sorely distressed, he always showed his greatheartedness by word and deed.

The original compositions performed at his concerts and published later, were at first held for impracticable by all other pianists. But Liszt gathered about him in Weimar a circle of pupils of both sexes, familiarized them with his new manner of holding the hand, his fingering, and style of playing, repeating emphatically, that to be effective the style must be full of soul and character, and that the artist "should not appear before the audience like the accused before his judges, but as a witness to eternal truth and beauty".

To Liszt's most effective **Concert Compositions** belong the following Fantasias on motives from various operas: *Grande Fantaisie dramatique* sur des thèmes de l'opéra Les Huguenots, Berlin, Schlesinger; *Réminiscences de Robert le diable*, ditto; *Réminiscences de la Juive*, ditto; *Réminiscences de Don Juan*, ditto; *Fantaisie sur des motifs de l'opéra La Sonnambula*, Leipzig, J. Schuberth & Co.; *Réminiscences de Norma*, Mainz, Schott; *Réminiscences des Puritains*, ditto; *I Puritani*, Introduction and Polonaise, ditto; *Fantaisie* sur la Tyrolienne de l'opéra La Fiancée, Vienna, Mechetti; *Réminiscences de Lucrezia Borgia*, 2 books, ditto; *Réminiscences de Lucia di Lammermoor*, Leipzig, Hofmeister; *Marche et Cavatine* de Lucia, Mainz, Schott; *Illustrations du Prophète* de Meyerbeer, 3 books, Leipzig, Breitkopf & Härtel; 2 pieces from Wagner's *Tannhäuser* and *Lohengrin*, ditto; 3 pieces from *Lohengrin*, ditto; *Andante and March* from the opera *Alfred* by J. Raff, Magdeburg, Heinrichshofen; *Deux Motifs de Benvenuto Cellini* de Berlioz, Brunswick, Meyer; *4 Concert Paraphrases* on "God save the Queen", Ernani, Rigoletto, and Il Trovatore by Verdi, Leipzig, J. Schuberth & Co.; *Hochzeitsmarsch und Elfenreigen* from the *Sommernachtstraum*, Breitkopf & Härtel; *Marche funèbre* de Don Sebastian, Vienna, Mechetti; *Valse de bravoure* on Motives from Gounod's Faust, Berlin, Bote & Bock.—To these may be added the following effective **Salon Pieces:** *Tarantella di bravura*, Vienna, Mechetti; *Gaudeamus igitur*, Breslau, Hainauer; *Hussitenlied*, Leipzig, Hofmeister; *Leier und Schwert*, after C. M. v. Weber, Berlin, Schlesinger; *Capriccio alla turca*, Vienna, Mechetti; *Ungarischer Sturmmarsch*, Berlin, Schlesinger; *Venezia e Napoli*, Mainz, Schott; *Zwei Balladen*, Leipzig, Kistner; *Scherzo und Marsch*, Brunswick, Meyer; *Drei Caprices-Valses*, Vienna, Haslinger; *Heroischer Marsch* in Hungarian style, Berlin, Schlesinger; *Goethe-Festmarsch*, Leipzig, J. Schuberth & Co.; 2 characteristic *Polonaises* and a brilliant *Mazurka*, Leipzig, Senff; a seductive *Valse-Impromptu*, Leipzig, J. Schuberth & Co.; and finally *1 Galop chromatique* (Leipzig, Hofmeister), sweeping onward with demonic wantonness, and executed by Liszt in an incredibly rapid tempo.

The original compositions in the *Années de pélérinage*, suites de compositions pour le Piano, 1e année, Suisse; 2e année, Italie (Mainz, Schott) breathe now the most ardent devotion, now the deepest melancholy of a youthful, impressionable nature lost in wrapt survey of the natural beauties of those countries; while a grand *Concert Solo* in *E*-minor (Breitkopf & Härtel), and still more a *Sonata* in *B*-minor dedicated to Robert Schumann (ditto), rank with Liszt's grandest and most original works by reason of their peculiar form, fantastic spirit, and venturesome modulutions.

A species of music-piece invented by Liszt are the **Transcriptions for the Pianoforte,** in which not only the melodies treated take on a warm, living *colorit* conformable to their character, but the poems, too, on which they are founded are charmingly and spiritedly illustrated by music closely following the thread of the story. Franz Schubert's songs, in particular, first became generally known and popular in Germany through Liszt's spirited transcriptions for piano. Of these there have been published: *Twelve Songs* by Franz Schubert, transcribed for the Pianoforte, Vienna, Spina; *Schwanengesang*, 14 Numbers, Vienna, Haslinger; the *Winterreise*, 10 Numbers, ditto; *Die Rose* and *Lob der Thränen*, ditto; the *Müllerlieder*, transcribed for pianoforte in easier style, 3 books, Vienna, Spina; *Six Melodies*, Berlin, Schlesinger; the *Sacred Songs*, Leipzig, J. Schuberth & Co. — To the same class belong *Beethoven's Songs* for the Pianoforte, 12 Numbers publ. by Breitkopf & Härtel and 6 Numbers by J. Schuberth & Co.; *Songs by Mendelssohn*, 7 Numbers publ. by Breitkopf & Härtel and 2 Numbers by Kistner in Leipzig; *Songs by Robert Franz*, 3 books, Breitkopf & Härtel; *Liebeslied* by Schumann, *Schlummerlied* by C. M. v. Weber, and *"O du, mein holder Abendstern"* from Tannhäuser, Leipzig, Kistner; *Buch der Lieder* by Liszt, four Pianoforte soli, Berlin, Schlesinger; *Polish Melodies* by Chopin, ditto; *Soirées de Rossini*, 14 Numbers, Mainz, Schott; *National Melodies* from the Ukraine and Poland, Leipzig, Kistner; *Soirées de Mercadante*, 6 Numbers; *Soirées de Donizetti*, 3 Numbers, Mainz, Schott; *National Melodies* from Russia, Hamburg, Cranz; ditto from Béarn, 2 Numbers, Mainz, Schott.—A similar species of transcriptions is formed by the *Valses-Caprices d'après F. Schubert* (Vienna, Spina), overflowing with fun and frolic, wit and humor; and finally, the effective transcriptions of Seb. Bach's *6 Preludes and Fugues* for the Organ (Ped. and Man.) Leipzig, Peters.—Novel in form and exciting in development are the following original compositions: *Episodes* from Lenau's Faust; *Nächtlicher Zug* and *Mephisto-Walzer* (J. Schuberth & Co.); the *Elegies* and the *Legends* (C. F. Kahnt); *Ave Maria, Waldesrauschen*, and *Gnomenreigen* in the Lebert-Stark Pianoforte Method (J. G. Cotta).

In sensitive, glowing colors appear the following works arranged by Liszt for Pianoforte and Orchestra: Weber's *Polonaise* in *E*, Berlin, Schlesinger; Schubert's *Fantasia* in *C*, Vienna, Spina; *Capriccio alla turca* on motives from Beethoven's Ruins of Athens; *Hungarian Rhapsody* in *E*-minor; and also two grand *Pianoforte Concertos*, products of most ardent inspiration, in *E*♭ (Vienna, Haslinger), and in *A* (Mainz, Schott), which, by reason of their lofty and intensely effective spirit and their supremely beautiful form, must be reckoned among the grandest, most powerful, and brilliant works in Pianoforte Literature.

As Chopin glorified his own nation in his moving Polonaises and Mazurkas, Liszt most faithfully portrayed and sang the nature and doings, the life and love of the Gypsies of his native land, in a series of attractive musical poems issued under the title of *Rhapsodies hongroises*. We unfortunately possess no complete edition of the same; for Nos. 1 and 2 were published by Senff, Leipzig, Nos. 3 to 10 by Haslinger of Vienna, and Nos. 11 to 15 by Schlesinger of Berlin. Liszt lived at various times for considerable periods among the Gypsies in Hungary; and these untamed children of Nature, too, were carried away by the might of his music, and admired and revered him wholly. His studies on their character are found in the book: *Des Bohémiens et de leur musique en Hongrie*, Paris, Bourdilliat et Cie. (German by Peter Cornelius, Pesth, Heckenast). This interesting work forms a commentary, so to speak, on his Hungarian Rhapsodies, as he himself suggests in its course as follows: "The charm which the music of the Gypsies has exercised upon us since childhood, familiarity with its peculiar sound and sense, comparable to no other kind, this gradual penetration into the secret of its life-springs, the ever-deeper insight into the nature of its form and the necessity of its perseverance in an eccentricity, any abatement of which would mean a renunciation of its character, a denial of its individuality, naturally led us very early to adapt many of its fragments for the pianoforte. And leisure hours soon amassed a goodly number of such adaptations, yet quite without an ulterior aim. But very far from satisfying our *penchant* or noting a diminution of our interest, we grew more and more absorbed in the work, and felt an ever-growing desire to transfer to our instrument the eloquent admonitions, the wierd effusions, the reveries, revels, and extravagances of this coy Muse. But with each step forward the task waxed immeasurably; at last no stopping-place, no bounds could be found. A crushing load of material weighed us down. Then arose the need of comparing, choosing, polishing, setting off! And amidst these endeavors the conviction strengthened within us, that these fragmentary, scattered melodies were the wandering, floating, nebulous parts of a great Whole, that they fully answered the conditions for the production of an harmonious unity, which would comprehend the very flower of their essential properties, their most unique beauties, and which, on the strength of the internal confirmation attempted by us at the beginning of these pages, might be regarded as a kind of national epic, sung by this people, who in all their ways follow an unwonted, unusual course, in an unwonted and unusual form and speech. From this new point of view we soon perforce became aware, that the wellnigh innumerably different forms of the Gypsy music, such as odes, dithyrambs, elegies, ballads, idyls, gazels, disticles, hymns of war, burial songs, love-songs, and drinking-rimes, might be united to one homogeneous body, to a complete work, its divisions to be so arranged that each song would form at once a whole and a part, which might be severed from the rest and be examined and enjoyed by and for itself, but which would none the less belong to the whole through the close affinity of subject-matter, the similarity of its inner nature, and unity in development. The isolated fragments of Gypsy music already published by us were subjected to renewed scrutiny; they were modified; blended, combined, conformably to our design of a Whole, which thus presented in its structure a work approximately realizing our idea of a Gypsy Epic, such as our fancy had portrayed".

Liszt's earlier-mentioned **reform in the holding of the hand** in piano-playing is propagated by his numerous pupils; his **peculiar fingering,** aiming foremostly at a more vigorous touch and a more even execution of passages, we often find indicated where necessary in his pianoforte compositions. The earliest style of holding the hand was such that the player, whose elbows when quietly seated before the keyboard were below the level of the keys, was fairly obliged to draw the latter down with the fingers; a coin laid upon the back of the hand would therefore have slid off into the player's lap, or to the floor. Much the same posture we see, for example, on the title-page of the Theoricum opus musicæ disciplinæ, (second edit., 1492), by Franchino Gafori, this celebrated musician being seated at the organ. In the earliest clavier works, which down to Frescobaldi resembled the scores for four-part vocal music, the fingering followed as best it might the progression of the four independent parts, and the black keys, whose tones sounded tolerably pure only in certain keys on account of the prevailing system of unequal temperament, were therefore used but seldom. The fingering did not become more difficult until compositions intended for the clavier began to be written with livelier runs and passages, and when, after Seb. Bach's appearance, the introduction of the equal temperament made it possible to use the black keys like the others. Before Bach's time, the thumb was employed only in wide stretches; it was therefore allowed to hang down, so as not to impede the stiffly outstretched fingers. For the clavier works of Bach, however, which were written in all keys, the thumb was "suddenly elevated from its former inactivity to the position of chief finger". (Essay on the true Method of playing the Clavier). In Germany, C. Ph. E. Bach was the first who attempted to reduce his father's fingering to rule. In the work just alluded to (third edition, 1787) he says: The hands should be held suspended above the keyboard in a horizontal position. One should play with bent fingers, without nervous straining; the commoner this fault, the more heed should be given to it. For whoever plays with straight fingers and tense nerves removes the other fingers, by reason of their length, too far from the thumb, which on the contrary ought constantly to keep as close as may be to the hand; they thus quite prevent this chief finger from doing its duty. The black keys are shorter and lie higher than the white, and therefore naturally belong to the three longest fingers. "Hence arises the first principal rule, that the little finger should touch the black keys seldom, and the thumb do this only in case of necessity." Where the fingers do not suffice, the thumb is turned under, being naturally designed thereto by its flexibility and shortness. "Passing over is effected by the other fingers, and is facilitated by passing a longer finger over a shorter one or over the thumb, when the fingers come to an end, as it were. — The passing of the thumb under the little finger, of the second finger over the third, of the third over the second, the fourth over the fifth, or of the little finger over the thumb, is reprehensible."

According to Clementi's method a silver dollar laid on the back of the hand should not fall off while playing. Francesco Pollini taught, on the contrary, in his Clavier Method (1811) mentioned earlier, that the hand should be held in a horizontal position, but *arched* (rotondata). And finally, Liszt did not hold his hand horizontally, but with the wrist higher than the front part, so that a coin laid on the back would slide down to the keyboard. If the fingers then rise to the height of the wrist, they gain all the more strength for the down-stroke upon the keys. Liszt sometimes played a strongly marked series of tones with the more powerful second finger alone, and a similar octave passage with the thumb and the third or fourth fingers; for a sustained or loud trill he used not only two adjoining finger, but pairs separated by others, such as first and third, or third and fifth; the right hand executed such trills in suitable places even with the following fingering: 1-4 2-3, 1-4 2-3, etc. He likewise produced a sharp trill in sixths or thirds by playing the main notes with the right hand, and the subsidiary notes with the left, with equal power. For a passage regularly repeated in different octaves, he chose the most convenient fingering in *one* octave and repeated the same in the following octaves, when it frequently occurs, in opposition to earlier rules, that the thumb is passed under the fifth finger, or the latter over the thumb. In his compositions, besides, we meet with chords whose width or full harmony seems to require the co-operation of both hands, whereas one of the latter is at the same time occupied in another way. In this case they are to be executed as broken or arpeggio'd chords by an accelerated crossing of the hands. He brings out two motives, at first treated separately, together further on; and, finally, sometimes performs a melody in three or fourfold octave unisons, while interweaving the same with the most brilliant passages, taking up the whole range of the keyboard, or accompanied by fullest-toned harmonies. The full harmony of the chords written by Liszt is produced especially by the favorable acoustic setting of their parts, in which the tone-waves formed can propagate in freest vibration all accompanying overtones and tones of combination. Each of Liszt's pianoforte compositions also proffers us new combinations and striking effects of tone, many of which years since became the common property of all pianists. But no one can form a definite conception of his marvellous performances except those, who have themselves heard him; Robert Schumann, after hearing him in 1840 at Leipzig, pointedly writes in a long article on his playing: "The instrument glows and flames under its master — it is no longer pianoforte-playing of this or that kind, but the veriest manifestation of a dauntless character, to whom, for ruling and conquering, Fate for once allotted instead of dangerous implements the peaceful ones of Art."

[Liszt lived out his life of nearly 75 years fully and wholly, creating, teaching, and helping to his last breath. In the churchyard at Bayreuth there stands, since Oct. 22, 1887 (his 77th birthday), a mausoleum over the grave of the artist whose name and fame filled the world, and are written in indelible characters in the book of the history of Art. Among the works left by Liszt is a method of study in three volumes, which has been issued under Alex. Winterberger's supervision by J. Schuberth in Hamburg. Difficulties with the publisher prevented the intended earlier publication of the work, already prepared for the press; Liszt's pleasure in the work was spoiled, and thus a final revision of the same by the master himself was not undertaken. Furthermore, a Pianoforte Concerto in *E*-minor with string orchestra has been found, which Liszt presumably composed during his stay in Switzerland (1835—1840). This work, named by himself "*Malédiction*", appears to have been left unfinished, as the score is not completed for full orchestra, and the pianoforte part shows a great number of alterations and variants in Liszt's hand. In form it resembles the *A*-major Concerto, and contains many beautiful, poetical touches. Liszt's pregnant writings, done into German by L. Ramann, have been published in six volumes by Breitkopf & Härtel, and mirror the wide knowledge, the rich experience in art, the lofty artistic standpoint, and the noble heart of this unmatched genius, so worthy of reverence both as an artist and as a man, in a truly dazzling light. A minute and intelligently written biography of Liszt, by Lina Ramann, has been published by Breitkopf & Härtel in 2 volumes. **O. L.**]

Liszt's Pupils and Contemporaries.

Among the pupils of the universally revered master, Franz Liszt, the one most nearly approaching him in truth and clearness of conception, in nobility and finish of execution, is

Hans von Bülow,

born at Dresden in the year 1830. He has also published a succession of brilliant salon pieces and more serious characteristic works, which exhibit him, in this aspect as well, as a thoroughly trained musician with an exquisite sense of the Beautiful. We mention: *Marche hongroise*, op. 3 (Mainz, Schott); *Rêverie fantastique*, op. 7 (Breslau, Leuckart); *Ballade*, op. 11 (Mainz, Schott); *Au sortir du bal*, op. 24 (Bote & Bock); *I Carnivale de Milano*, op. 21 (Barth. Senff); and a charmfully sparkling, flower-scented, deftly and airily flitting "*Elfenjagd*" (Leipzig, G. Heinze). Further, in his paraphrase of Wagner's "*Tristan and Isolde*", Bülow has produced a master-piece in pianoforte arrangement. Not only are the various orchestral effects reproduced in piano-style with a wealth of brilliant colors, but not one of the often intricately interwoven melodies of this overflowing score is slighted. All virtuosi preceding him had celebrated their most signal triumphs by the performance of their own original works; but he, familiar with both early and recent clavier literature, gifted with an astounding memory and a surprising keenness of conception, resolved to win renown through the vivid interpretation of masterworks of the past and present. And he became the miraculous resuscitator of the creations of the venerable Sebastian Bach, the profoundest expounder of Beethoven's last revelations, the most fiery declaimer of the fantastic tone-poems of Franz Liszt. As the latter had delivered all his performances free from memory, Bülow in like manner so assimilates the compositions of the masters of his choice, that he plays them as if improvising in inspired moments. He reproduces the Preludes, Fugues, and Suites of Bach and Handel with the full vigor and independence of the parts; interprets Emanuel Bach and Mozart in all their freshness and amiability; reveals the depth and sublimity of the gloomful Beethoven; attracts us sympathetically through Chopin's soulful poems, leads us with Schubert's charming melodies into the swirl of the brilliant ball-room, and arouses our warmest enthusiasm by the dazzling tone-colors and storm-swept passages of Liszt's Fantasias. In the rich and choice programs of his pianoforte recitals Bülow sets himself the loftiest tasks, and in his execution of the same excels all his predecessors in this field. We have heard him play, besides Liszt's Études, concert paraphrases, and Hungarian Rhapsodies, the pathetic Sonata in *B*-minor from memory, faithfully and in finished beauty. He has also played Beethoven's 33 Variations op. 120, and even the same master's last five Sonatas op. 101, 106, 109, 110 and 111 in a concert given at Berlin in 1878, in such a fashion that the large audience followed the thrilling delivery of these romantically dramatic poems with ever-growing excitement.

Bülow, who besides his high pianistic attainments is also an eminent conductor, having among other things brought the art of conducting without score into vogue, has held in turn the position of Kapellmeister at Munich, Hanover, Meiningen, St. Petersburg, and Berlin; his own pianoforte recitals, beginning with a concert-tour through Germany and Austria in 1853, have won him world-wide renown. Among his pupils, several are distinguished as virtuosi or teachers, above all Frits Hartvigson in London, Max Schwarz in Frankfort, Mr. Hatton, Heinrich Barth in Berlin, Frederic Lammond in Glasgow, Miss Anna Haasters in Cologne, and others. His fellow-pupil

Karl Tausig

(1841—1871), whose career ended just as he had reached the pinnacle of virtuosity, was original in another way. Hardly any other pianist will ever exhibit even the will to reach the same perfection. In strength, endurance, and precision he surpassed all his rivals. The tasks which he set himself were always accomplished in a wonderful manner. He relieved the romantically sentimental Chopin of his *Weltschmerz*, and showed him in his pristine creative vigor and wealth of imagination. He led his hearers into the awful depths of Beethoven's works, laid bare new veins of precious metals in their gloomy shafts, and displayed the treasures so found in the most brilliant fire and magical splendor of color. Tausig's *Nouvelles Soirées de Vienne*, published in Vienna and dedicated to his teacher Franz Liszt, are full of the most astonishing flashes of fancy; they pursue with wanton humor the Strauss waltzes on which they are built up, bombarding them with most graceful banterings, piquant passages, and striking harmonies.* In 1866 Tausig founded in Berlin a "*Schule des Höheren Clavierspiels*", in which at the outset Franz

* Comp. "Der letzte Virtuoso", by C. F. Weitzmann. Leipzig, C. F. Kahnt.

Bendel, and later Adolf Jensen, Louis Ehlert, Carl Bial, Franz Kroll, and Otto Lessmann were engaged as teachers. The most distinguished pupils issuing from this school were Rafaell Joseffy (b. 1852 at Pressburg, now living in New York), Max Pinner (b. 1851 at New York, d. 1887 in Davos), Oskar Raif (Berlin), Oskar Beringer (London), Vera Timanoff (St. Petersburg), Gustav Weber (d. 1887 in Zurich, published a valuable Pianoforte Quartet), and others.

Other of Liszt's most eminent pupils are **Hans von Bronsart** (b. 1830 in Berlin), whose *Trio* in *G*-minor for Pianoforte, Violin, and Violoncello shows the thoroughly trained musician, and whose *Pianoforte Concerto* in *F*♯-minor is also valuable musically;—**Dionys Pruckner**, who may be termed the classicist among more recent pianists, in that he combines faultless accuracy of execution, uncommon fullness of tone, and complete technical mastership with measured repose in the clear and organically contrasted exposition of the musical contents of the work in hand. These refinements have won for his playing not only most gratifying recognition from the narrower circles of thorough musicians, but likewise most brilliant successes in his public performances at Vienna, Pesth, Munich, Stuttgart, and other places;—**Franz Bendel**, who, both by his inspired performances and several attractive and genial compositions, has won a good reputation. To the works already mentioned may be added an extremely interesting *Ballade* (op. 31, Berlin, Challier), and among his posthumous works, published by the same house, a very melodious *Sonata* for Pianoforte and Violin in *E*-minor, and an animated *Trio* with Violin and 'Cello.

To this list may be added, as worthy fellow-pupils, Franz Kroll (1826—1877), who has also published various attractive pianoforte works, the (already mentioned) composers and pianists Salomon Jadassohn, Xaver Scharwenka, and Theodor Ratzenberger, together with the artists Karl Klindworth and William Mason; and finally the latterly very prominent artist **Giovanni Sgambati** (b. 1843 in Rome), who has written *1 Pianoforte Quartet*, *2 Quintets*, *F*-minor, op. 7, *B*♭-major, op. 5, *1 Pianoforte Concerto* in *G*-minor, op. 15, and many solo pieces; in all these Sgambati proves himself a highly gifted and ingenious composer, formed no less under the influence of the neo German tendency, than under that of the German classics. A *Prelude and Fugue* have been issued by Schott, Mainz.

Among the younger masters of pianoforte-playing, a long list of fine pupils of Liszt's later years have won distinction. First of all we must name.

Moritz Rosenthal. Despite Anton Rubinstein's dictum (in "Art and Artists") that the age of the great virtuosi came to a final end with Tausig's death, the question involuntarily arises on hearing Rosenthal, whether such perfect finish and mastery of every technical nuance and shade of expression could ever have been surpassed. Rosenthal was born at Lemberg in 1862; at the age of 8 years his natural bent for pianoforte-playing was so strongly developed, as to attract the attention and secure the aid of Mikuli, the Director of the Lemberg Conservatory. Two years later, Raphael Joseffy initiated him into Tausig's advanced method, and at the age of 14 Rosenthal gave a concert in Vienna, playing brilliant compositions by Weber, Beethoven, Chopin, and Liszt. On a concert-tour to Roumania he earned the title of Royal Pianist to the Roumanian Court. From 1878 onward, Liszt took the leading part in his pianistic education; Rosenthal followed the master on his yearly migrations to Weimar, Pesth, Vienna, and Rome, a faithful companion until Liszt's death in 1886. Thus he is both one of the last and youngest of Liszt's disciples in art. In 1887 he made his first concert tournée in America, and has since then created a furore in various European musical capitals. He throws into the shade all other competitors in the field of pianoforte virtuosity, whether as regards the boldness, the fairly astounding accuracy, or the overwhelming power of his technical performance. But he commands, besides, the entire scale of charming effects in touch and tone, and in the fullness of contrast found in modern romanticism no living contemporary is his rival.

Eugène d'Albert (b. at Glasgow on April 10, 1864) is the son of a French musician, a teacher of music and dancing in England, and of a German mother; he received his first musical instruction from his father, then becoming a pupil of Ernst Pauer in London. In the year 1880 Hans Richter took the highly talented youth to Vienna and introduced him to Liszt, under whose guidance the unusual gifts of the young artist developed with astonishing rapidity. d'Albert's first concerts at Vienna and Berlin justly created a sensation, for the effect of the youthful virtuoso's brilliant technique was enhanced by the intellectual maturity of his interpretations—an infallible sign of one of those few chosen from among many that are called. *1 Suite* in five movements for Pianoforte, op. 1 (Bote & Bock), and *1 Pianoforte Concerto* in *B*-minor, *Songs*, *Piano-pieces*, *2 Overtures*, etc., reveal the fine creative faculty of the young artist, who in the course of a few years has won European renown. In 1886 d'Albert settled in Eisenach. (It may be of interest to note, in view of his exuberant vigor and great powers of endurance, that d'Albert is a strict vegetarian).

Among Liszt's younger pupils we name further Arthur Friedheim (b. Oct. 26, 1859 at St. Petersburg), who for many years profitted by his master's instruction in Weimar, Rome, and Pesth, and in regard to brilliancy and precision of technique has few rivals. He is in the main a Liszt player, and with reference to the latter's works is a reliable maintainer of the direct tradition.—Bernhard Stavenhagen, too (b. 1862 at Greiz), after finishing his course of study in the *Hochschule* at Berlin, and masterfully developing his artistic individuality from 1885 under Liszt's influence, speedily gained a high reputation in Germany and England. Stavenhagen's style is distinguished for brilliant technique paired with great warmth of expression, which advantages he shares with Emil Sauer, at present living in Dresden. The latter, like another Liszt pupil of the younger generation, Alexander von Siloti, had previously studied under the guidance of Nicolas Rubinstein at Moscow. Other concert players of note are Alfred Reisenauer of Königsberg, Conrad Ansorge of Weimar (b. 1862 in Lieben), Max van de Sandt, Carl Schuler, Bertrand Roth of Dresden, Carl Pohlig, Jules de Zarembski (b. 1854 in Schitomir, Russia, d. Sept. 15, 1885 in Brussels as the successor of Louis Brassin at the Conservatory).

As well known as these, though in a different field, is Martin Krause of Leipzig, whose celebrity as a teacher of the pianoforte is due mainly to his faithful and scientifically exact maintainance of the Liszt tradition. — Martin Krause was born at Lobstedt near Leipzig in 1853, of a musical family; under the strict instruction of his father, a cantor, he was able at the age of 8 to play the organ in church and transpose chorales at sight, and on Sundays bore a part in quartets with his brothers and sisters. When 13 years old he went to Borna, attending the seminary there from his 15th to 19th year, and graduating as the first in his class both in music and letters. Here he obtained, from the piano-teacher Fuchs, the first ideas of his present technique. Coming to Leipzig, he attended the University down to his 22nd year, hearing lectures on musical and scientific subjects; he also entered the Conservatory in 1873, having instruction from Reinecke and Wenzel, to the former of whom he owes his initiation into the "art of a singing execution", and to the latter the theory of "the loose wrist". Undecided whether to devote himself to music or to letters, the opinion expressed by Reinecke after thoroughly testing Krause's powers, "that it had never before been so easy for him to give advice in such a matter", finally turned the scale in favor of art. Six months' teaching in an institute at Montreux, Switzerland, and a prolonged stay at Detmold as private tutor in a family, where he had a chance to practise from 8 to 11 hours daily, so far ripened his powers, that in 1878 we find him making a concert-tour in various towns of Holland and Germany, meeting everywhere with great success. In the Spring of 1880 he returned to Leipzig, played in Blüthner's hall, but then broke down from the strain of over-practice, and was nervously prostrated for two years. He made Liszt's acquaintance in 1882, and played before him for the first time in 1883. Thenceforward he was often, sometimes for a month at a time, in Weimar, in constant communication with the master and his pupils, eagerly observant of the minutest technical and artistic details, and taking infinite pains to learn from the older pupils — those of the time when Liszt still gave careful instruction in the minutiæ of technique — all details which could throw light on the master's marvelous facility. Krause, whose own specialty as a player was Beethoven, lays peculiar stress on Liszt's wonderful faculty for recognizing and bringing out each pupil's strong point and special capacity. In 1885 Krause, the Russian Siloti, Frau Moran-Olden, and others gave two grand concerts in Leipzig, at which Liszt was present, and which led to the foundation that same year of the famous "Lisztverein" (Liszt Society), of which Krause was the chief promoter and is still the chairman and manager. Since that year he has been settled in Leipzig as a teacher and writer, and in both these branches his thorough scientific and practical education in letters and art afford a firm foundation for a growing reputation. A work now in preparation by Krause on "Phrasing" will be eagerly awaited by all knowing his views on this highly important subject — a subject which the abstruse would-be scientific treatment frequently accorded it only tends to render confusing and disheartening to the average student-mind. In recognition of Krause's distinguished services to the cause of art, the Duke of Anhalt bestowed on him, in June, 1892, the title of Professor.

Among Liszt's lady pupils we name Vera Timanoff in St. Petersburg and Martha Remmert in Weimar, who have won recognition as virtuosi in concerts given at home and abroad. Emma Grosscurth of Cassel.

and Emma Koch of Munich, both of whom finished their studies under the supervision of Liszt and Bülow, have in numerous concerts proved themselves thoughtful *pianistes* of good musical taste.

Concerning the ladies, the term "pupils of Liszt" unhappily took on a somewhat unpleasant aftertaste during the last years of the master's life, a large number of immature or mediocrely endowed ladies having walked through the salon of the growingly indulgent artist, in order thereafter to give themselves out in highly inflated puffs not only for pupils, but for "favorite pupils", of Liszt. Thus it is too easily explainable, that critics and public alike finally became suspicious of the once so honorable title; still, enough genuine pupils of either sex uphold their master's memory, through the striving to serve true art in his spirit with seriousness and honest zeal.

Raff, Brahms, and Rubinstein.

These three masters elevated themselves to the culminating point of their productivity, not by pianoforte works alone, but also in particular by larger sacred, dramatic, and symphonic compositions. These larger works are among the finest of modern times; a selection from their pianoforte compositions has for a considerable period adorned the racks of our foremost pianists. **Joachim Raff** (b. on May 27, 1822, in Lachen on the Lake of Zurich, d. June 24/25, 1882, at Frankfort) made no name as a pianoforte virtuoso, yet his works in this category always show the most convenient piano-style, and all display a teeming imagination and thorough musical science, intelligently employed in a free and unconstrained way. For a time he dwelt near Liszt in Weimar, then settled in Wiesbaden, and in 1877 was appointed to the directorship of the Hoch Conservatory at Frankfort-on-the-Main. His diversified piano-pieces are for the most part, both in regard to conception and execution, accessible not merely to the grasp and powers of a virtuoso, but to any pianist of ability.

Attractive grace and freshness are exhaled, for example, by Raff's "*Frühlingsboten*", 12 piano-pieces, op. 55 (Leipzig, J. Schuberth & Co.). The first piece, *Winterruhe,* bears us to the sociable hearth of a cozy room, where we listen to the tender converse of a happy couple. In the second piece Spring is ushered in with all his songful messengers and fragrant flower-bells, repeating more and more urgently the cry: "Die Fenster auf, die Herzen auf!" (The windows ope, your hearts ope wide). In No. 3 we hear an earnest chorale in the Doric mode; then follows a warmer, livelier movement, wherein the theme of "the Oath" bears a warning part as *canto fermo*. No. 4, with its animated rhythms and exciting suspensions and deceptive progressions, constantly increases our feeling of "Unrest"; in No. 5 a sweetly caressing melody seeks to bring about a "Reconciliation" between the resentful lovers, but No. 6 renews the quarrel, gathering up its threads in a lively fugue. Like happily and artistically treated character-pieces are also found in the second half of the work, which contains very interesting figuration. With equally loving care are also wrought the piano-pieces of the following collections: *Album lyrique*, op. 17 (J. Schuberth & Co.); *Schweizerweisen*, op. 60 in 9 books (ditto); *12 Romances* en forme d'Études, op. 8, Breitkopf & Härtel; *Angelens letzter Tag im Kloster*, a cycle of epico-lyric fragments for Pianoforte, op. 27, Leipzig, Kistner. Of his other pianoforte works we mention several books of finely wrought *Suites*, published in Winterthur by Rieter-Biedermann, and in Leipzig by Peters; *Scherzo*, op. 3, Breitkopf & Härtel; *4 Galops brillants*, op. 5 ditto; *Morceau instructif*, Fantaisie et Variations brillantes, op. 6, ditto; *Impromptu*, op. 9, ditto; *Capricietto*, op. 40, Kistner; *Romanze*, op. 41, ditto. The works following require the skill of a virtuoso: *Hommage au Néoromantisme*, grand Capriccio, op. 10, Breitkopf & Härtel; *Sonate avec fugue* in *E*♭-minor, op. 14, ditto; *Capriccio*, op. 64; Three pianoforte soli, *Ballade*, *Scherzo*, and *Metamorphoses*, op. 74 (dedicated to Hans v. Bülow), J. Schuberth & Co.; and *Chant de l'Ondin*, grande Étude de l'Arpeggio-Tremolando, op. 83, Leipzig, Peters;—whereas the charming *12 Piano-pieces* of the set op. 75 (Leipzig, Kistner), are dedicated "to little hands". Raff shows himself a master of the broader forms in his five grand *Sonatas* with Violin, op. 59, 73, 78, 128, and 129; also in the *Trio*, op. 102, and the *Quintet* with Strings, op. 107 (all publ. by J. Schuberth & Co.), and in the two *Quartets* with Strings, op. 202, two books (Leipzig, Siegel). We must also mention the *12 Morceaux à 4 mains*, op. 82, separate or in 2 sets; *3 Sonatillen*, op. 99; *Deux Caprices de concert*, op. 111 (all Leipzig, J. Schuberth & Co.); *Erinnerung an Venedig*, op. 187, 6 books; *Reisebilder* for 4 hands, op. 160, 10 books (both publ. by Siegel, Leipzig); *Vom Rhein*, op. 134 (Fr. Kistner); *Am Giessbach*, op. 88; *La Gitana*, op. 110 (Rieter-Biedermann); *Polka de la Reine*, op. 35 (C. F. Peters), *Orientales*, op. 175, 8 books (Leipzig, Rob. Forberg).—Most of the earlier works here named have been revised and polished by Raff himself, so that we now possess them in carefully finished form. [As a composer Raff developed uncommon activity, which even among his opponents earned him the name of a copious writer. While it cannot be denied, that among his works many are found (especially among the minor ones for pianoforte) which hardly awakened, far less survived a passing interest, we must on the other hand take note of the fact, that Raff created many more works of enduring value, in which he ranks with the foremost composers of our time. To these belong many of his *11 Symphonies* and his *Overtures.* For Pianoforte and Orchestra he wrote *1 Concerto* in *C*-minor, op. 185, *1 Suite* in *E♭*, op. 200, and the *Ode au Printemps,* op. 76, the *Tageszeiten* for Pianoforte, Chorus, and Orchestra, op. 209. Of his later works we note *1 'Cello Sonata,* op. 183, *1 Chaconne*, op. 150, and *1 Fantasia,* op. 207a for 2 Pianofortes. **O. L.**]

Johannes Brahms (b. March 7, 1833 at Altona), at the instance of Robert Schumann, who instantly recognized in him the "musician by the grace of God", came forward in his very first compositions as one of the boldest neo-Romanticists. His initial work, the *Sonata* in *C* (Breitkopf & Härtel) is marked by exuberant, glowing flights of fancy, and wild, still unchecked youthful vigor. Only by degrees has he ordered the contents of his pianoforte works more intelligibly, discarded the harsh modulations and progressions found therein, and moulded their outward form to one more practicable for the player. This improvement already begins in the *F*♯-minor *Sonata*, op. 2 (ditto), and the *Scherzo* in *E♭*-minor, op. 4 (ditto), and shows still more in the *Variations with a Fugue* on a theme by Handel, op. 24 (ditto). In the *Waltzes* for 4 hands, op. 39 (Rieter-Biedermann) and also in the *Liebeslieder,* Waltzes for 4 hands with mixed chorus, op. 52 (Berlin, Simrock), he already presents himself in his full amiability as a German composer; and in the two books of *Studies,* Variations on a theme by Paganini, op. 35 (Rieter-Biedermann) he proffers the player a bright display of brilliant pyrotechnic passages, many-colored figuration, and surprising effects of tone. Of his larger compositions not yet named there have been published, by Breitkopf & Härtel, *Trio* with Violin and 'Cello, in *B,* op. 8; *Variations* on a theme by Robert Schumann, op. 9; *Ballades,* op. 10; — by B. Senff, *Sonata* in *F*-minor, op. 5;—by Rieter-Biedermann, *Concerto* with Orchestra in *D*-minor, op. 15; *Variations* for 4 hands, op. 23; *Quintet* with Strings in *F*-minor, op. 34;—by Simrock in Bonn, *Quartet* with Violin, Viola, and 'Cello in *G*-minor, op. 25; a second in *A*, op. 26; and a third in *C*-minor, op. 60.—Brahms has also published a second *Pianoforte Concerto* in *B*♭, op. 83; the *Rhapsodies*, op. 79; *1 Violin Sonata*, op. 78; *Liebeslieder* in 4 vocal parts with pianoforte accompaniment for 4 hands; *Hungarian Dances* for 4 hands (4 books); and more recently *1 Violin Sonata, 1 'Cello Sonata*, and *1 Pianoforte Trio*—perhaps the most clarified of all his works as yet published. Concise, though finished in form, they are marked by a wealth of melody and strong natural feeling.—For the introduction of Brahms to wider circles of musicians and the public, Hans von Bülow has rendered services, both as a conductor and a pianist, which can hardly find a parallel.

As a pianist, Brahms always strives to set the merits of the composition in hand, rather than his own virtuosity, in the best light; nor does he deign to lend to the products of his own fancy a dazzling outward brilliancy; for solely through their earnestly and warmly uttered poetical thoughts should they seek to win the sympathies of the hearers, and will therefore always find more favor in the intimate and congenial circles of friends than before larger and less homogeneous audiences.

Thoughtful and artistic in his compositions, bold and vigorous in his pianoforte performances—such is the character of **Anton Rubinstein** (b. Nov. 30, 1830, at Wechwotynetz near Jassy). Furnished by Nature with all the gifts that distinguish the master-musician, he so developed them through untiring industry even in early childhood, that in his tenth year he was already prepared to undertake a professional journey to Paris with his teacher, Alexander Villoing. Here he met with a friendly reception, and also with warm interest on the part of the hero of the day, Franz Liszt, whose advice and instruction were of the utmost advantage to him during a stay in Paris of a year and a half. Since 1848 he has lived chiefly in St. Petersburg, where as previously mentioned, he founded the Conservatory of Music, and whence he undertakes frequent tours,* partly for the rehearsal of his operas and other large works, partly to appear in successful soirées, or to arrange the publication of new manuscripts. In 1872 he travelled through America, and a year later we find him in Italy on a concert-tour, everywhere winning new laurels. Rubinstein

* Anton Rubinstein has given up public performances as a pianist, and at present devotes his energies to the management of the St. Petersburg Conservatory. O. L.

moves wherever he goes in the highest circles of society, a circumstance which affords a clew to the subjects of many of his works. The larger and more important of the same bear the character of the self-confident favorite of the aristocracy, mastering and illuminating his surroundings by intellectual flashes—of the potentate often shaken by violent storms, but always escaping unscathed and triumphant. On the other hand, the *Albums* dedicated to the fair sex—the *Portraits*, *Barcarolles*, and *Ball-scenes*—exhibit the gallant, engaging, and refined artist, now toying and chatting, again touching more serious topics, but always in a winning manner. In his concerts he plays by preference his own compositions, the larger of which, accompanied by the orchestra, often upsurge in thundering billows, then suddenly hold the hearers spell-bound by a wierd, *volksthümliche* melody, finally dragging them again into the wildest swirl, or leading them triumphantly into the haven ardently sought.

Rubinstein has published *5 Pianoforte Concertos*, the first in *E* (C. F. Peters), the second in *F* (Vienna, Spina), the third in *G* (Bote & Bock), the fourth, a special favorite with pianists, in *D*-minor (B. Senff), and the fifth, perhaps the grandest of them all, in *E♭* (ditto). Of forceful grandeur are the *Fantasie mit Orchester* in *C*, op. 84 (B. Senff), the *Fantasie* for two pianofortes in *F*, op. 73 (ditto), and the *Sonata* for 4 hands in *D*, op. 89 (ditto).—The first of the *Sonatas* for Pianoforte solo, in *E*, was issued by C. F. Peters; the second in *C*-minor, and also the third very noteworthy one in *F*, by Breitkopf & Härtel.—The *Sonata* with Violin in *C* was published by Peters, that in *A*-minor by Breitkopf & Härtel.—*1 Sonata* with Viola in *F*-minor, and two with 'Cello, have been issued by the latter firm.—*Trois morceaux* de salon with Violin, ditto with Viola, and still others with 'Cello, were issued by J. Schuberth & Co.—*Trios* with Violin and 'Cello have been published by Fr. Hofmeister, B. Senff, and by Lewy in Vienna;—*1 Quintet* with wind instruments by J. Schuberth & Co., and another with Strings by B. Senff;—and an *Octet* with strings and wind by C. F. Peters.

Of the numerous salon pieces for Pianoforte solo, op. 1, *Ondine*, an Étude from Rubinstein's childhood, is published by Schlesinger in Berlin;—*Album de Peterhof*, 12 morceaux, op. 75; *Fantaisie* in *E*-minor, op. 77; the very interesting *Miscellanées*, 9 books, op. 93, the last book containing the charming and easily executable *12 Miniatures;* and also the *Étude in false notes* in *C*, and the *Valse-Caprice* in *E♭*, by B. Senff;—Spina in Vienna has published *Russische Fantasien*, op. 2; the much-played *Deux Melodies*, op. 3; the *Polish Dances*, op. 5; the *Acrostic Laura*, op. 37, and several other piano-pieces.— Bote & Bock have published the very popular *Album de danses populaires*, op. 82, in a new edition revised by the composer; also *Le Bal*, en 10 Numéros; the attractive fourth *Barcarole* in *G*, and *Six Études.*—Schott's Söhne of Mainz have issued *Album de 24 Portraits* en 3 cahiers; *1 Suite* en 10 cahiers, op. 38; and *Points d'orgue* pour les concerts de Beethoven, op. 15, 19, 37, and 58;—Breitkopf & Härtel, *2 Sonatas, 3 Caprices*, and *3 Serenades* in one volume in stiff covers, red;—Kistner in Leipzig, *Deux Marches funèbres*, op. 29, and *Barcarole* with *Appassionato*, op. 30;—C. F. Kahnt in Leipzig, *Characterbilder* for 4 hands, op. 50, equally interesting and attractive for player and listeners; *Soirées à St. Pétersbourg*, six morceaux, op. 44, likewise warmly to be recommended;—C. F. Peters, *Préludes et Fugues* en stile libre, op. 53; and a new edition of the *Études*, op. 23 and 24;—Rózsavölgyé & Co. in Pesth, *Fantaisie* sur des mélodies hongroises.

Of the composers mentioned in this Section, Raff perhaps approaches him in fertility, but is an unimpassioned classic compared with Rubinstein, the most fiery of Romanticists. Among the younger pianists, only Hans von Bülow is his peer as an infallible virtuoso; but the latter quite sinks himself in an objective reproduction of the master as a faithful interpreter, lending through his own virtuosity merely the most animated coloring and characteristic illumination; whereas Rubinstein is always subjective, though his own personality irradiates in such manifold and charmful colors, that his imposing artistic skill everywhere appears as the soul of the character-piece chosen for interpretation. In any event we must recognize in these two masters of independent originality the most gifted and active pianists now living.

Grieg, Saint-Saëns, and Tschaikowsky.

Three artists still remain for mention who are in the full flower of productive activity, and an estimate of whose true value must therefore be left to the future. They are not of German parentage, but their compositions in part already lie before us in print, and are well calculated to invite closer scrutiny and to awaken a desire to know more of their most promising authors. **Edvard Hagerup Grieg** is a Norwegian (b. at Bergen June 15, 1843); **Camille Saint-Saëns** a Frenchman (b. at Paris Oct. 9, 1835); and **Peter Tschaikowsky** a Russian (b. April 25, 1840, at Wotkinsk in the government of Wiatka, Ural District). The influence of each on the musical life of his native land will doubtless be important; but it cannot as yet be determined, whether this influence will make itself felt abroad.

Grieg is not a pianoforte virtuoso of prominence, neither do his pianoforte works afford special difficulty to the player. The *Concerto* in *A*-minor with Orchestra, op. 16 (Leipzig, E. W. Fritzsch) is written in a cheerful vein and with brilliant passages; but harmonic harshnesses and sharp cross-relations are sometimes disturbing. The first movement closes in *A*-minor, and the following short Adagio begins, quite without connection, with the *D*♭-major chord. Even if the hearer conceives this latter as the *C*♯-major chord, the affinity between the two harmonies must first be constructed very sophistically through *A*-minor-*A*-major, and *C*♯-minor-*C*♯-major. The final Allegro is intelligibly and pleasingly written, but the oft-repeated and decidedly worn commencement of its principal theme makes an ill impression. In his easily executable *Lyrische Stückchen* for Pianoforte, op. 12 (Edit. Peters)—and also in the second and third sets or books of the same, op. 38 and 43—Grieg employs, as in many of his other compositions, Norwegian motives interesting both in melody and rhythm; but in them, too, the ear is often unpleasantly grated by striking, though unlovely, incorrectnesses; e. g. in the *A*-minor *Waltz* the major sixth *f*♯ frequently occurs instead of the minor sixth *f* proper to this key. The *Ballade* in the form of Variations on a Norwegian melody, op. 24 (same publ.), exhibits in both parts of the theme ill-sounding parallel fifths, which, even if written purposely, prove a lack of friendly counsel and aid. Of his other Pianoforte Works there have been published, by Breitkopf & Härtel, *Sonata* in *E*-minor, op. 7, and *Sonata* with Violin in *G*, op. 13;—by Rieter-Biedermann, *Fantasia* for 4 hands, op. 11;—in Edition Peters we find *Poetische Tonbilder*, op. 3; *Humoresken*, op. 6; *Nordische Tänze und Volksweisen*, op. 17; *Aus dem Volksleben*, op. 19; *1 Sonata* with Violin, op. 8; and *Symphonische Stücke* for 4 hands.—Other works are op. 35, *Norwegian Dances* for 2 or 4 hands; op. 36, *Sonata* for Pianoforte and 'Cello; op. 37, *Walzer-Capricen* for 2 or 4 hands; *"Aus Holberg's Zeit"*, Pianoforte Suite; op. 41, *Pianoforte Transcriptions* of his own songs; op. 45, *Third Sonata* for Pianoforte and Violin, in *C*-minor. (Comp. p. 178, foot.)

Camille Saint-Saëns, who from early youth played Bach's "Well-tempered Clavichord" by heart, who accompanied prima vista from the score a *Scena* just written by Richard Wagner for a lady singer, at whose wish he transposed it into a lower key, is also recognizable in his own works as a thoroughly trained musician. His *Premier Concerto* pour Piano in *D*, op. 17 (Paris, Durand, Schönewerk et Cie., Successeurs), of a majestically dignified character, develops a design sketched by a master-hand. Its modulations are unconstrained, the development flowing and artistic, and the piano-part, independent throughout, now enters into strenuous rivalry with the orchestra, and anon alternates peacefully with it. The Andante in *G*-minor is followed by a Finale con fuoco, in which the principal subject of the first movement finally resounds once more in triumphant jubilation. For the performance of this piece the skill of a virtuoso is not requisite, but all the more the delicate touch of a thoughtful and poetically impressionable pianist, who is able in the proper place vigorously to stem the tide of the full orchestra, and to show himself its master. The *Troisième Concerto* in *E♭* (same publ.) begins with high-surging pianoforte arpeggios, gradually joined by the orchestral instruments taking up the main motive one by one, and developing and illuminating it melodically and harmonically. At length the pianoforte takes it up, strongly and sonorously emphasizing it as the foundational motive of a work quite as grandly designed and wrought out as the concerto first described. The ingenious and well-skilled artist is likewise discernible in his smaller published salon pieces. The attractive piano-piece, op. 34, *Marche héroïque*, is bold and striking in progression and modulation; and the *Gavotte*, op. 23, flows on unconstrainedly in the ancient style, though taking advantage of modern technique. These pieces also do not demand the skill of a virtuoso, and, like op. 40, the *Danse macabre*, have been published in Paris by the above firm.—[Saint-Saëns, who was made a knight of the Légion d'honneur in 1867, and an officer of the same in 1884, is always the same incomparable pianist . . . . such receptions as he has received in the Conservatoire, in Russia, *in Leipzig*, and in London prove him to be one of the most remarkable and earnest pianoforte players of the day.—Other of his works are two further *Pianoforte Concertos* in *G*-minor and *C*-minor; *Quintet* for Pianoforte, 2 Violins, Viola, and 'Cello; *1 Trio*, and *1 Quartet* for Pianoforte and Strings; *1 Suite* for Pianoforte and 'Cello; *Sonata* for Pianoforte and 'Cello; *Berceuse* for Pianoforte and

Violin; *Allegro appassionato* for Pianoforte and 'Cello; *Romance* for ditto; *Septet* for Pianoforte, 5 strings, and trumpet *obbligato;*—and for Pianoforte solo:—Op. 3; 11 (*Duettino* in *G*, 4 hands); 21 (first *Mazurka); 24* (second *Mazurka); 35 (Variations* sur un thème de Beethoven, for 2 pianofortes—a gem); 52 (*Études); 56 (Menuet et Valse); 59 (Ballade,* 4 hands); besides several transcriptions of classical or popular airs and 12 transcriptions from Bach's cantatas and sonatas. **Grove.**]

The gifted Russian, **Peter Tschaikowsky,** has painted, in his *Concerto* in *B*♭-minor, a gigantic canvass of his people's period of storm and stress. In conception, form, and technique, it seems like a confident challenge to his competitors. It is dedicated to Hans von Bülow, who was the first to recognize his eminent and artistically developed creative vigor. It can still be had only of the publisher Jürgenson of Moscow, and in an edition wherein the orchestra, as in many similar recent works, is represented by a second pianoforte. After a promising Andante in *D*♭ ($^3/_4$ time), the animated principal movement in *B*♭, Allegro con spirito, begins ($^4/_4$ time). This is followed by a more tranquil Andantino semplice in *D*♭ ($^3/_4$ time); and the close is formed by an Allegro con fuoco, which surpasses the concerto-finales of all his predecessors in the fervid glow of the pianoforte passages and the orchestral colors. His earlier pianoforte compositions are by no means of such a heaven-storming nature, but quite as original. Only his first work, the *Scherzo à la russe*, still shows the specifically Slavonic temperament; even in the *Scherzo*, the second number in op. 2, he exhibits a strong individuality imitating none of his predecessors. Of the remaining piano-pieces we name the passionate *Romance* in *F*-minor, op. 5; the wantonly teasing *Humoresque*, op. 19; the *Souvenir de Hapsal*, op. 2, including as No. 1, *Ruines du château; Valse-Caprice*, op. 4; *Valse-Scherzo*, op. 7; *Capriccio*, op. 8; *Trois morceaux*, op. 9; *Nocturne and Humoresque*, op. 10; and *Six morceaux*, the last number of which is the *Thème original et Variations* (all published by Robert Forberg, Leipzig). All these neatly wrought salon pieces are peculiar in their progressions, intelligible and attractive in conception, and convenient in piano style; they justify the highest expectations with regard to the future works of this original composer.

[A second pianoforte *Concerto* by Tschaikowsky in *G*, op. 44, and a *Pianoforte Fantasia* with orchestra in *G*-minor, op. 56, are on a level with the first *Concerto* in their freshness and inventive originality, though both works win less applause for the soloist than this latter. We also note a *Pianoforte Trio* in *A*-minor, op. 50; a *Pianoforte Sonata,* op. 37; many books of *solo pieces,* pieces for Pianoforte and Violin, *Variations* for Pianoforte and 'Cello. Tschaikowsky has an astonishing productive faculty; contemporary with him a neo-Russian school of composition has arisen, including really distinguished talents. Alexander Borodin (1834—1887), Cesar Cui (b. 1835), Anatole Liadoff, Nicolaus Rimsky-Korsakoff (b. 1844), Balakirew (b. 1836, an eminent pianist, who in 1862 founded a "Free Music-school" together with Lamakin, composed an *Oriental Fantasia, "Slamey",* for pianoforte, many piano-pieces, etc.), Alexander Dargomirski (1813—1869, distinguished pianist), Modest Mussorgski (1839 to 1881, wrote besides operas many pieces for pianoforte and for the voice—*Danse macabre, Scènes d'enfants,* etc.); all of whom enthusiastically joined the neo-German movement headed by Liszt-Wagner-Berlioz, and were followed by younger musicians of talent, as N. Stcherbatcheff, Alexander Glazounow, and others. To the Russian school also belongs the Bohemian Eduard Naprawnik (b. 1839), who in 1869 became first Conductor of the Russian opera at St. Petersburg, and has composed a large number of Pianoforte Works—*Trios, Quartets,* a *Fantasia* for Pianoforte and Orchestra, op. 39, etc. **O. L.**]

Down to our day Beethoven has remained, in his symphonies, string-quartets, piano-trios, sonatas, and other extended works, the ideal of all unbiassed musicians. His pianoforte sonatas, manifolded in countless editions, have not been pushed aside by later composers, and all attempts at writing such compositions in the more brilliant style suited to the present standpoint of virtuosity, have proved repugnant to the genius of the sonata. To produce a work rivalling Beethoven's sonatas, would be possible only to an equally profound thinker, keen-sighted knower of the heart, and thoroughly equipped musician of universal and versatile talent, as was Beethoven himself—who, though sketching his ideas in moments of inspiration, developed and matured them afterwards in seasons of quiet contemplation and inexorable self-searching. Our most popular composers, on the contrary, are ready with their pens at any instant, and straightway consign, to their prejudice, their pieces in an unfinished state to the publisher. Moreover, they often spin out their melodies to infinity, whereas now, at this very day, the characteristic melody ought to be reinstated in its rightful place.

The *Concerto*, which employs the manifold colors of the orchestra, and portrays the more agitated moods, fiercer struggles, and violent passions, may call the full artistic skill of the performer into play, in order to attune the hearer's mood to deep melancholy or glad jubilation by animated or pathetic runs and passages suited to the subject of the work. The most illustrious composers now living have presented us with admirable works of this class, which would be brought out oftener by the younger pianists did the demands on the virtuosity of the performer not frequently overpass his ability.

The *Character-pieces*, *Stimmungsbilder*, and *Novellettes* reveal progress in the striving toward truth of expression. They choose a more diversified and unusual subject, and clothe it in conformity with its spirit in a form as new, characteristic, and attractive as possible. Humor in music, in particular, has been duly reinstated, as is shown by the humorous and piquant Humoresques and Scherzi recently issued.

The *Pianoforte Methods* of to-day are better calculated for a many-sided training of the pupil, the Études and exercises are more practically and tastefully written, and great masters have provided friendly gifts for little hands as well. [To the Pianoforte Methods an exceedingly valuable addition has latterly been made by **Lina Ramann.** Her broadly planned School of Pianoforte Technique has been published by Breitkopf & Härtel; its logical development of the entire material of instruction from the beginning caused Liszt to award preference to this work above all others. As fresh material of instruction this School introduces the Hungarian Scale—extracted from Liszt's Rhapsodies hongroises—with minor third, augmented fourth, and minor sixth. **O. L.**]

We notice with pleasure, that since the first edition of this book more attention has been paid to the earlier clavier literature, as proved by the *Collections* of the compositions of celebrated old masters published since its appearance. But much precious ore yet remains to be dug out and brought to light; in this connection we again urgently advise that such compositions should not be falsified by means of any "arrangements" whatever. This remark holds good in the case of Folk-songs and Folk-dances of various nations still to be published, which, if given unperverted, form a well-spring of new melodies and rhythms.

Low-priced *Popular Editions* of recent valuable pianoforte compositions are now issued by almost every considerable publishing house; the critically revised, larger *Éditions de luxe* of the Complete or Selected Works of Mozart, Beethoven, Schubert, Mendelssohn, and other masters, have found enterprising publishers, as we have regularly noted in the proper place. [To the Popular Editions of the pianoforte works of Mozart, Beethoven, Schubert, and Mendelssohn have lately been added those of Bach, Chopin, and Schumann. The Chopin Edition by Klindworth (Berlin, Bote & Bock), and the Schumann Editions by Dr. Hans Bischoff (Hanover, Steingräber) and Dr. Otto Neitzel (Cologne, Tonger), which meet all requirements in regard to critical revision of the works and practicalness of the explanatory notes, together with the admirable Beethoven Edition by Bülow, have already been mentioned. An excellent edition of Beethoven's Sonatas, by Klindworth, has also been issued by Bote & Bock of Berlin. Bach's Clavier Works have been published by Steingräber of Hanover in an admirable critical Teacher's Edition by Dr. Hans Bischoff; the same editor has also recently issued through the same firm the first three Pianoforte Concertos by Mozart in an instructive and critically revised edition. The editions of Mozart's and Beethoven's Sonatas by Dr. Hugo Riemann have created a stir, for the reason that the Editor's Theory of Phrasing is practically and consistently adhered to in them. The movement in this hitherto almost neglected department of tuition has doubtless already brought forth good fruits, although it cannot be denied, that the supporters of the movement themselves embarrass their meritorious work in a measure by minutiæ and singularities. **O. L.**]

The *Science of Counterpoint and Fugue,* in its strict purity and with its mysterious convolutions, is apparently in its decadence, being now practised by but a few able masters. The Science of Harmony, on the other hand, at least as applied by unbiassed composers, now recognizes the formerly unnoticed distinction between "chord" and "key". That is, each separate *chord* may naturally (diatonically) belong to seven different keys; it represents one definite *key* only when brought into combination with its two dominant chords. Only thus do the chord-progressions now looked upon as irregular licences find logical justification.

Virtuosity has attained through Liszt, who forced it to follow his most fiery pulses, a height, the transcending of which would endanger the player's accuracy, and leave to good luck the success of the desperate ventures expected at his hands. The virtuoso of today has at his command all nuances in the tone of his instrument, which under his fingers must never cease to sing, from the softest *piano* up to the strongest *forte.* For him difficulties ought no longer to exist in the composition chosen, and he should be so profoundly immersed in the poetry of his music, that he can interpret it free from all rhythmic fetters. Like an inspired *improvisatore* he is upborne by the feeling, that he captivates and irresistibly carries away his hearers by the potency of his heartfelt delivery.

HISTORY OF THE PIANOFORTE

by

C. F. WEITZMANN.

Supplement to the History of Pianoforte-playing **and** Pianoforte Literature.

TABLE OF CONTENTS.

PREFACE.

From an insignificant embryo, and after long centuries of constant fostering, the pianoforte has become the universal instrument of to-day. This latter epithet is fully appropriate. In its present form, further perfection of which is hardly imaginable, it is found in the capitals of Europe and America in nearly every house, and frequently several together. Its tone is full and resonant, in volume it vies with the full orchestra, and the player has at command every shade from the gentlest breath up to the most penetrating *forte*. The mechanism of the pianoforte excels that of all other instruments for the convenient execution of the most rapid runs and passages, and the singing tone of our present piano is equally adapted for the delivery of an expressively shaded melody with a most diversified harmonic accompaniment, or for the performance of polyphonic pieces in contrapuntal style. In its ability to lend living expression to all phases of emotion for which language lacks words, the pianoforte is the favorite instrument of the lonely mourner, and of the solitary soul whose joy seeks expression. But in the brilliant concert-hall, too, the pianoforte is gladly welcomed. Its objective character resembles that of the string quartet; it follows each changing mood, and the concert grand, with its distinguished, festal tone, does not lose in power even in alternate play with the full orchestra.

It will be of interest to every musician, and especially to every pianist, to learn of those masters in their often adventurous careers, to whose experiments and enduring perseverance we owe this influential and now so universally popular instrument.

To the general history of the pianoforte I have prefixed a short description of the separate parts common to nearly all its species, to avoid any later interruption of the historical narrative. After this follows the story of the origination of the various kinds of claviers, and of their further development down to the modern concert grand pianoforte.

The Clavier, and the earlier instruments related to it.

CLAVIER is the generic name for all the various kinds of musical instruments, within whose horizontal or perpendicular bodies of a three-cornered, four-cornered, or otherwise fashioned form strings are stretched across a sounding-board in such a way, that they can be tuned by means of pegs around which one of their ends is wound, and can be set in vibration by means of a series of levers, called keys or digitals. These keys rest near their front end, the actual digital pressed by the player's finger, on the *balance-rail,* being held in position upon this latter by the *balance key-pins,* fixed metal pegs which do not hinder their free movement. To the rear end of the key-lever is fastened either a stout perpendicular metal pin flattened on top, or a wooden *hopper* playing easily on springs (equivalent to "*jack*"), carrying a quill at the end. By striking the key the quill is caused to twang the string, whereupon the spring hopper instantly falls back to its former place. One side of the sounding-board is open, so that these quills, or the metallic *tangents,* when the keys are pressed down, can set in vibration the corresponding single strings or double or triple unisons. Not until the 18th century were the strings struck by little wooden *hammers,* which were either fastened to the keys themselves, or could play on spindles on a wooden rail placed above the keys, or whose shanks were fastened by strips of parchment to the rail. The hammers were driven against the strings by a spring jack on brass wire, and instantly fell back after the key was struck into their former position by the aid of a spring *hopper.* For a long time the jack and the hopper have formed only one connected, individual mechanism, the "action" of the pianoforte. When the key-lever impels the hammer against the string, it also lifts from the latter its *damper,* which is made of either cloth or felt, and which, as soon as the finger quits the key, again touches the string in order to hinder after-vibration. The *forte pedal,* which lifts all the dampers from the strings at once, thus intentionally allowing after-vibration, is a modern invention; like the *soft pedal*, which brings under the string a rail bearing projecting strips of cloth, against which the hammer then strikes, thus producing a softened effect of tone. Another style of soft pedal employs the *Verschiebung* (shifting of the keyboard), which permits the hammer to strike only one *(una corda)* of the two or three strings composing a unison; a third kind lessens the striking distance of the hammer.

The Clavier took its name from the *claves* (keys) which either directly or indirectly set the strings in vibration. This key-mechanism was borrowed from the organ, known long before the clavier.

Like the lute and harp, the clavier belongs to the class of musical instruments of percussion, whose tones are produced by a blow. Like them, too, it is classified among the many-stringed instruments *(polychorda)*, but is however distinguished from them by its keyboard *(claviarium)*, by virtue of which it belongs to the family of the many-keyed instruments *(polyplectra)*. Finally, we have to distinguish between the three essentially different species of the earlier Clavichords, the Harpsichords, and the more recent Pianoforte, which in turn exhibit very various kinds of claviers.*

This instrument, found in our day throughout the civilized world, and in high favor among all classes, did not suddenly appear as the invention of any individual, but owes its development into its present exceedingly practical and sonorous form to many tentative experiments at first little noticed, which led very slowly up to perfection.

On comparing the already published attempts at a history of the pianoforte, we find sharp contradictions in regard to the period of origination and the earlier character of this instrument. The reason for this lies in the various and often ambiguous names which it received from its first appearance in Italy, Germany, France, and England; and still more in the fact, that the authors writing on this

---

* The following illustrated hand-books treat of the build of the modern pianoforte: *Kutzing, Carl,* Theoretisch-practisches Handbuch der Fortepiano-Baukunst; Bonn and Chur, 1843, 8va, with 6 Tables.—By the same: Das Wissenschaftliche der Fortepiano-Baukunst; Bern and Leipzig, Dalp, 1844, 8vo; with illustrations.—*Welcker von Gontershausen,* Der Flügel etc. A comprehensive exposition of the art of Fortepiano-making; Frankfort, Winter, 1856; with illustrations.—By the same: Der Clavierbau etc.; Frankfort, Winter, 1870; 8vo, with illustrations.—*André, C. A.,* Der Clavierbau; Offenbach on the Main, Joh. André, 1855; 8vo.—*Blüthner and Gretschel,* Lehrbuch des Pianofortebaues etc.; Leipzig, 1875.

subject have regarded, and consequently treated, two instruments which, though similar in outward shape and mode of playing, were utterly different in origin, inner arrangement, and tone-production, as instruments differing only unessentially from each other.

However, before going further into detail, it will be necessary to cast a glance at the instruments already in existence previous to the advent of the claviers, and therefore able to serve as prototypes for the latter in their separate parts or the combination of the same.

To these belong, in particular:

The *Monochord*, an instrument already employed by the theoreticians of antiquity for the determination of the several intervals.

The *Psaltery* and the 35-stringed *Simikon;* many-stringed instruments known to the ancient Egyptians, and resembling our modern harps and lutes; likewise the medieval instrüments belonging to this family, as the Dulcimer, Spinet (Espinette), Hackbrett or Cymbal (salterio tedesco), and others.

Finally, pneumatic organs provided with keys had been known since the time of Theodosius (379—395); and in the year 757 the Byzantine Emperor Constantine sent to Pipin as a present an organ after the pattern of which Charlemagne had an organ built in 812 for the cathedral of Aachen.

In the earliest work on this subject by Virdung, printed in German in 1511, which we shall examine more closely further on, we find a cut of a large organ having 33 black and white keys in the modern arrangement, with a compass from **A** to **f**; also of a *positiv* with 2 hand-bellows, a *regal* with 3, and a *portativ* with one.*

These three styles of organ, intended for home use, enjoyed wide popularity on account of their easily managed keys, especially in the 15th and 16th centuries. But their bellows were very inconvenient to handle, having to be kept in constant motion either by the hand or both feet of the player, or by a second person, to supply the windchest. Nevertheless, they remained in vogue until

---

* *Portativ* (organum portatile) was the name of the smallest organ, to be carried by a strap around the neck, and played while walking or sitting, one hand working the bellows and the other pressing the keys. The *Regal* was a little organ with a single rank of horizontal reed-pipes. The *Positiv* possessed several different registers with upright pipes, was easily transportable, and placed for playing on a table or other convenient piece of furniture.

increasing success rewarded the endeavors to set tense strings in vibration by the aid of keys, and thus to construct a more practical and convenient instrument for the room.

Origin of the Clavichord.

The Monochord.

The testimony of earlier authors agrees in this:—That the simplest and meanest of all musical instruments, the Monochord, which was originally intended not for practical music, but only for speculative research, was the germ which slowly developed into the pianoforte, which in volume and wealth of tone replaces a full orchestra. Even in earliest antiquity the monochord was, as remarked, an indispensable instrument for all investigating theoreticians. It consisted of an oblong sound-box, over which was stretched a string tuned by means of a peg. A bridge (magas) touching the string could be shifted under any given nodal point marked beneath, and thus each interval of a scale having the whole string as its key-note could be determined with mathematical accuracy. E. g. if a string tuned to *G* were shortened, by means of the movable bridge, by a ninth, the remaining eight-ninths would give, when set in vibration, the major second *A* of the key-note; four-fifths of the string would give the major third *B;* three-fourths, the fourth *c;* two-thirds, the fifth *d;* three-fifths, the major sixth *e;* nine-sixteenths, the minor seventh *f;* one-half, the octave *g:*

G	A	B	c	d	e	f	g
$^1/_1$	$^8/_9$	$^4/_5$	$^3/_4$	$^2/_3$	$^3/_5$	$^9/_{16}$	$^1/_2$

If it were desired to compare an interval so determined with the tone of the entire string, the movable bridge had first to be shifted; but the consonance of two or more tones could not be produced on this single-stringed instrument. For this reason several other strings were soon added to that of the original monochord, tuned in unison with the first, and likewise provided with movable bridges. The theoreticians Claudius Ptolomæus and Aristides Quintilianus, who lived in the second century of our era, mention a four-cornered instrument having 4 strings tuned in unison, called the Helicon, and used for determining intervals. Although Johannes de

Muris teaches, in his "Musica speculativa" written in 1323, the use of the single-stringed monochord, he also recommends that with four strings for testing the harmony of the consonances, because it admitted of striking 2, 3, or 4 strings at once.

In using the monochord the continual shifting of the bridge was very troublesome. For this reason the instrument was furnished, probably as early as the 11th century, with a row of keys, the rear ends of which were provided with upright tangents, which struck the strings when the keys were pressed, thus setting them in vibration, and at the same time shortening them at the given nodal points, thus taking the place of the movable bridge. The simultaneous sounding of the other part of the string was doubtless prevented, even at that early time, by an adjustment like that shown by later instruments of this class. While the first key, the tangent of which struck the string at its extreme end, would sound the tone of its whole length, *G*, the second key, shortening the string by a ninth as in the above example, would give the tone *A*, corresponding to eight-ninths of the same. The third key shortened the string by one-fifth in like manner, and the four-fifths then set in vibration would sound the tone *B*; etc.

Guido d'Arezzo (b. about 995), who appears to have been the first to use the monochord in giving singing lessons, in order to illustrate the various intervals for his pupils, may have already added a simple key-board of this sort to the instrument, or perhaps made use of an existing invention. In the first instruction which he gives to the intending student of music, in his "Micrologus" (Gerbert, script. eccl. de Mus., Tom. II, pag. 4) he recommends emphatically "to practise the hand in the use of the monochord".* But the mere shifting of the bridge under the string of the instrument could hardly have called for special manual dexterity; and in order to give singing pupils a definite idea of the intervals of a melody, an instrument surely could not suffice, which necessitated a tedious shifting of the bridge for each separate tone.

Both strings and keys of the monochord were gradually multiplied; for in order to produce all the tones of the Guidonic system, 22 such were required, which subsequently became far too few. But the name of monochord was borne by this species of clavier down

---

* "Igitur qui nostram disciplinam petit, aliquantos cantus nostris notis pescriptos addiscat, in monochordi usu manum exerceat", etc.

to the 16th century,* when the instruments of the derivation described above began to be termed Monachord, Manichord, etc., and in general *Clavichord.*

The 22 *plectra, claves,* or keys of the earlier Clavichords were of a white color, and produced a diatonic series of tones from great *G* up to two-lined *e''*. Only the two higher octaves had an extra black key between *a* and *b* for *b*♭. Seven strings then sufficed for the production of these 22 tones. They were tuned to the lowest tone of the instrument, *G*, this tone being sounded by the *first* key, which set the entire length of the *first string* in vibration.** The *next* key, by means of its tangent or broad metal pin, shortened this same first string on striking it by a ninth, and consequently sounded the tone *A*. The third key in like manner shortened the same string by a fifth, thus sounding the tone *B*. The fourth key was the first to strike the second string, shortening the same with its tangent by one-quarter, thus causing three-quarters of the string to sound the tone *c;* etc. In the higher octaves, e. g. where only one-quarter of the string was to sound, the other three-quarters would have sounded louder than the smaller part required; but to hinder such vibration a strip of cloth was wound about that part of the string not intended to vibrate.

The tones *G, A,* and *B* being, as we have shown, produced by the same string, they could never be sounded in combination, and the tones *G* and *c* therefore formed the first consonance from below. On the other side, this imperfect clavichord had one advantage which explains its long continuance in tune. If the instrument-maker

---

* Nicola Vicento, on p. 103b of his work "L'antica musica ridotta alla moderna prattica", publ. in Rome, 1555, reckons the monochord among the keyed instruments of his time. Zarlino also classes the monochord with modern instruments in his "Istitutioni harmoniche" of the year 1558, saying in Cap. 41, p. 125: Et se bene nel mostrato Monochordo (the single-stringed instrument) si ritrovano le forme vere ed naturali di tutte quelle consonanze, che sono possibili da ritrovare, per questo non dovemo credere, che nelli *moderni istrumenti*, come sono Organi, Clavocembali, Arpichordi, *Monochordi* ed altri ancora tali consonanze si ritrovino nella loro vera ed natural forma. —Also comp. p. 97; the close of Cap. 27; and likewise p. 344, where he says: "He (the student of art) must be able to play the monochord and arpichord sufficiently well, if not perfectly."

** Even after the later multiplication of the strings, they were all tuned in unison. Proof of this we shall find further on, when discussing Virdung's work.

—at first apparently the cabinet-maker*—had adjusted the tangents of the keys at exactly the proper places, it was merely necessary to keep all the strings tuned in unison, in order to play the then still untempered diatonic scale in the utmost purity.

With the growing development of harmony, however, it became necessary to increase the number of strings on the clavichord at least so far, that each of the consonances of the diatonic ecclesiastical tones then still exclusively employed could be sounded together. But even after clavichords were built, whose keys sounded the tones in chromatic succession, the black and white keys then alternating as in the modern keyboard, three or four keys still struck one and the same string with their tangents at different distances from its end. It was a long time before the so-called "bundfreies" clavier was constructed, having an individual string for each key.

We still find clavichords with strings tuned in unison in general use as late as the 16th century. Such are those which Virdung described in 1511, and Zarlino called monochords in 1558. In view of the many tones of chromatic instruments of large compass, the numerous *frets* on the keys and the unison tuning of the strings necessarily became very inconvenient. On this account there was added to the clavichord, after the pattern of the *clavicembalo* of the 15th century, a wooden bridge beneath the strings, crossing diagonally the rectangle of the instrument, and furnished with short upright metal pins against which the strings were pressed on tension, and which gradually shortened the latter up to the highest tones. Now more practical, shorter and thinner strings could be assigned to the higher tones, and longer and stouter ones to the lower; but with the abolishment of the unison strings, and setting aside the exclusive control of the diatonic church modes, there began the search, which busied all theoreticians and practical musicians, after a rule which should likewise secure as pure a temperament as possible for the secular keys then constantly gaining ground. In a subsequent chapter this important matter will be treated in detail.

Despite the multiplication of its strings and keys, and the progressive improvement of its tone through more suitable sounding-boards and tangents, the clavichord retained its original form, that

---

* "I will not describe how the Clavichordium and other instruments are to be made, for that concerns architecture or the *handicraft of the cabinet-maker* rather than music." Virdung, 1511.

of an oblong box, which was at the outset placed on a table, but later obtained legs of its own. Claviers of this kind, derived from the monochord, still lingered in the first half of the 19th century, when the Hammerclavier or Pianoforte gradually ousted all the earlier species.

Origin of the Harpsichord.

Psaltery and Cymbal.

The clavichords described had, even in their latest perfection, only a delicate, hesitating tone. Amidst their growing popularity a plan was therefore devised for the construction of an instrument, whose strings could be set in stronger vibration by sharper tangents, by which means a fuller and steadier tone could be obtained.

Among the polychord instruments which might serve the end of combination with a keyboard, there were known in the middle ages, besides the harp, two others which especially concern us here, namely, the Psaltery and the Cymbal.

The harp-like Psaltery, constructed in a three-cornered, four-cornered, or round-cornered form, was carried by a strap around the neck, or set for playing on a table. Its strings were plucked with the fingers, with a metallic plectrum, or with *quills* attached to rings on the player's hands. Similar instruments, whose strings were however struck with two sticks or small wooden mallets, were contemporary with these under the following names: Dulcimer, Sambuke, Barbiton, Tympanum, Symphonie, Spinet, and Cymbalum.

The direct predecessor of the Clavicembalo, the Cymbal or *Hackbrett*, was also called the German Psaltery (salterio tedesco). It had a sharp, incisive tone, and consisted of a square box, upon which metallic strings were fastened and tuned in diatonic succession. At first its compass embraced from two to three octaves, and later four, the tones of which, beginning with great *C*, ascended in chromatic succession, with 2 or 3 unisons to each. In his hands the player held two wooden mallets, one end of which was covered with cloth in the later development, to render the tone produced less harsh. After the 18th century we find it almost exclusively in the hands of the peasants in Little Russia, and of the Gypsies in Hungary; the cymbal and the fiddle still form the chief instruments of the latter.

From the accounts of earlier writers we can only approximately determine the time at which there were added, to the psaltery and to the cymbal possibly derived from the same, keys whose tangents served instead of the fingers or mallets of the player to set the strings in vibration. From these accounts we also gather, that the clavichords or monochords were the earliest claviers of all, not followed until later by the clavicembali. And first, the following report of a trustworthy author will be of weight for us.

The celebrated philologist J. G. Scaliger, born 1484, lived until his forty-second year in Northern Italy. In his work Poetices libri VII, Lyons 1561, cap. 48, he narrates that Simius, who lived at the time of the decadence of ancient Greek music, invented the 35-stringed instrument called the Simicon, from which were derived the instruments popularly named Monochords, whose tones were produced by means of regularly ordered *plectra* (tangents) springing from below against the strings. These plectra were subsequently armed with sharp crow-quills, to obtain a distincter tone from the metal strings. In his childhood this instrument was called *Clavicymbalum* or *Harpsichordum,* but afterwards *Spinett,* from the sharp quills.*

The pianist and author Georges Becker has published, in the *Revue et Gazette musicale de Paris,* an article on "L'Épinette. Son origine, son étimologie", which was copied soon after its appearance by English, German, and American music journals, and also by the *Guide Musical* (Brussels, Schott frères) of Aug. 8th and 15th, 1878. Becker had found, in the book *Conclusioni nel suono dell' organo* etc., by Adriano Banchieri (Bologne, 1608), the following passage: "The spinet takes its name from the inventor of this oblong shape, a Venetian named Giovanni Spinetti, and I have seen such an instrument in the possession of the organist Francesco Stivori..... bearing the inscription: Joannes Spinetus Venetus fecit, A. D. 1503".

M. Becker now accuses the learned Scaliger of two mistakes contained in the quotation given above, hitherto used by all writers on musical history.—Firstly, the spinet was already known before Scaliger's birth; but this fact has been called in question neither by

* Fuit et Simii commentum illud, quod ab eo Simicum appellatum, quinque et triginta constabat chordis; a quibus eorum origo, quos nunc monochordos vulgus vocat, in quibus ordine digesta plectra subsilientia reddunt sonos. Additæ deinde plectris corvinarum pennarum cuspides: ex æreis filis expressiorem eliciunt harmoniam. Me puero Clavicymbalum et Harpsichordum nunc ab illis mucronibus Spinetam nominant.

Scaliger nor by any more recent author. — Secondly, it did not derive its appelation from the pointed crow-quills, but from its inventor Giovanni Spinetti. But this assumption, before accepting it a as certainty, must be supported by further proof than the discovered clavier of the year 1503 made by one Spinetus, and Banchieri's assertion put forward over 100 years later, that Spinetus was the inventor of the spinet. It tells against this assumption in the first place that Scaliger, who lived in Venice and Padua until 1526, and whose excellent memory is lauded, should not have heard the name of the pretended inventor, of whom Venice was the native place; and further, that none of the contemporary writings on this subject should mention him.

The clavicembali spoken of by Scaliger appeared at first in square form, but after the 17th century the larger ones had almost invariably the present "wing-shape". The latter occurred under the following names: Flügel, Kielflügel, Harpichord, Steertstück, and Schweinskopf,* and in upright form took the name of Clavicytherium. In a smaller, three or four-cornered form, the clavicembali had special names, and at first no legs of their own, being placed, like the earlier clavichords, on a suitable piece of furniture; e. g. the spinet and the virginal. These smaller instruments usually had a more limited compass than the Flügel, often only the higher octaves of the latter. In Italy, under the general name of "Cembalo", the Clavicembalo or Gravecembalo was always understood. To the larger styles of cembalo belonged the Arpichordo, to the smaller the Spinetto, Buonaccordo, and Virginale. In France, too, the general name "Clavecin" or "Clavessin" commonly referred only to the Clavicembalo, whereas the more popular, smaller kind was called *Espinette or Épinette.* In England the name *Harpsichord* was given to the larger Clavicembali, and *Virginals* to the smaller ones.

In Germany the general name "*Clavier*" always referred to the Clavichord specially affected there. Earlier names of the class, already mentioned in part, were *Monocordo*, *Monacordo*, *Manicordo*, and *Cembalo clavicordo.* In France they were called *Manicorde, Manicordion, and Clavicorde.* A Latin manuscript of the 15th century describes the *Dulce melos* or *Dulcimer* as a clavichord having an equal number of strings and keys, the tangents consisting, not of metal pins or wedges, but of wooden wedges.**

* Comp. Adlung, Mus. mech. org. II, 113, 114.

** Comp. Fétis, Hist. générale de la Musique, Paris, F. Didot, 1876; Tom. 5, pp. 202—3.

Before continuing the history of the two species of claviers, it will be expedient to give a concise statement of the distinctions characteristizing them.

On the *Clavichords* the player could bring out a softer or louder tone corresponding to a gentler or firmer touch of the keys; in the *Harpsichords* (Virginals, Spinets), on the contrary, the quill twanged the string with uniform power, thus permitting of a sharp outline, but no shading of the tones. On the former the tones could be executed either *staccato* or *legato;* while on the latter a *staccato* and vanishing sweep of single tones or full chords was always heard. The *Clavichord,* by reason of its delicate nuances of tone and the effect of the *Bebung (balancement)* peculiar to itself, which could be produced by moving the finger back and forth upon the key, was capable of the highest expression under the hand of a good player; whereas the *Harpsichord* always retained the same uniform, penetrating tone, and was therefore employed especially for concertos with orchestral accompaniment, or for accompanying vocal chorusses.

The *Pianoforte,* appearing in the first quarter of the 18th century, was brought only step by step to a perfection which united in itself the good qualities of its predecessors; the Clavichord consequently remained in Germany, down to the 19th century, the keyboard instrument generally preferred by masters and pupils.

Notes on the Claviers of the 16th and 17th centuries.

In the following extracts from ancient printed works we shall notice the earliest evidences and confirmations of the accounts already given concerning the origin and the later development of the clavichord and clavicembalo (harpsichord). We shall find both species of clavier in practical use as early as the beginning of the 16th century, shall examine their different interior arrangement more closely, and thus attain to a clearer insight regarding the difference of origin evidenced thereby.

An extremely rare book, indeed the earliest printed work to which we can refer here, bears the title: “Musica getutscht und ausgezogen durch Sebastianum Virdung Priesters von Amberg”. From the Preface, “geben zu Basel uff zinstag Margarethe Tusent funff hundert und XI Jar” (1511), we perceive that it is a German condensation of a larger Latin work by the same author. It is furnished with many neat woodcuts, and written in the form of dialogues between the author Sebastian and his friend Andreas Sylvanus. Though often quoted, this book seems never to have been exhaustively utilized; for it contains so many hitherto unnoticed disclosures, especially concerning the earlier claviers, that it will be of interest to let the priest Sebastian speak for the most part for himself in the following. He begins his instructions by classing instrumental music in three genera: (1) Stringed instruments; (2) instruments sounded by wind; (3) musical instruments made of metal or other resonant material. He then speaks of the genus of stringed instruments, and remarks, that certain of the same have *claves* (keys), by means of which they are governed and played upon according to rule. Of this kind are the instruments with *clavieren* (keyboards). Then follow illustrations of four different kinds of claviers. The first three, *Clavicordium*, *Clavicimbalum*, and *Virginal*, appear in the form of shallow, oblong boxes, whose lids are held open by supports in order to show the inner arrangement of the strings. The fourth illustration, the *Claviciterium*, exhibits an upright harpsichord, which, like the other instruments, is not provided with feet, and had therefore like them to be set on a suitable piece of furniture. In all these claviers the keys are shown without any bed or keyframe, projecting freely out in front, whereas their division into white lower and black upper keys remains the same at the present day.

The Clavicordium has only 7 strings of equal length for its 38 keys, which include the compass of male and female voices in chromatic succession from *A* to b^2.*

In the Clavicimbalum, Virginal, and Claviciterium the strings, which are already equal in number to the keys, grow shorter towards the higher notes, and in regard to the upright Claviciterium Virdung gives the following information: "This is like the Virginal, but has other strings of sheep-gut, and nails which *make it harp* (twang the strings?), and also has quills like the Virginal; it was *recently* invented, and I have seen only one of them".

In the following illustrations of a square and three-cornered Psalterium, each of which has 10 strings, our author remarks: "The Psalterium, *which is still in use,* I have never seen otherwise than

* Fétis, in his Hist. de la Musique, Tom. V, p. 201, gives the same compass and the same description of the claviers of the 15th and 16th centuries, but not from our source.

three-cornered. But I think that the Virginal was formerly derived and copied from the Psalterio, although it is now played and touched with keys, and furnished with quills; though the same is now made in the shape of a long box, like that of a Clavicordium, it is nevertheless more comparable to the Psalterium than to the Clavicord, *since one must have to each key a separate string;* each successive string must likewise be drawn higher than the one preceding, and also become shorter in the same proportion. The strings thus successively shortened therefore form, even in the (square) box (of the instrument), a triangle. But neither is it strange that the Psalterium Hieronimi is square; for not the form of an instrument, but only its mode of stringing and tuning, is of importance". Further on, Virdung gives his friend this advice: "Let thy first choice be the Clavicordium, next the lute, and thirdly the flute; for what thou learnest on the Clavicordio, thou canst also play well and easily on the organ, the Clavicimbel, the Virginal, and on all other keyboard instruments".

On folio E (1) Sebastian observes: "Hie facht es an zu lernen"; and then proceeds: "It is the Clavicordium, I believe, which Guido Aretinus called the Monocordum on account of its single string, and which he calculated or measured, described, and regulated according to the diatonic genus alone. — But I could never find out who it was, that after him invented or devised, that according to the same gauge and for each point a key was made to strike the string at the exact point measured off, then producing just that tone and no other, than the natural gauge ought to yield at that same point. Neither do I know who it was that named the instrument Clavicordium after these keys".—Andreas then asks, how many keys and strings the Clavicordium should have, and Sebastian answers: "I can tell thee no number which it must have; but as the instrument comes from the Monochord, I should think that one might put in as many strings as one has a mind".

A. "But when it has more than one string, it can no longer be called a Monocordium, but, from the number of strings, Tetracordum, Pentacordum, etc."

S. "The number of strings makes no difference; for look, the whole matter is, whether there be many or few strings on the instrument, *that they stand all together in one unison, or in like pitch, no one being higher or lower than any other*".

A. "Why must that be?"

S. "As the gauge of the whole Monocord serves only for one

string, if there were several such not of equal pitch, the gauge of these would be quite wrong, and would produce false notes."

A. "Then would *one* string be enough for the Clavicord?"

S. "No, there must necessarily be more than one, because on one string alone one cannot sound a consonance *simul et semel*, together and at once, but only in succession. Consequently one necessarily employs numerous strings, in order that one may be enabled to hear therefrom the sweetness of the simultaneous consonances in two, three, four, or more parts."

A. "How many keys ought it then to have?"

S. "When Guido wrote on the Monocord, he treated only of the diatonic genus; and therefore the Clavicordium had for a long time not more than 20 keys".

In the woodcut inserted here by Virdung there are 20 white keys, together with two black keys for the tones *b*♭ and b^1♭ in the higher octaves, so that it does not show 20 keys, as the author says, but 22.*

Sebastian then continues: "But afterwards others found a still more subtle device; they read Boetius, too, and divided the Monocord according to the chromatic genus.—Now they make Clavicords of just three octaves, though some add a key and a half-tone more, so that now we usually find, for both genera (the diatonic and chromatic), 38 keys (from low *F* of the male voices up to high g^2 of the female voices)".

The last observations of the priest of Amberg pertinent to our subject are as follows: "Another arrangement is now made of the Clavicordia, for which reason I did not care to state a number of strings at first. Commonly, however, three strings are now taken to a unison, so that one need not stop playing if a string snap. Each unison usually has 3 keys which strike on it, so that only those two keys (tones) cannot be struck together which would be dissonant. Some empty unisons, on which no key strikes, are also put in—on account of the resonance. Brass naturally sounds coarse, but steel fine ("cleyn"), therefore brass strings are taken for the lower

---

* The cause of this contradiction, which also occurs in other early works when mentioning the Guidonic system, lies in the fact, that in the hexachord on which Guido founded his system *either* the *B quadratum* (our modern *B*), *or* the *B rotundum* (our *B*♭), was taken *alone*. Consequently the system, without its two *B*♭'s, consisted of 20 tones, and included just the same number when *B*♭ was substituted for *B*.

unisons, and steel strings for the higher. The strips of cloth woven betwixt the unisons of the strings prevent them from jangling and sounding on, so that the strings sound no longer than one holds the key down for a *tempus* (i. e. beat of the pulse). But on lifting the finger from the key, the tone ceases, even in the runs ("läufflin")— the cloth strips effect this".

Five-and-twenty years later the book just quoted was republished in Latin, retaining the original woodcuts, but provided with additions and a new appendix, under the following title: "Musurgia seu praxis Musicae. Illius primo quae Instrumentis agitur certa ratio, ab Ottomaro Luscinio Argentino duobus Libris absoluta. — Argentorati apud Joannem Schottum Anno Christi 1536."

It is evident that even then the claviers were considered the most perfect musical instruments, from the following remark of Luscinius concerning the same: "All these instruments have keys (as they are called), which strike the strings in various places; when the keys are set in motion by the hands, they sound the full euphony of harmonies, so that one could desire nothing further to be added to these instruments".

In the years 1615 and 1619 Michael Prætorius published his *Syntagma musicum,* consisting of three parts, followed in 1620 by a *Theatrum instrumentorum* with 120 illustrations of various instruments. The author knew and drew upon the work by Virdung; we therefore quote only that which he communicates in the second part, *de Organographia,* on the improvements in claviers made down to his time.

At first (Prætorius says in the 36th Chapter) there were made for the Clavichordia not more than 20 claves, *in genere diatonico,* among which were only 2 black keys, *b*♭ and *b'*♭. After this, however, there were added more *semitonia* according to the *gencre chromatico,* the compass being extended from *F, G, G*♯ up to *f', f'*♯. But now, he observes, all Symphonies and Clavichordia begin below with *C* and end on *a'', c'', d''*, or even *f''*.

For him, the foundation of all keyboard instruments is the Clavichordium, neither does it give so much trouble with the quilling and the tuning. Clavichordia are often met with, he proceeds, which stand in tune for years. In all Clavichords 2, 3, or even 4 keys (which *propter dissonantiam* must not be touched at the same time) are always used for one unison of strings.

Concerning the other claviers of his period Prætorius gives the following account:

A *Symphony*, and likewise a *Clavicymbalum, Virginal* or *Spinet*, are designated in common parlance indiscriminately by the term "instrument" (though quite wrongly).

Spinetta is a small square instrument, which is tuned an octave or a fifth higher than the right pitch, and which is usually placed on or in the large instruments. Both the large and the small square ones are named in Italy *Spinetto*, in England *Virginal*, and in France *Espinette*.

Clavicymbalum or *Gravecymbalum* is a long (longer than broad) instrument, called by some a *Flügel* (wing) because of its shape, by others, *sed male*, a *Schweinskopf* (swine's-head), because its end forms a point like a wild boar's head. It has a strong, bright, and almost more pleasing resonance and tone than the others, on account of the double, threefold, or even fourfold strings; and I have seen one with 2 unisons and a fifth and octave as empty *(eitel)* strings, all of which sounded together most pleasingly and charmingly.

I have seen at Prague, Prætorius reports further on, at Herr Carl Luyton's (the organist), a Clavicymbel (Clavicymbalum universale seu perfectum), which was made accurately and carefully in Vienna thirty years ago (i. e. about 1589), in which not only all the semitonia, as *b♭*, *c♯*, *d♯*, *f♯*, *g♯*, etc. were doubled, but also an extra semi- or semitonium was added between *e* and *f*, which must have been necessary in the *genere enharmonico*, so that it had, in the four octaves from *C* to three-lined *c‴*, 77 claves all told.*

Among the illustrations given by Prætorius in his *Theatrum instrumentarum* we find claviers with four, five, and six sides, including a Clavicymbal "a fourth lower than choir-pitch", in wing-shape; furthermore, an Octave-Spinet and an Octave-Clavichord of a small size corresponding to their compass of but 3 octaves, and also an oblong "gemein (common) Clavichord" of 4 octaves (from *E* to three-lined *e‴*) and strings of equal length.

Regarding the status of claviers in Italy, we gain some information from a work issued in Perugia in 1695, by G. A. A. Bontempi, *Historia musica*, p. 47. Here we learn, that Girolamo Zente had

* More than 30 years before, similar chromatico-enharmonic instruments had already been constructed, and then described by Nicola Vicentino in his previously mentioned book published in Rome, 1555: "L'antica musica, ridotta alla moderna prattica"; and also by Zarlino in a book likewise already referred to, published in Venice, 1358: "Istitutione harmoniche", p. 140. We find an illustration of such a wing-shaped clavier in this latter, p. 141.

invented the newest Clavicembali. Their form was nearly that of an isoceles triangle; they had 2 keyboards and from 2 to 3 draw-stops, took up little room, and yet sounded fully as loud as the long Clavicembali. Bontempi remarks further, that the keyboards of the new instruments were capable of being shifted to the right or to the left by a tone higher or lower, which arrangement, however, was aimless so long as the claviers possessed only 13 strings to the octave of 13 keys. But after two strings without keys had been added to the octave of 13 keys, giving the tones between *d♯ and e,* and between *g♯* and *a*, which could be struck by one or the other key on shifting the keyboard, these instruments had likewise *"attained the highest pitch of perfection"*.

The intermediate tones mentioned by Bontempi were actually necessary, in order to present with tolerable purity the tone-relations in the new keys arising from the shifting of the keyboard, as the tuning of all the claviers hitherto discussed still lacked the modern equal temperament.

The Tuning of the Clavier-strings.

Equal and Unequal Temperament.

The impossibility of establishing an absolutely pure system of harmony is a well-known fact mathematically proved. Even in the following series of pure fifths (2:3)

a♭ e♭ b♭ | f c g d a e b | f♯ c♯ g♯

the tones *a♭* and *g♯* (aside from the inequality of the thirds, sixths, and other intervals arising therefrom) form no pure octave; for the tone g♯ is by 74/73 higher than *a♭*. And should one continue the series of pure fifths to infinity, no tone would ever be reached which would stand to a preceding tone in the proportion of a pure octave (1:2). But just in the octave the ear cannot bear the slightest deviation—a fact recognized even by the two opposing theoreticians of antiquity, Pythagoras and Aristoxenos, together with their adherents.

The Pythagoreans, in establishing an harmonic system, insisted upon the purity of the fourths (3:4) and fifths (2:3).

Fourths: B E A D G C F.

Fifths: F C G D A E B.

From these established tones they formed the diatonic tetrachord:

B C D E

and also the united tetrachords

B C D E F G A

to which was subsequently added a whole tone (8:9) at the lower end

A, B C D E F G A . . . .,

In this "pure diatonic system of harmony" the fourths, fifths, and octaves obtained their natural proportions, but not the major thirds (4:5), the minor thirds (5:6), and their inversions, the minor and major sixths.

Aristoxenos recognized, as an umpire in musical matters, not only the reflective faculty, which judges merely by figures, but gave preference to the ear. This theoretician (about 320 B. C.) sought to adjust the Pythagorean system to the practical needs of musicians by dividing the tetrachord into thirty equal parts, giving to each semitone 6, and to each whole tone 12, of these parts.

Diatonic: *B C D E*
6 12 12

Chromatic: *B C D♭ E*
6 6 18

When, as shown above, the tetrachords were extended to an octave, the latter was divided according to Aristoxenos' plan into 12 semitones of precisely equal value. The fifths, however, were at the same time diminished by $^{1}/_{12}$ of a diatonic comma;* for only by this means could the pure octave be obtained in the harmonic system now comprising twelve steps.

Aristoxenos was thus the first theoretician to establish in music an "equally tempered system of harmony", although it did not find general practical application until more than two thousand years later, after many hardly-contested battles.

Since the 11th century, and more particularly by Guido d'Arezzo and the succeeding theoreticians, attempts were resumed to institute a system which should at least establish sufficient purity in the harmonic relations of the diatonic ecclesiastical modes then exclusively

---

* Twelve successive fifths overstep the octave of their starting-point by a "comma". Each of these fifths must therefore be diminished or tempered by 1/12 of this narrow interval, in order finally to reach the pure octave.

employed. The various ways of dividing the monochord, which were proposed to this end by Guido d'Arezzo, take no account, however, of pure thirds and sixths, because in the 11th century and a long time thereafter these intervals were held to be dissonant.*

But when, after the 15th century, the harmonic construction of the compositions became more pleasing and intelligible, the tuning in pure fifths and fourths without regard to the quality of the thirds and sixths no longer sufficed, even when using the ecclesiastical modes almost universally in vogue until towards 1700. Even the theoreticians were obliged to allow the singers to raise or lower chromatically certain notes in their parts, in order to avoid harsh melodic progressions, such as the tritone *f-b* or the so-called "false" fifth *b-f*, or to reach the leading-note (subsemitonium modi) in "perfect closes", as the composers did not yet venture to sully the purity of their diatonic measures with chromatic signs.

Toward the middle of the 16th century the "chromaticists" (Zarlino, Ist. harmon., parte 3, cap. 80) grew continually bolder, and the need became felt to tune claviers and other keyed instruments already arranged chromatically in such a manner, that the thirds and sixths would also obtain their due share of purity, they having been finally admitted by the theoreticians to the station of "imperfect consonances".

The clavier-tuners, at that time the clavier-players themselves, had already attempted to come at a satisfactorily pure temperament by ear. Now, however, the theoreticians also began the search after suitable and stable rules for temperament.

The Florentine Piero Aron, whose clearly and carefully written work *Toscanello in Musica* ran through five editions** from 1523 to 1562, gives the division of the clavier, which he styles *Monachordo*, into tones and natural and accidental semitones, treats in Chapter XLI

---

* The first theoretician to recognize the consonant character of the thirds was Franco of Cologne, in the 13th century(?). As perfect consonances he names the unison and octave, as medium the fifth and the fourth, and as "imperfect" the major and minor third. In the 14th century, de Muris still reckons the major and minor thirds to the imperfect consonances, but adds to these the *major* sixth. Philippe de Vitry, a contemporary of de Muris, finally designates both the major and minor third and the major and minor sixth as "imperfect consonances".

** I quote from the Venetian edition of 1529, Cap. XL: Divisione del Monachordo per tuoni, et semituoni naturali et accidentali; also Cap. XLI: De la participatione et modo d'accordare l'instrumento.

of the temperament (participatione) of this "instrument", and gives directions for tuning the same. He remarks, that everything formerly written on this topic was hard to understand, even for the learned, and gives, to begin with, a description of the clavier of his time, as follows: In the "instrumento organico" there were, as usually arranged, 29 natural tones, called according to general custom "white keys", and 18 accidental tones called "black keys or semitones". The compass of the instrument was 4 octaves with all tones in chromatic succession from low *F* of the male voices upward, in which only the two black keys for low *F*♯ and *G*♯ were wanting. Aron gives the following directions for tuning the clavier: First tune the tone *C* at a pitch taken at pleasure (con quella intonatione che a te piacerà), then the higher pure octave of this tone, and also its pure major third *E*; after this the fifth *C-G* rather lower than quite pure, as also the fifth *G-D;* now the octave of the last tone, and the fifths *D-A, A-E,* and *E-B,* though all a trifle narrower than pure, i. e. somewhat too low and not quite perfect. Now take the fifth *F* below the tone *C*, but tune it, in contrast to the others, rather higher than pure in order to "attain the right and pure temperament and tune". Then tune the fifths *B*♭ below *F*, and *E*♭ below *B*♭, in the same way as the fifth *F-G;* the remaining semitones, (black keys) however, as thirds; the tone *C*♯ in like manner, striking *A* and *E*, and *F*♯ tuned to *D* and *A*, etc.; until finally the remaining octaves are tuned, and one thus attains the true temperament.

Zarlino, the astutest theoretician of his period, and an authority in all branches of music during two centuries, also gives in the above-named work instructions for the temperament of keyboard instruments, based on the division of the string of the monochord.

In the organs, Clavocembali, Arpichordi, Monochordi, and other modern instruments, he says, the consonances are not met with in in their natural and pure proportions, but in tuning the same are *tempered* by musicians, i. e. augmented or diminished according to necessity, but not so as to hurt the ear. This process of temperament, latterly called "participatione", is employed in order that the intervals of the major and minor third, which were earlier not reckoned among the consonances, may also sound as such.

Zarlino's first direction for obtaining the purest temperament possible for the tones of the diatonic genus, runs as follows: By tuning the fourths *B-e, e-a, a-d′*, in their true proportion (3:4), then the pure minor third (5:6) *B-d*, the tones *d-d'* will not form a pure octave, the proportion of which is 1:2—

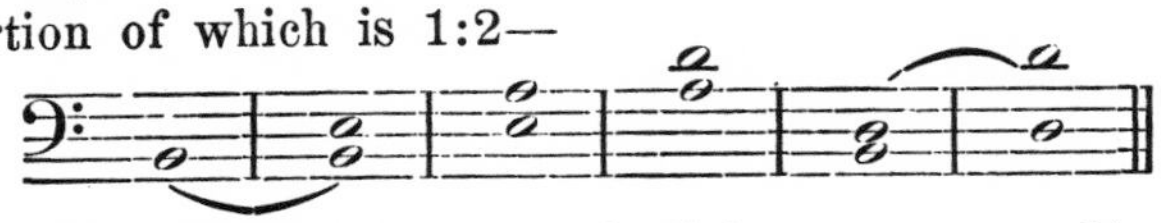

The difference between *d* and *d'* is a comma; this is divided into 7 parts, which are so distributed among the 7 intervals of the 8 tones forming the octave, that finally the two tones of different sound, *d* and *d'*, blend to a single tone.

The octave, Zarlino teaches, must invariably be pure. It consists of a fifth and a fourth; the former is to be diminished by $^2/_7$ of the comma, the latter augmented by the same amount. The pure fifth consists of one major and one minor third; each of these is diminished by $^1/_7$, and consequently each major and minor sixth augmented by the same. The major third consists of one greater semitone and one greater whole tone; the former is augmented by $^3/_7$, the latter diminished by $^4/_7$.

Zarlino also mentions, that to the best of his knowledge he was the first to treat of temperament, and to lay down rules therefor.

Further on in the aforesaid work he gives instructions for the construction of a clavicembalo on which not only the diatonic genus, but also the chromatic and enharmonic genera, could be played.

In the year 1548 Zarlino had a "Clavocembalo" made in Venice by the admirable builder of such instruments, Dominico Pesarese, a picture of which he gives on p. 141.* It exhibits the modern wing-shape, and has a compass of two octaves of the male voice from *A* in the great octave up. The lower white keys are arranged as in our pianofortes; but between the tones *b* and *c*, and likewise between *e* and *f*, there also lies a white upper key, and between the remaining tones are found two upper (short) keys, one of which is always black and the other white; so that within the space of each octave there lie, not 12 keys as at present, but 19 different tones. But, our theoretician observes, had one cared to add even more tones, one would nevertheless never have achieved perfect purity of all the intervals, nor have been able to produce more pleasing harmonies with the same than those hitherto known.

We have already remarked that both in Italy and Germany various attempts were made to construct such "Arcicembali" and

* Beside the cut we find the following quotation: "Difficile est, nisi docto homini tot tendere chordas".

"Universalinstrumente", through the aid of whose chromatic and enharmonic keys the purest temperament possible should be obtained. The Florentine F. Nigetti was perhaps the last to manufacture such an instrument, called "cembalo onnicordo" or "Proteus", about 1650, which was provided with five keyboards arranged stepwise, together with numerous draw-stops. It is said that on this instrument one could distinguish the enharmonic tones, and play in all keys without being disturbed by improper dissonances.

The unpracticalness of the difficult make and tuning of these instruments always quickly relegated them to the background; but their chief aim—the production of the various keys in as nearly equal purity as possible—was striven after in other ways.

Since the 16th century, particularly in Germany, many schemes were brought forward for rendering tolerable the tuning of keyboard instruments furnished with 12 different tones to the octave. Thus, among others, the organist E. N. Ammerbach of Leipzig, in his "Orgel- oder Instrument-Tabulatur"* published there in 1571, gives in Chap. V directions for the pure tuning of claviers. First, he tunes to the great *F* a pure octave *F-f*, followed by the fifth *f-c'*, the fifth *c'-g'*, and the minor third *a* below *c'*; then the octave *a-a'*, from the last tone downward the fifth *a'-d'*, and in like manner the fifth *d'-g*, the minor third *g'-e'*, and the major third *g-b* of the small octave.—One may, he remarks, begin either in the treble or the bass, tuning the other octaves according to the tones established. The tones still missing, *c*♯, *f*♯, *g*♯, are added as major thirds, and the tones *b*♭ and *d*♯ (*e*♭) as minor thirds, to the tones already tuned, forming the respective intervals. Now, if one octave be tuned after another, the clavier will, in his opinion, be very well tuned.

It soon was apparent, that with Ammerbach's pure tuning of the fifths it was impossible that the other intervals should likewise be natural and pure. During the 17th century there consequently appeared numerous schemes for unequal temperament, which, while producing *certain* intervals in perfect purity, gave others in a decidedly tempered form. But not until the 18th century was a system of *equal temperament* established and introduced, in which, although only the octaves were perfectly pure, the remaining intervals deviated but slightly from mathematical exactness.

---

* Described in detail by C. F. Becker in "Die Hausmusik in Deutschland", Leipzig, 1840, p. 20 et seq.

Two highly meritorious writers on the temperament of keyboard instruments were Andreas Werkmeister (1645—1706), organist at Halberstadt, and Joh. Georg Neidhardt (d. Jan. 1, 1739), Kapellmeister at Königsberg. Werkmeister was also one of the first who battled successfully against the employment of the ecclesiastical modes, which had for a long time not been applied in their original purity. In his work (Aschersleben, 1698) on "The necessary observations and rules for the proper treatment of the Bassus continuus, so that anyone having some slight knowledge of music and the clavier can learn it by himself", he remarks on p. 50: "In modern composition, too, one could get along very well with two modes, if they were applied to the tempered clavier, and if there were erected on each key the one mode, that commonly called major, and thereupon the other, that called minor; then we should have 24 *triades harmonicas*, and could play through the circle on the clavier".—"The two modes must, however, (thus he writes further on) retain their accuracy in the *ambitu, repercussion, clausulis formalibus*, etc. (i. e. sound well in tune throughout the repetitions and modulations of the fugued movement) according to modern style, that no disharmony may creep in".—"In their way, the old musicians already had their *digressiones*, and nevertheless they regarded as sacred the order maintained in music by the modes; and although modern musicians are still hardier in their digressions, they nevertheless keep to a certain mode as a norm or guide, so that they can remain in order, and not make confusion worse confounded".—"All digressions or modulations must have a rational motive; thus the beginner should follow approved authorities, not scribbling at random whatever may come into his goose's-head(!), and mutilate, spoil, and bring into discredit the noble art of music; such are assuredly degenerate children and changelings, as the late Dr. Martin Luther terms the abusers of music. Indeed, every thing not ordered according to the laws of Nature, is monstrous and inapt. In brief, as confusion reigns throughout the world, such is at present the case with music: Whatever sounds well and finely is flouted, what sounds bad and wrong is esteemed. Confused heads love confused music, and bewilder and madden the minds of the hearers: as divers sage and learned men confirm".

After these angry attacks upon the unnatural innovations and daring ventures in the music of *his* time, such as we find repeated at *all* times by the most eminent theoreticians, Werkmeister gives on p. 64 brief instructions for tuning and well tempering a clavichord, which follow in concise form below.

Anyone wishing to tune the clavichord according to the diatonic chromatic genus, which is most employed now-a-days, to temper twelve keys in an octave, and to regulate the whole clavier accordingly, may take as starting-point the small *c* either in *chorus pitch* or *chamber pitch.** Tune to this the pure octave c^1, and then the fifth *g*, which must be held a trifle lower than its true pitch to *c*. To this *g* tune its fifth d^1, likewise holding it a trifle lower than pure to *g*. Now the lower octave of d^1, quite pure; to this *d* its fifth *a*, also held a trifle low; to *a* its fifth e^1, held a very little lower than true. Now compare this e^1 with c^1 or *c*; should this third be tolerable, and not altogether too high, this first trial results satisfactorily, for all major thirds must be held somewhat high when struck with their fundamental. But should the tone e^1 be too sharp or high, the fifths must be corrected and let down a little, until it becomes tolerably sharp. Then tune to this e^1 its lower octave pure, then the fifth *e-b* as before a trifle low, then *b* as the major third of *g* as above, testing it with $g\text{-}b\text{-}d^1$, and taking this third *g-b* as the second proof of correct tuning. Then tune $b\text{-}f^1\sharp$, holding it decidedly low, and to this $f^1\sharp$ its pure lower octave. Now the thirds $d\text{-}f\sharp$ and $d^1\text{-}f^1\sharp$ can be tested, the major third $f\sharp$ having to be somewhat too high. To $f\sharp$ then tune $c^1\sharp$ as a fifth held a trifle too low; to $c^1\sharp$ its lower third *a*, which like all major thirds must be held somewhat high to its fundamental. Tune to $c^1\sharp$ its pure lower octave $c\sharp$, and then the fifth $g\sharp$, almost pure. As a test, take the major third below. This $g\sharp$ is usually rather sharp to *e*, but in view of its function as $a\flat$ it cannot be otherwise $(f\text{-}a\flat\text{-}c^1)$. To $g\sharp$ the fifth $d^1\sharp$ is tuned, which may be held a very little high, so as to form a fair consonance in the major thirds $b\text{-}d^1\sharp$ and $d\sharp(e\flat)\text{-}g$. Then tune to $d^1\sharp$ its pure lower octave $d\sharp$, and the fifth $d\sharp(e\flat)\text{-}b\flat$, which may also be held a trifle high, in order that the major third $b\flat\text{-}d^1$ may be tolerable. Then tune f^1 to $b\flat$, again a trifle high, or even pure, according as the lower octave *f* may sound with c^1 or in the triad $f\text{-}a\text{-}c^1$ as a final test. Should one or another fifth appear too high or too low, it must always be corrected. The remaining tones of the clavier are finally tuned as pure octaves of tones previously tuned.

This topic is grasped more definitely and scientifically by the above-mentioned Neidhardt. His first work on the subject bears the

* The chorus pitch was that of the organs of the period, being a whole tone higher than the chamber pitch of secular music.

following title, explaining the contents of the book: The best and easiest temperament of the *monochordi*, by means of which the *genus diatonico-chromaticum* employed now-a-days is so regulated, that all intervals agree in proper proportion and uniform vibration, and therefore the *modi regulares* can be transposed into each and every key in agreeable uniformity; preceded by a treatise on the origin of musical ratios, on the *generibus musicis*, their faults, and the shortcomings of other improvements. The whole writ down thoroughly, orderly, plainly, and briefly, according to mathematical principles, in academical leisure hours. Jena, 1706.

This treatise the author followed up with several others, each improving on that preceding, and all aiming at establishing an equal temperament.

Mattheson also recommends an equal temperament for claviers in his book "Das beschützte Orchester" (The Protected Orchestra), Hamburg, 1717, p. 85, and condenses his opinion on the subject in his "Vollkommener Capellmeister", (Hamburg, 1739, p. 55) as follows:

"Temperament is such a regulation of the intervals on the claviers, that the one is somewhat lowered, the other somewhat raised, from its true pitch, in order that all may agree in as full concord as possible. The tempering of the clavier is therefore a matter of necessity, because no moderation (alteration of the intervals) can be effected on this instrument either with the breath or with the fingers; which is, on the contrary, easily done with the human voice and all other sounding instruments".—"Only the claviers and harps, being divided and measured-off instruments, are subject to this difficulty, that in tuning them one must have recourse to tempering, concerning which such a stir is made in many books as if the welfare of the whole world were bound up in the clavier alone. For the human voice, or wind and bowed instruments, require this makeshift so little, that they can hit the right pitch by the aid of the breath, the fingers, or other natural agencies. Thus we may easily imagine, that any tuner of the clavier, organ, or harp will regulate this temperament as his ear is accustomed, and after his own ideas; for but few of these people are capable of giving a reason why, or explaining how, they do anything.— —The commonest manner of tempering which, in vulgar parlance, will do, depends on the following three principles: 1. *The octaves, minor sixths, and minor thirds, must always be pure.* 2. *To the major sixths and the fourths a trifle is added.* 3. *From the fifths and major thirds, however, a trifle is taken.* But how much or how little this trifle shall be is another question, which very few instrument-tuners know anything about".

"But, regarding a more exact temperament, we have works thoroughly and painstakingly written by Andreas Werkmeister, Johann Georg Neidhardt, Johann Arnold Vockerodt, Christoph Albert Sinn, etc., of which amateurs may take counsel on occasion—the second is more especially to be recommended".

A pioneer in the theory of music, the author and composer J. P. Rameau of Paris, was the first practically to perfect the subject in hand, his method soon being universally adopted in Germany as well. His first theoretical work appeared at Paris in 1722 under the title: Traité de l'harmonie réduite à ses principes naturels. A plain explanation and simplification of the same, "Éléments de musique théorique et pratique suivant les principes de M. Rameau", by M. d'Alembert, followed in the year 1752, and secured for this theoretician, previously appreciated by but few, the recognition which he merited. In this book (Part I, Ch. VII, § 72) we find the following directions for tempering keyboard instruments, which surpass all earlier methods in the uniform vibration of the intervals, and which are still followed in the main by piano-tuners.

Take (so teaches Rameau-d'Alembert) any key of the piano, for instance *C*, tune its fifth *G*, at first quite pure, then lowering it imperceptibly; tune to this *G* its pure fifth *D*, and then lower it likewise a trifle; continue in like manner with all fifths ascending in succession. On arriving at the last fifths *a♯—e♯* and *e♯—b♯*, the last tone, *b♯*, must exactly coincide with the initial tone *c*, that is, form its pure octave. If this be so, one may be sure that the clavier is well tuned. But if the last fifth *e♯— b♯* (*f—c*) is too flat, the preceding fifths, or some of them, have been too far diminished; if, on the other hand, the last fifth is too sharp, the preceding fifths have not been sufficiently diminished, and one must go back to make this error good, until all 12 tones of the octave are correctly tuned by this method. One has then merely to tune the octaves of these tones exactly true, in order to have a well-tuned clavier.

Friedr. Wilhelm Marpurg, who published d'Alembert's work in German (1757), says on p. 35, in a note concerning Rameau's temperament:

Although one finds fewer altered thirds in the temperament usual in Germany than in that of M. Rameau, the fifths are, on the contrary, all the worse in the former, and likewise many thirds, so that on a clavier tuned in this way there will be five or six intolerable keys in which nothing can be played. In M. Rameau's temperament, on the other hand, all the keys are equally good.*

In his epoch-making work, "The Theory of the Sensations of Tone", (Fourth Ed., Brunswick, 1877), Helmholtz has written in a erudite and liberal spirit on the advantages and disadvantages of the tempered tuning of keyboard instruments (pp. 508—533, Appendix XVIII). From his theories, which are always the outcome of personal experiment and experience, I quote the following (4th ed., p. 506):

"Starting from *C*, as shown before, we pass through a series of pure fifths to *b*♯, which differs from *C* by only about one-half a semitone, namely by the interval of 74/73. *Descending* from *C* through 12 successive fifths we reach *d*♭♭, which is as much lower than *C* as *b*♯ is higher. Taking *c*-*b*♯-*d*♭♭, and dividing the slight deviation of 74/73 equally among all twelve fifths of each circle, each fifth will be about 1/60 of a semitone impure, which is, indeed, a very slight deviation. Thus all differences between the degrees within an octave are derived from the 12 degrees, as we have them in our modern keyboard instruments". — "The thirds and sixths in equal temperament are more nearly pure than the Pythagorean intervals".

"There can be no question", Helmholtz observes further on, "that the system of equal temperament, on acount of its simplicity, possesses extraordinary advantages for instrumental music; that any other system would require a far more complicated mechanism of the instruments and render them far more difficult to manage, and in con-

---

* Contributions to the literature of Temperament are contained in Adlung's "Anlagen zur mus. Gelahrtheit", 2nd ed., pp. 318—337, and in "Mus. mech. organoedi", II, 22, same author. In the systematic chronological view of musical literature by C. F. Becker (2 Parts, Leipzig, 1836 and 1838), including the similar work by Forkel, we find over 85 treatises dating from 1688 to 1838 on the division of the monochord, and on the tuning and temperament of keyboard instruments. This list contains the works of Werkmeister, Neidhardt, Kirnberger, the Abbé Vogler, Marpurg, Türk, and Scheibler. The invention of the latter, the establishment of equal temperament by means of vibrations, was first made known and intelligible through the essay by Dr Löhr, "On the Invention of Scheibler" (Über die Scheibler'sche Erfindung). The "Catalogue de la bibliothèque de F. J. Fétis", issued at Brussels in 1877, also contains 39 treatises on our topic in German, French, English, and Italian. M. Hauptmann published a valuable essay on Temperament in the "Jahrbücher für mus. Wissenschaft", 1863.

sequence, that the high development of modern instrumental music was possible only under the domination of the tempered system of tuning. But one must not think that the difference between the tempered and natural systems is a mathematical subtility of no practical value. Actual observation at a suitably tuned instrument immediately shows, that this difference is striking enough to be noticed by persons of very ordinary musical talent. Moreover, we see directly that the same thing was felt by earlier musicians who were still accustomed to the pure intervals of vocal music then very carefully studied, when we cast a glance over musical treatises of the second half of the 17th and first half of the 18th centuries, at which time the introduction of various systems of equal temperament was the subject of warm controversy, when methods on methods were invented and rejected, aiming at conquering the difficulty, and most ingenious styles of instruments were contrived for the practical realization of the enharmonic differences between the degrees".

A mathematically pure musical system can neither be worked out theoretically nor carried out practically. True, in the diatonic system of Pythagoras the fifths and fourths, and likewise the octaves, are all fixed in exact and pure proportions; but the thirds and sixths formed of the tones *F C G D A E B* deviate more, as we have learned before, from their natural purity, than those of our equal temperament.

When musically gifted vocalists sing without accompaniment, they always strike pure intervals only; but with a melodic series of tones, or a succession of chords executed with exact purity, they are unable to maintain the pitch at which they began.

Even the following short example proves that a singer taking its intervals with mathematical purity will, on reaching the fifth tone, no longer be in unison with the tone of the same name on which he began, but must have flatted by a comma (81 : 80).

80 96 72 108 81

5 : 6 4 : 3 2 : 3 4 : 3

Here the lower figures give the pure proportions of the intervals, and the upper ones the corresponding division of a string.

When the singers, however, are supported by a trained orchestra, they not only execute the melodies and full chords in naturally pure intervals, but also hold the pitch established by the orchestra. For the orchestral instruments, wielded by human hands, are able like the singers to reinforce the pure fifths and octaves by pure thirds and sixths, or to sharp or flat these latter slightly in case of necessity. But when so-called "enharmonic transitions" are executed with harsh impurity by singers and instrumentalists, this is always the fault of the composer, who has placed two keys side by side on an equal footing which stand in no rational degree of relationship one to the other. Only the well-tempered pianoforte, with its fixed tones, can easily and intelligibly reproduce such enharmonic modulations, because the hearer does not perceive the change of key, but follows up the harmony first heard, which, it is true, ought finally to lead to a satisfactory close, this being unhappily often not the case.

While it is impossible for the unaccompanied singer to maintain perfect purity in the intervals, without at the same time leaving the original pitch, the pianoforte, on the other hand, can never attain perfect purity of tuning by a multiplication of its tones and keys. Equal temperament, however, avoids both these dangerous reefs, and deviates so imperceptibly from absolute purity that our most eminent composers have always given preference to the well-tempered pianoforte, and have dedicated to it their most pregnant works.

Further Development of the Clavichord and Harpsichord.

Far from being content with "the highest pitch of perfection in the clavier" lauded by Luscinius in 1536 and Bontempi in 1695, endeavors were continually making in Germany, France, Italy and England to render the instrument more practical and agreeable in regard to compass, tone, and touch. Thus the strings were sometimes of brass, sometimes of steel or gut; the soundboard was variously adjusted and enlarged, each tone was furnished with 2, 3, or even 4 like-tuned strings (unisons), which were set in vibration by tangents of metal, whalebone, or leather. Furthermore, these instruments were frequently provided with several keyboards, one often being in the relation of an octave to the other, and capable of employment either separately or "coupled". Finally, they were also furnished with stops, combinations, and registers, which damped or reinforced the tone, or united the keyboard with an organ, or even with bells, cymbals, or drums.

During the 17th century harpsichords were often imported from France into Germany, where the clavichord was peculiarly affected; about the year 1680 the clavichord-maker Mietcke of Charlottenburg near Berlin was one of the first to succeed, after many attempts, in building harpsichords of equally good quality. He palmed off his first successful harpsichord as a French instrument, and received for it the sum of 300 thalers. But when it became known that he himself was the maker of these instruments, their price fell so that, although generally admitted to be excellent, only from 60 to 80 thalers were paid for them.

Mietcke's contemporary Mattheson, who records this fact in the copy of the "Neu-Eröffneten Orchester" now in my possession, calls attention to it on page 213 of this work by the following censure:

"In almost all matters a shameful state of things prevails here at home — that we perversely choose to favor everything coming from abroad, not invariably because it is fine and good, but simply because it is foreign, above our native persons and things, not because the latter are bad or common, but simply and solely because they are home products; to favor and honor creatures, who are often not worth powder and shot, and who worm themselves in by intrigue and plots (if they are only foreigners); and on the contrary to despise and slight much that may be found in our own country, in our town, our house, even though on careful examination it may excel."

Further on in the above work, which was published in 1713, Mattheson remarks (p. 262) that the full-toned *(vollstimmigen)* claviers surpass all other instruments, and that the two brothers Rücker (Ruckers?) of Brabant had done good work and gained a reputation as the makers of square and wingshaped harpsichords; also that the fine and workmanlike clavichords of von Brocken, Middleburg, and Fleischer, with their strong and clear resonance, were held in high esteem. He says, moreover, that the harpsichord, with its great versatility (Université), furnished an almost indispensable foundation in accompanying sacred, theatre, and chamber music, but that pieces with modern and showy technique *(Hand- und Galanterie-Sachen)* could be brought out best and cleanest on a good clavichord, as the latter produced the singing tone far more plainly, sustained and softened, than the harpsichord or spinet, with their even resonance of tone. "Whoever would hear a delicate hand (fist!) and clean technique (so he exclaims), must seat his candidate at a well-made clavichord; for on a great harpsichord, provided with 3 or 4 stops or registers, much slurring will escape the ear, and one will hardly hear the graces distinctly".

In the clavichords, as remarked before, the tangents or pins of 3 or 4 neighboring keys struck one and the same string in different places, and therefore produced, on striking, just so many different tones. Now these tones could be struck in succession, but never played together. All works touching on our topic name D. T. Faber as the inventor, who first made (about 1732) a *bundfreies* Clavier, in which each key had one string or one set of unisons allotted to it. This item, however, is taken in all cases from Walther's "Musikalisches Lexicon", issued in 1732. But the article in question reads literally: Faber (Daniel Tobias), organist at Craylsheim, "has invented a clavichord which is *Bundfrey* throughout, and can be modified by various adjustments in three ways so as to sound (1) like a lute, (2) like one, in which the resonance is undamped, and (3) like a muffled *Glockenspiel* (set of small bells). See Extract from the *Coburgische Zeitung* of April, 1725, p. 78".

Should this last-named source not enter more into detail, Faber's invention would seem to consist either only in the clavichord built *bundfrei* "throughout", or even simply in the lute-stop and bell-stop added to the same. For it is highly probable that attempts were made even previous to the date of this extract to obviate the difficulty complained of.

Even in those clavichords which were *bundfrei* throughout the keys were still fashioned in the strangest curves, to enable the tangents to strike their proper strings. The organist K. Lemme, living at Brunswick about 1780, was the first to succeed in giving the keys a straight action, and consequently a lighter touch. In the year 1771 he and his father also invented the *pressed* soundboard so firmly united that it could not be torn apart. Lemme also built clavichords of a pleasing, oval-round form, with a fine strong tone.

The pedal, invented for his instrument* by Bernhard Murer (called Bernadino), organist at Venice in 1445, in order to lend greater power to the bass tones of the organ through the additon of lower octaves, was early added to the clavichord and harpsichord as well, both of which doubtless profited by such a reinforcement. As we have seen, Virdung mentions the same as early as 1511, and Adlung describes the pedals of the clavichord in detail in both of his works given above.

* See Caffi, Storia della musica sacra, Venezia, 1855, Vol. II, p. 14.

The stops or registers sometimes added to the clavichords were controlled by the player's hands or feet, and were intended to soften or reinforce the tone of the instrument. For instance, the in any event mild tone of the clavichord was still further damped by shaping its metallic tangents somewhat broader than usual, and then covering one half of each with leather or cloth. The celestina or lute-stop would bring this softer half to bear on the strings, whereas a pantaleon or harp-stop made sharper pins or metallic jacks strike the latter.

In Germany continuous efforts were made to perfect the clavichord there in general use, the harpsichord being employed almost exclusively as a support for vocal choruses, and seldom as a solo instrument accompanied by the orchestra. C. Ph. E. Bach published, among other pieces, Concertos for harpsichord in 1745 and 1752.

In France the clavecins, and their smaller size, the épinettes, were preferred to the clavichords, and the Parisian instrument-makers were mainly occupied in their improvement, also finding frequent sale for them abroad.

At first the harpsichords had but one keyboard, like the spinets. Later they were provided with two, lying stepwise one above the other, and then two unisons were added. Sometimes each of these two strings had a separate jack. In this case, when the upper keyboard was played on, only one string would be plucked, while the lower keyboard coupled the upper, thus setting both strings in vibration and giving the harpsichord a redoubled tone, especially when, as often happened, the upper keyboard was tuned an octave higher than the lower.

One of the oldest and most renowned clavier manufactories, that of the Ruckers family at Antwerp, is often mentioned with praise by the earlier writers in Germany, the Netherlands, France, and England.*

Hans Ruckers, the first master in this family, built harpsichords and spinets as early as the latter half of the 16th century, which, according to detailed accounts by Hüllmandel, the celebrated pupil

* Compare W. de Burbure, Recherches sur les facteurs de clavecins et les luthiers d'Anvers. Bruxelles, Hayez, 1863.—Fétis, Biogr. des mus., VII, 246.—E. van der Straeten, la Mus. aux Pays-bas. Bruxelles, Muquardt, 1867, p. 65 etc.—Encycl. méth., Musique, Paris, 1791, p. 286.—Chouquet, Le musée du conservat., Paris, Didot, 1875, p. 46.—Burney, The present state of mus. in Germany. London, 1755, I.—Cramer, Magaz. I, 392.

of Em. Bach, excelled all former instruments of this kind. He gave the harpsichords a stronger, fuller, and more brilliant tone by adding to each pair of strings tuned in unison a third string, shorter and of finer wire, tuned to their higher octave. For the low tones he used copper strings, for the higher ones steel strings, and extended the compass of the harpsichords by four tones, by giving them four full octaves, from contra-*C* to three-lined $\underline{c}'''$. Ruckers added a second keyboard to his harpsichords, one keyboard sounding all three strings, and the other but one string. He paid most careful attention to the broader or narrower grain of the soundboard, and also to its thickness, in order to obtain a tone of the greatest "carrying" power, and altogether brought the low and high tones into an harmonious relation unknown in the older harpsichords. His claviers were well-known and sought for not only in the Netherlands, but were also shipped in considerable numbers to France, Germany, and England.

Of the make of this Hans Ruckers "le vieux" the museum of the Paris Conservatory possesses, as No. 221, a harpsichord (clavecin) of the year 1590, with two keyboards. No. 222 is a similar instrument, made by Hans Ruckers "le jeune", the under side of the cover and the finger-board being ornamented with admirable paintings by masters of that period. Fétis owned a spinet, by Ruckers the Elder, with two keyboards (épinette double), the upper being tuned an octave higher than the lower; they could be played either separately or together "with the finest effect". The instrument bore the inscription: Hans Ruckers me fecit Antverpiae, 1610.

Three sons of the aforesaid firm kept alive their father's brilliant renown. They were named Francis (b. 1576), Hans "le jeune" (b. 1578), and André (bapt. 1579), who later assumed the to-name of "le vieux" to distinguish him from his son, André Ruckers le jeune. The instruments of this last master are said even to have surpassed those of his predecessors in fullness of tone and excellent workmanship. The best artists of Antwerp, more particularly the painter of flowers and animals, Franck, adorned them with neatly executed paintings, for which reason they often brought 3000 francs. These adornments, however, were later frequently the cause of the demolition of the instruments, being detached from them and turned to account as independent paintings.

The clavecins made in Antwerp still enjoyed high favor till toward the end of the 18th century. In 1750 a manufactory was established there by J. D. Dulcken, a Hessian by birth, whose clavecins ranked among the best of that period. From his workshops came J. P. Bull, whose harpsichords sold for 100 ducats, and were highly extolled, especially by Burney. The latter terms them "double harpsichords", which simply means a harpsichord having two keyboards. The Museum of Antiquities at Antwerp possesses one of these with the inscription: Joannes Petrus Bull me fecit Antverpiae anno 1779.

To avoid, or at least to simplify, the tedious and expensive "quilling" of the harpsichords, many experiments were made during the 18th century in Germany, France, and Italy. Thus the instrument-maker Wiclef of Anspach, about 1740, used small brass adjustments instead of quills. To his harpsichords he also added bells, tuned true by turning.

Of wider influence, however, were the "clavecins à buffles" or "en peau de buffles", invented by the Netherlander Pascal Taskin at Paris in the year 1768. He employed, for one register or stop of his trichord clavecin, bits of ox-leather instead of quills, and the French recorder of the invention praises it by saying: "Il ne pince plus, mais il caresse le corde" (it no longer plucks, but caresses, the string), and adds, its sweet, velvety-soft tone swells at pleasure under the pressure of the player's hand. By means of various stops, governed by the pressure of the knee and later of the foot, either the quills or the leather tangents could be made to act separately or together, and the strings sounded softly or loudly at will.

A German eye-witness, Kapellmeister Vogler of Paris, writes concerning the new invention: "They are harpsichords of the finest make. Each has 2 keyboards with three strings, the third tuned in the octave, with the lute-stop. Herein they do not differ from other harpsichords. The new invention, however, adds to the above another row of a so-called "jeu de buffle", through which the bass obtains a magnificent double-bass effect hitherto unknown". — The price was from 1500 to 3000 livres.*

From the following accounts of German and Italian clavicembali, reaching well into the æra of the pianoforte, it is evident that Taskin's invention was both known and speedily imitated outside of France.

---

* See La Borde, Essai sur la mus., 1780, I, 346 et seq.—Cramer, Magazin der Music, 1783, I, 209.—J. H. Mees, Abrégé hist. sur la mus. moderne etc., Bruxelles, 1828, p. 60.

The harpsichords built subsequently to 1773 by the instrument-maker Joh. Chr. Oesterlin of Berlin were eagerly sought for and widely disseminated. The harpsichords which he furnished with a newly invented kind of leathern tangents were special favorites. The *cembalo angelico*, invented at Rome about 1778, also had tangents of leather, which were covered besides with velvet, in order to obtain as soft a tone as possible.

In the year 1775 J. G. Wagner of Dresden advertised a newly invented "clavecin royal", which, though built in clavichord-form, was said to have the full tone of a harpsichord. It had 4 pedals, which swelled or diminished the tone at will, and which were intended to imitate the harp, lute, pantaleon and pianoforte. His co-worker and surviving younger brother, Ch. Sal. Wagner, is said to have obtained the *forte* and *piano* effects in his harpsichords "by means of the cover"*, and besides this to have added 3 combinations without pipes, yet "imitating to illusion" the flute, clavichord, and bassoon. How far this illusion went may be gathered from the fact, that the bassoon-stop, for instance, let down a narrow roll of paper upon the lower strings, the latter then giving out a jarring tone when struck. Up to 1796 he had built no less than 772 harpsichords, the finest of which cost some 600 thalers.

The shifting of the keyboard was known as early as the beginning of the 17th century. Praetorius, in his *Syntagma musicum* (1614), mentions a clavicembalo whose key *C* could be shifted by a stop to come under *C♭*, *D♭*, *D*, *E♭*, *D♯*, and *E*, thus affording a convenient method of transposing within this compass, and also, by reason of the enharmonic tones present, of playing in nearly perfect tune. Adlung, in his Mus. mech. organoedi, gives a detailed description of such a "transposing clavicembalo", praising it especially because one could play both in the chorus-pitch and, by shifting the keyboard, in the true chamber-pitch $1^1/_2$ tones lower as well.

We have no exact description of the "cimbali piegatori" of Gioseppe Mendini in the 17th century, but can get a notion of them from the "clavecins brisés" which the instrument-maker Marius

* This was probably the adjustment also called, when occurring later, the "crescendo", in which the cover above the strings was similar to the soundboard. This cover consisted of several thin, narrow layers of wood, which could be spread apart or brought close together like a fan by means of a pedal stop, the resonance of the strings thus issuing loudly, or being stifled by the apparently closed cover.

"invented" in 1700, and which probably resembled them not only in name but also in arrangement. Of these latter a specimen is still extant in the Museum of the Paris Conservatory, as No. 224. Its three parts, when placed one above another, find room in a small trunk. The inventor, according to his advertisement, even stowed the instrument in a wig-box, and states its weight at only from 10 to 12 pounds. The longest of the strings, which were set in vibration by metallic tangents, was but two feet in length, though having, as he says, the tone of clavichords 7 feet long. Marius, in 1716, laid before the Paris Academy 4 models of hammer-claviers (clavecins à maillets), to which we shall return further on.

Altogether, during the 18th century, so many "new inventions" were advertised, which were intended to reinforce the tone of the clavichord, soften that of the harpsichord, improve tone and touch of the recent hammer-clavier, and perfect all these instruments by "new combinations", registers, and stops, that the musical periodicals had standing headings devoted to the topic. Striking names were bestowed upon the claviers provided by their inventors with innumerable contrivances, in order to attract purchasers, and the foremost clavier-makers of the time held it to be a point of honor to add something new and peculiar to their instruments. "The gentlemen are so fond of inventing, even though it be naught but new names!" cries Cramer in 1783 in his *Magazin der Music,* replete with such striking advertisements.

The plainly perceptible endeavor to give the clavichords and harpsichords a fuller and more singing tone was, at the same time, a struggle for existence on the part of these instruments. The hammer-clavier invented before 1711 by Christofori, and since then incessatly more effectively developed, crowned the aforesaid endeavor with success, while bringing the two other instruments alluded to, until then universally esteemed, into desuetude.

A History of the Clavier cannot pass by unnoticed the efforts made to keep alive the interest in the earlier claviers by means of improvement and alterations. The most striking of these "inventions" will find brief mention below, although they were in great part soon forgotten again, while but few of them were of use to the new pianoforte.

Joh. Christoph Fleischer, an instrument-maker living at Hamburg about 1718, in praise of whom Mattheson is quoted above, was the inventor of the so-called *Theorben-Flügel** with 16-foot tone, i. e. pitched an octave lower than the ordinary claviers with 8-foot tone. This contra-harpsichord was furnished with 3 registers, one sounding the gut strings and the other the metal strings. Moreover, he made "Lautenclaviere" (lute-claviers) of ordinary compass, having gut strings tuned in pairs, and took from 60 to 1000 thalers for his insruments.

Franz Jacob Spath of Ratisbon presented to the Elector at Bonn in 1751 a "Tangenten-Flügel" without quills, having 30 combinations, and in 1770 even made one with 50 combinations, having a piano-stop, forte, echo, gut-string, harp, and other stops.

Forkel mentions, in his *Musikalische Bibliothek*, I, 298, that the clavier-teacher M. de Virbés of Paris invented in 1771 a "clavecin acoustique", which could imitate 18 different instruments, and this merely with the ordinary strings of the harpsichord. This imitation was said to be so exact, that a symphony could be played with the same effect as if executed by a great orchestra; except that the nature of the instrument caused all sounds to be heard as "pincés". About 1777 de Virbés again announced a new instrument under the name of the "clavecin harmonieux et céleste", having much the same character, imitating 14 instruments, such as the lute, harp, flute, oboe, clarinet, bassoon, celestine, harmonica, etc., and producing the tones either *pianissimo, crescendo,* or *fortissimo.*

Among the instrument-makers who strove to add new inventions to their already excellent work, we also find J. G. Jürgensen, who flourished in Schleswig about 1783. He built clavichords "ranking in singing tone and power with those of Friederici, Krämer, Lemmi, and of Möller in Copenhagen." He also invented a "clavecin royal", which, as he announced, afforded 12 changes or combinations imitating the sound of the harpsichord, fortepiano, harp, lute, and other instruments at the player's discretion, by means of 2 draw-stops and as many pedals, and produced a more powerful *forte* by opening the cover above the strings. The instrument was in clavichord-form, 1¼ ells long by a scant ell broad, and cost 60 ducats. Besides this instrument, Jürgensen also exhibited a "belsona real" having 5 draw-stops, which were said to produce over 48 changes by their various combination.

Forkel reports, in the *Musikalische Bibliothek* for 1779, that the instrument-maker Hofmann of Gotha had contrived a "double clave-

* The great bass-lute was named "Theorbo".

cin". On either side of the same were two keyboards, to be played by two executants together, or, when coupled, by one player. Joh. Andreas Stein, who will receive special mention in the History of the Pianoforte, also invented at Augsburg a double harpsichord, which he named a "vis-à-vis". On occasion of a journey to Paris in 1758 he contrived a concert instrument combining the harpsichord still most in favor there with the pianoforte, and in such fashion, that each of these instruments had its strings and soundboard independent of the other.

J. P. Milchmeyer, mechanician, clavier-teacher, and author of a pianoforte method, invented about 1781 a "mechanical flügel", with three keyboards and no less then 250 combinations, said to be produced by combining the several stops, which were nearly always alike in all the "new inventions" so portentously puffed. The mechanician Mercia of London alone succeeded, in 1783, in producing a harpsichord with really *new* effects, having hit upon the device of titillating his hearers' ears by "delusively imitated trumpets" and real drums.

Despite all these noises happily not heard, but only read of, we have nevertheless not yet reached the summit of the Parnassus of wonder-instruments. For upon that height there shines a work of art, which must needs be described at length, left unfinished by a bell-founder of Prague, and finished by the Doctor of Philosophy and Medicine Vincenz von Blaha, Professor in the University at Prague. The latter not only finished the said instrument, which combined a hammer-clavier (with which we need not occupy ourselves here) with various other instruments, in the year 1795, but likewise furnished it with original and doubtless highly important additions. The instrument was in the ordinary shape of a harpsichord, beneath which, behind green curtains, the entire apparatus for Turkish music, such as a drum, triangle, etc., was placed, and set in motion by a pedal. Herr von Blaha, when showing off this work of art himself, would also sound the drums and fifes alone, singing to the same, or playing "a real bassoon" -accompaniment thereto by the aid of a little tube in his mouth. Above the keys of the hammer-clavier was set, besides, a separate keyboard controlling two rows of organ-pipes, and a pedal worked the bellows providing these pipes with life-giving wind. For amateurs our doctor also let loose the droning bagpipe and rattling castanets. But all this was surpassed by the suddenly in-rushing, howling stormwind, the plashing sleet, and the rolling thunder with fearful thunder-claps, to which he sang a lovely descriptive aria, until the war of elements was tranquilized. But this silence was truly refreshing, as he naïvely remarks.—To incredulous readers I commend the source quoted by Gerber: *Literarischer Anzeiger*, 1798, No. LI, p. 531.

The Piano-violins, and the Pantaleon.

The attempts to contrive a keyboard instrument which could produce tones more sustained than those of the clavichord and harpsichord, began early in the 17th century. As a prototype, although a very imperfect one, of the class, we might name the hurdy-gurdy (veille), which was known from the 9th century onward in Germany, France, and Italy.* It bore the form of a small lute or viola, strung with 3 or 4 gut strings. Over the strings was a wooden cover, on one side of which were fixed 8 or 10 keys whose tangents, like those of the clavichord, "stopped" one of the strings at various points, thus shortening it. By means of a projecting crank the right hand turned a wheel which, being rosined, set all the strings in vibration. When touched by the left hand, the keys could then produce a melody within a range of 8 to 12 successive diatonic tones, with a running accompaniment by the doubled or simple tonic and dominant.

However, the Piano-violin (Geigenwerk) contrived by the organist Joh. Heiden of Nuremberg, about 1600, might be regarded as a really new invention; in it the keys when touched pressed their corresponding wire strings against small rosined wheels. These wheels were kept revolving by a pedal, sounding the strings touched as in a bowed instrument.

Later imitations of this instrument do not appear to have met with much favor. The "Gambenwerke" made toward the middle of the 18th century by G. M. Rish of Ilmenau had better success. His improvement of the "Nuremberg Geigenwerke" is found chiefly in the simple substitution of gut strings, like those of bowed instruments, for the wire strings. He undertook professional tours with his Gambenwerke, and sought purchasers for them on the way.

---

* In different countries this instrument was also known under the names of *lira tedesca, viola da orbo, Drehleier, Bauernleier,* and Latinized to *lyra rustica* or *pagana;* etc.

In 1754 Johann Hohlfeld exhibited to King Frederick II at Berlin a piano-violin (Bogenflügel) strung with gut strings, beneath which was a bow furnished with horsehair. On pressing the keys the strings were drawn by little hooks against the bow, the slow or rapid movement of which the player controlled by a pedal-stop, in order to sound the string in proportionally weak or powerful sustained tones.

This instrument of Hohlfeld's was materially improved and perfected 15 years later by J. G. Greiner of Wetzlar. At the desire of the Abbé Vogler he added to it an ordinary pianoforte, which was set upon the piano-violin strung with gut strings, and could be coupled or connected with it. The length of this pair of oblong instruments, which found room on a table, was 3 feet 8 inches, the breadth 1 foot 8 inches, and the height 1 foot. Greiner named the instrument the "Bogenhammerclavier", and sold it in Copenhagen for 600 thalers.

In 1794 C. A. von Meyer, at Knonow, conceived that he could improve the Bogenflügel, by providing for each of its gut strings a separate horsehair bow. The frame holding these bows was moved up and down by a pedal, and each key pressed the bow allotted to it against the string to be sounded, which remained in position.

The renown and description of such claviers with a sustained tone penetrated to Moscow, where the instrument-maker J. Ch. Hübner invented a "clavecin harmonique" about 1801, which accurately reproduced the sound of a string quartet. His fellow-workman Pouleau gave the name of "Orchestrine" to a still further improved *Bogenflügel* of full and powerful tone, and gave performances on it at Paris in 1808, and later in Brussels, with extraordinary applause.

To the class of these bowed instruments also belong the Celestino of Walker, the Sostenute-Piano of Mott in London, and the Orphica or Xänorphica of Röllig in Vienna.

None of the instruments described have proved practically and permanently useful. The oft-required renewal and tuning of the strings was as expensive and tedious as the regulation and repairing of the bows and of the wheels setting them in motion. In the course of the 19th century attempts at their improvement were consequently discontinued.

The Dulcimer is another of those instruments, the power of whose tone is controlled by the player's hand. Upon being furnished with keys, as narrated above, which plucked the strings through the medium of quills, the instrument was transformed into the clavicembalo, on which, however, to the regret of musicians, the music produced was always of a rough and grating quality. The earlier mode of playing the dulcimer with hammers was therefore resumed, its resonance being bettered to begin with, softer sounding gut strings taken instead of the sharp-set wires, and the hammer-heads covered with soft leather, thus enabling the player to shade his performances in an artistic manner. The dulcimer, when thus improved, surpassed, as we are assured, both the clavichord and clavicembalo in fullness of tone and capacity of shading, and from this very circumstance is said to have given direct occasion for the invention of the pianoforte. For soon after the brilliant appearance of the new dulcimer, the new invention of the pianoforte appeared almost simultaneously in Italy, France, and Germany. The following account will enable the reader to judge for himself of the probability of a transition from the perfected dulcimer into the—at first—very primitive hammer-clavier.

Pantaleon Hebenstreit, born in Eisleben, is first heard of at Leipsic, where he gave lessons on the clavichord and in dancing. Being deeply in debt, he escaped his importunate creditors by flight, concealing himself in the house of an intimate friend, a country parson in the Merseburg district, whose children he instructed in clavichord playing. In the village inn he often heard the dulcimer played, made one in the improved style described above, and attained to such extraordinary virtuosity on the instrument that he journeyed in 1705 to Paris, to give public performances on it. He won great applause when playing before Louis XIV, who was so enchanted by his masterly performances, enhanced by the most diversified tone-colors, that he loaded him with marks of favor, and gave the instrument its inventor's baptismal name Pantaleon (Pantalon), under which it became more and more widely known. Hebenstreit made an equally favorable impression when performing on the Pantaleon before Ninon de Lenclos. The Abbé Chateauneuf, who was present, describes the instrument in his 'Dialogue sur la musique des anciens', and is full of praises of the artist's extraordinary performances and brilliant mental powers. In the year 1706 we find Hebenstreit as Kapellmeister, soloist on the Pantaleon, and Court Dancing-master at Eisenach; and when our celebrated composer Telemann was engaged there in 1708 as Concertmeister (first violin), Hebenstreit induced him to play with him concert pieces for two violins composed by the latter. Of these Telemann writes in his Autobiography that he always had to prepare and refresh himself for several days, that he might in some measure approach in strength the "not sufficiently to be praised Herr Pantaleon Hebenstreit" in such contests. However, this universal genius soon relinquished to Telemann his position as Kapellmeister, and repaired with his favorite instrument, the Pantaleon, to Vienna. Here he played on it before the imperial court, and was rewarded with a gold chain, on which the Emperor's portrait hung. He now proceeded to Dresden, and after the king had heard him, a concert was arranged at the court, in which all the German and Italian *Kammervirtuosi* took part. "As soon as Herr Hebenstreit began," recounts Forkel, "and performed only a short prelude, the whole court was astounded at this new and admirable music, and even the jealous foreigners had to confess that they had never heard anything grander or more perfect on a single instrument. Herr Hebenstreit had the art of bringing out full-scored music ("volle Musik") on his instrument as expressively as if 20 different instruments were playing. Augustus immediately engaged Herr Hebenstreit as royal Kammermusicus; paid all his debts; made him besides a munificent present in ready money; and allowed him an annual salary of 2000 thalers".

As finally perfected the Pantaleon appeared thus: It was 4 times as large as the ordinary dulcimer, and oblong in shape. It had 2 soundboards, as of two instruments standing close together, was strung on one side with steel and brass wires, on the other with gut strings, and the 2 wooden mallets in the player's hands were sometimes used with the softer side, sometimes with the harder.

After Hebenstreit's death in 1750 at Dresden his instrument, which was hard to keep in order on account of its 185 strings, difficult to tune, and still more difficult to play successfully, was practised by only a few of his pupils.

But it can be asserted only with probability, and never with certainty, that Hebenstreit's incontestably brilliant success on his wonderful instrument, together with the wide-spread fame of the latter, actually instigated experiments in substituting wooden hammers acted on by keys for the hand-hammers of the Pantaleon, and thus bringing about the invention of a keyboard instrument to be played *piano e forte.*

The Hammer-clavier or Pianoforte.

In Germany, France, and Italy the celebrated organ-builder Gottfried Silbermann was generally held to be the inventor of the pianoforte, until the also highly esteemed organist and theoretician Ch. G. Schroeter in 1763 claimed for himself the honor of this invention — 10 years, to be sure, after Silbermann's death — and tried to establish his claim by documents and drawings. This, however, could not rob Silbermann of the merit of having materially improved the pianoforte, and thus being the first to effect its further popularization.

But extracts have recently been published from Italian and French archives, which for the first time set Schroeter's and Silbermann's participation in this invention in its true light, by enumerating the names of the inventors of the pianoforte as they appeared in quick succession, and establishing with diplomatic accuracy the year in which the invention was publicly announced. We owe this important information — which, taken together with the resurrected pianofortes of that period, calls for a complete re-writing of all histories of the pianoforte previously published — more particularly to an Association in Florence, which decided to arrange a celebration, on May 7, 1874, in honor of Cristofori, the first and wholly independent inventor of the "clavicembalo with the piano and forte". This instrument, known since the year 1711, was styled "pianoforte" after the designation bestowed on it by its inventor, which name has been retained outside of Italy as well. For a long time after his death the inventor was only cursorily mentioned as Christofani, Cristofari, Cristofali, etc. His true name, however, now lies before us in a certified facsimile, in the work published by Leto Puliti, "Cenni storici della vita del serenissimo Ferdinando dei Medici, granprincipe di Toscana etc. Estratto dagli Atti dell' Accademia del R· Istituto musicale di Firenze, 1874, pag. 108". The original of this is to be found in the list of instruments belonging to the inheritance of the abovenamed Prince, and witnesses to their surrender to the custodian by the following signature of Sept. 23, 1716: "Io Bartolomeo Cristofori ò ricevuto in Consegno tutti li sopradetti Strumenti et in fede mano propria". Among these instruments, which were confided to Cristofori's keeping before the Prince's death, were Antwerp harpsichords, French *clavecins brisés*, and also a large number of Italian clavicembali and smaller and larger spinets, many of which were ornamented with costly painting and gilding. The makers of these claviers were, with few exceptions, the then most celebrated Italian masters — Domenico da Pesaro, Girolamo Zenti, Cortona di Roma, Guiseppe Mondini, and Bartolomeo Cristofori.

According to recent researches, Cristofori was born at Padua on May 4, 1653. Here he attained to such great renown as a clavier-maker, that Prince Ferdinando dei Medici, a patron of art and especially well-versed in music, induced him to come to Florence, and enter his service as Court Clavier-maker and custodian of his collection of instruments.

Now, in a publication* issued at Venice in the year 1711, was noticed the invention, hitherto regarded as an impossibility, of a *gravecembalo col piano e forte,* happily achieved by Bartolomeo Cristofali (*sic*), the salaried cembalist of the Prince of Toscana, of which he had already made three equally good, and of the ordinary size of other harpsichords. A point mentioned with special commendation was, that in this new instrument it depended upon the degree of strength with which the player touched the keys, whether the tone should be soft or loud, in all possible gradations. Many musicians, continues the reporter, Marchese Scipione Maffei di Verona, withhold the praise due to the invention, because the tone is too soft and dull, although one easily becomes accustomed to it, and soon even prefers it to that of other harpsichords. The chief objection, however, made to the new instrument is, that one must first habituate oneself to its touch, even if already a practised player on other keyboard instruments. But this being, in point of fact, a new instrument, says Maffei, its characteristics must first be studied in order to bring out its peculiarities with skill and taste.

The construction of these harpsichords shows, Maffei remarks further, instead of the usual jacks plucking the strings with quills, *a row of little hammers striking the strings from below.* According to the description and accompanying drawing, the hammer-heads are small wooden cubes like dice, covered on top with "buckskin", and penetrated by the shanks of the hammers. All the hammers are placed *above and independent of the key-levers*, on a wooden frame. The lower end of the hammer-shank is connected with a round disk,

---

* Giornale dei letterati d'Italia. Tomo quinto sotto la protezione del serenissimo principe di Toscana. In Venezia MDCCXI, appresso Gio. Gabriello Ertz. Articolo IX.

by whose aid the hammer can play easily, and on pressing the key a hopper drives the hammer with more or less force against the string. Instead of the escapement of our newer pianofortes, a spring of brass wire on the hopper permits the drop of the hammer to a position of rest instantly after the stroke; and instead of the check likewise added later, the hammer here falls upon two cross-threads of silk. A cloth-covered damper rests on the string, not letting it vibrate freely until the key is pressed.

Maffei describes this instrument at great length; and specimens still extant, of the years 1720 and 1726, which were exhibited on the occasion of the Cristofori celebration, one being accurately described by Puliti and both later by Ponsicchi*, prove that its inventor continually strove to improve it. The first of these two shows on the finger-board the following engraved words: Bartholomaeus de Cristoforis patavinus inventor faciebat Florentiae MDCCXX, but it appears to have been remodelled at a later period, the form of the hammer-heads, for instance, strikingly resembling the modern ones. The pianoforte of 1726, on the contrary, evidently contains only improvements made by Cristofori himself. In it the hammer-heads consist of small hollow pasteboard cylinders covered with leather, and the whole hammer is no longer held in position and at rest by silk threads, but by a contrivance resembling our modern check.

Cristofori retained until his death in 1731 his position as custodian of the aforesaid collection; in May, 1876, the committee in charge of the festivities in his honor erected a memorial stone to the inventor of the pianoforte, in the convent of Santa Croce at Florence.

At that time, however, the pianoforte seems to have been disseminated no further, either in Italy or beyond its boundaries, for we possess no accounts of attempts at improving Cristofori's invention. The chief reason for this is probably to be sought in the objection raised by the clavier-players, that its manipulation was decidedly more inconvenient than that of the harpsichords then in vogue in Italy, and its tone much less penetrating.

Marius, the maker of the clavecins above alluded to, is the second, and in all probability equally independent, inventor of a hammer-clavier. In 1716 he laid before the Royal Academy of Paris the drawings and descriptions of four different models of claviers in

* Il Pianoforte, sua origine e sviluppo (con tavole) etc. Firenze, G. G. Guidi, 1876.

which wooden hammers were substituted for the quilled jacks.* By this means, says the report of the Academy, he avoids the constant repairing of the ordinary harpsichord, obtains a finer and more powerful tone, and by graduating the force or lightness of the touch lends to the instrument an expressiveness hitherto wanting to it. Further, M. Marius has also invented a keyboard with hammers (clavier à maillets) for the harpsichords hitherto used, which can be put into or taken out of the latter without necessitating any alteration. M. Marius also employs two other simpler and more practical devices to replace the jacks by hammers. "Tout cela a paru très bien pensé". With these words closes the brief report of the Paris Academy.

However, in the published Proceedings of the Academy concerning reports on machines and inventions, we find a more detailed description and 4 illustrations of the "clavecin à maillets inventé par M. Marius" in the year 1716.** The drawings are supposed to represent the mechanism of four different kinds of hammer-claviers, but appear to be mere rough experimental suggestions, which might have led to the result proposed by the "inventor" after successive successful improvements. The drawing of the first model, in conjunction with that of the second, exhibits the key, consisting of a long, narrow strip of wood, and playing in a fork on the front balance-rail, as the lever of a wooden hammer adjusted above it on a rail. Like the key, this hammer consists of a long, narrow slip of wood bearing on its end an upright cube of wood, which strikes the proper string, when the key is depressed, like the metal pin on the key of the clavichord.

It is thought, says the reporter, that with keyboards of this make the power of the tone can be modified by skilfully graduating the touch. According to this theory (so closes the description of the first model), the hammers have been adjusted in various manners and positions. — The second model was intended to show how the hammers could strike the keys from above or below, two rows of a trichord adjustment of the strings being employed. The third model proposes an improvement of the first, the string being struck from

* See Histoire de l'académie royale des sciences, Année MDCCXVI, à Paris de l'imprimerie royale MDCCXVIII, p. 77. (Compare L. Puliti as above.)

** See Machines et inventions approuvées par l'accadémie royale des sciences. Tome troisième, depuis 1713 jusqu'en 1719. A Paris MDCCXXXV, pag. 83. 1716. No. 172. With drawings of the 4 models by Marius.

below by a round wooden peg instead of a hammer, the troublesome quilling of the harpsichord being thus avoided. The fourth model is intended to show that both the hammer adjustment and the former quill adjustment could be put into one and the same harpsichord, and played upon either separately or simultaneously.

All four models are explained at great length,* but their unpractical character is so glaringly apparent that probably no attempt was ever made to apply them in practice. The entire invention was soon forgotten, and even Fétis did not consider the inventor worthy of a separate article in either edition of his *Biographie des musiciens*.

Walther, in his Musikalisches Lexicon published at Leipsic in 1732, mentions neither a pianoforte nor any hammer-clavier whatever, nor does a similar work published at Chemnitz in 1749 yet notice instruments of this class. Not until 1767 does the Court Composer Joh. Friedr. Agricola of Berlin write, in his annotations to Adlung's Musica mech. organoedi (Vol. I. p. 212): — "Hr. Gottfried Silbermann is celebrated on account of his fine flügel and clavichords, the invention of the Cimbal d'Amour,** and the improvement of the *Piano forte*. True, the first attempt at this piano forte was devised and carried out in Italy; but Hr. Silbermann has improved it so greatly that he himself is hardly less than its inventor".

Silbermann, of whose highly influential labors we shall speak at length directly, died in 1753, and in 1763 the above-mentioned organist Ch. G. Schroeter of Nordhausen published, in Marpurg's "Kritische Briefe", the "Circumstanial description of a newly invented keyboard instrument, on which one can play loudly aud softly in different degrees, together with two drawings, 1763". He professes to have been chiefly impelled to this "new invention" by the Pantaleon of the "world-renowned virtuoso Hebenstreit", having made attempts as early as 1717 to contrive a keyed instrument which should set the strings in vibration by means of mallets or hammers instead of the metal pins or quills hitherto used. He recounts further, that in 1721 he laid two models before the Dresden court. In one the hammers struck from below, in the other from above. Both were furnished with dampers, and on either the strings could be sounded loudly or softly. The models met with the king's approval, and he

* Both the models and the French description of them are given in full in the work by L. Puliti mentioned above.

** A description of this instrument is given further on.

ordered that a working model should be made of the under-striking kind. The order remained unexecuted, and when Schroeter was about to leave Dresden he failed, despite all his attemps, to get his models back again. He asserted, that they became known in Germany without his knowledge and consent, were clumsily imitated, and styled "pianoforte".

Even if we give full credence to Schroeter's statements, we must, on the strength of documents now accessible, regard his claim to the invention of the pianoforte as wholly baseless. For Cristofori had made a complete pianoforte as early as 1711, and Marius had exhibited four models of like instruments in 1716, while Schroeter, as he himself asserts, first attempted to build a clavier playing loudly and softly in 1717. Neither could Silbermann have made any use of Schroeter's model-drawings, these not being published till 10 years after Silbermann's death. A glance at the latter's active life will suffice to convince us, that to his persevering labors we owe the production of an instrument which, by reason of its practical usefulness and convenient management, soon attained to the widest popularity.

Gottfried Silbermann, born at Frauenstein in Saxony in the year 1683, was the second son of a reputable carpenter. Despite his early fondness for music it was decided that he should follow his father's trade. But his lively diposition soon bore him away from carpentering, neither could the workshops of other masters, in which he was subsequently placed, confine him for any length of time. Mischievous pranks even brought him into jail, whence he escaped, however, overnight, to flee from an awarded punishment. He fled to a relative in Böhmisch-Einsiedel, who provided him with means to travel to Strassburg, the adopted home of his elder brother Andreas, the celebrated builder of the organ in the Minster at Strassburg, who gave him a friendly reception. In his flourishing establishment he taught him the art of organ-building, and after 3 years spent here by Gottfried in zealous work, his brother entrusted the thoroughly trained young master with the principal work on an organ in the church of a convent near by. Gottfried labored industriously at his task, and during this time made the acquaintance of a young, lively French lady, who had been forced to take the veil, and yearned to regain her freedom. Ardent mutual love ripened their decision to attempt a bold escape. One moonlight night she had even climbed the wall, and he had already thrown her a rope-ladder, when her absence was remarked in the convent, and she was forcibly carried back into the garden. He himself escaped from the hands of a servant of the convent only after a prolonged struggle, and took refuge in the drying-loft of a cabinet-maker, his friend. As soon as he deemed himself safe from any ill consequences of his adventure, he journeyed back to his native town. In Frauenstein he now completed the first organ built wholly by himself, which met with so favorable a reception that he was commissioned to build an organ for the cathedral at Freiburg. The extremely successful construction of this organ won him the name of the foremost organ-builder in Saxony, which was thoroughly well deserved, as the numerous organs made by him testify.

The long sojourn with his serious and strict elder brother had brought Gottfried's earlier levity within the proper limits, and lent to his restlessly aspiring mind an energy and perseverance which no obstacles could daunt, and which never relaxed until the goal aimed at was gained. These traits are also plainly apparent in his experiments in constructing a pianoforte as perfect as possible. "With him everything had to be good and genuine; he never worked for looks, and defective work, even finished pianofortes, he would batter to pieces with an axe".*

Agricola, whom we quoted above concerning Silbermann's influence, gives the following additional information for the History of the Pianoforte in Vol. 2 of the work alluded to (S. 116):

"Hr. Gottfr. Silbermann had at first built two of these instruments. One of them was seen and played on by the late Kapellmeister Hr. Joh. Seb. Bach. He praised, and was even filled with admiration at, their tone, but raised the objection, that it was too weak high up, and far too hard to play. Herr Silbermann, who could bear no faultfinding with his work, took this extremely ill. For a long time therefore, he felt resentful towards Herr Bach. And nevertheless his conscience told him, that Herr Bach was right. Therefore — to his great credit be it said — he thought it best to turn out no more of these instruments; but, on the other hand, to bestow the more careful attention to bettering the defects noticed by Herr Bach. On this he labored many years. And I doubt the less, that this was the true cause of the delay, because I have heard Herr

* See the Sketch by Ludwig Mooser, based on church and official documents: "Das Brüderpaar die Orgelbaumeister Andreas und Gottfried Silbermann". Strassburg, printed by Gustav Silbermann, 1861.

Silbermann himself admit it. Finally, Herr Silbermann having really invented many improvements, especially in the matter of touch, he again sold one to the court of the Prince of Rudolstadt.—Shortly afterward H. M. the King of Prussia ordered one of these instruments, and on its meeting with his Majesty's approval, several more were ordered of Herr Silbermann.* Anyone — especially one who, like myself, had seen either of the two instruments — could see and hear very readily from all these how industriously Herr Silbermann must have worked to improve then. Herr Silbermann likewise was moved by a laudable ambition to show one of these instruments, his newer work, to Herr Kapellmeister Bach, that he might test it; from whom it now received unqualified approval".

From this report by Agricola, who knew Silbermann personally, it would seem to be beyond doubt that we owe the construction of pianofortes for practical use, and their wide popularization, solely to the tireless energy of the Saxon Silbermann.

Silbermann earned the high esteem of all musical circles not only by his admirable organs, neatly and durably constructed clavichords, harpsichords and pianofortes, but also by the invention of the Cimbal d'amour. On this last instrument the tone of the clavichord, to whose class it belonged, was brought out more fully and sustainedly. Its strings were twice as long as in the ordinary clavichord, and the tangents on the keys struck exactly in the middle of the strings, thus sounding the octave of the whole string on both its halves. The tone thus gained in mellowness and fullness; indeed, this invention, now quite forgotten, might perhaps be resuscitated to advantage in our modern instruments for the low and medium tones by the addition of a flageolet-stop lightly touching the middle of the strings.

The greatest musicians of their times, Sebastian Bach at 1737, and Mozart at 1777, recognized the value of the invention of the pianoforte; nevertheless it was long before it could take its due rank among the other keyboard instruments. As in the history of music throughout, we see in this case, too, the battle of progress against the conservative element, the resistance of usage to innovation. Thus the anonymous author of the Musikalisches Handbuch, issued at "Alethinopel" (Leipsic) simultanously with Forkel's Musikalischer Almanach by Schwickert, does not yet yield the preference to the

* Frederick II paid 700 thalers for each of these pianofortes. Silbermann usually sold the less elegantly finished instruments of this kind for 300 thalers.

pianoforte. Firstly, he justly censures the usage of composers in writing on the title-page of their works: "Sonatas for the Clavier", without naming the special instrument intended, although each of these has its peculiar character. On the harpsichord, he observes, the heart can not speak, one can not paint, not lay on light and shade, but only produce a plain, well-defined sketch. It is suitable for checking or hurrying the flow of the music — in a word, for accompanying. The Fortepiano, he continues, ranks higher, especially when it is one made by Friederici or Stein. On it the heart can speak, and express manifold emotions, can paint, and diffuse light and shade. But is lacks the medium tints and minute beauties, being thus on the whole the instrument for concertos and quartets. — The clavichord, however, ranks highest of all. Though excluded by its character from public concerts, it is all more the confidant of solitude. On it I can express the emotion of my heart, and shade, tone, disperse, and blend the tones through all their undulations. To become acquainted with a virtuoso (so he closes his observations) one must hear him at the clavichord — not at the fortepiano, and still less at the harpsichord.

Forkel, in the above Almanach for 1782, also ranks the clavichord above all other kinds of claviers, though giving prominent mention to the delicacy of execution and diversity of shading possible on the Spath pianofortes.

Chr. Fr. Daniel Schubart, highly esteemed both as a poet and musician, also writes at length on the claviers of his period in his "Ideen zu einer Aesthetik der Tonkunst" (Ideas on the Æsthetics of Musical Art), penned during his imprisonment at Hohenasberg and announced in 1785, although not published by his son until 1806. From this we give a few quotations as a supplementary characterization.

The harpsichord twangs the strings either with crow-quills, or, though more expensively, with golden points. It exercises the hand in accurate musical delineation, therefore the beginner should first practise on the harpsichord.

The admirable fortepiano, he exclaims, is — *Heil uns!* — another invention of the Germans. Silbermann pondered over means for lending expressiveness to the harpsichord, and he and his successor contrived the instrument which yields *forte* and *piano* to the pressure of the handwithout stops. The management of the fortepiano is very different from that of the quilled harpsichord. The latter requires merely a light touch, while the keys of the fortepiano must be touched with a spring or glide. The musical *colorit*, however, can by no means be given in all its nuances on the latter.

The clavichord, that lonely, melancholy, unspeakably sweet instrument, is, if made by a master, preferable to the harpsichord and the fortepiano. The swelling and dying away of the tones, the mellow trill expiring under the fingers, the *portamento*, in a word, all shades of feeling can be definitely expressed by the finger-pressure, the vibration and trembling (Beben) of the strings, by the lighter or more powerful touch of the hand. The clavichords, (thus Schubart closes his remarks), have at the present day almost reached their climax; they embrace from 5 to 6 octaves, are *gebunden* and *ungebunden* (having several keys to a string, or but one), with or without lute-stops, and for a player of feeling it would hardly seem possible to add a perfection to this instrument.

We perceive, that even while the pianoforte was coming into more general use, the clavichord was preferred for a long time. Should a skilful instrument-maker undertake to resuscitate this formerly much lauded instrument, we are convinced, therefore, that a gifted artist employing it in his performances beside those on the concert-grand, would create a great effect even to-day. Of course, the compositions selected would have to be adapted to the romantic chiaro-oscuro of the clavichord tone. Masters of composition and practising pupils would likewise find it pleasant to possess an instrument whose tone does not carry far, which takes up little room, can be easily transported, and might be bought for a very moderate price.

Silbermann's fortepianos at first all appear to have been in grand-piano form, for it is narrated of Ch. E. Friederici of Gera (d. 1779), one of the earliest makers of such instruments, that he constructed them in clavichord form, and styled them *Fortbien* to distinguish them from the others. On account of their admirable workmanship they spread, as we are told, over half the world. The Fortepianos, too, which Joh. Adam Spath (d. 1796) of Ratisbon constructed in grand form and sold for 40 ducats, were held in high estimation in Germany. They were especially praised because the dampers lay *upon* (on top of) the strings, being lifted from the latter as long as the player pressed the keys. The instruments of this meritorious master were later surpassed by the pianofortes of Johann Andreas Stein (d. 1792) of Augsburg. Mozart, on becoming acquainted with these latter, chose them principally for his performances, whereby this instrument was first brought into general notice and vogue. The following account of Stein's instruments is given in a letter written by Mozart at the age of 21 to his father (Augsburg, 1777):

"Now, to begin with, I must tell you about the Stein pianoforte. Before seeing any of Stein's make, I liked Spath's claviers the best, but now must give the preference to Stein's; for they damp far better than even those from Ratisbon. When I strike the keys hard, whether I let my fingers lie or lift them, the tone ceases in the same instant that I sound it. However I may touch the keys, the tone will always be the same, it will not 'block' *(scheppern)*, it will not go easier at one time and harder the next, or even fail altogether; in a word, everything is even. To be sure, he does not sell such a pianoforte under 300 florins; but the trouble and pains he takes are beyond price. His instruments have the special advantage above others that they are made with an escapement, which not one in a hundred troubles his head with; but without an escapement the pianoforte will inevitably block and continue to sound. When one touches the keys, the hammers drop at the instant they spring against the strings, whether the key be held down or released. When he has finished such a pianoforte (so he himself tells me), he first sits down to it and tries all sorts of passages, runs, and leaps, and scrapes and works until the action will do anything; for he works only for the good of music, and not simply for his own benefit, else he would be done directly. He often says: 'If I myself were not such an ardent admirer of music, and could not perform a little on the pianoforte, I should long ago have lost patience with my work; but as it is I am an admirer of instruments which do not bother the player, and are durable'. And his pianofortes are really durable. He guarantees, that the soundboards will neither crack nor burst. After he has made a soundboard for a pianoforte he exposes it to the air, rain, snow, sun-heat, and all devils *(sic)*, that it may crack, and then glues shavings into the cracks to make the soundboard strong and very firm. He is really glad when it cracks; for then one may be sure that nothing else will happen to it. He often even cuts into it himself, and then glues it up, and strengthens it thoroughly. He has 3 such finished pianofortes, and I have just played on them again to-day. — The machine (knee-pedal) which one presses with the knee is also better made by him than by others. I barely need to touch it, to make it work; and as soon as one withdraws the knee a little, not the least after-resonance is heard". — — —

Joh. Andreas Stein, the master thus praised by Mozart, was born in 1728, went through his training in Silbermann's workshops, and later made a name by several inventions of new instruments of the organ and clavier class. But the most valuable service rendered by him to art was the invention of a new hammer-mechanism for the pianoforte. In Cristofori's Italian action the hammers were adjusted *independently of the keys* upon a separate wooden rail; whereas in Stein's "German action" the hammers were set *on the keys themselves.* In the latter there stands on the tail of the key a metal pin bent backwards, on which is fastened a brass cap. The bill-shaped shank of the hammer, with its spindles, is accurately fitted into this cap, but can readily play within the latter. On depressing the key, the butt of the hammer-shank is caught in a spring-catch which is adjusted behind the key, lifts the hammer up to strike the string, and instantly lets it drop again to a position of repose. A check received it and held it in the right position, and the leathering of the hammer was so practical that the player could graduate the power of the tone by a gentler or stronger touch of the key. When Stein's children Andreas and Nanette removed the business of their deceased father to Vienna in 1794, where it was successfully continued, the aforesaid mechanism in the pianoforte was styled the "Viennese action".

A material influence was exerted on the flourishing business of the Stein family in Vienna by their acquaintance with Andreas Streicher. He was born in indigent circumstances at Stuttgart in 1761, and a pronounced talent decided him to devote himself to music. In his twenty-first year he had scraped together a small sum by teaching, which he considered sufficient for a journey to Hamburg, in order thoroughly to learn the true method of playing the clavier under the guidance of the renowned C. Ph. E. Bach. However, before carrying out this decision, a copy of Schiller's "Räuber", first printed in 1781, fell into his hands, which so moved him that he became eager to make the personal acquaintance of its author, who was at that time regimental physician under the austere Duke Karl of Württemberg. Andreas, with his ardent veneration for the gifted poet, and Schiller, attracted by the faithful, impressionable, warm-hearted Swabian, speedily became intimate friends. This friendship was soon put to the proof, as Schiller, incensed at the Duke's harsh command to forbear from writing, fled from Stuttgart, aided and accompanied by Andreas. After prolonged wanderings, often on foot, the money of both was exhausted, and Andreas was forced, as he said, "to forsake Germany's noblest poet alone and in misfortune". The journey to Emanuel Bach had to be given up, and Streicher went to Mannheim, to earn a living by giving clavier-lessons. He had unexpected success, and both here and in Munich, whither he repaired after a time, he was loved and honored as a virtuoso, teacher, and composer. On repeated business trips to Augsburg he made the acquaintance of Nanette (Marie Anna), the daughter of J. A. Stein. Since earliest childhood she had learned to give her father's pianofortes the finishing touches, and was also highly esteemed as an expressive pianoforte player. Streicher's bearing, frank and inviting confidence, won her love, and their union was a source of unalloyed happiness to both. At Streicher's desire his wife and her brother removed the business to Vienna in 1794. Here Streicher's musical gifts also found general favor, and the pianoforte manufactory, conducted on the principles of the elder Stein, became so flourishing that Streicher found it necessary to aid personally in carrying it on. From 1802 onward the business was conducted by the two equally esteemed firms of "Geschwister Stein" and "Nanette Streicher, *née* Stein", to which latter "and Son" was later added. Streicher, grown more familiar with the make of the pianoforte, invented the mechanism in which the hammer strikes the string *from above,* which was likewise practically employed as improved by Pape, in Paris. Streicher's house in Vienna was a rallying point for the most eminent artists, foreign and native, and Nanette was the soul of the company. Held in estimation as an excellent pianoforte player, as a lady of high mental cultivation, and as a wife and mother, she was likewise the faithful friend of Beethoven when he was most difficult of access, and untiring in her care for the household of the great master. She died in January, 1833, universally mourned, and followed only four months later by her equally honored spouse. Their son Johann Baptist maintained the renown of the firm, and Liszt, Thalberg, Clara Wieck, and Dreyschock chose their concert grands at Vienna in preference from this factory, which to-day still sustains its high rank under the grandson of Andreas, Emil Streicher.

It is a remarkable fact that we owe just to Schiller the perfection of the modern concert grand which Andreas Streicher was especially active in bringing about. For had Andreas journeyed to Hamburg to be trained as a virtuoso by Emanuel Bach, instead of throwing in his lot with Schiller, he would propably never have known and married Nanette, who induced him to take an active part in pianoforte making. And on the other hand, without Streicher's watchful care and friendship, Schiller might easily have met the fate of the unfortunate Daniel Schubart, whom he greatly rejoiced by a visit during his ten years' captivity in Hohenasperg.

Pianoforte-making in England.

In the year 1680 the instrument-maker Tabel, who had been trained in the celebrated workshops of the Brothers Ruckers at Antwerp, came to London, and founded there the first noteworthy factory for claviers. The Swiss Burkhardt Tschudi (later always called Shudi) worked in Tabel's Factory, and founded in 1732 a very lucrative business of his own in London.* John Broadwood, a Scotchman, entered Shudi's manufactory about 1763, and so distinguished himself by fine workmanship and ingenious inventions that Shudi gave him his daughter in marriage. Shudi subsequently made over his large and prosperous business to Broadwood, who had already conducted it for a considerable time.

About 1766 a German, Johann Zumpe, brought over "Silbermann's invention", the pianoforte, to London. This instrument, in his very neat and workmanlike make, immediately found great favor there and soon won such renown that its services were even impressed to enhance the brilliancy of a "benefit" performance. On a theatre-bill of May 16, 1767, is found the announcement: "End of Act I Miss Brickler will sing a favourite song from Judith, accompanied by Mr. Dibdin, on a new instrument call'd Piano Forte." A year later the "London Bach" (Johann Christian) played the pianoforte in public for the first time in a concert.

Great influence was exerted on the popularization and perfecting of the pianoforte by the fact that in the year 1775 Muzio Clementi not only employed one in a concert at London with brilliant success, but thenceforward also adapted his brilliant compositions to this effective instrument, for which the Saxon Ambassador at London, Graf Brühl, devised the blued steel strings in 1774, of fuller tone and less liable to rust than the ordinary ones.

* Kirkman (Kirchmann), likewise a clavier-maker of repute, was also trained to independence in Tabel's workshops.

The foremost clavier manufacturers of London strove to improve the newly invented instrument more and more, constructing it both in Square and Grand form. The Silbermann action, in which the hammers were independent of the keys and rested on a separate rail above the latter, were so essentially improved, especially by Backers, Stodart, and Broadwood, that it became known and widely employed as a new invention under the name of the "English action". On depressing the key it impels by means of its jack, which at the same time acts as an escapement (hopper), the hammer against the key, through an aperture in the soundboard, and lets it drop instantly back into its former position. In 1808 the last-named manufactory assumed the firm-name of *Broadwood and Sons*, and the pianofortes since turned out by them attained such world-wide renown that as early as 1856 their workshops were the most extensive of all then existing. Some 500 employees were then working at their tasks, "from the first saw-cut of the rough log up to the finest work on the finished pianoforte." From a descriptive pamphlet written for the "International Inventions Exhibition" at London in 1885, and kindly furnished by the firm to the Editor, the following list is taken.

Number of Pianofortes of all kinds made by the Broadwood Firm from 1780 to 1885.

Full Grands	1780 to 1885	22,093
Short Grands, including separate series of Semi, Bichorda, Boudoir, and short Drawing Room Grands	1831 to 1885	17,875
Cottages	1819 to 1885	62,857
Old Upright, or Vertical Grands	1799 to 1831	940
Cabinets	1812 to 1856	8,963
Squares	1780 to 1864	64,161
		176,889
To which add Harpsichords, 1732 to 1793 (approximately)		1,200
	Grand total	178,089

Pianoforte-making in France.

In Germany the clavichord was preferred, as remarked before, to the pianoforte even long after the invention and popularization of the latter, while in England marked favor was shown to the pianoforte immediately after its first appearance there in 1766. The French had grown so exclusively accustomed to the tone and action of the harpsichords in wingshape (clavecins) and square form (épinettes), that the pianoforte did not find acceptance and favor in France until long after its full naturalization in Germany and England. La Borde relates in 1780 that the few pianofortes coming from London to Paris, although pleasing in the upper register, were hard and dull in the lower. He remarks, besides, that their square shape (illustrated in his work, I, 346) could not be transformed into the French wing-shape, and that they were frightfully dear as well.

In the year 1768 Sébastien Erhard (later he always wrote his name Erard) came from Strassburg to Paris. Here he entered the workshop of a clavier-maker, and proved to be such a judicious, enterprising, and persevering workman that his name was soon known in all Paris. Being a clever mathematician and mechanician, he invented in 1776 the "clavecin mécanique", a harpsichord with stops shifting the stroke from quilled jacks to jacks "en peau de buffle". The instrument also had two pedals, one of which stopped the strings in the middle, thus raising the pitch by an octave, while the other combined the above changes. At the request of an influential patroness, the Comtesse de Villeroy, he constructed his first pianoforte in 1777, which met with great favor in her soirées. About this time Jean Baptiste Erard came to Paris, and participated thenceforward in his brother's work. Their establishment in Paris soon became well-known and patronized. The inexhaustible inventor Sébastien constructed for Queen Marie Antoinette a "piano organisé" with two keyboards, one of which played a pianoforte, and the other an organ, a "jeu d'expression" being attached to the latter. A second stop transposed the instrument as much as 3 semitones higher or lower. Space is wanting to name all the inventions contrived by him for the pianoforte, and likewise for the harp, which he completely transformed (double-action harp with fork mechanism); for his active mind was incessantly occupied with plans for perfecting both instruments.

The terrors of the outbreaking Revolution drove Sébastien to London, and the harp and pianoforte manufactory established there soon became as flourishing as that in Paris, continued meantime by his brother. In 1796 he returned to France, and there constructed the first grand pianoforte after the improved English system. Its touch being considered too heavy, he made renewed attempts to better the action. Dussek, equally admired as a composer and virtuoso, played on one of his concert grands in 1808 with brilliant success; and Choron, in the Supplement to his Dict. hist. des musiciens, reports in 1817 on a new grand pianoforte of the brothers Erard: "It has a compass of 6 octaves, and under the hands of the player its tone appears either full and mellow, or loud and brilliant". —Erard has won lasting fame in the history of pianoforte-making by his invention in 1823 of the hammer-action "à double mouvement" or "à double échappement", which thenceforward was used in all concert grands with the English action. In this action, when the hammer has struck the string, it may again be thrown upward by the slightest pressure of the finger by the aid of a second lever (hopper) with similar escapement, thus yielding most conveniently the *pianissimo*, *crescendo*, and extreme *forte* to the player's will.—Sébastien Erard, the eminent promoter of pianoforte-making, died in 1831 at his castle 'La Muette', whither he had withdrawn from active life some years before. His nephew Pierre was already the manager of the London factory. After the decease of his uncle, who made him his heir, he came to Paris, and conducted both the extensive factories with energy and success until his death in 1855. Schäfer of Paris then continued the business. The world-renowned Erard factory, established in 1780, has reached a grand total of 89,000 instruments (down to end of 1890), namely 19,000 Grands, 61,000 Uprights and 9,000 Squares. In the year 1890 there were made 400 Grands and 1300 Uprights, or 1700 in all. Here, too, the Squares seem to have gone quite out of favor. The Erard establishment employs about 500 hands on an average.

After successful tours through Germany, Italy, and England, the celebrated composer Ignaz Pleyel settled in 1795 in Paris, where his easily executed symphonies, string-quartets, and clavier-sonatas were received with such unusual enthusiasm that he decided to publish them on his own account. In addition to his music shop he opened, in 1807, a pianoforte manufactory, thus laying the foundation of the business later raised to the highest pitch of prosperity by his son Camille Pleyel in particular, even rivalling that of the Erards. The instruments of Pleyel's make are distinguished by a sympathetic tone, and stimulate the performer by admitting of the most delicate shading of a composition. Chopin characterized the instruments of these two equally meritorious firms in the words: "Quand je suis mal disposé, je joue sur un Piano d'Erard et j'y trouve facilement un son fait. Mais quand je me sens en verve et assez fort, pour trouver mon propre son à moi, il me faut un Piano de Pleyel".* August Wolf (d. 1877) conducted the business with circumspection after Camille Pleyel's death, and has been quick to adopt all new improvements of the instrument.

The skilful Swabian pianoforte-maker Heinrich Pape (b. 1789 at Sorstedt, d. 1875 at Paris) came to Paris in 1811, where he organized and managed for some years the pianoforte factory of Pleyel. In 1815 he set up for himself, and his factory was soon in a condition to compete with the two firms mentioned above. Thinking that the strings of the pianoforte would yield a clearer tone if the soundboard beneath them were enclosed on all sides—i. e. if the aperture through which the hammers struck the strings were done away with—he readopted the action already employed by Streicher, in which the hammers struck the strings from above. This action proved peculiarly advantageous for square pianos and "cottages", and was therefore soon generally adopted in the latter, as well as in the "pianinos" (cabinets) afterwards taking their place. Pape introduced the felted hammer instead of the leather-covered one, and also devised the overstrung pattern.

Pianoforte-making in Germany etc.

The names of the pianoforte-makers, and of the inventors and improvers of separate parts, are legion, and their number is swelling year by year. In the following résumé, therefore, only a few of the most prominent firms will be mentioned.

The instruments of Bechstein in Berlin enjoy a world-wide reputation. The founder of the factory, Karl Bechstein, was born at Gotha in 1826; after working in various German piano factories he acted from 1848 to 1852 as foreman for Peran of Berlin, then made a tour of observation to London and Paris, where he worked for Pape and Krügelstein, and established himself with modest means at Berlin in 1856. Within a short time the factory attained to such prosperity, that the greatest masters of pianoforte-playing began to take an interest in Bechstein's make, so that he was enabled more and more to turn his attention to the construction of large concert grands. Business gradually increased to such an extent, that Bech-

* Karasowski, Friedrich Chopin. Dresden, Ries, 1877. II, 96.

stein now employs several hundred workmen, and turns out over a thousand finished instruments annually. Herr Bechstein, whose instruments enjoy a wide European reputation, has manufactured down to Oct., 1891, 26,900 in all; the number made in 1890 was 2600, of which 1100 were grands and 1500 pianinos. From 500 to 550 workmen are regularly employed by him.

Bechstein's chief competitor in Germany is Julius Blüthner of Leipsic, born in 1824 at Falkenhain near Merseburg. He founded his factory at Leipsic in 1853 in 1856 took out a patent for improvements in the construction of the pianoforte, and speedily raised his establishment to high reputation. The "Aliquotflügel" are a specialty of Blüthner's, their tone being reinforced by an octave-string stretched above the unisons belonging to each tone, which octave-string is not touched by the hammer, but vibrates in sympathy with the tone given out by the strings below it. Blüthner's instruments have repeatedly received the highest awards (Paris 1867, Vienna 1873, Philadelphia 1876, Sydney 1880, etc.). It would appear that the factory of Commercienrath Blüthner is at present the leading leading establishment of its class on the continent of Europe. Down to the end of 1890 the total number of instruments made was in round numbers 35,000, about 20,000 of these being Grands, and 15,000 Pianinos. For some 20 years no more Squares have been manufactured, and only about 500 in all down to the time of their discontinuance. Of the famous "Aliquot" Grands nearly 7,500 have been finished; of Pianinos with the Jankó keyboard, some 50. In the year 1890 there were made altogether 2500 instruments, Grands and Pianinos in equal numbers. 600 workmen are regularly employed. Sufficient proof of the interest excited in musical circles by the Jankó keyboard is found in the fact, that it has been introduced among the instruments regularly taught at the Leipzig Conservatory, with a special instructor, Herr Hofpianist Wendling. The latter, himself a virtuoso on his instrument, has also had good success in teaching its peculiar techniqu͜e, as was shown by the highly successful début of one of his lady pupils at an *Abendunterhaltung* on Oct. 30th, 1891. The instrument used, from Blüthner's factory, exhibits great improvements in regard to both action and tone.

Theodore Steinway of New York has established a branch factory at Hamburg, in which the several parts of the instruments, sent in a finished condition from New York, are put together.—In Brunswick the factory still flourishes which Heinrich Steinway, on his removal to New York, made over to his eldest son Theodor; the latter carried it on till 1865, in which year he also went to America; the present firm is Theodor Steinway's Successors, Helferich, Grotrian and Co.

In South Germany the instruments made by J. L. Schiedmayer and Söhne of Stuttgart have won a well-earned and wide reputation, being distinguished by excellent workmanship, a fine tone, and facile touch. The pianos of A. Biber in Munich enjoy equal popularity by reason of their durability and simple, readily answering action.—The renown of the Viennese pianoforte factories is maintained in our day, among many others, by the following makers: Carl Stein, Ernst Streicher (both descendants of the masters previously mentioned), Conrad Graf, Ludwig Bösendorfer, and M. Schweighofers Wittwe. The factory of Herr L. Bösendorfer is at present the largest in Austria; it was founded by the father of the present owner in 1828, and carried on by him till 1859, down to which time the instruments were not numbered. Since 1859, 12,430 pianofortes have been made, but hardly 1% of this total were pianinos, all the rest being grands. The Bösendorfer grands are the only make used by virtuosi in Austria.

In Switzerland the Huni and Hubert Pianofortes of Zurich are in great demand; while in Italy, the native country of the instrument, Cristofori's invention long remained utterly neglected, Germany undertaking the perfection and popularization of the same. As a consequence, all the leading Italian manufacturers construct their pianos on the "Prussian" system, as Roeseler of Turin, Colomba e Grimm of Milan, Maltarello of Vicenza, Niccola Lacchin of Padua, Sievers* oj Naples, etc.

The Modern Pianoforte.

Although the instruments of the makers named above fulfil the requirements of modern pianoforte virtuosi in their extraordinary performances, carried up to a dizzy height by the fiery inspiration of the unrivalled champion, Franz Liszt, the pianoforte-makers of Germany,

* G. F. Sievers has likewise published a very complete Handbook of Pianoforte construction entitled "Il Pianoforte, guida pratica etc". Napoli, Benedetto Pelerano, 1868. With numerous drawings, and an Atlas in folio, containing illustrations of the English, Streicher, Pleyel, Erard, and Steinway actions in their natural size.

France, England and America strive incessantly to perfect the construction of the separate parts of the instrument.

The unheard-of force exerted by Liszt and his numerous pupils occasioned the instrument-makers to construct the wrestplank with the tuning-pins of the strings, and the string-plate, in the best possible manner, to obviate getting out of tune as far as might be. To this end both supports of the ends of the strings were screwed fast to iron plates, and held at a proper distance apart by cross-bars. A patent taken out in 1820 by Thom and Allen for such an arrangement was first practically applied later by Stodart in London; and a still more practical invention was a cast-iron frame combining the said iron plates and cross-bars in a single piece of metal of the same kind.

The strings of the concert grand, which formerly sometimes snapped under Liszt's titanic grasp, withstood it after being made of the toughest material, cast steel. The English strings of Webster in Manchester, formerly universally employed, were later surpassed in tension-power by those of Miller in Vienna. Furthermore, the tone of the pianoforte has lost all sharpness and gained in fullness, since the hammers have been covered with specially prepared felt instead of leather.

Ingenious as was the Erard action with double escapement, its manufacture and repairing have always been attended by great difficulties. Modern piano-makers therefore spare no pains to simplify this hammer-action, or at least to render it as durable as possible, without sacrificing its lightness of touch.

Besides the great Concert Grands, with a compass frequently exceeding seven octaves, Parlor Grands and Semi-Grands are also made; and the Square Piano, still a favorite in England and America, has in Germany been almost entirely superseded by the Pianino or Upright Piano. This latter instrument, evolved from the upright grands or "cottages", has an overstriking action, the hammers of which are centred on a separate wooden rail, the strings being overstrung as in the grands. The overstrung pattern of Steinway and Sons in New York has now been almost universally adopted as the most practical one for Grands, Squares, and Uprights.

A recent invention for the pianoforte deserves more attention than it has hitherto received, for it will become indispensable to all pianists whenever gifted composers shall recognize it as an effective means of expression, and apply it in their compositions. This is the "pedale de prolongement" (prolongation pedal) practically employed in 1860 by Debain of Paris, in 1862 by Montal of London. It was simplified and improved by Steinway of New York in 1874. By its aid a tone or full chord, when struck, can he sustained even while both hands of the player are executing suitable runs and passages, and while the soft and loud pedals are used at pleasure. The sustained tone or chord continues singing until the foot releases the pedal by which it was taken.

Other recent contrivances for the improvement of the pianoforte have been, in part, attempted earlier without finding favor, or were too complicated in construction to remain permanently in serviceable condition, and were consequently slighted as worthless or unpractical from the beginning.

The double pianofortes, on which two persons can play at once, each on a separate keyboard, appear from time to time, though without meeting with success. One of the latest pianos with two keyboards is the "Piano Mangeot" (à deux claviers renversés), played on in 1879 by Jules de Zarembski at the Paris Exposition. Whereas in the former double-keyboard grands the keyboards ran parallel like the organ manuals, and could also be coupled, the keyboards of the Piano Mangeot, though lying stepwise one above the other, are in opposition, the tones of the lower ascending as usual from left to right, while those of the upper ascend from right to left, so that a scale, for instance, played in contrary motion sounds in parallel motion or even in unison. The attempt to give the same color to all keys having the same name, e. g. all *C*-keys blue, all *D*-keys red, etc. has probably found no imitators. The Society "Croma", which has tried for years to introduce a so-called chromatic keyboard having six white keys in regular alternation with six black ones, likewise appears to remain "exclusive". On the other hand, Eduard Zachariae's "Kunstpedal", which by means of various combinations lifts the dampers from lower, medium, or higher groups of strings, thus allowing them to sound on, has found some little practical application.

Henri Herz of Paris, like the composers and virtuosi Pleyel and Kalkbrenner, established a pianoforte factory, and in 1851 publicly exhibited a "Piano éolien", whose tones could be sustained and swelled by means of a current of air directed against the strings by a bellows worked by a pedal. The piano-maker Schnell, 62 years earlier, showed a similar instrument, at first in Paris and later in

Germany, which won him great applause; but neither this "Animocorde", nor Kalkbrenner's "pneumatisches Saiteninstrument", became popular, despite their wondrously affecting tone. The reason for this can be sought only in the great difficulty of constructing them, and the frequent need of repairs.

An arrangement of the keyboard which has latterly attracted much attention, and which stands in distant relationship to the chromatic" keyboard before alluded to, is the invention of Paul von Jankó. On this keyboard the scale of *C*-major no longer occupies the lower row of keys exclusively, as in the ordinary succession *C, D, E, F, G, A, B, c*, etc. The first three of these tones are presented by white keys, and the other three by black keys *on a level with the white.* The black keys answering to *C♯* and *D♯* lie slightly elevated between *C-D* and *D-E*; between the white key for *E* and the first black key for *F* lies, also elevated, the white key for *F*; and in like manner, between the black keys *F-G-A*, the white keys for *G♯* and *A♯* while between the black *A*-key and the white *c*-key is found the (elevated) white *B*-key. Taking capitals for the white keys, and small letters for the black ones, the following arrangement would show the grouping of the octave.

Upper row of keys: *c♯ d♯ F G A B*
Lower row of keys: *C D E f♯ g♯ a♯ c*

Thus, to play this octave chromatically, the keys in two rows lying one above the other have to be touched alternately. The entire keyboard, however, consists of a triple series of keyboards paired in the above manner, and presenting to the eye six different and apparently independent rows of keys ascending stepwise, as shown

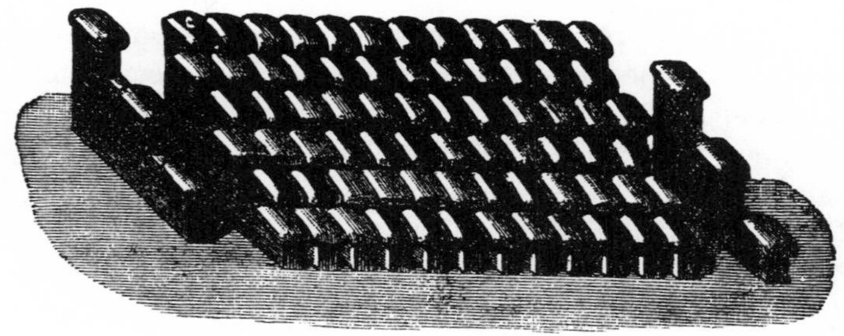

in the accompanying cut, which exhibits a section of the keyboard embracing about two octaves.

Each tone of the old keyboard is given three times on the Jankó keyboard, as it can be struck by means of the same key-lever at three different places lying one above the other, as the unattached keys on either side of the cut show. This construction, it is contended, accommodates itself better to the shape and natural position of the hand than the ordinary keyboard, because in any given case one can choose that key, of the three sounding each tone, which is most convenient for the hand at the given instant. The inventor commends, as a peculiar advantage of his keyboard, the point that only one fingering is needed for all the scales, and that the stretched hand commands a wider compass than on the ordinary keyboard, the playing of music in full harmonies or polyphonic style being this materially facilitated. The width of an octave on the ordinary keyboard corresponds exactly to that of a tenth on this; on the latter large hands can conveniently stretch a thirteenth, or even a fourteenth (*c'*—*a''* ♯). Despite its very apparent advantages for transcendant execution, it remains to be seen whether the new keyboard will win general popularity; at any rate the invention is an extremely ingenious one, and the attention paid to it by various manufacturers is deserving of commendation. The first grands with the Jankó keyboard were made by R. W. Kurka of Vienna, who was followed by R. Ibach Sohn of Barmen, Duysen of Berlin, J. G. Vogel and Sohn of Plauen, Kaps of Dresden, and others. The latter took pains to lighten the touch, which was too heavy in the pianos first turned out, by means of technical improvements. O. L.]

The numerous devices for noting down the tones of performance on the pianoforte, by the aid of a revolving drum or an advancing strip of paper, in the form of dots and lines of varying length, which signs could then be written out in notes of corresponding height (pitch) and length — have failed on account of their complicated form and liability to get out of order. The first note-writing machine of this kind was theoretically described, though never made to work in practice, by a London clergyman named Creed, in the Philosophical Transations for 1747. The mechanician Hohlfeld of Berlin was the first to construct one, which he delivered to the Berlin Academy for trial in 1852. He was followed at intervals by Englishmen, Germans, and Frenchmen with similar inventions, bearing the names of Piano sténographe, Melograph, Pianographe, etc. Most of them were loudly praised on their appearance, but have nevertheless not won general favor. Even the celebrated "Notograph" of Schmeil, a teacher in Magdeburg, has met the same fate as the rest. The electric "Melograph", in which the depression of the piano-keys closes a circuit, causing the music to be recorded on a strip of paper in much the same way as a message is taken by a Morse telegraphic apparatus, is perhaps the most successful of all these inventions; the music so noted down can be transferred to a stiff sheet of cardboard, and then reproduced in the "Melotrope".

The Augustinian friar Engramelle of Paris probably did not think, when he published his work on "La tonotechnie ou l'art de noter les cylindres etc." (The art of registering the cylinders of barrel-organs) in 1775, of ever employing it for noting a piano performance. It happened that a friend of his, a musician named Baptiste, once praised the compositions of an Italian pianist, and regretted his refusal to make them public. Engramelle requested that the Italian might be introduced to him, and on this occasion the virtuoso executed his celebrated compositions. During a second visit from the two musicians Engramelle exhibited a little hand-organ (Serinette or bird-organ), which startled the Italian by reproducing with astonishing accuracy the compositions he had so jealously withheld. Engramelle, as it proved, had fastened underneath his piano the cylinder of a barrel-organ, covered with white paper, and so connected with the keyboard that the tones produced by depressing the keys were noted on the cylinder. At each revolution, the cylinder advanced by a line, to present a blank surface for the next series of note-signs. These signs were then filled out with little pegs and ridges of wire, and the cylinder thus prepared was placed in the box containing the pipes and the crank-action, on turning which latter the music would immediately be reproduced.

Here another invention must be mentioned, which, though having no influence on the construction of the pianoforte, has from time to time been thought important in teaching pianoforte-playing. This is the Chiroplast or Hand-guide invented by Logier in England about 1814. Two smooth wooden rails, adjusted in front of and higher than the keys, held the hands, when the latter were passed between them, at the proper distance from the keys, while a pair of open gloves kept the fingers in the most correct position. In spite of many opponents, the Chiroplast won the approval of eminent piano-teachers in London. Kalkbrenner joined Logier later, and made innumerable partisans for the hand-guide, but in the sequel perceived its deficiencies; for the two rails between which the hands moved did not even admit the passing under of the thumb or the passing over of any finger. He therefore discarded the upper part of the arrangement, and then recommended the improved Chiroplast under the name of "guide-main". Liszt proposed that it should be more appropriately named "guide-âne", thus dealing a death-blow to the invention.

Nevertheless similar appliances, altered and improved, reappear now and then, and but a short time ago an "automatic piano hand-guide" constructed by W. Bohrer of Montreal, intended to constrain the pupil to hold the arm and hand correctly while playing, found the approbation of noteworthy teachers. In our opinion such mechanical aids ought never to come into general use, but be chosen only in special cases when the pupil's individuality demands them, and employed for a longer or shorter period.

As soon as the earlier clavichords and harpsichords became capable of sounding full chords distinctly, they were used by composers, by reason of their easier management and more pleasing tone, in preference to the zithers and lutes previously predominant. The clavichord, on account of its weaker tone, was to be found only in private apartments, whereas the more brilliant harpsichord appeared in public soon after it had assumed a presentable shape.

Early in the year 1600, when one of the first dramas in the recitative style provided throughout with music, Jacopo Peri's "Euridice", was given at Florence, the composer thought the clavicembalo already sufficiently important to reinforce the accompanying orchestra. In the same year a sacred musical drama composed by Emilio de' Cavalieri, "La rappresentazione di anima e di corpo", was brought out at Rome in the oratory — hence the general name of such musical works, *Oratorio* — of the church *della vallicella,* in dramatic style and interspersed with dances, on a stage furnished with decorations. The accompanying instruments were stationed behind the scenes, reinforced as in the opera mentioned above by a clavicembalo, together with lutes of various kinds, violins, and flutes. Even in the 17th century, after the bass-viols, viols, and violins had taken the leading place in the orchestra, a cemballist was still specially engaged in the theatres for executing the harmonic accompaniment to the opera recitatives. In the 18th century the pianoforte was sometimes substituted for the harpsichord; in this century the original Russian composer Glinka introduced it into the orchestra as a solo instrument in his romantic opera "Russlan and Ludmilla."

The pianoforte has such a peculiar tone, that even in the opera it might well suggest new shadings, incisive arpeggi, and effective combinations with the other orchestral instruments, as the pianoforte concertos of our classic masters convincingly prove.

In the music-rooms of composers of all nationalities we find the pianoforte, which can audibly reproduce the pictures of their fancy, thus providing a sketch for the future painting. In the Museum of the Paris Conservatory of Music are several such instruments once belonging to celebrated composers; for instance No. 231, in which Meyerbeer inscribed the fact that at this piano, placed at his disposal by his friend Peter Pixis (1835 at Baden), he composed a great part of his opera "The Huguenots".

Franz Liszt, to whom we owe not merely the present high pitch of pianoforte-playing, but in consequence of it the great development of the modern concert grand as well, kindly wrote me a letter, concerning his own instruments, which possesses permanent value on account of its mentioning the most admirable pianofortes of his time, at the head of which there stands, since 1873, a magnificent Steinway grand. Its reproduction therefore forms a fitting close to my History of the Pianoforte.

To C. F. Weitzmann, Berlin.

Weimar, Aug. 14, 1861.

.... In reply to your question touching the Beethoven pianoforte and the Mozart spinet, I can give you the following information.

The Beethoven pianoforte (from C to C) was selected for the great man by Ries, Cramer, Knyvett, Moscheles, and Kalkbrenner in London at Broadwood's, and furnished with the signatures of these gentlemen and a Latin inscription by Broadwood. Schindler, in his for the most part repulsive biography of Beethoven, mentions this present, which gave B. great pleasure, and always served in his room as a show-piano, although people in Vienna averred that He generally used it untuned, and without having the snapped strings restrung. After his death it was bought by Herr Spina, with whom I grew to be on friendly terms through my editorial connection with the publishing house of Diabelli (whose main stay he was) — and in 1845 Spina presented me with this art-relic at Vienna.

The Mozart spinet is of far less value. I cannot now remember just how many octaves it has — probably not quite 5. — Nine years ago it was announced for sale in the music-journals, and presented to me by the Princess of Wittgenstein through the agency of Bartholf Senff of Leipzig (about1 852 or '53 at latest). Mozart being, as you are aware, more of a traveler than Beethoven, a larger number of pianos and spinets used by Him are extant. The one you saw a short time since at the Altenburg came from Salzburg to Leipzig and Weimar, accompanied by several authenticating documents. In Salzburg and other places there are similar pieces of furniture of Mozart's, the most appropriate place for which would seem to be the Germanic Museum at Nuremberg.

Finally, honored friend, with reference to pianos of my own, there are the following at the Altenburg: — 1 Erard in the reception-room in the first story — 1 Bechstein in the little parlor adjoining — 1 Boisselot (Marseilles) in my study or workroom. N. B. Louis Boisselot was a friend of mine, and accompanied me on the whole trip through Spain and Portugal ('45 to '47). He died soon after — I kept this piano, which besides underwent some other remarkable vicissitudes of fortune which I will relate to you when occasion serves. In the state it has been in for several years it can hardly be played on by any one else, yet I can neither make up my mind to put it aside, nor even to place another beside it in my study.

In the so-called Musik-Salon (2nd story) there stand two Vienna grands made by Streicher and Bösendorfer, and in the other room a Hungarian grand made by Beregszazy. . . . . —

Postscriptum.

Weimar, May 24, 1878.

To the above, written in 1861, I may add, that in my present domicile at Weimar ("Hofgärtnerei") there shines every year a Bechstein grand, and during my winter sojourn in Pesth one or two Bösendorfer grands (as my apartments there have room for several pianofortes). Chickering's grand, which I used in Rome, now stands in state in Hungary, and that made by Steinway frequently appears here in concerts.

F. Liszt.

APPENDIX I.

CLAVIER COMPOSITIONS

OF THE

SIXTEENTH, SEVENTEENTH, AND EIGHTEENTH CENTURIES.

TABLE OF CONTENTS.

I. Claudio Merulo. 1532-1604.

Toccata.

Toccate d'intavolatura d'organo. lib. I. Rom, 1598.
F. J. Fétis, Traité complet de la Théorie et de la Pratique de l'Harmonie.

II. Girolamo Frescobaldi. 1588-1645. (?)

Canzona in sesto tono:

3
3
3

Il primo libro di Capricci, Canzon francese, e Recercari, fatti sopra diversi sogetti et arie. In Partidura (sic) di Girolamo Frescobaldi, organista in San Pietro di Roma. Novamente ristampati con privilegio. In Venetia, appresso Alessandro Vincenti MDCXXVI. (1626.) Four-part score with bars.

III. Bernardo Pasquini. 1637-1710.

Sonata.

Arpeggio.

Siegue :

Pensiero.

Manuscript of the year 1732 in the British Museum at London.

IV. Francesco Durante. 1684-1755.

Sonata.

1.
Adagio.

3. Giga.

Manuscript of the year 1732 in the British Museum at London.

V. Pier Domenico Paradies. 1746.

Sonata.

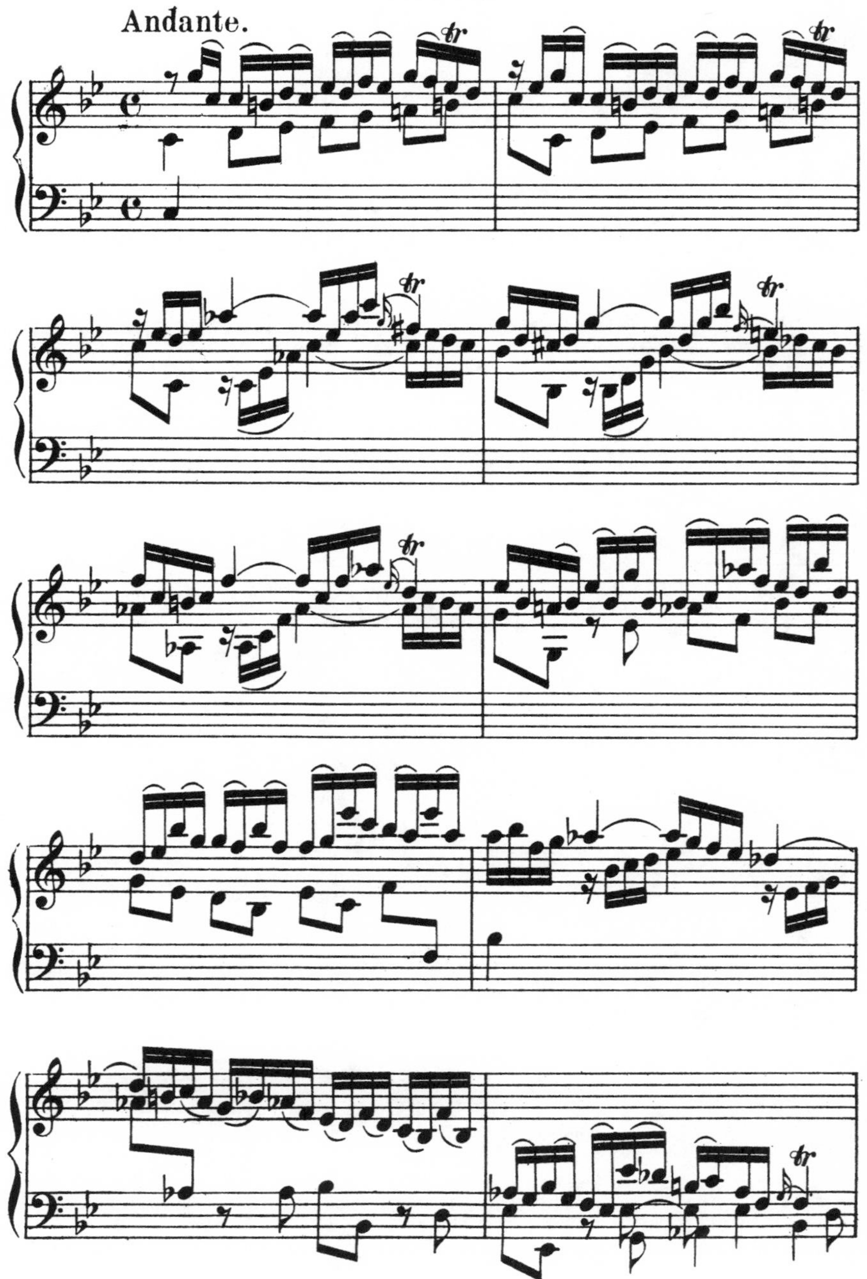

tr
1.
2.

tr
tr
tr
tr
tr
tr
tr
1.
2.

Minuetto.
3
tr
tr
tr

Sonate di Clavicembalo -- da Pier Domenico Paradies Napolitano. London, J. Blundell (1746-1747.)

The above two movements form the fourth of the 12 Sonatas in this part.

VI. Thomas Tallis. d. 1585.

Lesson, two partes in one.

Musica antiqua, by John Stafford Smith. Vol. I. p. 70. London, Preston.

Some notes of the soprano, in the first measures of this 2-part canon, are marked with trill-signs, which are, however, of no importance, as they do not occur further on.

VII. William Bird. 1538-1623.

The Carman's Whistle, No. 58 in "Queen Elizabeth's Virginal book."

Var. 5.
Var. 6.
tr
tr

tr
tr
Var. 7.

Ch. Burney, General History of Music, Vol. III, 89.

VIII. Orlando Gibbons. 1583-1625.

The Queene's Command, 20th Lesson, from Parthenia, or the Maydenhead of the first musicke that euer was printed for the Virginalls, London, 1655.

J. St. Smith, Musica antiqua, Vol. I, 75.

IX. Henry Purcell. 1658-1695.

Riggadoon from Musick's Hand-maid by Playford, 1689.

J. St. Smith, Musica antiqua, Vol. II, 185.

X. Jean Henry d'Anglebert. 1689.

Allemande.

Pieces de Clavessin etc. liv. I. Paris, 1689.
The agrements of the above Allemande have been written out in modern notation.

XI. François Couperin. 1668-1733.

Prélude.

L'art de toucher le clavecin par Monsieur Couperin, dédié à sa Majesté. Paris, 1717. Pag. 54.

XII. Louis Marchand. 1669-1732.

Gavotte.

A History of Music, by Thomas Busby, German translation by Ch. F. Michaelis. Band II. Leipzig 1822, Baumgärtner.

XIII. Johann Jacob Froberger. 1635-1695.

Phantasia supra *ut, re, mi, fa, sol, la,* Clavicymbalis accommodata.

A. Kircher, Musurgia, Rom, 1650. T. I, 466.

XIV. Gottlieb Muffat. 1727.

Sarabande and Fugue.

Componimenti musicali per il cembalo di Theofilo Muffat. Wien, 1727.

Fuga.

XV. G. Heinrich Stölzel. 1690-1749.

Finale from the Enharmonic Clavier-Sonata.

From the Musikalisches Allerley (edited by F. W. Marpurg.) 14. Stück 1761. Berlin, F. W. Birnstiel.

XVI. Schobert. d. 1768.

Fragment from a Clavier-sonata.

Oeuvres mêlées, contenant VI Sonates pour le Clavessin. J. U. Haffner à Nuremberg. (1760-1767.)

XVII. Carl Philipp Emanuel Bach. 1714-1788.

Claviersonate; first movement.

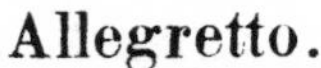

p
f
p
ten.
1.
2.

p
f
f
p
f

Musikalisches Vielerley. Edited by C. Ph. Em. Bach. Hamburg, 1770. 21. Stück.

XVIII. N. Joseph Hüllmandel. 1751-1823.

IVe Divertissement.

p
rinf.
p
rinf.
p
cresc.
p
rinf.
rinf.
rinf.
p
p
1.

Un poco Adagio.
2.
cresc.
f
p
smorz.

mf
rinf.
f
p
f
p
f
p
cresc.

Six Divertissements pour le Pianoforte ou le Clavecin, Oeuvre VII. Paris, Saunier.

XIX. Agréments

in earlier Clavier Compositions, and their execution according to the following authors.

J. H. d'Anglebert, 1689.

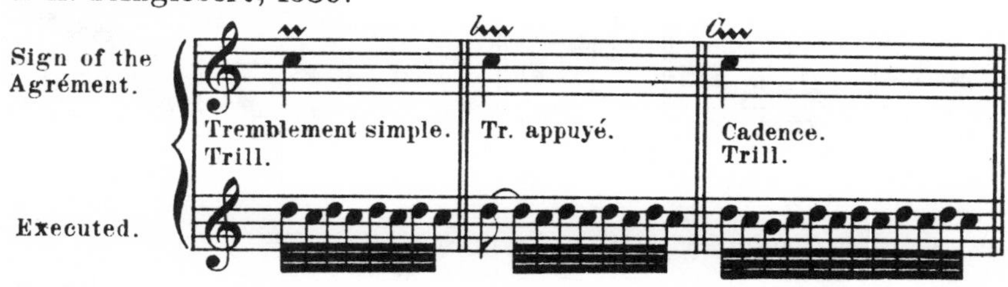

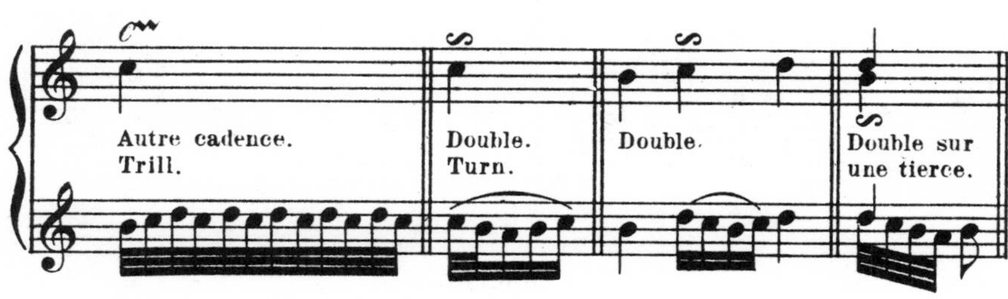

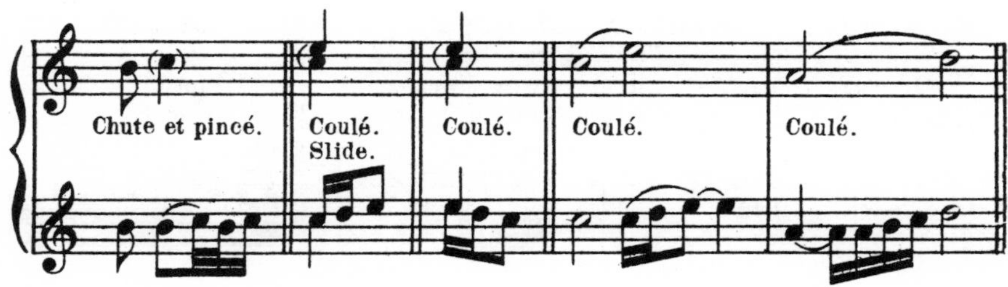

Coulé.
Chute.
Arpège.
Arpège.
Arpège.
Acciaccatura.

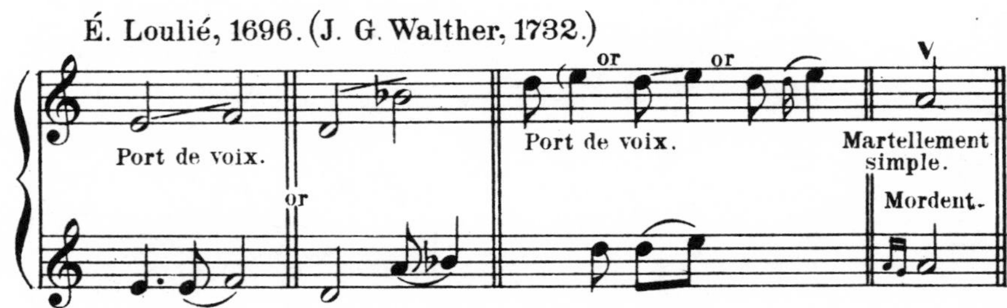
É. Loulié, 1696. (J. G. Walther, 1732.)
or
or
Port de voix.
or
Port de voix.
Martellement simple.
Mordent.

F. Couperin, 1713.
M. double.
M. triple.
Pincé.
Pincé.
Mordent or Beisser.
Tremblement.
Trill.

F. W. Marpurg, 1762.
Tierce coulée.
Port de voix.
Appoggiatura.
Appoggiatura.
Vorschlag.
Pincé.
Mordent.
or
3

Pincè renversé,
Inv. Mordent.
Tremblement
Trill.
or
Acciaccatura.
Zusammen-
schlag.
Doublé. Turn.
J. S. Petri, 1782.
Doppelschlag.
Turn.
Turn with Trill.
Getrillerter Doppelschlag.
Trill.
G. F. Wolf 1783.
Double Trill with.
After-slide.
Nachschlag.
Double Trill with
Fore-slide and After-
slide.
Appoggiat.
Appoggiat.
Ordinary Trill.
Trill from above.
Long Mordent.
The same 1789.
Trill from below.
Turn.
Turn with Inv.
Mordent.

C. P. E. Bach, 1787.
Vorschläge.
Appoggiaturas.
Trill.
tr
Turn
F. Pollini, 1811.
J. P. Milchmeyer, 1797.
Gruppetto.
Gruppetto.
Appogg.
Small Notes.
J. G. Walther, 1732, and others.
Small Notes.
(38.)
Aspiration.
N. de S. Lambert, 1697.
Suspension.
F. Couperin, 1713.
Passing shake.
Callcott, 1817.
(Clavichord.)
Balancement.
Turn.
Turn from below.
Springing Nachschlag.
Milchmeyer, 1799.
Slide.
or
tr
3

The value of the notes determines the duration of the Trills, Inverted Mordents, and Mordents (the number of the beats or vibrations of the same). (Couperin.)

The note with which a *Vorschlag* (fore-grace, appoggiatura) is performed, whether it be long or short, legato or staccato, ascending or descending, must always fall on the beat of its main note. (Marpurg.)

Not the main note, but the subsidiary note above it, always begins the Trill. (Petri.)

To the first note of those forming an agrément, all the other parts must be struck together.—All appoggiaturas are struck more strongly than the following note, and *drawn up* (bound) to the latter.—At times the harmony determines the value of the appoggiaturas (fore-graces).—A Trill upon a note of some length always takes an after-turn. Even with shorter notes, staccato notes, or notes progressing by seconds, the after-turn is played, and executed with the same rapidity as the trill.—Triplets, and descending short notes, take by preference the Trill without after-turn. (C. Ph. E. Bach.)

APPENDIX II.

ILLUSTRATIONS

TO THE

HISTORY OF THE PIANOFORTE.

TABLE OF CONTENTS.

The Precursors of the Clavier.

After illustrations from the beginning of the 16th century.

Claviers from the beginning of the 16th century.

The Hammer-action of the Pianoforte.

The Precursors of the Pianoforte.

After illustrations from the beginning of the 16th century.

Fig. 1.

The Organ.

Compass from A to f. Keys projecting freely, as in all keyed instruments of that period. The player had a low seat, and struck or drew down the heavily answering keys with the fingers, the wrist hanging down below the keys.

Fig. 2.

The Psaltery.

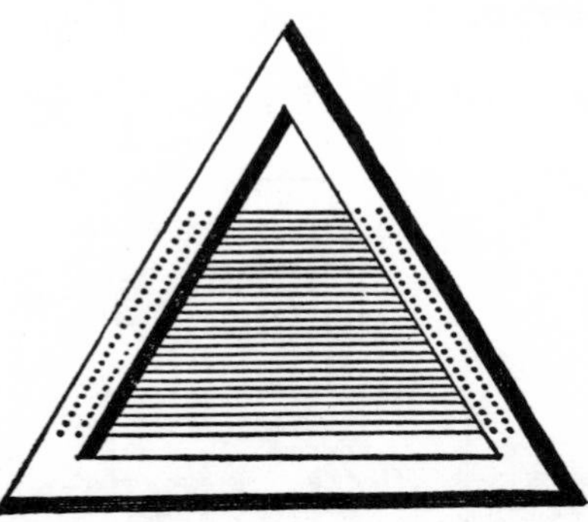

This instrument also occurred in a square and other forms, and had metallic strings, varying in number from 6, 10, 12, 15, up to 38 double strings.

Fig. 3.

The Cymbalum.

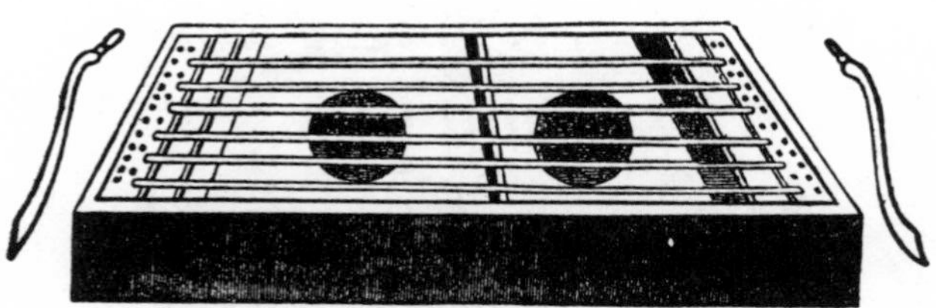

The metallic strings, varying greatly in number, were struck by two wooden plectra.

Claviers from the beginning of the 16th century.

Fig. 4.

The Clavichord.

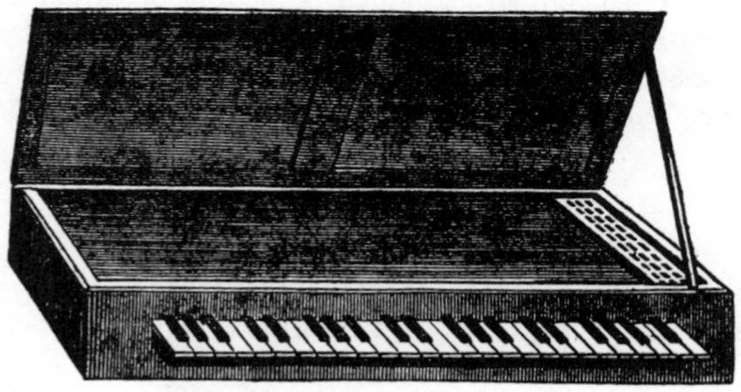

The metallic strings, varying in number, were all of like length and like pitch. At first the clavichord had 20 or 21 keys, but later considerably more. The keys were furnished with upright metallic tangents, which struck against the strings from below, allowing them to sound, sometimes in their entire length, and sometimes shortening them at certain nodes, to make the string yield the tone corresponding to the place of the key in the keyboard. Thus 2 or 3 keys often struck one and the same string.

Fig. 5.

The Harpsichord.

(Spinet, Virginal.)

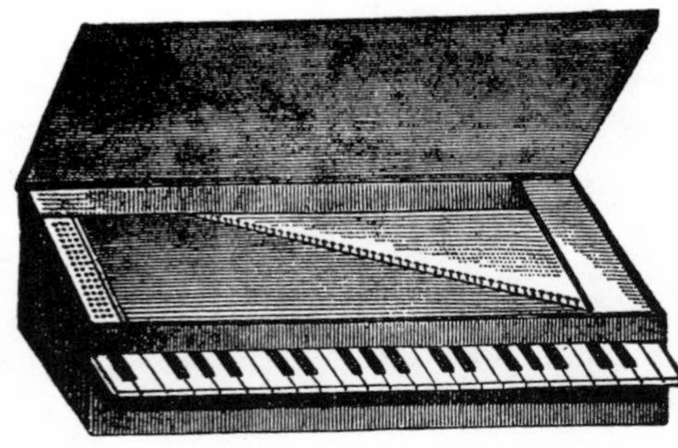

Each key has a separate string, which is plucked or twitched by the quill of a spring-jack set on the rear end of the key-lever. Later, side by side with the clavichords in square form, the Harpsichord occurs in Germany only in the wing-shape (grand-piano form).

Fig. 6.

The Clavicitherium.

An upright harpsichord. It was furnished, like all the claviers depicted here, with metallic strings, and when wanted for playing was set, like the others, upon a suitable piece of furniture. In this figure the lower tones are assigned to the shorter strings, the higher to the longer ones; for this and other irregularities the draughtsmen of the 16th century are responsible.

Fig. 7.

Harpsichord of the year 1590.

Wing-shape, with two keyboards.

After the large and elegantly fitted up Harpsichord made by Hans Ruckers of Antwerp in the year 1590, now in the Museum of the Conservatory of Music at Paris. It has two keyboards, and its original compass of 4 octaves was later extended to 5. Hans Ruckers' instruments were distinguished by their full, even tone; his harpsichords were bichord, the lower strings of copper, the higher of steel, and the sound-boards show most careful workmanship.

Fig. 8.

I. Pianoforte action by Cristofori, 1711.

Bartholomaeus de Christophoris Patavinus inventor faciebat Florentiae MDCCXI.

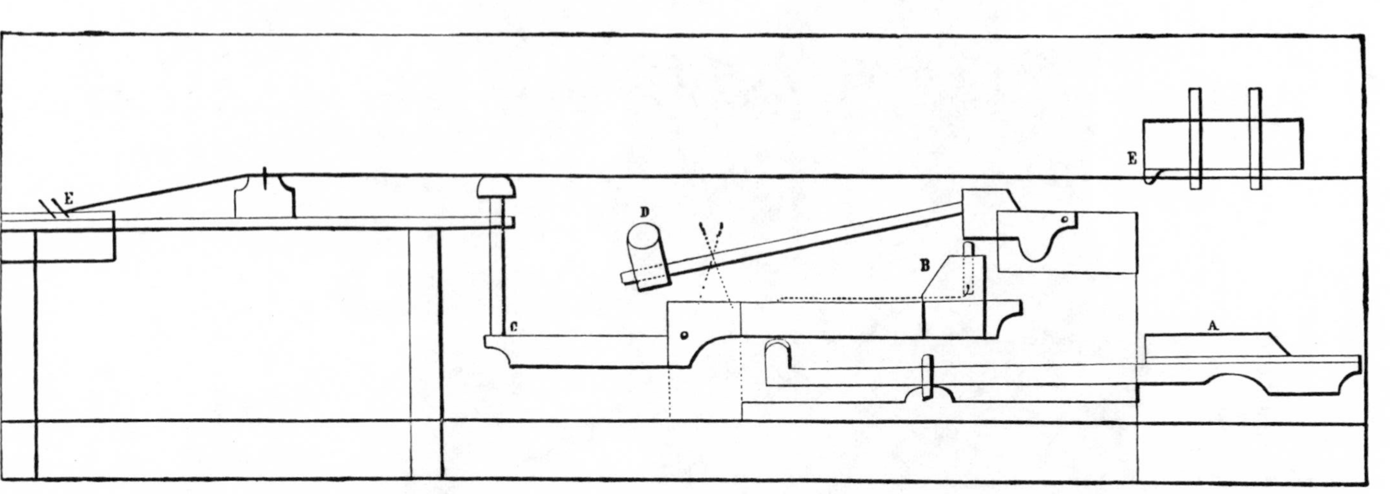

A is the key, the first lever of the Cristofori hammer-action; B the hopper (on springs) on the second lever at the end of which the damper C is fixed; D is the hammer, centered on a special beam, with the head resting on silk threads; it is impelled by the hopper against the string E-E, then dropping immediately into its former position. D, the hammer-head, is a hollow pasteboard cylinder, padded on the upper end with leather.

Fig. 9.

II. Hammer-action by Marius, 1716.

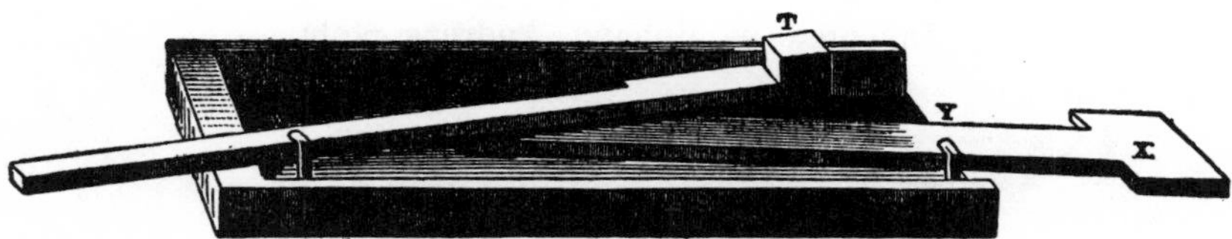

Clavecin à Maillets, inventé par M. Marius. Cette deuxième Figure est pour faire voir comment on peut établir un clavier à maillets pour tirer le son en-dessous. Le maillet T est mobile au point V, et la touche X mobile en Y; en ce cas il faut que la tête T du maillet soit plus pésante que la queue.

No Hammer-clavier seems to have been built according to Marius' models. Silbermann had made pianofortes for practical use as early as 1726, and not until 1763 did Schröter make public his models, which were exhibited at Dresden in 1721, but afterwards lost.

Fig. 10.

III. Pianoforte-action by Schröter, 1721 (1763).

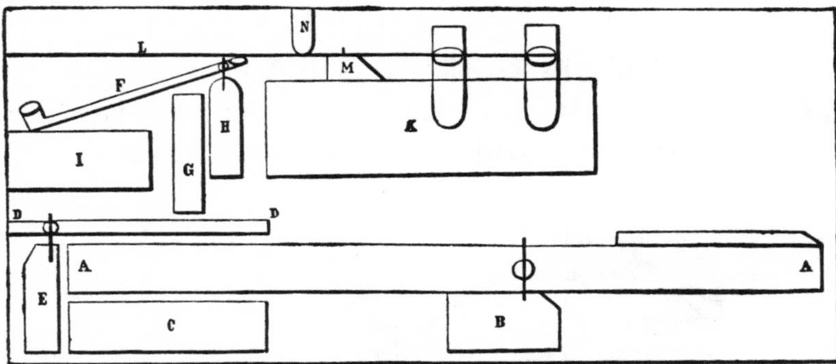

A—A is the keyboard. B and C are rails on which the keys lie. D—D the "driver" (second lever); its long front end lies on the key, its short rear end plays on a pin in the beam E. F is the hammer, whose head is covered with leather; the tail of its shank acts at the same time as the damper, being covered with velvet. H is the cross-section of a beam rounded on top, upon which is adjusted a row of pins on which the hammers are hung. I is the cross-section of a rail on which the hammers rest; the latter rise to the strings between two pins not given here. G, the hopper, stands on the long front end of the second lever D—D; it is held to a straight course by two rows of thin pins not shown here, which reach from beam I over to beam H. K is the stout wrest-plank. L is the string, held in position by little pegs on the bridge M. N is a strong, smooth iron bridge, rounded underneath, which must press firmly on the strings, as they would otherwise yield but a faint, weak tone.

Fig. 11.

IV. German or Viennese Action.

Invented by Johann Andreas Stein.

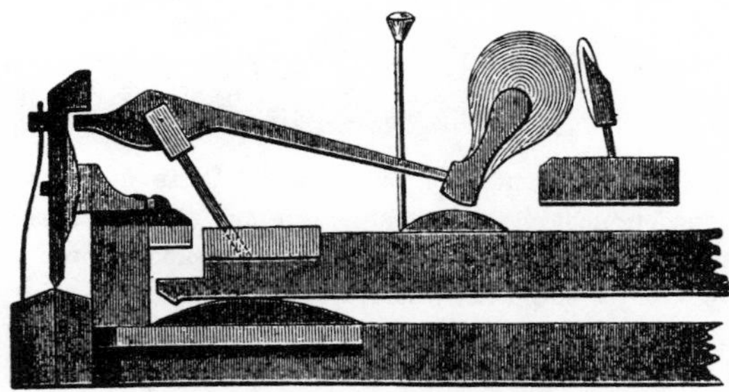

The shank of the hammer plays in a brass socket fixed on an iron pin, which stands on the key-lever itself. On pressing down the key, the hammer-butt catches in the spring-flange of the hopper behind the key, is lifted by it against the string, and instantly drops into its former position.

Fig. 12.

V. The so-called English Action,

already employed by Cristofori, and thereafter variously improved by Silbermann, Streicher, Broadwood, and others.

The hammers are adjusted upon a separate rail over the keys, and are driven against the strings by a jack, which is fastened to the rear end of each key-lever by a strip of parchment, and is at the same time a spring-hopper. The hammers are provided with checks and the strings with dampers, but these variously adjusted appliances are not shown here, in order to exhibit more clearly the chief features of this action.

INDEX.

D.

E.

N.

O.

P.

Q.

R.